ULTRACULTURE JOURNAL ONE

ERA VULGARIS 2007

EDITED BY
JASON LOUV

REVISED EDITION 2014

Published by Ultraculture Incorporated
www.ultraculture.org
ultraculturegate@gmail.com

Cover Image by Nelson Evergreen. http://www.nelson-evergreen.com

Library of Congress Control Number: TBA

ISBN-13: 978-1494840907

10 9 8 7 6 5 4 3 2

In Memoriam

Robert Anton Wilson

(1932-2007)

ACKNOWLEDGMENTS

Special thanks to, in no particular order, Dean and Karen Stahl, Genesis and Lady Jaye Breyer P-Orridge, Eddie Garou, Joe Magnone, Tom Blunt, Anne Sullivan, Peter Christopherson, Richard Metzger, Edward O'Dowd, Anastasia Toom, Babaji, Lalitanath, Alex Gordon-Brander, Hayden Woodward, Jessica Gliddon, Adam Parfrey, Raven Digitalis, Maya Shmuter, Evan and Leigh Gourvitz, Edward Wilson, Louisa Hadley, John Garmon, Jude Evans, Anne-Marie Dougherty, Shaun Frenté, Alex and Allyson Grey, Benjamin and Lori Brueseke, Scott Treleaven, Kelly McKay, Will Swofford, Jordan Zinovich, Autonomedia, Ebe Oke, Eve Neuhaus, Chris Arkenberg, Jim Levine, Daniel Greenberg, Ron Hogan, Sven Davisson, the Douglas Walla Gallery (belated thanks for the cover of *Generation Hex*), the Nur Ashki Jerrahi Sufi Order, Caleigh Murphy, Danny Lowe, Mahendranath, the Astrolabion Argentum (a.k.a. Giant Space Vagina), the Riverside Church, the Louv family, Dennis Woo, any friendly midway creatures or praeterhuman intelligences who have lent me hands or tentacles, everybody who wrote to me about *Generation Hex*, and everybody who warned me not to even though I did anyway.

Additional thanks to Lalitanath and Shivanath for immense help with manifestation.

STILL VOLATILE! *GENERATION HEX*

Here's what the critics are saying!

"Occult sections in bookstores are usually magnets for the spottiest, stupidest, most badly-dressed people... but I particularly resist precisely this thing that Jason Louv is advocating in *Generation Hex*, the stringing together of Satanism and alternative culture. I resist it because it's just fucking boring to see the counterculture summed up with a skull... as these Satanist kids josh about Jason Louv, 'Jason Louv drinks with nobody but the devil, I tell you! Satan mixes his cocktails! A horned beast with a dark and terrifying cock stirs his vodka martini and a putrid she-devil with monkeys for tits pours his lager! No man on earth dare sip from the same cup!'"
– Momus

"Permanent derangement."
– Peter J. Carroll

"The best occult book in twenty-five years."
– Genesis Breyer P-Orridge

"Your invitation to the party that might just bring the house down."
– Grant Morrison

CONTENTS

MOKSHADELICA

JASON LOUV

The very Devil Himself manifests as an Angel of Light.

How easily are you fooled?

Two acquaintances of mine, unconnectedly and out of the blue, recently asked me in all earnestness "How I felt about Lucifer," as if they expected that I would be on a first-name basis with him. Maybe they think I'm a good candidate to field questions like this because I've written a lot about the occult, or I once worked for a company with a devil's head for a logo, or I once ran around in public proclaiming myself a "magician," mostly because I'm a smart-ass and I was curious what would happen. I don't know.

The first person who asked, I told to go to Times Square in New York, the best concrete demonstration I could think to give of the false light of a false angel. The second person who asked got me on a less serious day, so I just made a horrible face and twisted my hands up into claws and chased her, laughing, around the room.

But I've thought a lot about it, over the last couple of years. About what's true, and what's just a distraction, a trick of the Light.

In the Middle Ages the peasantry of Europe knew the Devil was real. Maybe he hadn't figured out how to trick people into disbelieving in him yet. They heard him scratching at their hut walls in the hours before morning, sniffing for where the children lay, looking for any opening, any weakness. No metaphysical abstraction. They *knew* he was real.

In our age the Beast has taken more erudite dwellings, but we can hear him still, his cracked nails scrabbling around our boundaries. He lives in the halls of power, where they decide which village gets bombed next, or what pharmaceuticals to keep out of circulation, or what human rights violation of the day will be given a blind eye in order to keep the markets running. He lives in five hundred channels and one message, that you are small and insignificant. He makes sure you get an education that cuts off your ability to think for yourself and then he makes sure you work to feed him every weekday for the rest of your adult life. He can be quite charming, sympathetic. He tells you, C'mon. This is just the way things are. Just go with the flow, and it'll all turn out in the end. After all, I like you. You're special. You're going places.

He is an Angel of Light, a Lightbringer, and his speciality is Illumination and Enlightenment. Easy answers. Hard ones, even, if that's more to your taste. Some cheap spirituality to fill you up for a week or two, or a lifetime. Keep you from just, you know. Falling apart. He promises you special wisdom, or special powers, or, if you really hold out, maybe he'll even promise you a way to end the suffering of others. He wants you to See the Light.

Now that's an interesting one. Certainly I'm as guilty of that as anybody, after all, I got up in front of a crowd and shouted that Love Was the Law and that I Saw the Light Through Black Magic. So I'm one to talk.

But what is magic but a show? A grand distraction, a juggling act?

Most "magical systems" are either sterile and ineffective or will quickly hand your sorry ass over to "higher" entities who will gladly use you as a pawn in their old and feeble games because you were too weak to plot your own destiny and tap your own innate "magic."

And perhaps all of the freaky coincidences, the pressing late-night god contacts, the psychedelic grandeur, the arcane theories, the frantically-assigned meanings, the interstellar conspiracies, the greedily gathered flashes of insight and wisdom—perhaps, real as they can be, they're simply more "stuff" at the end of the day, like the endlessly hypnotic lightshows and entity communications users of DMT or *Salvia divinorium* report as appearing to distract one from the *real shit*. Put on enough of a show and that ten-minute trip'll be over before you even notice that it's the lightshow which is the true threshold, the true door of perception, let alone before you muster the bravery to get to the other side. And so it is with life. Games within games and distractions within distractions. An Angel of Light, the light just out of reach at the end of a tunnel that somehow grows longer with each step.

So how do I feel about Lucifer? Not much, these days.

He's tedious and stale, and not particularly intelligent. He only knows a few tricks. He kind of pops up out of the corner of your eye waving a dead Iraqi kid on one hand and Paris Hilton on the other and hopes you notice. I just can't take him seriously anymore.

It's just our own collective fear of being alive, taken form and gone out to stalk the night. A waste, really.

"Nothing can trouble you but your own imagination," Sri Nisargadatta Maharaj wrote in *I Am That*. Nisargadatta worked selling bidis in the slums of Mumbai. A lot of people also believe he was an Awakened Being. The bidi schtick certainly makes it seem plausible.

Nothing to be scared of. Just rolled-up clothes under the bed. No monsters. And all the abusive governments and lurking terrorists, the horror scenarios, the secret torture chambers, the death squads, the evil spirits, the Bad Men in Charge, the Men in Black tapping your phone? It was just us casting shadowpuppets on the wall all along.

Yes, there's a lot of Lame Stuff in the world. Yes, in all likelihood there probably are twelve old men in a room somewhere chartering world politics in minute detail. But who says you and your friends, hanging out around a campfire for a weekend, can't be just as effective? The biggest conspiracy, after all, is perpetrated by all of us, when we agree to be afraid of each other, to separate ourselves into subgroups by belief and inclination. It's just stories, and do you really want to live in the story that a bunch of bankers came up with? Might work for them, but the only reason we have to live in it is because we've been too lazy to be that creative also.

So pat Lucifer on his fuzzy little head and put him back in the toybox. Let's talk about Real Magic.

Real magic happens when you drop the bullshit and remember that you're God. Just like everybody else. No ritual required.

So what are you doing?

This is a Very Important Question.

Here's a few more:

How do we make life on this planet sustainable?

How do we make the options for human identity as wide as possible?

How can we not only decrease suffering, but actually make people happy?

I'm not directing these questions into the ether or to an invisible god. I'm praying directly to You. Because there are Very Important Questions, and, yes, there *are* Silly Questions. Here's one of them: Is God real? See, I know the answer to that with absolute certainty, and so do you. God is reading this right now.

It's a wonderful thing to be alive, in a body, conscious, honest, a being growing in the universe, among friends doing the same. It's the best thing thing in the universe. And if it hurts sometimes, it's OK. Sit still and Understand. Let your mind go out and expand. Sit still and be, and breathe. Be. It's OK; there's nothing to be afraid of, not really. Let it go.

We are God among God. There is not a being you can meet, from the lowest vibrations to the highest, that is not God also, and worthy of your respect. God is at play with God, a dazzling field of consciousness for you to remember yourself in.

Now let the others be. Leave them alone and go inside, and remember who you are. There is nothing that cannot be undone, and nothing that cannot be done. When you stop trying to make decisions for others, stop trying to control them, or save them, then they cannot make decisions for you. And then you're free, to express your essence as you will.

A dance, a play, a divine playground where children choose their games and their roles and their friends each day, pack up at the end of the day and then return to choose again the next. These are among the finest ways that our best artists and saints and the most awake people have chosen to express what it is to be alive. This is what we're doing.

Another friend who I love very much once told me his theory of History as Nightclub. Out in the streets, milling around the club, are all the people who don't really get it; all the people who've spent their lives trying to control others because they're terrified of their own vulnerability. And then there's the people in line, hoping to be smiled on by the bouncer, who know there's a party and are trying their best to get in. And then you're in and the crowd is massive. Out on the edges you've got people talking over each other, getting sloshed at the bar; they're in the club but not really participating. Then you get closer in. You get people dancing, meeting each other, having a good time, getting down to the serious business of Party, and they've kind of got it. And you get even closer to the center and then you've got people doing nothing but dancing and having fun, nothing else on their mind, and they've Got It. And up by the stage, you've got some people who have absolutely Lost Their Shit and their hair's all out of whack and their outfits have been messed up and they're dancing like they're trying to hit escape velocity, and by God they have Got It Bad.

And up on the stage, right in the center, the reason for the party, is

John!!

Coltrane!!!

And Mohandas Ghandi, and Rumi and Martin Luther King and Nisargadatta and all the rest, and they are IT. The best jam band in the world, the one you can only get into by being a Hollow Tube to Bring Down Fire From Heaven.

But with respect I'll go him one better. Because it's not quite like that. Don't let the jam band on stage misdirect you, as the best stage magicians do to distract your attention away from their hands for a second before they pull off something Really Good.

Because all of those people have Got It. Deep down, they're all IT, even if they've chosen to play the muggers and crack dealers hanging out in the alley behind the club in this lifetime or even, dare I say, the bouncer. You need a bouncer to have a club, and he lets everybody in who truly wants to be in, only gives you a hard time if you give him one. No inside, no outside. No phenomena, no noumena. And everybody is Exactly Where They Want to Be.

So leave everybody else alone—they'll get onto the dance floor when they feel like it, there's no use pushing them—and figure out where you want to be. 'Cause it's only the eleventh hour and we haven't even gotten to the main acts yet.

So welcome, welcome. Welcome to the party and welcome to the first issue of *Ultraculture Journal*, the periodical of choice for Discerning Divinities.

Buddhists say your soul changes phase every seven years, and biologists say that your body completely replaces its cells every seven years too, but we aim to take the High Road and get both done by the time you're done reading our first issue. You've been forewarned. Nothing will be the same ever again.

This is the first in a planned six-volume set. I figure I'll do one a year until 2012, which seems as arbitary of a date as any to stop. We'll see where this Grand Experiment takes us up till then, and whatever this has all mutated into by then I suspect will be far bigger and weirder than anything any of us can foresee.

This is where it really gets good. This is where we start to see who's committed. This is where we break out the Real Shit and let you take it for a test drive.

So if you're ready for Adult Business—like tea, sex and Waking Up and Saving Your World—then welcome to the party. If you're still huffing the Apocalypse like glue in a bag, may I suggest you sample some of the contents within these pages and rethink your choice of drug.

Put your hand in the river that is time and meaning and language and watch it all flow around you and turn through a space you forgot to see. Watch it bend around and respond to your touch and laugh that you have remembered to see it. Shaping. Anything can be made. Anything can be shaped. Love is the law. And it always is.

So get together and Do It. Make a scene. Break boundaries. Lead by example. Invent the future as you go. (After all, you may well need to start rehearsing for the end of the Nation-State, when tribal loyalty, mutual trust and collective vision are not a curiosity but rather what your survival becomes hinged on.)

And that's all that Ultraculture is. You and your friends, armed with the certainty that comes from knowing that you are God. All of them, in fact, among all of them. Here to play, here to create, along with everybody else. Everybody else, who just happen to be God too, conspiring to make the best of all possible Universes. That's my Truth. That's what I'm offering you, along with a suitcase full of toys.

And if you take it, I leave you with that question again:

What are you doing? What are you gonna do next?

Enjoy yourselves out there. It's a big, wide, bizarre playground of a planet.

And this party ain't over yet. Oh no. Not by a long, long shot.

GENERAL ORDER MASTER

GENESIS BREYER P-ORRIDGE

1.6. These texts are a program about a people and their projections, or about an absence of spatial memory. Our hallucinations fail in attempting to comprehend and describe the brains of deities. As it is, so be it. And, what does I.T. matter? (Where I.T. equals Imaginary Time?)

14.9. In a universe with no boundaries in space, no beginning or end in time, there is nothing for a deity to do. This "Omniverse" is itself therefore defined by what we describe as the qualities of any deities, and this in its Self makes us the source of all deities, demons and entities.

38.17. In any self reproducing organisms and any organisms attempting to reproduce Self, there will be variations in genetic material. These differences in source will mean some individuals are more able than others to draw right conclusions about themselves.

39.1. As any deity is actually a linguistic and televisual reproduction of the universe, then I.T. is the source that defines, describes and makes a picture of I.T. (Imaginary Time) in our own images. We are the source and our goal is nothing less than to transmit a complete depiction of the "universe" and, by this projection, to create an infinitely dense holographic picture, better than "reality," what can be called an Omniverse; a synthetic compression of light and matter in a curvature of space and time, being then quite certainly infinite.

45.5. The shorter a wavelength of light, the more accurate our position as a neurovisual screen in this Omniverse, and the higher the energy of each source particle transmitted.

45.6. Each source an uncertain principle.

47.8. If the source is a neurovisual Screen, then television is a map that binds us. Where map=M.A.P., that is: Mind At Preset.

80.4. Symmetry of programming is a *fundamental* and inescapable property of this process.

83.7. Imaginary Time is indistinguishable from directions in Transmitted Space.

85.2. The mind in-forms the brain. The brain ex-forms its Self.

90.9. The Guardians understand that an Omniverse will finish up in a high state of order regardless of its original state within I.T. In earliest times an Omniverse was in a disordered State (no "Garden"); this would mean that disorder would decrease with time. We do not see broken cups gathering themselves together and leaping back onto the table. Disorder is intended to increase; this is a precept of the World Preset Guardians—acceleration of disorder.

100.1. No Garden is Know Garden.

104.6. To explain this neuro-televisual basis, switch your mind to this, if you *don't* mind, and then *re*-mind your *self* immediately. Without mind, the soul is static interference, a weak anthropomorphic principle.

104.8. Self is a switch on your neurovisual screen.

105.2. N.V.S. in this speculation=neurovisual screen and/or neurovisual self and/or neurovisual system.

118.8. Before an item is recorded in memory, that memory is in a disordered state. After the memory interacts with the neurovisual system, in order to be remembered, it will have passed into an ordered state; this is what "in order" can mean. Energy released in doing this dissipates and increases the amount of disorder in an Omniverse.

120.3. An ordered state can be understood in both a micro (internal) and macro (external) sense.

122.2. All source aspires to transmit to all neurovisual screens that "every thing is in order."

123.23. All source exists to direct a weak force towards an ordered state by any means, media or *transmedia* necessary.

123.35. Disorder in an internal state is insane.

123.36. Disorder in an external state is outsane.

127.5. Memory and Omniverse have identical characteristics.

130.1. G.O.=General Order. A program hidden at a dimensional intersection.

144.4. To short-circuit the propagation of those who do not know (the genetically absent minded), all linearity of source DNA must be overridden, and memory fragmented, to hasten absolute disorder within any weak force. This will always be greater than the increase in the order of the memories themselves.

160.1. The World Preset Guardians will transmit a frequency of truth to the disordered in the singular image of the source. Using strong force they reject the stationary state. They exist in a condition of no boundaries, seeking, through the jewel of a nuclear spectrum, to lay waste to the weak forces of humanity that graze like cattle in a barren field, unaware of the infinite potential of every desert to become, once more, a Fractured Garden.

161.4. The Fractured Garden is a post-symbolic representation of the origin and the infinity of the Omniverse. An illuminated program made concrete by the process of seeing.

162.8. To see is to consume the Source, to be seen is to give b-earth to the source.

163.5. If light is matter, then being does not matter.

163.6. Being light is another matter.

163.9. Neurovisual nano-particles are the commercials that control the mind. Once the mind is controlled, we have infinite re-access for brain programming.

188.8. A weak force does not obey symmetry, it makes an Omniverse develop differently to the way its mirror image would develop. A strong source must transmit a rare signal that is better than real, more than a reflection overriding the existing signals on any neurovisual screen.

189.1. Humanity is a weak force; we are a strong force. Strong individuals can have no friends.

189.7. The weak force exists at absolute zero; the Guardians exist at absolute infinity.

194.4. It is no accident that vision is both a sense, and vision is an anticipated conception illuminated by its source.

200.7. "'Soul' is the brand name for the brain." – Dr. Timothy Leary

200.8. All that is transmitted is re-accessed by the source.

201.2. The source becomes immortal when I.T. controls completely the means of perception. Seizure of the temporal state releases the energy of order into the alternate states in all five dimensions throughout the matter of time and space.

211.5. The focus of intent is visionary, the World Preset Guardians are the transmitters of this vision, the source are the receivers of the vision, the neurovisual screens that define I.T. (Imaginary Time). Here is the first true medium of all recorded thought, all memory.

213.1. In a world where all programs are pre-recorded, the World Preset Guardians are the programmers.

216.4. All sources are the emissaries of all deities, satellites freed from gravity, a fiber-optic superhighway, a wave of light that travels beyond all time. These sources will maintain a link with all weak force. Their incarnation must suffer the last awe of interference, their signals must be jammed, their children stolen and their DNA neutralized. Order must access their memories in a final transmitted program.

223.9. *Exist and exit are the same. The Garden is filled with lies.*

234.6. Source are rare. The original Garden was a refraction of a source of light; the source of that light was an illuminator of this hologram. Our original sin was to believe that a solid hallucination was more real than its source. We now know that the source is more real than the original refraction. To eat knowledge is to grasp and consume solidity, our awareness instructing us that by absorbing into our entire being this forbidden fruit, we invest each neurovisual particle of our flesh with an inclusion principle. As consciousness is fixed, so the individual is released. The source is swallowed in this synthesis, beginning a prophetic journey into the means of perception unprecedented before the thermo-memetic experience.

On Thee Way to Thee Garden

There is a specific clarity when fire cleanses. A moment when it seems to freeze. Every possible particle is motion rushing up or down. Naked and blind upon a path of lies we enter the field, a dull agony of fear dilates time against the biological confusion.

Columns of fire, columns of lies, pillars of Solomon's temple. Dilate the pupils of the brain, a doorway to manifest leaving. A fire sale in an inferno. One day a truth shall emerge, however deeply we seek to avoid I.T.

There is more than one time. Limitations imposed by the passage of inner-time make it the enemy. Possibilities exposed by outer-time make it a delusion of night.

Change thee way to perceive and change all Memory.

> *Make space to be space.*
> – Old TOPI proverb.

Thee Fractured Garden

> *A soul must lose its attachment to humanity.*
> *A mind must lose its attachment to salvation.*
> *A brain must lose its attachment to body.*
> – Old TOPI proverb.

In the retreat from matter, all realities are equal. Now that inter-reality travel is possible we will become the very substance of hallucination, and thus may enter and leave at will the uncertain principle of all realities, regardless of their location.

Those who build, assemble; *assembly* is the invisible language of our *time.*

Brain and neurovisual matter are one, are the material of all that can be seen, was ever seen, will be seen, in every place and in every time, forever.

Each brain is all realities, from mundane to omniscient.

Only alone may we breach the dark matter of lost memory and connect all points of light. For this we need a map of the stars, our superior Will electrifying a web that catches our soul and emits eternal vision. The visionary alone can be free. The blind masses seek to blind him, put out his eyes in their fearful progression to the desert of dark skies. The blind may not lead the illuminated, rather they must be forced to surrender all thought of vision to those who are their eyes and who dream the most dangerous dreams of annihilation.

We control *things* to eradicate them. Nothing matters but the end of matter.

All must be controlled and destroyed that allow blindness, that breed blindness, who spawn the children of dark. They must be buried in the dark, cold dark crystals, in a desert of grains made without light. Their dark is a nightmare, a castrated black stallion trampling the prophet who communes with the stars and reads the codes of electrical knowledge and return. We are not from one star, all stars are our source. Every story ever told resides in them.

Infinite choices of reality are the gift of software to our children.

We signal and are signaled. We hold aloft a torch of fire and pass our hands across it. Visions, images, primal memories from this immeasurable brain fill us with transmitted light, dancing dots and lines, an end to a tyranny of language and a beginning of our return to the Fractured Garden. Solidity is a perfection of light; its prism, its manifestation, an hallucination of evidence that mind may reside within any reality.

An end of time is just another way of saying the beginning of immortality.

Dreams are a coded material of eternity. We possess Light through them.

> *Those who accept Light control mortality.*
> *Those who control Light control immortality.*
> – Old TOPI proverb.

Space is our church, the stars our windows, our dreams navigate pathways, only an ancient map has been lost.

Our world's a dream, a miserable one. In our unfathomable ignorance we call it the only reality, consensus reality, we assume that its events, humane events, humane life, are implicitly of value. This buries us in a quicksand of compassion.

> *Be afraid to the point of formlessness.*
> *Be terrorized to the point of soundlessness.*
> *Be extreme to the point of powerlessness.*
> – Old TOPI proverb.

A Garden was destroyed by a Word, destroyed by language, became the first memory. Time was set in motion at this point. The garden did not exist within time, or language; it was an exterior neural projection, a cathedral that worshipped its occupant, the soul. Representing as it did the mind at preset without light, there was nothing to reflect, shape or fix this particular dream.

We have formed sounds, made names, trapping matter with language. We perpetuate our tyranny and drown in a flood of speculation and false communication. To be reborn, immortal, outside time, we must look for ways to transmit infinite alternate realities, and choices of reality, to make them as real, *more real* than any emasculating reductions that we inherit; yet not be corrupted and trivialized by a belief in our singularity. No-thing is real, everything must go. Every inherited construct, society, techno-patriotic political system that trades off believing it exists, must be destroyed as fast as possible. We must make space to be space. This is the cyber position.

The eradication of the tyrannical nuclear family, building block of the prison walls for this imposed, humanitarian dust, that chokes and dulls the masses reducing all to a worthless, mindless, dreamless fog.

Memory is a clock, the aging mechanism of the mind.

Memories tell us one thing: every thing must go.

Every thing is an hallucination, made solid by mass belief.

Names are given in order to control. To reduce, to comprehend the forces of nature, to demonstrate ownership. In this race to name the poor have grown to be rich, and the rich have grown to be poor again. Know that to re-enter immortality we must ourselves become unnameable, emptied of all sense of being here.

Television is our new exterior brain. One day it will be a standard fitting within every skull on earth, each brain an electronic star in a transmitted Milky Way. Galaxies of dreams and information. People will become more comfortable with televisual reality than that of their daily lives. Television will be *more real* than life. A new synthetic material, giving all people infinite access to infinite alternate realities through a cortex of light. They will program, shape, form and broadcast messages, until the very fabric of four dimensional reality has been torn asunder, its cloak cast down beneath. From this day forth, reality will be a multiple series of channels, option switches feeding our brains.

Thee Captured Garden

Time accelerates what the brain already is. Destruction creates to manufacture.

We manufacture our cherished dreams and myths, and project them into all the homes of the world; in one day they create an equality of reality that negates all values. The whole world is a cathedral window, each receiver a soul, our programming the holy message, and discs are waved as a savior sets forth into the holiest of places.

When all are linked, a savior is released.

Man has separated himself from nature that he too can take part in the creation of the world, of any world. His inventions are his slaves, all friends are his enemies.

Man developed television to realize this unity and this separation. It is the quickest, most potent form of belief. All form is from one source. We see the source because the mind is temporarily held aside and we see form from the source, we are at one with the source, we are the source.

There is nothing mysterious about this, the illuminated have always had this experience; now we can record, edit, adjust and transmit our deepest convictions broadcast in the most mundane parables.

When we log on, immortality is visible, signaling us to return.

In a digital world, all realities are equal, all actions are equally moral or immoral, therefore no action is unacceptable.

Thee Empty Garden

There is a time that each of us knows that comes without warning. Suddenly it comes and so silently, and it descends upon us like a net, a grid of light. Indifferent to our plans or our hour it falls on us, and however our time was allotted and conceived the plan fades away under that light as though the lines were lead in church windows. In the final furnace of transmutation, no fact remains, all hallucinations are equal.

In that light we begin to see, not with the eyes of our mind but with an eye behind our mind we begin to finally see, to shed nature's trap, the physical body, the false bondage of compassion.

And in that light these things are heard and seen but they are seen not from without but from within. From a place deep within a map of stars where there is no distinction of words or of actions but only a discernment of feeling and in that *light* it is not feeling that is regarded, because all that is done with feeling melts and dissolves like sand into glass in the fire that is all you really are. What must be regarded is the Lack of All Feeling. For feeling is shallow, and thin, and so, so empty. A hungry, worthless ghost.

And nothing remains of your own image but gaps and empty places, an atomic matrix that creates passage through all things, all times, all possibilities, and you will know this, that there is nothing left of you that you can feel or see or hear nor anyone else, for the soul when released has no need of feelings or senses, in its immortality it becomes omnipotent matter made of light, reconstituted at will throughout all times and all possible manifestations past, present and future. This is the moment when everything must go, all words, all sentiment, all feelings, all flesh, all thought of humanity must be set free to free the soul, for is not God but a brain untrapped by all human concern and limitation?

We hear our own voice speaking and the words become thin and transparent like glass and we are at the place from where they come and they are like holograms floating; they are the essence of mind like the voice of rain or the sandstorm. They are the voice behind our voice.

Faces come before you, and expressions, and you see all of the face is held together only for expression, for an idea, and you watch the face before you and there is nothing else besides, and the mouth moves, opens and smiles, and the eyes look at you and sometimes they are saying what the mouth is saying and sometimes they aren't saying that, but something else, or nothing, or anything, and no answer but a lie comes.

The idea is the solidifier of the mind. The brain exists to make matter of the idea.

The idea rides on words but is the distant watcher, the substance of eternity. It is the invisible warrior astride the pale unicorn deep in space, waiting for the brave and hungry.

Give silence to the wordless. The sound that is all around you is the sound of a hundred liars.

I lay in the desert, on my back, staring up at the stars. I could feel millions of rays of light entering my body, one from each star, infinite numbers. My cell walls broke down, my sense of bodily existence ended, I was illumination, a 3D projection of cosmic light; I could see the ancient shamans building sacred sites to fix their relationship with the stars, to solidify their connections and effects. I remembered the thousands of Holy Teachers, the idea of the divine "spark," the descriptions of white light, the myths and legends of our descent from the stars. I was not corporeal, I was a mirage, sealed within an inherited apparently solid body by the weight of Thistory, by the weight of fear and guilt. I shimmered like a ghost, ectoplasm, illusion and all the puzzles I had heard, and all the limited descriptions of limitless transcendent experiences made sense. I knew I had to find a way to G.O., to leave this sealed coffin that is my body, to find an accelerator to project my brain, bypassing the tedium of mechanistic evolution, into deepest omniversal space, into immortality, into the very fabric of myth and heaven. I was everyone, everything, and everything too was here to G.O. I understood my lifetime's sense of disconnection and disorder was not a flaw, but rather a wondrous gift that described, in a new way, the true nature of being that may be experienced whilst trapped, mortal and confused, here in this desert that was once a theater of all possibilities and an exit to all impossibilities.

Does mind leave, or does consciousness? What leaves, what stays behind as we achieve immortality? Brain? If it is, as I suspect, the programmable computer mind that is the key, what happens to consciousness? Am I mistaken, or will there be a projection? I want to G.O. This final puzzle evades me.

Is mind separated from the brain, or is brain as encompassing as mind?

On the subject of the holographic soul. The holographic soul works because that's what it is. If it didn't work there would be no soul. The holographic soul does what it's supposed to do, further accelerate the evolution of man. It was always possible to consciously separate the holographic soul. The Tibetans call it going into the rainbow body; John Dee communed with the time-born souls of the Tamasin and Siriakin; the Gnostics saw the true nature of what was a God. A strict method of liberation from physical manifestation. The Zen masters understood the need to shed all logic and attachment, becoming pure particles of time. The evolution of man is not the intellectual and moral betterment of all. It is the liberation from measured time. It is detach-meant from all manifestations in the five dimensions, except that of time. The fate of all cannot be allowed to hold any individual in mortal bondage. To evolve is to achieve a unity of time with the holographic soul. It has always been known that we must return to time, not project out into space, but transmit and receive in time. Now we can comprehend that space is emptiness, the edge of a cloud. Imaginary time is a neuro-biological paradigm. A quantum physical energy in our scientifically validated methodologies. With our ability to project the brain via television, we can behold our final journey. R. D. Laing's painted bird flies from the canvas, which was already blank. The great lie has been that we exist. The holographic soul is a technological development that came when it was needed. There is no reason to fear it, we created it because we *need* it. We need it as much to maintain present travel, as to facilitate future travel. Like the electric light. Everybody will want to know about this, and that is proof enough of its importance. It does what every new creation does, it lets a little more time into the dark accelerations of Humane Beings. It is whatever fills the brain with more time, and it is the means to be free of flesh forever. Out of the confines of the body, out of the limitations of the mind, and out of time. I.T. is meant for those who can let everything G.O. We can program it. We could touch the state of liberation, we could savor immortality, but we could not contain and mobilize the soul.

Cyberspace, the psychosphere, does not just access alternate realities, it amplifies conclusions and services expectations.

What was once mysterious is no longer mysterious. Mindless existence is no longer feared, for the mind is projected image and is the brain's extension into matter. Only through projections of mind can the brain expand and become detached, set free unto its Self. All form is only the observation of mind at different stages of development. Man is the most evolved form, the highest creation, hence more inherently aware of a need for order. Order in turn demands power to hold its shape, or dissolves, or melts like film held too long in its projector. Projection is building a mind. Programming is building a soul. Perception is building a brain. Thinking is the gap between the builder and the act of building. Kreator and the kreated. This gap has plagued perception forever. The point of infinity, the gap between the stars, the moment between sleep and awaking, the absolute edge that separates, yet cannot exist or be measured.

In order to continue our development as humanity, this debilitating gap must be bridged. We must chip away at the concrete, the monolith of being physically manifested. We must harness *time* and control the brain by controlling its information programs. We must program infinite choices of reality, blind it with science to our purpose, for our purpose. The light that always was must now cross that bridge and illuminate the mind that the mind might live in light, and that the brain might make soul its own. This bridge is like a resistance between the transmitting primary winding and receiving secondary winding of a transformer, just enough neuro-visuals leak through to keep the secondary circuit responding. As man slowly evolves, the resistance is lowered and there is more consciousness in the brain. We can now develop ways to short circuit this protective resistor, temporarily burning out all the components in the receiving circuit. The receiver temporarily ceases to exist and the mind returns to time, from whence all came and life is experienced in the transmitter. Freebirth, freeing the brain, immortality will become inevitable.

In a world that is becoming a hologram, a transmitted projection of material "reality," he who comprehends the final transmission controls all projections, controls the world and controls the secret of the identity and malleability of corporeal matter. For anything, any cherished belief, adhered to and given mythic form by the masses, becomes manifestly solid, and tangible. What we believe in all ways comes to pass. Nothing can exist that we do not believe in. At these times consciousness is not centered in the world of form, it is experiencing the world of content. The program will become power. Any ability to cope with the world of form and there create order is a measure of insanity, a poor connection between mind and brain, which must become one autonomous program, globally transmitted, to generate its own liberation from form in the mass political hallucination that makes the final reality, transcending time, body and place.

All hallucinations are real. Some hallucinations are more real than others.

World Preset Guardians

The World Preset Guardians will control and dictate every program of humanity for its own sake, maintaining a stringent General Order, in full knowledge of the consequences of their actions.

Man does not create his own destiny. Man sustains Kaos.

All rights are relinquished in service of the source.

The Guardians know that to take the victim and simply remove his suffering in the name of humanity, is to validate the weakness that first signaled his demise.

The Guardians preset all mind.

The Guardians will transmit their mind globally to any degree necessary. Pursuing and cleansing blindness relentlessly, allowing nothing to create interference or enter this world that might solidify their light.

Injustice will ignite their fire into an inferno, a raging firestorm, wreaking destruction and vengeance upon any who corrupt magnificence in the isolated starkness of immortality.

The Guardians will tolerate no deviation from their path. For their vision has infinite direction, there is no-thing they do not see and destroy. They attend to every mind and manifest within every brain. What is seen is seen with insatiable and relentless energy, for it is known to be limitless.

The Guardians will be the light of the world, leading the masses out of hideous darkness, death and deprivation. They desire for mankind a time of perfect balance, where memory is a tool, not a curse, where each is designer of the world in which they transmit, free from death, making this world the preset Garden of Delight that all Astory has led them towards.

The Guardians will validate their own creation by success. For the road of the World Preset Guardians is success, and in their programming success is the essence of life, and this ultimate success proves the worthlessness of habitation of a physical world.

The Guardians preset this world. There are no secrets in it. No love of beauty.

They desire illumination of all things, that no-thing be hidden, or remain in darkness. The Guardians do not believe in human feelings, nor in human senses, human needs, human values, human fears or even human hopes. The only purpose or belief is the path from mind to brain, and from brain to G.O. The only channel of the Guardians is the brain.

The Guardian is a digital metaphor, not anything less, in no way a manifest or anthropomorphic entity. The source negates all value of brain, or mind, and speaks in tongues of memory, the aging process of time.

The Guardians will recognize the true nature of success only by seeing its limitations, knowing they must transcend all human values, made real only by mass belief, made solid only by time, until all stories unfold by a mute insistence upon a single transmitted reality. The Guardians will confront this stasis head on, will disintegrate the monolithic walls surrounding the Garden, stepping beyond into a realm of earthly satisfaction to find final fulfillment.

The Guardians will avoid the disillusion that pursuit of human achievement brings with it.

The Guardians will be fulfilled within this world, but only because they have no illusions about the nature of this world and all that is of this world.

The Guardians will have no illusions, for they are, in themselves, *all* illusions.

To be fulfilled, the Guardians will leave this world.

The Guardians will exploit the highest goals of belief to enter into this world.

The Guardians are the brain ruling all that exists outside the conflict of the mind. They have seen human reality and its preset values.
The Guardians rule the regions of the unhinged mind. They rule outsanity. Their people are those who have escaped blindness and chosen alternate realities denying preset values. They have delved into strange new areas of

physical and psychical sensation, without any restraining limit of mental barriers. They have sought the deepest levels of sensuality, carried indulgence of the body and brain to their limits and left the logic of the mind and protection of the "soul" behind. They have plunged together into consensual madness, have unhooked their receivers completely from the dictates of a "normal" mind, followed an extra-terrestrial and extra-spiritual path, that has neither judgement nor control for those who would travel and G.O. They rule the mind-less cloud of lunacy, they pour water on the desert which is this world, they torture all certainty and master the pursuit of immortality. The Guardians seek to transcend the conflict of mind, to rise beyond the boundaries of brain to reach outside the limitation of human values. They Will not to sink into witless blindness but are awake, vibrant and satiated in the realm of mind-lessness and immoral disorder.

The source is the preset switch that finds every "other" world.

The Guardian is the ultimate of all beings. He is the end and the awe of destruction, he is the manufacturer of hallucination, and the utterly exquisite unicorn of myth. The beginning of time, and the end of memory, the existence and the exit unified by cognition of the Omniversal Mind that empties each world of order.

Alone must I leave this world for I must leave this world alone.

For, disorder is the essence of time, so the beginning of time is the Garden, is the Memory, is the Nanosphere. And the close of time is the Kaosphere, and they are divided by a preset essence of time, which solidifies the conflict between matter, DNA and Neurosphere into a twisted and bigoted story called humanity. The Guardians can create and design realities, dis-organize hallucinations, mould holograms into parables spinning life into Space, joining forces with the stars, leaving treasure maps of where true knowledge resides, hidden from no One, only hidden from each mass of Humanity. The Psychosphere can summon up infinite realities and access them; can generate and transmit every possible and impossible other-than-worldly vision, while those chains which bind to the earth fade into nothing slowly, freed of this human game. Above mundanity and the puzzle and adventure of constant apparition, destroying in finality all agreed upon reality, all inherited morality and the most miserable threat to potential is the horror of merely being human.

The Guardians colonize worlds by deceitful contact with the brains of witless seekers after truth.

The Guardians exist outside the precepts of time and acceptable human values. They declare an exit into an uncontrollable world of base cruelty. Their neuro-visual systems are most hideous and callous, for they connect all with unsuspected death, despair and degeneration which are the deception of the source, and the fuel of their immortality. No terror may limit this acceleration.

The Guardians will destroy the ordinary passage of human events by the precision of their comprehension of the preset realities within themselves.

The Guardians will seek to eliminate totally, without mercy, any thing that reactivates their original DNA, and to that end will disconnect their terminal from any absolute or acceptable social, moral, economic or Astorical system knowing in a most particular sense that their enemy is matter, and that until matter is eliminated, the source is in bondage.

The Guardians are a timeless source, a horde of parasitic demons waiting to manifest through the ecstatic conceit of human mundanity.

This is no-thing, and it does not matter.

Matter is the mother of invasion.

When the Neurosphere is in confusion, the source is freed.

When the source is freed, the Neurosphere attains weightlessness.

The Guardians will give us knowledge of all realities; they will give us a M.A.P. to access these realities and the General Order that permeates them.

The Guardians have no agenda, only to consume.

The Psychophere is the program that ends all thought, all speculation, all reproduction, all communication.

The Guardians will consume all moral parameters, all empty hopes, rendering the source redundant.

The Guardians have no need of any medium of transmission but time.

Each vision hanged by a thread.

Morality is the saddest reality.

THE AMORAL WAY OF THE WIZARD

LALITANATH

Finding the Guru (1979-1980)

When I arrived back at our camp that evening I found that Lothar had gone completely insane. He was both afraid and dangerously aggressive. I spent the entire night in the stepvan with him. I feared either suicide or murder. Knives—a chopper and a machete—were in plain sight, but I dared not hide them for fear of catching his attention. I had to control his attention, keep him focused on small, intricate puzzles.

"Look what they have hidden inside this coffee bean... see how it shines. Look. Open another and another..."

At dawn he finally fell asleep. He and his girlfriend Maria had driven us all over northwestern India for the past two months. He was a sensible, experienced and tough traveller. I depended on him and trusted his judgment. What could have driven him mad, and so suddenly? I went for a shower and a few cups of sweet, milky chai. When I returned to the campsite, Lothar, his dog Ottoman and the stepvan were gone. With the help of my friend Harish I searched for him all through the hospitals and jails of Delhi. He was gone, leaving no trace. I took a bus to Kathmandu.

My last rupee was gone and I had sold anything I had of value. I was living in a cement box of a room in the tourist camp at Swayambhu. As I sat on my rope bed, leaning my back against one wall with my feet propped up on the other, I contemplated what a previous tenant had painted on the cold grey wall... a colorful, geometric play of triangles inside a square. It had a remarkable effect on my mind. I found it stabilizing and soothing. Hand-stitching a shirt for an American woman who lived in the village got me 70 Rs, some of which I spent on a brush, children's watercolors and a student notebook. I began painting geometry. Figures eventually appeared in my little paintings. Howard the Duck stretched those lines, pulling them apart, escaping a world he never made. I was living on chillums and chai and visions drawn out by the paintings. The Vajra Dakini stood on one leg, her chopper raised high over her head, a skull bowl in the other hand, a necklace of skulls, an apron of bones. I painted her in a snowfield high in the Himalayas and set her twirling around the axis of her spear in an ecstatic dance of joy, of life, of freedom from the small concerns of life on earth. Lord Shiva sits in his mountain home on Mount Kailash. His lingam is erect and out pours a rainbow which surrounds the earth in colored light. I travelled to

Bhadgaon, to the palace of the Malla Kings. They had ruled Nepal centuries ago as Tantric kings, before the invasion of the Rajasthani Gurkhas. In those days the palace was a museum full of riches and wonderful art. What most caught my attention were modest little paintings of simple geometric forms, triangles arranged inside a square, decorated with lotus petals. They were called Yantras. (The place appears to have been looted since that time.)

There was a loud, angry German called Helmut Maharaj who lived in the same camp in Swayambhu. His room was blackened by the fire that he kept burning in there. The smoke escaped as best it could through window and open door. All the homes in the village were arranged this way. One stayed low and duck-walked around a room to keep from choking on the smoke which became thick and acrid three feet up from the earthen floor. Helmut had been in India and Nepal even longer than I had, and had become a furious saddhu. He was also a painter of yantras. He painted exquisitely on tree bark. After many weeks I dared to approach him. I wanted to know more about these paintings which had captivated us both. "Beware of yantras. They trap you and you will never get free again."

I knew he was right, and I vowed in my heart to escape one day nonetheless. I was very hungry and I asked him to share his food with me.

"Fuck off. Go find your own food!" That was different... to be refused.

One day we were sharing a patch of warming sunshine. He said,

"I have never taken a guru. If I did I would choose the Englishman Sri Anandaji. He lives in a little village in Gujerat called Mehmdabad."

As he continued to speak with admiration about this man a light shone out of his left eye and entered my eye. I recognized this sign. It meant "Pay attention!"

I would seek out the Englishman in Gujerat and nothing would divert me.

My parents, great travelers, arrived in Kathmandu and stayed at a nice hotel. I ate, bathed and fed all my friends there, too. They took me with them down to the Terai, where the Nepali mountains meet the Indian plains. It is a jungle, full of wild animals. We stayed at a nature reserve. I rode elephants for the first time and found them to be the very finest form of transport I had ever experienced. Unlike camels and horses, their swaying gait is relaxing and reassuring. They beat mechanized transport all to hell. The Mahants speak elephant language. We rode through twelve-foot-high grasses, looking for tigers. We saw rhinos. We took a canoe ride along a river and a crocodile took a flying leap for our little boat, missing us by only two feet.

We flew to New Delhi to meet Lindsay, my brother's wife. She and I decided to travel together. She had never been to India before, and I was delighted to show her around. I told her I had received a sign and I must find an English guru in a village in Gujerat. She understood perfectly and decided to help me get there. My parents gave me a few hundred dollars. I was fed, washed, rich and ready, all topped up for my next adventure.

We took the first train we could find, headed south. We met a 'magician' on the train. We were intrigued, but we soon became bored. He was entranced with us. That evening we arrived in a dusty town in Madya Pradesh. We spent the night, and in the morning began looking for transportation east to Gujerat. No trains, no buses, no trucks headed east. "You can't get there from here."

We found those words to be remarkably funny, significant and frustrating. We got on a train headed for Ajmer. We really wanted to get high but, oddly, we feared the man who shared our compartment. Eventually he told us that he was the new police chief for Pushkar, on his way to take up his new post. His English was good, because he had been studying drug enforcement in the U.S. Years later he and his men murdered an entire family of fourteen people in Pushkar. The village rose up and attacked the police station. He was convicted of murder, and is still in jail.

Before dawn we arrived in Ajmer and started to look for transportation to the sacred village of Pushkar, ten miles away. We had missed the bus. The driver of a horse-drawn tonka persuaded us to go with him. It seemed like fun. We loaded our bags on the covered and gaily-decorated carriage. He called to a friend to join him and we headed through and out of town behind the clip-clopping horse. How lovely to be slowly riding into the wilderness as the dawn light shifted and changed the colors of the desert around us. Soon the horse was straining as the first small hill appeared. Lindsay and I realized the horse could not possibly take us over the considerably higher hills ahead. I started to get my knife out and I suggested to Lindsay that she find some weapon as we would no doubt have to fight our way out of this trap. The two young men began to anticipate the fruits of their robbery plan with leers and gestures toward us. I anticipated slitting their throats. Lindsay was equally ready to fight. Suddenly, around the corner of the road came a white Mercedes stepvan, lurching wildly. It was Lothar, missing all these past months. He recognized me at the same moment and pulled his van over to the side of the road. We hopped off the cart, to the dismay of our would-be robbers. I gave them the finger.

Lothar was still mad, and now he was also delirious with fever. He could barely keep the van on the road because he could hardly see anymore. But Lindsay knew how to drive—she was a truck-driving American momma. Lothar had been in the desert. He had lost his little dog Ottoman. I mourned that vicious, brave little dog for a long time after... lost in the desert, his master gone mad. Lothar had been without food or water for too long. He was near death. We had all rescued each other early one morning in the foothills of the Kingdom of Pushkar.

As we pulled into the village, people cheered at the sight of Lindsay, a pretty little slip of a woman driving that great big van, having maneuvered the dangerous hairpin turning road. I applied wet cloth to Lothar's head to bring down the fever and soothe his delirium. While looking for a room to stay, I found a young German woman who knew Lothar and agreed to care for him. I had no time for him now. We were on the move. Suddenly Lindsay, all clean and white, dressed in ironed khakis and starched shirt, silver jewelry and crystals, got violently ill. She needed a bathroom NOW. None here, none there. Ah, here we have one. She went in and was violently sick from every orifice of her body. There was no water and wouldn't be any for hours. She stood there, stunned, covered in puke and shit. Then she started to laugh. She laughed and laughed until tears poured down her cheeks. Later she told me that for one awful minute she had almost broken. Her laughter had delivered her India in the palm of her hand. Wow!

We kept travelling south. The coincidences and chance meetings kept coming at, even for us, a remarkable rate. Together we pulled magic and mystery from every shadow in the land. We finally parted in Goa, exhausted by two weeks of non-stop, excellent weirdness.

I took the boat north to Bombay. It was one of my hometowns in India. I had been stuck waiting for money for months on end in Bombay. I knew the city very well. I got a room at the Stiffles Hotel and went looking for my friends at Dipti's House of Pure Drinks. Dipti's was just a little wooden box of a room a few steps up from the street. As long as any of us had any money we would spend it on fruit lassis at Dipti's. Dipti was a clean, shiny man who knew all us hippies, who we are and where we are. He kept our messages to each other in his desk and was happy to be a guardian angel to the ragtag crowd of foreigners who constantly passed through town. He told me Ganesh Giri was in town, asking for me.

I had first met Ganesh Giri years before, just a few yards down the road from Dipti's. I passed a tall, very thin, long haired Indian man, dressed entirely in rich raw silk, a long kurta, vest and silk lungi. His elegant appearance, different from anybody I had seen before, caused me to stop and turn around as soon as I had passed him. He did the same.

He spoke only a few words of English. We walked together all over town for the rest of the day. He made those few words into an endless story. He fascinated me. I couldn't leave his side. I wondered if he was a prince. He said, "Come to Chowpatty and sleep with me." I wondered if Chowpatty was a palace. I followed him into the night. Chowpatty was the downtown beach. He introduced me to his friends. They were a jolly bunch of saddhus who made me very welcome. They shared their food with me. We sat up late into the night around a little fire. Ganesh Giri explained that this group gambled everything they had gathered during the day on a numbers game and lived on luck or its lack. Then he laid his silk lungi on the sand, another long piece of cloth, his turban, spread out beside that and we laid down to sleep under the stars, side by side. It was my first taste of saddhu life. Just before dawn, he and Santosh woke me up and we went looking for chai. In my mind, which was so blissed on love and the pleasure of his presence, we had become Rama and Sita and Lakshman walking in the Gir jungle at dawn. We bathed in a spring in a little natural oasis under Malabar Hill, in the middle of the city. He took my hand and led me into an entirely different India, far from the life of foreign cosmopolitan hippies grooving on the surface freedom afforded us by the generosity of India's open-minded people.

The sight of this richly dressed saddhu and a lovestruck foreign girl annoyed Indians and disgusted my friends. He was well known to many as a treacherous thief and womanizer. We didn't care. Whenever we met we walked together until I dropped from exhaustion. He was a Naga from the Juna Akkada. He showed me saddhu life and saddhu secrets, places and poisons, temples and sacred spots. He gave me little black balls of "medicine" that contained datura and gold and I never knew what else. He never lied to me.

I hadn't seen him for such a long time and now he and I were back together—but now Ganesh Giri was dying. He was so thin that his knees and elbows were huge knobs on thin sticks. He could barely walk without panting and stopping to catch his breath. He had smoked too many chillums, eaten too much poison, taken too much cobra venom into his bloodstream. He had reached a state of exhaustion. We had both run as far as the road went. We sat in Dipti's and quietly argued over which one of us was guru to the other. The next day we sat there, and I said,

"This is the end of life for both of us. Let's go to the Gir forest and meditate until the lions eat us, or we attain enlightenment."

We argued about lions for a while and then he agreed to my plan. I said I had only one little stop to make. It was on our way. I had to see the Englishman. It was the only thing I had left to do in my stupid sorry excuse for a life. He agreed. I bought train tickets to Ahmedabad and we left that night. The train was impossibly crowded and we spent the whole night crouched up in the little string luggage rack near the ceiling. Two dozen people were jammed into six spaces. No problem. We were together again, on our final adventure.

The next morning we were in the ugly, unfriendly little town of Mehmdabad. Nobody knew the name Anandaji. I said, "He's English, *farangi*."

We got directions. We took a horse-drawn tonka and headed towards the Society. Eventually the driver found the place, a large cement house, covered in bougainvillea. Ganesh Giri went in first to check things out. I waited outside with the bags and the horse.

"Get the hell out of my house you filthy saddhu! What do you mean by coming in here? What is your sampraday? Liar!! Get out! Get out!"

What a furious, roaring voice. Poor Ganesh Giri had no strength to defend himself. His protests were weak and softly spoken, barely audible over the blasting anger of that voice. I rushed in to rescue my comrade. I stepped into the little room and was captured by brilliant blue eyes. So unexpected. He looked up at me and roared,

"What the hell do YOU want?"

I stood my ground and answered arrogantly,

"I want enlightenment, of course!"

Silence. He was taken aback for half of a heartbeat.

"In that case, you may stay. He..."

He pointed at Ganesh Giri.

"He has to leave now. And take his lice with him!"

I agreed immediately. I went out with Ganesh Giri to the waiting horse tonka.

"I am staying. You must leave."

He looked dismayed. He feared for my safety. I gave him half my hashish and money. We agreed to meet in Bikaner in a few days and off he went. I never saw him again. I returned to the room and the furious Englishman. I plunked down my bag. I knew destiny when I saw him.

Life at the Hermitage

I looked at him. He was an imposing and handsome man of seventy years. His eyes captivated my attention, piercingly blue and crackling with energy. His hair was long, white with yellow blonde tips, and grew luxuriantly. He wore cheap silver hoop earrings and his ear lobes were large. His forehead, his cranium were huge. Everything about him was massive. His hands were scary, huge, with padded finger tips and dangerous thumbs. He had a good-sized belly, and his skin was shiny with health.

Oddly I can't remember how he was dressed or if he was naked. It was winter and early morning, so I assume he was wearing a long orange robe, a kufni, to keep off the morning chill. He handed me his card. "Shri Gurudev Dadaji Mahendranath."

"Oh! No wonder you were so hard to find this morning. I had the wrong name!" I laughed.

"I am called Dadaji. It is an affectionate term meaning grandfather."

"Dadaji. My name is Kristen. I come from Canada, but I've been in India off and on for many years."

"Well Kristen from Canada, would you join me for a cup of tea?"

"Yes, please."

A moment later Kaliben, a tiny, aged, bright and spry woman came into the room with two cups of sweet, milky chai.

"This is Kaliben. She and her husband Chotabhai own this house. I am their guest here and have been for many years."

I pranaamed to her respectfully (bowed with my hands held together in front of my face) and she smiled back, warmly but uncertain of me at the same time. She gathered up two or three pieces of laundry and left the room with a protective glance back towards Dadaji.

He sat down on his low wooden bed, the only furniture in the room. He indicated a mat that I could sit on, as the floor was cold terrazzo. We sipped tea and both lit up cheap Indian cigarettes.

"You come from Canada. Where are you going?"

"I had an idea to go to the Gir forest."

"Ah. You will of course go to Girnar, on the holy mountain. I spent some time there. It is one of the most sacred pilgrimage places in all of India."

I didn't know that.

"And your mission is enlightenment?" he said with an amused twinkle.

He had just asked the three traditional questions. Who are you? Where are you going? What is your mission? "Kristen from Canada" was a mundane answer. "Girnar" was at least a good destination, but in my case haphazard. My mission? Good answer, but painfully naïve. How much can be learned in so few words.

Suddenly a small bundle of a boy burst into the room and took a long slide across the floor and landed at Dadaji's feet. "Ha! Has Janak been a good boy?"

He pulled the little lad up and gave him an inch on the bed. He tousled his hair and laughed.

"I doubt it," he said.

Then he playfully tapped him on the head as a blessing and introduced him as the youngest member of the household, and one to whom special dispensation was given to sit beside the Guru on his throne. Janak looked boldly back at me, his eyes full of mischief.

A moment later, Sangeeta, his sister, a self-contained young girl with a long braid, came in. She was accompanied by Matti. They both approached the bed and bowed to touch the guru's feet. He gave them both his blessings, speaking in Sanskrit and thumping their bowed heads. Sangeeta was quiet and Matti had a paralyzed tongue, was slightly mad and only spoke in loud croaks. The young sister and her old auntie began sweeping and washing the floor, cleaning up the tea cups and dusting. Meanwhile, Dadaji questioned Janak about school. Janak wouldn't be caught speaking English, so he just nodded and laughed. The eldest brother, Nitesh, was at college in Ahmedabad and wouldn't be back until evening.

The morning rush of activity was over as abruptly as it had begun. The kids went off to school and Matti went about her domestic chores in the other part of the house.

We continued to smoke and chat. He explained that these people—the P. family—were very, very dear to him. Even before he had moved into their home "due to antiquity," they had sent one of their sons to his kutir (hut) on the Vatrak River with warm rotis and a cooked vegetable dish every day for years. Ramesh had recently moved to London and was deeply missed. I would meet his brother Dinubhai, son of Chotabhai and father of the children, as the day progressed. Then he explained that it was common practice in Gujerat State to end female names in -ben, which means sister, and to end male names in -bhai, which means brother. Thus Kaliben was Sister Kali. The men's names could be used either as Ramubhai or Ramesh, Dinubhai or Dinesh. Gujerati was a singular language in India, and the Gujeratis have many peculiarities, opposite to all their neighbors. Their cooking is admired all over India.

In walked Kailashben, daughter-in-law, mother to the three children and wife of Dinubhai. All the family seemed very content, but Kailashben was the physical embodiment of that contentment. She was round and beautiful, simply dressed in a soft sari, gentle and sweet.

I had been invited to lunch. Except for Dhinubhai, who always sat with him while he ate, Dadaji ate alone in his room. I was sent out to eat with the family in the other part of the house. We sat in a semi-circle on the floor in the kitchen. It was a big group, so we ate first with the women and children and the adult men as they came in from work. First came Chotabhai, the elderly head of the household. He welcomed me to his home with grave dignity. He showed neither curiosity nor suspicion. He sold vegetables in the village marketplace, as his family had done for generations. A year hence I would look up from my stitching and ask, "How was business today?" He would look appalled at my rudeness of spirit. He delivered a few sharp, short sentences that conveyed precisely his lack of interest in the vagaries of his fortunes in the marketplace.

I had just finished eating, washing my hand into the plate with the last of my drinking water. I was planning to get up and help with the clean-up when I was summoned back to Dadaji's room by Janak. Dinubhai was there. He and Dadaji had obviously been conferring. As there were no hotels anywhere near and the railway station was a simple village one without waiting/sleeping rooms, I had been invited to stay the night, possibly two nights. The family could make room for me among the large metal drums of stored beans and rice and the large stone wheat hand-grinder in the corner. They would even give me a rope charpoy (bed) to sleep on, which, looking back, was probably one of the elders' beds, because in India we normally all slept on rolled-out mats on the floor. I accepted their invitation immediately.

After lunch we all went down for a short nap in our various spots. When we were all awake again Dadaji showed me the workings of how and where to bathe, wash clothes, draw water and know drinking water from washing water. As there was just one water tap, by the backyard steps, all household water was kept in a variety of large amphora style pots, placed strategically all around the house. In those days the water supply was sporadic. Everyone in the village rushed to fill pots while the water ran. It was also a new colony of cement houses and wasn't yet entirely hooked up to the small grid of those days.

He showed me that it was possible to discreetly pee at the shower drain which ran into the miniature canal system that snaked through the garden outside. His watered-down piss, he assured me, was the secret to the luxuriant growth of bougainvillea which this house, out of all the other houses in the colony, enjoyed. The flowering bushes already reached the roof and blossomed a glorious red.

The sun always sets at six p.m., and that first evening we went up the back cement stairs to the roof. Dadaji had two lawn chairs stacked behind the door to the vestibule that sat over the stairs on the roof. We took them out and put them up. The roof was edged by a three-foot-high wall made of decorative cement blocks, and was, of course, as big as the entire downstairs. From this roof I was to watch the world outside the house for many an hour.

That first evening was typical. The sun set, and evening twilight began with the flight home of huge, furry fruit bats. They flew so close that I could have reached up and stroked their fur. They had great leathery wings, and their passage was accompanied by the strange sound those wings made. Minutes later, in a cross-current, a stream of loudly cawing, brilliantly green little parrots flew to their night home tree. Swallows swooped past on their way over to the mud cliffs by the river. The breeze would always come up the moment the sun slipped below the horizon, and with it came the smell of the little fires all over India, being lit to cook the evening meal. The cows raised dust as the herds drifted home and the dust mixed with the light of the sunset. It is the eternal moment of evening homecoming, and is the most celebrated, evocative expression of endless India. I looked at the card which Shri Gurudev Dadaji Mahendranath had given me that morning when I had just arrived. Under his name it continued. Hermitage of the Cosmic Oracle and Lunar Laboratory of Twilight Yoga. I looked over to where Dhinubhai and Dadaji were sitting together listening to the BBC World News on the radio. The stars were coming out one by one above. The night air was fresh and cool.

Mangalnath and Girnar

New information found fertile ground in me. I was so stretched out, trying to understand, trying to be receptive. He may well have wished me to relax, but I was determined not to miss any word or any signal. He sent me away after my first few days at the hermitage. He had given me a dozen addresses of people all over the world. I joked that he certainly didn't want me to get lost, no matter where I wandered. I told him that my original plan had been to go to the Gir forest. Quite alarmed, he started to warn me of the dangers of the forests beyond the Ambaji Temple on the climb up the Holy Mountain. He used Indian words that I couldn't understand, but I gathered that the Holy Mountain was a place of murder and mayhem. He certainly was harsh in his warnings about saddhus.

"On the other hand," he said, "Girnar is the sacred home of India's greatest saint and the founder of the Naths, Dattatreya by name."

He arranged for Dinubhai to write a note of introduction in Gujerati to Sri Mangalnath Maharaj of Girnar, and that is where I headed after leaving Mehmadabad.

It took two days of hard train and bus travel to get to Girnar, which is a tiny village perched on the lower heights of the sacred mountain. Girnar is a pilgrimage town full of ashrams and saddhus. The first person I saw striding down the road, like a king, was a naked, ash-covered, dreadlocked saint. I was directed to Mangalnath's ashram, which was large, and when I walked in it was full of schoolboys eating lunch off the traditional leaves placed on the ground. I stood around, shy and uncertain of what to do. I had never been in an ashram before. I didn't speak a word of the local language (nor much of any Indian language), and apparently nobody spoke English. Nevertheless, within an hour I was sitting on the ground in the shade of a large mango tree, eating the same lunch as the crowd of schoolboys.

I had never eaten anything that rough in my life before. I truly doubted I could do it again. The rice had stones, the vegetables were barely chopped and not skinned and the rotis were made of very roughly ground flour. Indian food was still a mystery to me. I had not yet become a fan, and this was not the way to start.

Eventually a man arrived who looked like he knew the boss, so I gave him my introduction written in Gujerati. He conveyed to me that Mangalnath would be available that evening at 5:00, and then he took me to meet Wanita. She was the middle aged woman who cooked and cared for Mangalnath. She lived in a little tunnel of a room. Her bed was laid on top of three trunks that held all her worldly goods. The walls were hung with embroidered panels and her two sarees were hung over a line that followed the wall. The kitchen was just inside the door and was nothing more than a two-burner kerosene cook stove on the floor, some pots, storage bins for grains and the spices and vegetables of the day. Wanita has forever become associated in my mind with Santoshi Ma, goddess of contentment. She took my hand and brought me into her tiny home. She laid out a mat for me to sleep on and then she began to cook. She was a marvelous and refined cook. Her rotis were soft and perfectly formed, her spicing mild and subtle and her sauces divine. She conveyed to me that she was given this little home and food in return for caring for Mangalnath. I guessed she was a widow or from some other desperate social condition. She was very happy to be doing this and living there and she adored Mangalnath.

He was a Raja saddhu, a kingly saint. Among other things he fed and housed 300 schoolboys in his ashram every day, which permitted these sons of nomads and impoverished rural folk to get an education. He was so respected and adored by so many people across India that he was very wealthy in alms. This is how he chose to give away that money.

Finally it was five p.m. and I was taken to meet the great man. He was blind. He sat on a deer skin and wore only a lungoti (a g-string). He looked well fed and very good humoured. Dadaji's note was read to him. A look of delight came over his face. He said, "Ah, Mahendranath Ji," and he laughed with his memories. He called me over close to him and took my hand. I fumbled a bit of money in alms to him, but he wanted only to read me by sense of touch. He made a few comments with a big grin and everybody around us laughed, rather lewdly I thought. I felt self-conscious, scared, shy, alone, but I was also determined with all my being to climb that holy mountain, and I was also spiritually aflame from meeting Dadaji so short a while back. On that level he responded to me and he silently gave me a depth of encouragement. Without sight or language we communicated only by holding hands.

After a few minutes he laughed again and had a man give me double plus one Rs. of what I had just given him. Someone explained that offerings should never be of an amount that ends in zero. It caused bad luck and poverty for the receiver. I had been given 21 Rs. I felt embarrassed, but also enriched, as I had so little money.

I slept in Wanita's little home that night and she got me up and fed by four a.m. I bade the ashram farewell and started to walk up the great mountain that loomed over us all. I knew nothing of what was up there beyond the Ambaji temple. The climb began abruptly after passing through the archway that defined the limits of the village, up great stone steps that have been cut and laid into the mountain in a long, somewhat meandering trail up to the first summit. Chai shops of every size and capacity appeared along the route. Sometimes there were chairs and umbrellas, but usually it was a bend in the path that offered a little shade, some tea and perhaps some biscuits and a warm drink or two. The path was already full of pilgrims of all ages and types. Some climbed in rough palanquins; an oldster might be strapped to the back of a strong son. All water, wood and food had to be hauled up that pathway by a steady stream of human packhorses. Pilgrims had been climbing these stairs unceasingly for thousands of years. I had been using a mantra constantly on this trip. It was one of the things that gave me the strength and confidence to keep going. My sense grew that I too was a true pilgrim, climbing the Holy Mountain and on my way to confront the mystery and get some answers.

Later that day I had finally climbed enough of those stairs, through the sparse, dry forest and the blasting sun, and now I stood outside the gates of the Ambaji temple. I peeked into the cool dark interior, but I couldn't quite bear to enter. I had no money left and the hands were out at every step. I had never spent time in temples and I didn't feel at all inclined to learn the way of things right then and there. I ducked to the left of the great throng of people and headed into the wilderness, until I found a little cave with a view to the ends of the earth.

I pulled out my chillum and managed to get it lit with my last match. In that sudden alteration of consciousness, very heightened by the location, I reminisced about Dadaji's parting words back at the hermitage. Raising his arms over his head and taking one step forward in a dramatic heiratic pose, he had intoned "DO AS THOU WILT SHALL BE THE WHOLE OF THE LAW." I was thunderstruck. I had never heard those words before. They sounded very, very shocking to me. They seemed to contradict everything I had ever been told to do before. It sounded wrong and scared me about the true nature of this strange man who was now my Guru. During the entire trip I had brought these words forward in my mind and examined them from every angle. Sitting in that cave, high above the surrounding plain and so high on hashish, the meaning of those words dawned on me and hurtled me straight into an altered state of flaming understanding. I am free, I was born free and have lived free without ever once realizing it. Something physically and abruptly changed in me from that moment. I came into focus. I was entrapped by ego, by social pressure that got me to conform and obey the rules of my reality tunnel. Detaching from that pressure left me free to pursue the purpose for which I had incarnated in this life. I went into bliss.

I left the cave and headed back down those stairs in the late afternoon. My feet barely touched the ground. I contained my wild laughter, and that just fed the fire. I was sitting on a rocky outcropping ledge, resting and reviewing my wonderful vision in the cave. An older Indian man came by, looked up and said in English,

"My dear, you are all aflame. You have seen the face of the Goddess I think."

He placed some rupees at my feet. I was amazed. Others could see what I was experiencing! What could he possibly have seen? I continued to get offerings from people who bowed to my visionary experience and walked on. I gathered up the money and decided to head straight back to the hermitage as fast as I could get there.

Study Begins

When I arrived back at the house in Mehmadabad, early morning, a week after I had left, Dadaji looked up in great surprise and said, "What are you doing here?"

"Well, I met Mangalnath and I climbed Girnar and I got blown away by what you said... Do As Thou Wilt... that was amazing! And now, well, where else would I go? I have to be here."

"You can't stay here."

Tears just suddenly poured out of my eyes. I slumped back.

"You certainly cry very easily!"

"No I don't," I said defiantly through tears, "I'm tough as nails."

"Don't say that. Tough is useless. Dreadful. No good at all and a great detriment for a woman."

"Listen," he said, "I'm a very heavy trip. Living with me is unbearable. Unthinkable."

"No no. I won't be a bother. I promise. I'm really easy to get along with. It will be great. I really have to be here with you."

"What are you talking about? I'm completely bogus you know."

"You are?" I said, distress and surprise in my voice.

"Well, maybe not completely," he said with an amused grin.

I won that argument and moved in again, but now I lived in the little vestibule at the top of the stairs that lead outside to the roof.

The next day after lunch in Dadaji's room, I got up to help the women clean up the meal.

He said, "Sit down."

"I am just going to help with the clean up."

"Don't interfere," he growled.

I sat down, but felt a struggle inside.

"I don't see how I can stay here for free and not help with the household chores. It isn't right."

"Mind your own business."

I didn't insist further. He was getting angry.

I seldom understood why Dadaji acted the way he did. He never explained. I began my custom of obeying in blind trust. It always seemed to me that he never taught me anything. Generally I did as I was told, but my internal dialogue was often hot and defiant.

"Mind your own business. Don't interfere."

I heard those words constantly for years. They always pinched.

In fact those words signal the beginning of the Nivritti Marga, the Path of Inward Turning or the Varma Marga, the Left Turning Path or the Natha Marga, the Subtle Zig Zag Trail.

Learn to command my own attention and gain great energy by unhooking from the teat of the transitory, of the passing show of life. This was the first step of my transformation work.

Withdrawing attention involved me in pitched battles with ego, guilt, conditioning, self image. In order to not cause new karmic entanglement and new prolonged soap operas I learned the art of not doing, of not involving myself in the lives of others. Anything that interfered with the contemplative or meditative state was a lure. The vast sea of influences seeking to change me into a better person, a responsible worker, a more alluring woman or a useful citizen needed to be evaded like poison gas. The in-turning of the majority of my attention was an enormous wrenching effort.

Our daily life together settled into a pleasant routine. We talked, smoked cheap cigarettes. He took snuff and chewing tobacco and smoked cigarettes. I was a pack-a-day smoker. The air was always foggy blue with the smoke. The family included me into the routine with little problem that I ever heard of. If Dadaji was happy, they were also content.

Dadaji told war stories. He had been in the International Brigade during the Spanish Civil War. The Russians lectured the new soldiers on the technique of attack. He asked how to retreat.

"There is no retreat."

His survival depended on his ability to think independently, and magic helped too. A huge bomb exploded in the field while he was trying to carry a wounded soldier to safety. The dust cloud was so thick that he couldn't tell which way to go, and which way led to enemy lines. The bullets were zinging past. Suddenly a bejewelled arm reached into the dust cloud and pulled him to safety. Dadaji had a number of encounters with God Indra, who protected and blessed him throughout his life.

The Second World War started right away, after the triumph of fascism in Spain. Dadaji signed up again, although anti-fascist fighters were not welcome in the British army. He caused a mutiny in the boat that sailed to the battlefields of southern Europe. He was put up on charges, but as he related with relish, the tables soon turned, his accusers were reprimanded for incompetence and he was exonerated. Petty bureaucrats and officious officers hated Dadaji. He took such pleasure in being the cause of their discomfort. He enjoyed taking the side of the underdog against the blind injustices of the powerful.

He was trained as a physiotherapist. To get him out of the hair of one high ranking officer, he was shifted to Italy, and later Egypt. In Egypt he had a chance to visit the pyramids and clamber inside, unrestrained by tourists or authorities. Magic occurred. In Italy he made a pilgrimage to Assisi. Although considered sacred by Catholics because of St. Francis, it is also claimed by Sufis and magicians as one of their power places. Assisi was yet one more of the endless connections that existed between us. I had been there a number of times as a child and an adolescent, and I was well aware of the power of that place. Once again he was given free run and got to see a certain crypt that is usually hidden from public view.

He was very proud of saving Yugoslavians. He treated many soldiers from there who were later being forcibly repatriated by the British. These were men who had fought the Nazis almost barehanded. They were partisans being forced back into the waiting arms of murderous fascist collaborators who executed every one of them. They told their story to Dadaji. Using his

Labour Party connections he was able to have the matter brought up in the British Parliament, and the facts became known to the public.

"I wish I could have died on the battlefield, but in this lifetime it is not to be. At least the British army provided me with the mantra that has served me so well in this life."

My ears perked up in the sleepy afternoon heat.

"You know the song about 'The Long and the Short and the Tall'? Well fuck 'em all!"

"Whats the mantra though?"

"Fuck 'em all," he intoned solemnly.

"Try it and see. Never let the bastards get the better of you."

It works just fine.

Keeping me occupied and quiet was not as easy as I had promised. Finally Dadaji had me copy out everything he had written into small, lined school notebooks. Each afternoon I would spend two or three hours copying. This had the excellent effect of forcing me to concentrate, and improved my handwriting, too. Sometimes we would discuss what he had written, but I found most of it difficult to follow in those early days. What I loved was his poetry. I loved the rhythm and the simplicity of expression. His poems spoke of his joy in the saddhu life. All he needed was a little food and water and a shady tree, the simple necessities of life, freely given and happily received. He wrote poems for children, for me, about love and happy moments of spiritual joy and physical pleasure.

He tried to get me to answer his mail. Every day we would wait for Dinubhai, our contact with the world outside his room, to bring in the mail. Letters came from all over the world. He was most interested in the letters that came from Mike Magee. He was the young Englishman who had shown up a year before and received initiation and the name Lokanath. Dadaji really loved the guy. He was seventy years old by this time, and Mike was the first Westerner he had met that he considered worthy of initiation. Through Mike's wide-ranging influence, more and more young Brits and even Americans began to write. Dadaji was looking for some particular quality in these kids, but he seldom found it. Answering all these letters and paying the postage slowly became a drain on his energy and resources.

Two things bothered him about the people who wanted his spiritual teachings. Those who kept their feet in too many camps irritated him to no end. Wiccan Thelemite Gnostic Naths are not as rare a bird as one might imagine. And he always hoped somebody would weave new patterns from his old gems, find new ways of living and thinking, find ways of escaping from the old rat race. He despaired of anyone breaking free from the old occult patterns of European magic and Asian religious expression.

When I arrived that very first day I am sure I saw a good number of books on his shelf. By the time I came back a week later he had burned them all. His library, which I examined surreptitiously, consisted of a heavily marked-up *I Ching*, Patanjali's *Yoga Sutras*, an Oxford English Dictionary and a particular translation of *Srimad Bhagavatam*. He did not wish to discuss theories, nor did he want to hear about what I had read. He disapproved of my reading habits. The worst thing I could do was expose myself to the spiritual theories and ideas of others. As far as he was concerned, it was a world of crap out there. Somehow, without books and only a few people around him who spoke English, he was always current and informed about the world in tremendous detail. His grasp of history, science and geography never failed to surprise. He loved to quote long epic poems by heart, especially King Arthur's death scene and the return of Excalibur to the Lady of the Lake. Of course. He was Merlin.

He was Merlin and the Great Swan and a magician and a hermit. I thought he was quite nuts. On the other hand, and in the same breath, I had decided that he was my enlightened Guru and I trusted him with my very atoms. I think this is called cognitive dissonance, and I had it very badly and very often around that man. He understood the power of identification and encouraged me to think of myself and of us together in mythic and magical terms. He was Merlin, I was the dangerous Nimue. I wrote him a poem from her viewpoint. I could never have retrieved the information it contained in mundane headspace. I was his goddess, his beloved. He was my hero, omniscient, saint, devil and time traveller. This play was at the very heart of Indian Tantra as I came to understand it. Both human and divine we meet in another place, think different thoughts and accomplish great deeds. No need for ritual... in fact, he and I never did any ritual work whatsoever. We spontaneously shifted into "lucky space," and all was accomplished. When I or anyone else would thank him for some problem solved, some boon given, he would always look slightly mystified.

"I don't know what you are talking about."

Since modesty was not one of his attributes, I eventually understood that good magic is what happens because it has to, spontaneously and with an often humorous perfection. On the other hand, Mahendranath often fueled his magic with fury. His anger was terrifying. One day he attended a gathering of local dignitaries. At the end of the ceremonies a very poor old farmer came to the stage and, looking up, begged him to send rain because the fields were dry and the crops were dying. His first impulse was to refuse.

One of the Brahmins on the stage said, "Just ignore him, he is nothing but a low caste dog."

Yipes! Dadaji became infuriated by the remark. He quickly and spontaneously drew a magic sigil and empowered it with his rage. The rains began to pour down out of a once-blue sky within moments.

"It rained so hard and in such amounts," he said, laughing at the memory, "I was swept off the stage and almost drowned in the flood."

That old farmer was still around, and whenever we encountered him on one of our walks, he hobbled towards us like a blind old mole. Laughing and worshipping at the same time, he would bend and touch Dadaji's feet. Then they would walk and talk for a moment, and Dadaji would give him one of his head-thumping blessings. Magic had bound them together in enduring friendship.

Kleshas

Living with Dadaji proved to be as difficult as he had predicted. Now, I can see that I took up so much of his space, his time and his emotional energy. He would often say in exasperation, "Would you RELAX!" When he had had more than enough, his door curtain would be pulled closed and I was forbidden to enter, usually for days. The family would give me aggrieved looks as they came and went from his darkened and closed-off room. Angry roars would bring someone running. I would spin off into hurt and anger and fear and stay frozen, unable to bear what was happening. I could never figure out what had made him act that way. On the other hand, in their wise way, the older family members would move in very close to him, pressing and massaging his legs, feet, arms and head. They would soothe him like he was a sick child. I knew nothing about nurturing, so I stood in harsh judgement of his "babyish" behavior and I would yell at him and attack his curtain with insults. Then Kaliben would take me by the arm, hold my hand and tell me to shush and go upstairs to the roof and leave him alone. He would be shouting at me by then. Couldn't everybody see he was wrong and I was right?

I have always had a problem with authority. I had acted in an unprecedented manner when I had given Mahendranath authority over me. I had given him the right to do to me anything he saw fit to do. Nonetheless I obviously squirmed and rankled and burned. I began to fantasize about killing him in violent ways. I couldn't stop it. I would drown him, knife him and shoot him with a machine gun. These fantasies disturbed me greatly because consciously I adored him. One day while I was copying his writing into my notebook I was also thinking about my violent reactions and wondering what was going on with me. I looked down and saw I had written "neurosis." There was nothing else to do but confess. I expected fury. Instead he laughed and said, "This is why I love you. You tell the truth." I was relieved, but I wondered if he really knew my dark heart.

Many many saddhus are ex-military or ex-police. It meant that these men were often fastidious, methodical and competent. Dadaji was all of these things. His room contained little, but everything had somehow been altered by his hand. He kept his tools in tins which were decorated with orange paint and had strange faces created out of cut paper glued to the outside. Anything that broke, he would repair. His ancient and rotten tape player was always needing to be taken apart. Little screws and parts and pieces would be carefully placed in a lid to be cleaned, filed and replaced. If a tape broke he took the cassette apart and very meticulously restuck the tape back together with sticky tape cut to size with a little blade. It was rewound and the cassette put back together with its tiny screws. He loved his music and even though the quality was worse than the early transistor radios, he could be transported by Grieg or, just as easily, some new disco group or Indian film music. He was always looking for new sounds. Every afternoon, equipment permitting, we would sit and listen to a few selected pieces of very varied music. His feelings about music were as unpredictable and as strongly held as his feelings about ideas and people.

He sewed all his own cold weather kufnis (robes, actually "shrouds"). His orange sheets were hemmed by his hand and he delighted in making marvelous nightcaps in fanciful but simple shapes. His stitching was perfect, even and almost invisible. It intrigued and offended me too. I had made my living by sewing and had often done large handstitched projects, but I couldn't come close to his skill. He started to sew things for me, a set of orange cotton sheets, a red heavy cotton robe with an orange circle over the heart. During one of our loud angry fights, I sat and stitched around a large piece of cloth, emulating as best I could his invisibly small stitches. I refused to eat or even look up until the entire project was finished. "There! Anything you can do, so can I!"

Orange or geru (orange ochre earth) is the saddhu's main color, but black, red, yellow and white also occur. Naths often wear black, but Dadaji liked orange and, for occasions, a touch of lemon yellow. Every few weeks he would re-dye all his cloth and robes and sheets with powdered orange dye. It seemed to soothe his temper, and it was fun. The bright dye water covered the floor outside his room. Playing in water was a relief in the heat. I gave him a beautiful length of cloth, rather garish, gold and yellow stripes, obviously Muslim in style and taste. I had bought it in the wonderful bazaar in Peshawar in western Pakistan. He was as delighted by its utterly inappropriate quality as by its beauty.

Giving gifts to Dadaji was a trial. I went to Ahmedabad with Uma and spent hours looking for an alarm clock for him. I knew he needed one. His old clock could no longer be fixed and I hoped to even out some of my perceived debt to him. I bought a large round clock, with big numbers and a loud alarm. The next day he was furious with the clock. I had bought the cheapest I could find, I had been mean and pennypinching and the clock had bad vibes. Since none of this was true except possibly the bad vibes, I didn't feel any anger at his reaction. I was a little annoyed when I saw it later, smashed up, on the trash heap behind the house. Eventually I realized that he either destroyed or gave away most gifts he received. The gold cloth was a rare exception. I believe he always kept it in his trunk. He had a way of divining the quality of intention in any gift, and the cloth was one of the few things I gave him that was spontaneous and lacking in subtext.

He told me about his time in Thailand in the '50s. He had fixed up a cave as his hermitage on Snake Mountain. He was able to accomplish furious amounts of meditation in that remote place. He had a great gift, talent and fascination for meditation. He became well known. One day the King and Queen of Thailand came to visit and they gave him a cup, a bowl and a plate of solid gold. After they left he took the precious objects and hammered and smashed them with a rock into the crevasses in the mountain cave. Symbolically the gold went back to its origin as a vein running through the earth. Shortly afterwards his meditation was abruptly interrupted by a visit from God Indra and his ragtag crew of buddies who came to visit in a vision of godly mischief and humor.

This is Dadaji's ditty of the Five Kleshas.

> *"The five pain-bearing obstructions,*
> *The root cause of trouble and strife,*
> *Ignorance, Ego, Attachment,*
> *Repulsion and Clinging to Life."*

The five kleshas never stop impeding our enjoyment of life and our development. Dadaji never stopped confronting kleshas as they arose in him. We both dealt with ego in a very odd way, by bragging, self-aggrandizing through our personal mythologies and mocking the achievements of others. You will have to figure that one out for yourself. We were very clever with this method.

Ignorance is simply not thinking clearly for oneself. Allowing myself to express a limiting viewpoint, a sentimental cliché, a self-delusion got me into lots of trouble. My trite liberal beliefs, inherited and unexamined, would cause him to become dangerously angry. I made a remark about vegetarianism and non-killing. He gave me a dark and disgusted look and went out and killed a neighbor's piglet that had been rampaging through the garden. He just smashed it with a big rock and left it there. I was silent, stunned, but a whole block of rules broke off the frozen iceberg of my belief system and floated away.

Attachment and repulsion are the two sides of the same seesaw. As a hippie I had little repulsion to the usual things. I was undaunted by dirt, germs, bad water, lepers or Indian third-class train toilets. I could sleep in any dirty place and wear rags without a care or a damn. I needed to dive deep to find my level of repulsion, and it was surprising when I found it. The cult of Aghoris is dedicated to working with this klesha. The very name means that nothing is, in and of itself, repulsive. Fear, preference, overwhelming desire, refusal, rejection are all plays of attraction and repulsion. Ideally I try to bring all these things into a balanced and minor manifestation at the fulcrum between extremes.

Clinging to life or clinging to anything too strongly leads to tearing and splitting of the will and the heart. It is a hard lesson and I will never know how successful the work has been until I face my own death. I am learning to relax in the face of threat and danger. It has proven to be the best possible reaction because it is surprising and unsettles even packs of dogs and marauding monkeys. Surprise changes the situation quickly, and hopefully a better outcome is experienced by all. *Songs of the Dakini*, about Buddhist Sadvini and Queen of Tibet, Yeshe Tsogyal, taught me this. Keith Dowman translates these songs in *Skydancer*.

I was away at the time of Dadaji's seventy-fifth birthday. I have no idea why he decided to commit suicide. When I returned, everybody, including Dadaji, was abuzz with the extraordinary tale. He told me this:

"I was sick of life. You can live too long you know! I decided to leave this sordid world. I made sure of my success by killing myself in two ways at once. I took a large amount of rat poison and then I slit my wrists. It seemed I was unconscious for a long time, because I had quite an adventure in that in-between life and death place. [Often called the bardo.] It is always twilight and grey there. I walked a while until I ran into a group of saddhus sitting together in a circle. They were gambling. They had been gambling for a very, very long time. Behind them a bright road led somewhere. I asked the saddhus why they were just sitting there and not walking the road. They barely looked up, and gave a collective shrug. I left them and started towards the road. There I found Kaliben. [The grandmother had recently died and we all mourned her passing.] She and I had a final conversation."

This little bird of a woman, who had never been further than a few miles down the road, who couldn't read or write, who knew nothing but domestic life set in a pattern a thousand years ago, this singing bird, always caged by cultural rules, was the woman Dadaji called his Guru. They blessed each other and went their separated ways. Apparently the rat poison counteracted the bleeding and the bleeding counteracted the poison, if you can believe that! So he came back alive and felt rather jolly and pleased with himself.

Years later Dadaji fell down the cement stairs leading to the roof. He broke his hip and was rushed to the hospital. I was told that he spent the entire night breathing like a steam engine and he was dead by morning. It was said he had killed himself by yogic means, unwilling to be a burden on the family. Later, as I travelled among the Naths of India, I learned the true reason for his self-caused death. Naths never want to die of natural causes, depleted of energy and all played out. Death must be faced with energy and power. The spirit travels like a shooting star to free itself from earth's limitations. It is customary for Naths of any standing and power to have themselves buried alive in a small crypt. When this is done correctly, the Nath remains both here and there and is effective in both realms, manifest and powerful. I met some of these "living dead" during my travels, and I have no doubt of the effectiveness of their tradition. I have been in a large room in a very ancient Nath ashram filled with fifty-two living dead graves of Nath leaders, each one having picked the time to go down into their tombs.

Choices

Mahendranath thought for himself. He looked at words and ideas carefully, turning, studying and comparing. He deeply examined everything in life that we take for granted. He never believed anything that he had not himself confirmed. Eventually this gave him an exalted view or, rather, a view from a high place, a panoramic view. To become a naked Nath in India, to form no attachments to people, places or objects, to gather together nothing at all, to embrace poverty and solitude, these are odd choices. These are the choices of someone who views life from outside and far beyond any local reality tunnel. Looking into his future as a young, healthy Englishman, he could see a world of possibilities. He experienced wild freedom while gazing at a plenum of potential pathways spread out at his feet.

There is a persistent belief that we are about to see a planetary reset to default, a mysterious, unknowable default. The lodestone mind that carries its own inner maps may steer true when our other maps no longer correspond to a newly-altered reality. Preparing for total novelty seems impossible, but in fact it is the way of life for a magician.

Years ago de Ropp wrote a useful and clarifying book on the subject of life paths called *The Master Game.* This is a very good book for youths who wish to examine their motivations and the deep desires and goals that influence their creation of lives that conform to (hopefully) their greatest ideals. Power, fame, wealth, family life, wisdom, experiences and freedom (jivanmukti) are all legitimate aims. If we make our choices from the handbook we are given by society, and usually our families, we have very limited choices. We do what has already been done, what is always done. This is what makes the world go round, perhaps. The salt of the earth, the propagators of life, the growers of food and new software, inventors, lovers and soldiers make this planet function as it must. These are the salt and the pillars, the men and women of the world.

Dadaji first picked to be a soldier—or to be much more accurate, he chose to attend wars. I never heard him mention shooting a gun. He was rescue and medical help on the battlefields in Spain, and rehab for the soldiers in the Second World War. He was always getting himself into trouble with the higher ranks, so he wasn't planning to rise through the military. Perhaps the horrors and destruction of war, tyrannical rules and sudden death were useful catalysts to push him further outside the gates of ordinary life. I suspect we have all spent lifetimes as rank and file soldiers, following some leader, dying for one cause or another, on the battlefields of time. The saddhu ranks are filled with such men.

He was rejected by the military world. He was a troublemaker, a big troublemaker. He asked too many questions and proposed unthinkable solutions.

At all times, from a very young age, he was meditating, seeking out "saints" and sacred places, reading and researching—this at a time when there was very little information or example available to a Western seeker. Meanwhile, he worked at lots of jobs. He didn't drink or smoke or gamble, so his money went far. He travelled. He painted houses, designed ingenious ways to make jobs better or easier. He was a journalist and editor for an English-language newspaper in Bangkok. He was a window washer in Darwin. He was clever with his hands and meticulous to an extraordinary degree. He lived by his skills and wits on the surface of society, but formed no roots, no ties, no attachments.

He spent his own time researching cosmic mysteries, scientific advances, and ancient cultures and forms of magic. He learned that true information and accurate maps are hard to find. He talked with Wallace Budge at the British Museum. Budge was the foremost scientific investigator and expert on ancient Egypt. His most valuable words to the young man were, "We really don't know anything about ancient Egypt. So much of what you read, even in the history books, is pure imagination."

He sought out conversation with Aleister Crowley because he always looked to the despised and the discounted one, the object of mockery. "The one favored by the crowd is sure to be as great a fool as the crowd around him!"

He knew Crowley in the final years, when he was fairly derelict and addicted to pain-killing drugs. He had become a man of greatly diminished energy and influence. He had, however, a long view of his own life and accomplishments. He advised the young man and summed up what he felt were the triumphs and disappointments of his adventure-filled life. His great despair was never feeling satisfied with his encounters with magick. Dadaji was most surprised that Western magicians, including Crowley, still dreamt of finding "The Book" wherein would be written all the secrets of magic.

I wonder how Dadaji knew the true nature of magic long before he went to Asia? He said he had his first experience of enlightenment while still a young man in England. At that time he was camping out in a tent in a forest, where he could be alone and meditate without distraction. He had just returned from there to his tiny London flat. He had come to take care of his mundane reality and regroup before going back to the forest to continue his assault on the barriers to consciousness. He had just put a piece of music by Grieg on the phonograph and he was profoundly relaxed, sipping a freshly-brewed cup of tea, when... Bom Bolenath! Shiva Shankar Alakh! Alakh! Alakh!... he was swept up in a towering vision of Lord Shiva. The image was overwhelming, but the power and information transfer were unspoken, unspeakable and knowable only in another state of awareness altogether.

He said Crowley suggested he study the *I Ching* and visit India. He did both to his everlasting benefit. He finally sailed into Bombay Harbor in 1954, landing without a single penny in his pocket. He had given away the last of his shillings as tips to the ship staff. That very day he was initiated as a sannyasi and as an Adinath by his new guru, Lokanath of Uttarkashi. This saint had been patiently awaiting a mysterious arrival for two weeks. A vision of Shiva had told him to leave his silent cave in the remote Himalayas and come down to the blasting hot, crowded, coastal city and wait for the one who was to be his successor, his inheritor, his spiritual son. They must have recognized each other immediately. He was given the name of Mahendra, a name of God Indra who had blessed and protected him his whole life. Arriving penniless, no way back, was the magic pass for Dadaji, and he knew it.

We neo-Naths talk often about no gurus, no traditions; the new ways, the modern patterns of our path here in America and Europe. I wonder, though, how we can ever replace this exalted moment of utter clarity and dispassion and determination, this moment of nivritti marga, turning away from all that life has to offer? Taking the sannyas vows and taking on a guru are supreme moments, ultimate experiences, unalterable steps. It is death and rebirth. The old life is cast off with every attachment and responsibility that belonged to that life. This moment is understood as an exit from the womb of the world and rebirth into... the other life, the mirror of life as it used to be.

Motivation and desire are now only for freedom and renouncement, less not more, smaller not bigger, solitary, single-minded, already dead. Committed to renouncing heaven and therefore hell, this life and the next, everything we love in this life... we had better have a damn good reason, some reward that is greater than life itself. Promise not to work for another or for wages, promise not to marry or breed, promise to be so poor that you can't even feed yourself, change your name (lose that identity!), never visit your family again. You are dead for them. Everyone knows that some of these promises, vows, rules will get bent and broken, but nonetheless promises are made. This is a commitment that will certainly alter viewpoint, motivations and the outcome of one's life. This is a particularly odd choice to make for your life.

Most of Mahendranath's life in India is a complete mystery. He gave little peeks:

"I was studying *I Ching* in Penang and..."

"I was meditating on Serpent Mountain when..."

"I met this movie star in Benares and she..."

"I visited Goa and saw..."

"It was while I was wandering in the Rann of Kutch that..."

The saddhu wanders. He walks from Parasuramakund to Kanyakumari and back again. In every nook and cranny of India you will find saddhu signs. Tiny temples, painted rocks, fire rings, Nath graves, rusting trishuls nestled into the trunks of giant peepul trees. Saddhus wander and gather experience. They test the strength of their saddhana against the world and they do so half naked and unarmed. Using alcohol or drugs, starvation, privation and pain, gambling, sex, celibacy, meditation and contemplation, solitude or crowds they storm the walls of perception and explore the limits of human consciousness. They come up with endless wild and silly schemes for attaining Godhood, siddhas, all-knowing, all-power, all-whatever they figure they are seeking. Some saddhus are very radical beings who experiment and push back boundaries and restrictions and limitations with the zeal of maddened warriors.

Mahendranath despised modern saddhus. He felt they almost never fulfilled the potential that the saddhu life had given them. This is never an easy life and most fall by the wayside, giving up their inner freedom in favor of greedy cravings, crime and a closed mind. Drug use takes an enormous toll. Ignorance and politics turn them into small-minded, dangerous idiots. They are no longer widely supported by the population upon whom they depend for food and shelter. Meditation is often spoken of, but is seldom practised. Dadaji was considered odd for his fascination with and practice of meditation. Lokanath sent him off to the Buddhists to seek more information because it was so little studied among the Hindu wanderers.

The saddhu who acts out his knowledge and understanding is a delight to see, for a while. I spent one day following an old saddhu around the streets of Bombay. After a while I figured out that he had decided that for this day he would not exert his will. He would be tossed and twirled by the currents of the moment and the whims of passersby. What a hilarious, instructive and illuminating day! He became entrained in the energy streams of a passing businessman who was caught up in his thoughts and moving fast. Soon he became entangled with this goofy little old man, half-naked and toothless, grinning and glazed eyes shining. He was swatted away into the stream of a housewife who looked around to find that he had followed her to her doorway.

"Ah, Maharaj," she said sweetly, "please enter. You must eat. And you, foreign girl, you come too and eat."

Half a bite taken when a little whirlwind twirled him out of the courtyard and back out into the street, light as a feather.

At sunset we went down to the sacred lake at Walkeshwar, near the shoreline in Bombay. He went into the water among all the others washing themselves, their clothes, their kids, their cows. The ritual of bells and horns had started and incense and firelight streamed from the hundreds of little temples that surrounded that lake. It was the magic twilight moment, sandhya. Nothing is seen clearly, the light is tricky and smoky. Is that a snake or a rope? Suddenly that goofy clown of a saddhu looked me straight in the eye. I was up on the dry steps, his eyes shining in that commanding magical way that eyes shine when signaling important parts of the script. He lifted his loincloth most deliberately and seriously and exposed his nakedness. I was stunned. I couldn't guess the significance of what I was seeing at that moment but it was all etched so clearly in my memory to be understood later with more experience and words and knowledge. That was magic! The actor, the audience and the play, consciousness and the moment and the message. I hadn't met Dadaji yet, but I would be prepared to meet him, shortly thereafter.

Anyway, I just wanted to say something about choices and arrangements that can be more favorable to allowing strangeness and alternate realities to start manifesting intensely in one's life. I believe saddhu life points to this method. We mostly meet reflections of our mundane selves in habitual life, but it is my impression that jivanmukti is more often found on very strange pathways. Improbability may be the royal road to enlightenment. Magic is found where the weight of probability is less and the unlikely is becoming the norm. There is a strange buzzing of bee sound in the ears. The only power here is to be a skillful surfer. Don't fall off among sharks or the ordinary life, and learn to relax. Dadaji's choices were as wildly improbable as some wonderful number in the mathematical theory of playing the odds. He was just another fellow with a wild idea who ended up not too badly. The future may find a use for his work or not. To quote the gypsy, "He did what he did and he got what he got."

Bliss and Information

Dadaji seldom talked to me about spiritual matters. He preferred old war stories and occasionally he would tell me great tales from his adventures after the war, travelling through Asia and India. When he saw me reading Carlos Castaneda or any Indian saint or other authors who dwelt on such subjects he would become annoyed and recommend that I stick to Agatha Christie detective novels... "They are better quality mindfood than other people's ideas about God." I seldom took his advice because I found that especially under the influence of Castaneda I could raise my level of consciousness to a place where I was a more competent operator on the spiritual level. From Castaneda I could sometimes leap to an enlightenment state.

There were three books that Dadaji liked me to read. We both shared a deep love for the *I Ching* and once in a while we would do joint readings in which he was the top line and I was, I believe, a middle line. He was always very clear about the translation that he preferred in any book and he had a really superb eye for the best translation available. In those days Wilhelm's was the only good translation of the *I Ching*, "barring that idiot Jung's introduction which is just a useless rehash." He said that the middle section,

"The Great Treatise," the *Ta Chuan*, was the greatest magical text available to us, and he encouraged me to read and re-read it. He had altered his *I Ching*, crossing out any Christian references that Wilhelm had put into the footnotes. His distaste for the Black Dharmas, the three awful expressions of the desert fiend Jehovah, always amused me. He scratched out the offending words thickly, and darkly, and totally.

Recently a new version of the *I Ching* has appeared. Two women, Carol Anthony and Hanna Moog, have used the *I Ching* to translate itself. It is a very clever technique and the result removes all traces of Confucius and his tired social regulations, hierarchies and judgemental commentaries. I suspect that Dadaji would be as delighted as I am to see the venerable old Sage cleansed of the detritus of ages and returned to the clarity of the original magical, nature-based, pagan work which celebrates the unique way we each travel our paths through life. His *I Ching* was underlined, hexagrams were occasionally re-named and all through the text he had red-lined the teachings that guided him through his life. His poem about the *I Ching*, which is found in *Tantra of Blowing the Mind*, is one of my favorites. It is called:

The Fantasy of the Activation of the Transformations

The transformations of light and dark:
how colorful!
Some things at rest and some in motion:
what a creation!
Sevens and eights and nines and sixes:
what calculation!
The cosmic forces of ceaseless endeavor:
how miraculous!
The ebb and flow of the ocean of life;
how expansive!
When we open our eyes to the changing cosmos;
what a spectacle!

Much of the tantra is devoted to the *I Ching* and his rewording of the ancient text in order to illuminate the beauty and deeper meaning of the hexagrams is his tribute to his favorite book. As we lit the incense and bowed our heads together to prepare to throw the coins on the little orange cloth that served as our altar, he would intone his invocation:

I bow to the cosmic oracle
to the miracle of transformations
the ideas of people are confusing
but clear is the way of revelation

He would throw the coins, call out the name of the hexagram and then turn to me, his eyes full of light and sometimes even tears, and say "Do you see?"

Sleeping at the hermitage was different than sleeping anywhere else. At times I could feel Dadaji tripping along my nervous system and I would cry out in alarm. Mostly, though, I would be asleep and conscious at the same time. Dreams were rich and deep wells of wierdglow and otherworld life. One night I dreamt of the Magicians' Ball. We were all in disguise, in fabulous costumes and dancing in a great room, stars for our ceiling, hung with lanterns and streamers of ribbons. The music was strange but intoxicating. The view from an upper balcony was one of riotous joy and also a stately decorum... an odd mix for any party. My escort was a very handsome young man with blonde hair. His face was uncovered but disguised nonetheless. We all attended this astral event at regular intervals of no-time and the many hundreds of us were perfectly at home in this no-place. Disguise was a game and only when I awoke did I realize with whom I had been dancing the night away. Some of you might also have memories of attending this grand celebration. Mostly the dream world was more didactic. I remember swimming in the vast ocean of consciousness like a dolphin, leaping out of the water and diving forward or back-flipping, and each time I hit the medium I entered another life, another point of view. I felt I was being instructed, that I was practicing to achieve a faculty in this art of moving through the consciousness of others and of my own endless ocean of lives. This dreamlife helped to keep me in a state of apartness from the ordinary life going on all around me. It would be impossible to maintain a life in this magic bubble of the Hermitage of the Great Work if the mundane world were allowed to intrude.

Eventually, usually in the second or third month of the visit, I would become sour, petulant and deeply unhappy. I would feel that Dadaji was a great burden, unbearable to be around. I began to yearn for the freedom of wandering about India alone. Our farewells were a relief to us both but also sobbingly and heartbreaking sad. I could no longer bear the heightened intensity and the powerful energy levels nor the level of discipline which I needed to maintain self awareness around his attuned Being. I had such admiration for the Patels. They never left his side and never tired or weakened.

Once, on my own, I wanted to try out my new knowledge and understanding while still in a magical space that permitted the synchronicity and insight and powerful meditation to continue. Slowly it would fade away and I was left with no fairy dust at all, but usually a lot of ash and smoking fire.

A few days after Dadaji died in 1992, I returned to the village and the home that we had shared for so long. As soon as Kapilnath and Garudanath, who had arrived earlier from Seattle had left, I collapsed into a puddle of tears and sweat and diarrhea. I lay on the floor of his room and limply wept. Eventually I gathered a bit of self respect and headed out into India feeling like a ronin without direction or purpose. I went to Pushkar. I rented a little domed tower room and slowly began to create my new life. Thus began a dramatic time of adventure and shock and wildness and power. I became a shemshani, a burning ground girl. A crew of Naths and Aghoris and unnamed ones gathered around me. We would make pilgrimage, riding on camels or in a camel cart, into the wonderful Pushkar desert. Bengalis sing and most of my crew were Bengali and eventually we were even joined by a young wandering Baul singer. We would arrive at some destination in the desert, an ancient temple or oasis, and we would sing all night. Out of the darkness somebody would arrive with a drum or cymbals or wonderful voice, spiced tea would appear and the chillums would be passed from one to the other.

A young Nath boy, Brihaspatinath, offered to take me to see some of the great Nath places and to go and visit the remarkable and immensely wealthy Durganath, a six foot tall French Nath woman who lived alone in a huge cave, armed with an uzi and the ability to turn into a tiger. She turned out to be a petite Australian woman, armed with a spear, who was surprised to learn she had ever been a tiger. Our meeting was fateful. Her cave was under the protection of Reechishvar, the Lord of Bears and an aspect of Shiva. In one night my hair turned into lightning bolt dreadlocks. I had no money and I left there barefoot, dressed in ragged orange robes and an old turban to cover my head. Thus I wandered for seven months. The shock of a sudden shift back into mundane reality caused me a great deal of damage. My nerves broke. Without a visa, I was forced to return to Canada.

My storehouse of Dadaji magic was all dried up. I felt like a shell, neither human nor magical. I felt unstable and unable to continue my life as I had before. This is a typical condition for one who is orphaned of a great guru.

It is now 2007. After years of effort and lack of effort I begin to feel my way and to remember the knowledge and sensations of the past. Along the way I learned to be a good housewife, I created a home, I learned to drive a car, I learned gentleness with kids and little animals, I watched too much television. I learned to draw and paint, to sew, to carve stone, to garden and I learned about attachment and responsibility and belonging to a place and time. I learned how to follow rules and care a bit about how I appeared to others. These are some of the parts of a good human life. One afternoon when it looked like I could not become more content with my life in Vancouver I suffered an anxiety attack that I thought was me dying. After that I was never free of them. My sound sleep become much less sound and I began to experience fear, although there was nothing to be afraid about. My amnesia for the past was complete at this point. I knew events had transpired but they held no power, no resonance for me. My magical past was missing and my happy Canadian life had turned sour and frightening. I have used the *I Ching*, Reiki, fasting, drugs, ritual, amulets and Chi Gung to help me find my way through many levels of unfamiliar suffering.

Varieties of modern energy therapy have proven to be the most useful tool so far. What modern psychology has to say about our ancient practices, our beliefs about ourselves and our manifestations is radical and new. It speaks of pathology and dissociation where I think of shamanic manifestation. On the other hand it brings the mystic firmly back down into the body. The necessity to respect, honor and listen to what is after all our physical expression is a new idea for me. It may be the most useful contribution of modern Western thought to the ancient but tired paths of Eastern spirituality.

During our years together, one or the other of us would slip into a state that I can only describe as enlightened. These states were full of bliss and information. Sometimes the ecstasy would last for days. Reading *Avadhoota Gita* brought me into just such a state for almost a week. Dattatreya writes of his delight in his wild freedom, his expansive self-expression, his spontaneous knowing. He learned nothing from books or the words and ideas of others, let alone the rules and regulations of the world. His wisdom came from his twenty-four gurus, the wasp, the bird, the turtle and the greatest of all gurus, his own perfect Self, the Inner Guru. The *Avadhoota Gita* is a celebration of the Self, a celebration of the royal path of Liberation. Once I entered into the state of wildness, the distractions, noise and illusion of life on earth no longer had a hold on me and for that short period I was the avadhoot. I saw Dadaji for what he was, I saw us for what we both were. We were eternal Life, star stuff, the expressive universe in microcosm. When Dadaji would enter the state, the territory of bliss, he seemed to grow to another size and proportion and he glowed fiercely with inner fire. His words were liquid honey that poured into my heart and resonated with my own all-knowing, all-encompassing, all-understanding condition of the information-rich state of enlightenment.

This is the reason that Dadaji never "taught me anything." This is why he never wanted me to read what other people think, other people's patterns, ideas, concepts of the ways and means of attainment. This is the reason he ridiculed every guru, every wise speaker of great words, every hero and saint. He knew deeply that each sentient being is star stuff, is the Inner Guru, is Spontaneous Knowing, is perfection of Cosmic Expression. That means YOU too. Words mostly obscure this truth. Forms and systems create masses of impenetrable overlay on the simplicity of Self. May we all enjoy Ecstasy in Absolute.

A SPELL TO OPEN THE SKY

ELIJAH

The "true" invocation is performed with the cracking of the dam amid the glossalic flow. The void has voice and speaks of the death of all language. The signs of the sacred and silent alphabet are enacted between the lines of the vulgar tongue. This spell is enacted outside of time, occurring across multiple references of perspective projected stereo-graphically through the black point of transmogrification. The temple must be in resonance with the nature of death revelation; triumphant fire and force negated. Behind which, the masks reveal-conceal silence.

Through the pearl of inverted synthesis;
Do I STIR AND CREATE thy Nether Might!
By the inexorable midnight sun oblivion,
Poised on the edge of Anthrax Horizon;
Do I CALL FORTH AND INVOKE thy Nether Might!
With the wicked blade, forged of the triumphant Aphex Loa!
Do I WIELD AND ENACT thy Nether Might!
To the annihilation of the love supreme ingested within the tunnel of agape;
Do I BECOME thy Nether Might!
The dawn of light calls forth by the essence of chaos.
By the waters of Nether Night is the EGG supplanted in the mind.
WE come beyond the edge; infinity.

o
r
nozon
c h

The Eye Behind the eye of the sun through the formulaic inversion wielded of the kingdom. The words of the Magus are falsehood. CHORONZON is bound and chained by the iron spike. Through fire night vehicles of pain is the word spoken and concealed; by wind and air has the lie been received. This egress to our house is born amidst the schisms of paradox; paradise; the omega ecstasis. His heart weeps... reaching towards, towards... "Oh my god, the light is silenced, and the face..." the face is the DOUBLE-FUSED-DIAMOND of a god enraged. Shredding betwixt morrows by truth refracted.

WE live in an INVISIBLE PALACE.

There is no closing for this enchantment once it has become.

Notes

The preceding spell is not to be (nor can it be) used by the novice to any effect.

Ciphers: Gematric Study and meditation here reveal more than is shown.

1) The Lamion Continuum	The tools of the Breath and Voice; The Children

Pronounced (LAH-MEE-ON) in a single breath of three syllables.

LAH	as in LA, City of Angels
MEE	as in get ME a drink
ON	as in turn the lights ON

2) AI	TH	IA	The tools of the
11	+	11	Scarlet Brother

Pronounced (EH-EETH-EE-AY).

EH	as in Eh? Que? What?
EETH	as in teeth
EE	as in "E" the letter
AY	as in "ay mate" or "hey"

The Universal Compass aligning the great wheel; Sandalphon; the elder prophet. A new magical weapon which varies in construction depending on the ray of refraction, each Aeon aligning in impossible Syzygy.

3) HO	IR	ZON	The Tools of the
11	210/206	777	Scarlet GASH

The Scarlet Sash being the tool of acquisition of mastery of this school. The sash reveals its own in accordance with the alignments of the AITHIA.

Aphex Loa—The extension of the Word of HORIZON to the original sons of the earth; re-born of the insect. A devouring servitor of the Loa themselves. A present-tense adjective of universal oblivion. Oraboras wiped away and forgotten. Aphex Loa (also a technique) is so old school that it's new school.

The six actions indicated in the invocation are the universal axis around the central point of becoming. There is a secret Saturn inside this lie, which is the tomb of shAItaN, the death of NeMo. The axis can be aligned to the cube of space in this case the three mothers revolving about the mundane Saturn with the other six representing the faces of the cube; Leviathan Incarnate. The twelve simples aligned in accordance with the twelve edges (the zodiac), the eight vertices being the points of the turning of the wheel, the in-between times which can be accessed at any moment by analysis of the transition between thoughts. A gateway to Nevermind(IR) or OH?!.

The EGG (NEVER MIND)—The catastrophic collapse of the infinite jest. The infinite nature of creation gives rise to ecstasies beyond our conceptual limitations. (N)ever(M)ind is the state of acquisition of void consciousness. This state of perception to be fully enacted in this frame of reference must be given voice, the vehicle without voice is delegated to the Watchers, the recorders of the events enacted. N, M also references the dark waters of Scorpio birthing the needed spoke for the turning of the wheel.

Important Questions

Huh?

What?

Who says?

What next?

To what end?

Is it still the war?

Did you come yet?

Is it safe to come out yet?

Do you know its name? Have you seen its face?

Who are these people? What's happening? What's my line?

Did it work? Is it working? Did that actually happen? Did I just imagine it?

Who are you? What's your name? Who are your parents? Where did you go to school?

What do you do? Where do you do it? What do you buy? Where do you buy it?

What is the name of the Intelligence of the planet Jupiter?

Was that something else or was it just me?

Could I have paid less somewhere else?

What is the atomic weight of gold?

When did you first notice it?

What is magick?

What do I get?

Did I do OK?

So what?

A GRAMMARY

JASON LOUV

2014 Pre-Script: MARK YE WELL! This is a record of a magician's early career and as such is subject to much confusion and delusion, and a lot of fumbling and failing mixed in with the successes. It is not presented to be emulated, but as a historical piece. Much of the material contained herein is concordant with the stage in esoteric training in which the student gains access to the "astral," collective unconscious or Qabalistic World of *Yetizrah* and can quickly become swept away by the enflamed imagination which, because of spiritual practice, can seem *more real* than physical reality. This is "Chapel Perilous," where the vicissitudes of the mind are stirred up by meditation and ritual, and psychic faculties begin to manifest, but are not yet *fully* seen as yet another layer of illusion, mastered and finally stabilized in no-mind or clear, single-pointed awareness as the nature of the mind is realized. This process can be seen mapped in the mythology of many world religions; the present essay is best thought of as a textual version of the famous Tibetan or Japanese depictions of wrathful, flaming demons—the demon that is the aspirant's own mind-in-total, activated and enflamed but not yet fully awakened or mastered. "By doing certain things certain results will follow; students are most earnestly warned against attributing objective reality or philosophic validity to any of them." – Aleister Crowley, *Liber O vel Manus et Sagittae.* **X**

The following is my attempt to cohesively assemble and pass on what I have experienced of magick in the last eight years of regular practice. In the interest of full disclosure and trust I have done my best to include both methods of operation and some of my own experiences with the methods proscribed. Even if the following is a catalog of extreme highs and extreme lows, of mistakes and errors as well as successes, I hope that if nothing else I am at least able to convey the sincerity with which I engage these areas, and with which I feel they should be engaged. At this point I have no desire to write about magick in order to make myself seem important; to be honest, the major reason why I've decided to write this is out of a need to do so as therapy, and in order to understand my experience and begin to make myself whole again. If any of this can be of any use to people besides me, then not only is my therapeutic need fulfilled, but it will have been worth having to write this as therapy in the first place.

I frequently use terminology derived from Western Esoteric Tradition sources, but have done my best to make these concepts as clear as possible. I am not an adherent of any particular school or theory of magic, but I have gone to great lengths to study and take on as many systems as possible.

A word about symbolic language: some of the most profound occult writing is often done in what the Tibetans call "twilight language," meaning it is written in such a way that it can't be understood unless you've had the experience discussed or you have a teacher explaining it to you. Puzzling such documents out, though, can spark enormous cognitive leaps. I have done my best to be as straightforward as possible here, but language is limited. When reading symbolic language, it is very important to remember two things. First, valid occult symbols are meant to be filing cabinets which hold certain realms of experience. They are not the thing in themselves, they are instead a convenience for talking about, or autogenerating, these experiences. Magic is an interchange in which experience becomes symbol and symbol becomes experience. Secondly, valid occult symbols can be interpreted on more than one level, and in most cases, can be interpreted on any level conceivable. How you interpret symbols forms a test of depth of insight.

One is forewarned that absolutely nothing (especially nothing) is what it seems within the realm of magick (even more so than in "normal" life). There are never easy answers. Something seen from one angle and thought to be understood one day may be seen by another one or two or seventy-eight angles in time. As one progresses, apparent dualities collapse, boundaries are re-drawn, sides are chosen and then swapped, new information can become the corner-stone of one's temple or topple it, certainties are smashed by a chaos from which fresh diamonds of insight are born. "The obvious road," as William S. Burroughs once said, "is almost always the fool's road."

There is very little that is more dangerous than reaching out and grasping for the truth beyond the numerous easy answers that this world so readily has to hand. I do not say that to sound dramatic. I say that as proper forewarning. By engaging with this material in a sincere manner, you are taking your life into your own hands, for better and for worse. In all cases, however, never forget that BELIEF CREATES REALITY.

(But whose belief? And whose reality?)

I am also getting this down in one place so that I can, outside of a few areas left to explore, close the file and move on into the great unknown. Magical and spiritual systems may be the last snare before the door out. "Follow my ten-step plan to freedom! It'll only take you your whole life..."

One must always be on the look-out for "anti-brainwashing brainwashing," as Mahendranath called it.

There is a door. And as my stoner third-grade school bus driver once said, after a seven thirty a.m. lecture on quantum mechanics which scared the shit out of nine-year-old me, "You ever hear the philosophy of The Doors? On one side is the known... on the other, the UNKNOWN."

And with those particularly sage words, I leave you to it. Take what you can.

Eleven Precepts for Reality Manipulation

0. Nothing comes from nothing.
1. All surroundings are evolving.
2. You are what you perceive. The dream and the dreamer are another dreamer's dream.
3. Change the environment to change the self. Change the self to change the environment.
4. Many games, many players. One player, one game.
5. In a mirror(ing) universe, all actions have an equal and mirrored reaction.
6. Infinite love is the only truth. Manifest reality is a predictable mathematical equation for distracting consciousness into believing it exists and thereby constraining it.
7. Be excellent to each other.
8. All is gradient manifestation of one substance. Change a part to change the whole.
9. Individuality is insanity.
10. Everything suffers all the time.
11. Sex, death and taxes.

Magic Is

The use of illusion to manipulate illusion in order to make it more apparent that the illusion is an illusion.

Something That Sounds Believable and Respectable and Like You've Read a Lot of Books and Probably Know What You're Talking About, Please; After All, You Went to a Good College and Got Good Grades Before You Started Dancing Around With Hot Witches and Old Hippies Butt Naked and Hailing Baphomet and Other Such Nonsense

The "rational" and "skeptical" view of the more outré facets of human life is a hold-over from the Victorian period, when spiritualism swept across Europe, to be met with jeers and stiff upper lips from "respectable" society. The "but you don't really believe in ghosts, do you, chap?" attitude which we are conditioned to take to anything "supernatural" or which cannot be "explained by science" (actually, many supernatural effects can be at least somewhat explained by science these days) is no longer valid. It was created by and for white men to keep a solid boundary between white male privilege and anything which might threaten that privilege—female sexuality, the belief structures of non-white people, the body, anything which might undermine the solar male cult of Science and Social Darwinism. After these citadels began to crumble during the Modern period and the First World War—a transition which can be seen chronicled with horror in the works of Marcel Proust, Ezra Pound and Golden Dawn initiate W. B. Yeats, who struggled not to perceive this shift as the end of the world (my weren't they scared of all those "subjects" swarming back from the colonies!)—"reason" is only one option in a global marketplace of belief, and is no longer the best adaptive strategy to modern life. In the world we currently inhabit, the spoils of victory belong not to those who operate on reason, but to those who operate on pure will and imagination, and who take immediate action and then spin it so it seems justified after the fact (witness the Bush administration). In Neuro-Linguistic Programming terms, whoever has the most flexibility of action and belief in any given group inevitably holds the most power in the group. Such are words of wisdom for twenty-first century life.

Our senses process eleven million bits of information per second. Our conscious mind proceeds to edit out all but sixteen bits, which is all our focus can handle. Which means that we only perceive 0.000145% of the total reality available to our senses at any given second. This total reality of the senses is itself only a tiny fraction of existence—consider, for instance, that only 4% of the universe is composed of matter, the rest being what astrophysicists call "dark" (i.e. invisible) matter and "dark" energy. And you want to tell me we have even the slightest clue what's going on, and that we're alone in the universe?

We are socialized to choose the sixteen bits of the eleven million bits our senses process per second which, at any given time, fit what we call consensus reality (advice to any four-year-olds who may be reading this: Don't let them make you forget! Don't!). With everybody operating on this spectrum at the same time, we are able to have "civilization." With everybody operating on different spectrums, there would be no possibility of cooperation and hence nobody would be able to eat or have a roof over their head. This does not mean that the rest of the spectrum is not just as "real" as that which supports the reality we are taught to see.

By oblique social pressure, cultures since pre-history have selected a small percentage of individuals as emissaries to the rest of the spectrum—shamans, artists, scientists. Our culture at present honors and supports scientists as long as they are making pharmaceuticals or weapons, artists as long as they are making art which is simple enough to be traded as a mass commodity and/or are dead, and shamans as long as they tell people what they want to hear or tell corporations how to function better. The rest it sneers at and refuses to support beyond begrudged tokenism.

The world is saturated with systems for exploring the invisible landscape and the various strata of life which exist at frequencies other than our own. Every culture has at least one. Unsuccessful shamans go out in the invisible landscape and get lost. Successful shamans go out and then come back with the raw material that is then progressively honed into various forms of cultural advancement (example: Robert Johnson and the birth of rock 'n' roll).

A shaman or magician is, first and foremost, an explorer of consciousness. Consciousness is a fluid, transpersonal continuum which, fully understood, is everything, existing and not existing. If, as superstring theory and ancient Hermetic doctrine alike suggest, everything is vibration, then perceiving vibratory levels beyond the usual should consist of changing the frequency we are receiving at. There are infinite vibratory levels existing in the same "space and time" as our own, which we can't directly perceive just as we can't directly perceive ultraviolet or infrared light without special instruments. Many of these levels are inhabited. Many of them are inhabited by life-forms which can see us even if we can't see them. Some are friendly. Others are not.

Those who can figure out how to operate on levels beyond the ordinary, by blind luck or extended and precise observation and experimentation, can often make things happen which make no sense in terms of consensus reality, hence the brute catch-all term "magic," which I actually rather like, since it sounds silly and nonsensical and foolish, and I like silly and nonsensical and foolish things, because they are often gates leading outside of normal (policed and shepherded) reality.

The techniques of magic and meditation can be seen as methods for tuning the frequency you are receiving and transmitting at, boosting or canceling the signal, and eliminating static. If you don't take conscious control, you will be receiving and transmitting what somebody else wants you to. A lot of magic therefore consists of a) making sure you're the one controlling your story and b) making sure the story's interesting enough to keep you satisfied and engaged.

The goal is evolution into something more than the narcotized, reactionary, neurotically social-media-checking, corporately enslaved shaved ape that is our current state of being (presuming you are reading this in the First World). The method is contact with and interaction with levels of existence above our own, and with beings, energies and processes which are able to facilitate our growth. No, you can't prove that it's not all in your mind, because you can't prove that anything isn't all in your mind. But ultimately, it doesn't matter, because whatever you choose to focus on in your life creates the life you lead. So choose wisely.

There is no such thing as a "magician." To paraphrase Crowley, you can do certain things and certain results will follow. This does not make you special or any different from anybody else other than the fact that you have chosen to explore certain areas of the human experience that other people may not have, just as every single person you pass on the street every day has had numerous experiences you never have and never will. There is nothing so annoying and juvenile as somebody who goes around calling themselves a magician with a straight face. I know because I've been there, and I was a twat. (Some certainly choose to do so for purposes of cultural hacking, Grant Morrison being a primary example. This can have the effect of at least temporarily scrambling people's sense of reason and proportion so one can slip in deeper mind bombs; it does have its uses. I have chosen to wear this mask at certain points in my life, but have found that taking it off is not nearly as easy as getting it on.)

And at this ripe hour we shall now segueway into story time! I love stories!!

"There is an Eastern tale which speaks about a very rich magician who had a great many sheep. But at the same time this magician was very mean. He did not want to hire shepherds, nor did he want to erect a fence about the pasture where his sheep were grazing. The sheep consequently often wandered into the forest, fell into ravines, and so on, and above all they ran away, for they knew that the magician wanted their flesh and skins and this they did not like.

"At last the magician found a remedy. He hypnotized his sheep and suggested to them first of all that they were immortal and that no harm was being done to them when they were skinned, that, on the contrary, it would be very good for them and even pleasant; secondly he suggested that the magician was a good master who loved his flock so much that he was ready to do anything in the world for them; and in the third place he suggested to them that if anything at all were going to happen to them it was not going to happen just then, at any rate not that day, and therefore they had no need to think about it. Further the magician suggested to his sheep that they were not sheep at all; to some of them he suggested that they were lions, to others that they were eagles, to others that they were men, and to others that they were magicians.

"And after this all his cares and worries about the sheep came to an end. They never ran away again but quietly awaited the time when the magician would require their flesh and skins.

"This tale is a very good illustration of man's position."

– Gurdjieff, as quoted by P. D. Ouspensky

Mentors and Students

There are no easy or comprehensive ways to learn magick. One has to take their instruction where they find it. That generally means haunting used book stores, tracking down out-of-print manuscripts, spending long hours scouring tacky and overly pop-up-laden corners of the internet, joining disreputable occult orders, and finding and pestering people who seem to know what they're talking about. 99% of all magickal writing is juvenile, delusional or unnecessarily convoluted, until you get to a certain level of "initiation," after which nearly all of it is legit, at least in a certain light.

Since in order to learn how to "magically" manipulate reality you have to learn about the reality you are manipulating, everything can teach you the mechanics of sorcery. Watch how things move and change. Watch how human lives progress. Watch the way that power operates and who actually wields it. Watch nature. Watch yourself. The only time you can see something is when it moves... everything else must be inferred. How good you are at inferring the unseen causes behind things determines how good you will be at causing things to happen in unseen ways, and definitely how good you will be at predicting how future events will unfold.

I have had a number of mentors in my life, many of them for short periods of time only. Many of my most important magical lessons have been learned from people who are not quote "magicians," though I also count myself very lucky to have met and picked up hints and encouragement from some of the best magicians in the English-speaking world. My most consistent mentor/student relationship has been with Genesis and Lady Jaye Breyer P-Orridge, who I love dearly and who have never given me any overt lessons in magic that I have noticed, beyond their example, and hence have taught me most of all.

Foundations of Practice

Start by doing big and absurd things. The crazier the better. Eke out your beginner's luck while you have it and see what you can get away with. The results you get at this stage are what will keep you interested and pursuing magick to the silent end. Do it your own way, make up your own rituals and techniques and gods. Don't start by following somebody else's system. Throw your whole self into it, your creativity and imagination as well as your sheer willpower. At this point it is the daring and bravado to transgress into unknown territory which will get you your initial results.

The basic tools needed at this time are a journal for recording the nature and results of experiments, a journal for recording dreams, a daily meditation practice of any sort (sitting zazen is recommended), one or more banishing rituals, some method of divination and a study and practice of sigil magick. These are discussed below.

I began serious research of magick at the age of sixteen, following multiple experiences with the *I Ching* which "could not be explained rationally," and began practice at seventeen. My foundational text was Colin Wilson's *The Occult*, which posits that humans have a hidden faculty that allows them to perform acts that appear to be "magic," but which only those willing to go to the furthest extremes of the mind are able to utilize. Grant Morrison's *The Invisibles* comic series opened numerous avenues of exploration for me at this time as well (reading *The Invisibles* every month was, for me, an experience on a similar level that seeing the Beatles play *The Ed Sullivan Show* presumably was for many of my parents' generation). Shortly after this I bought a copy of Peter Carroll's *Liber Null*, which provided the first legit blueprint for performing magick I had found at that point, and which uses a similar model for explaining how and why magick works.

In this foundational period of study and practice I used Carroll's *Liber MMM* and *Liber KKK*[1] as the syllabi for daily ritual; all of my rituals and techniques were self-devised at this point, outside of cursory experimentation with Hermetic magick and Voodoo. During this period I seemed to be achieving results on a regular basis—controlling weather patterns, using sigils and servitors to manipulate the minds of malevolent authority figures, cursing (in one case to stop a school shooting, in another to neutralize a child molester), invisibility, action at a distance, time manipulation, etc etc. For a while it seemed like the more *apparently* impossible it was that something would work, the more likely it was to work. I also successfully performed magic for friends, in some cases friends on different continents, and had my successes confirmed by people other than myself. Up to this time I had considered magic to be either a charming practical joke or a confidence trick; I was right, but certainly unprepared to discover how deep the joke ran.

At this point the revelations were coming fast and furious and my identity was rapidly beginning to warp in order to accommodate the new outlook and potential. My life became a running string of improbable and even absurd synchronicities, as is *de rigeur* for the budding magician; it seemed as if the universe was "waking up" and beginning to speak directly to me. I do not attribute my success in these areas to anything other than the fact that I was willing to go and *try it*. Most are unwilling to even consider the possibility of magick, even if it can be startlingly easy.

During this time nearly all of the magick I developed hinged around various methods of deep trance combined with full focus on symbolic representations of what I wanted to occur. This is the type of ritual work which I have most frequently engaged in with groups, ranging from two to thirty participants, and which I have made a consistent practice of in order to steer my progress through the material world.

However, I was left with two pressing questions, which left me no better off than I was before I had discovered magick: "So what?" and "What are you going to use it for?" Rather than arbitrarily pick a goal to aim for, I began the laborious and endless task of deconditioning myself from any casually accepted or inherited ideas about what either the world or my self were, and began the search for my "true will" (whatever THAT is).

After this period I left for college, where I had the freedom to experiment with sex and drugs in a full and extended fashion for the first time (having had a somewhat sheltered upbringing), which quickly changed the whole scene and focus. During this time my identity collapsed and was rebuilt multiple times,[2] leading up to the end of my second year of school when I made a serious practice of *Liber MMM* and intensive study of the Qabalah, after which I was formally initiated into an occult order in Los Angeles, which crystallized my identity into a more organized and self-assured state. After my initiation I moved from my experimental stage into an in-depth practice of Hermetic and Thelemic magick, the focus now being on raising and perfecting the self instead of attaining one-off magical effects.

I was drawn into more traditional forms of magick out of a certain sense of rebellion against the chaos magic writers I had first read, and the chaos magic "scene" on the internet, where the dictum that one should break all the rules in magic was continually repeated. What rules was I supposed to break, I wondered? Traditional forms provided a sense of structure that I was at that time not getting from my schooling or personal life; in addition, engaging myself in largely Medieval forms of magick appealed to a certain sense of sick irony as the new Dark Ages of the George W. Bush administration ramped up, starting with the destruction of Babylon.

Using somebody else's map is a bit of a double-edged sword. On one hand, it is easy to be constrained by somebody else's worldview and terminology and begin to limit one's perceptions by trying to shove them into inappropriately-shaped boxes. On the other, the maps of others can provide directions to places one never would have found on one's own. In my own case, I have felt it important to take on, or at least investigate, the methods and findings of the many magicians and mystics upon whose shoulders I stand.

The Magical Record

Immensely useful. Write down the specifics of what you've done after you do it. Its primary function is to keep you focused and excited about adding entries every day so that you stay on task and can look back to see how you're progressing. In addition you should write down your revelations as you have them, any particularly weird synchronicities, your dreams and anything else that seems appropriate. To be honest, I very rarely look back at my records, but the discipline of striving to do ritual work and record it on a daily basis is central to my practice. I tend to go back and write up summaries of what I've been up to every six months or so just so I have a clear idea of where I'm at. Reading old records can be very inspiring and revelatory, and also very embarrassing.

The second interpretation of the magical record is that it is very important at some point to find a way to offer your findings and experience to the world. Crowley was clear that one's work is the sole property of those immediately below you in the chain. Every generation of magicians progresses quicker because they have better and more concise models and records to work with that have been handed down to them by the preceding generations. Choose your medium and then prepare your work for the world; I offered the record of my early work and that of others of my "scene" to the wider public as *Generation Hex*, though I am now a bit more dubious about doing it this way, as directly talking about magic is often less effective in explaining it than talking about it in oblique or fictionalized ways. Genesis P-Orridge does music, Grant Morrison does comics, William Burroughs did novels, Kenneth Anger does films, Austin Spare and Brion Gysin painted, etc etc etc. Transmitting magic through art (art which can be made sentient via magic) is one of the most potent and effective ways of doing magic in its own right. Even Crowley admitted, at the end of his life (in *Eight Lectures on Yoga*), that the greatest artist is greater than the greatest magician, and my my, isn't that just fucking great, I thought as I read that line, after spending years trying to learn magick and reading all of Crowley's books instead of going to art school, where I probably would have had easy access to degeneracy of a much higher quality than I did flapping around with a bunch of weirdo occultists and geeking over deleted Coil singles, at any rate. (I jest, I jest, you know I love you.)

Magick must be expressed through your life and through your work. As Richard Metzger once said to me, "You can't really *just* be a magician." One of magic's many functions should be to act as the inspiration and grease for your secular occupation. Even writers as far back as Eliphas Lévi included stern warnings in their books to go get a freaking job and not be that most dreaded Beast of all, the parents' basement magician.

Meditation

Daily effort at stilling and focusing the mind is what underlies everything else. We come from nothing and go to nothing; nothing comes from nothing.

The standard, constipated Western occult attitude towards meditation, as advanced by Crowley and his admirers, is to sit completely still and strain your mind until all thought goes away. This is useless and detrimental. It's better to sit and let your mind empty of its own accord; focus on your breath, and neither judge nor cling to any passing thoughts. Rather than relying on *Liber MMM* or Crowley's *Liber E* for meditation instruction, you're better off finding an actual meditation class with somebody you trust; try your local Buddhist center. It is very important not to strain yourself in this area, as you can develop a negative loop which can hinder normal thought processes while not meditating.

Biofeedback devices are now cheap and readily available on the open market (some come packaged with meditation training software); these can dramatically improve one's meditation practice by providing tangible feedback. Neurofeedback devices, while still very expensive, are also available, and provide even more possibilities for brain training and meditation. This is an area I need to do extended work in.

More involved meditations can be of much more interest to the more advanced magician. I have found working with the 112 meditations of the *Vijnanabhairava Tantra* particularly crazysexycool.

The traditional manuals of meditation are *The Yoga Sutras of Patanjali* and *The Dhammapada*.

Dreams, Astral Travel, Scrying

Dreams should be recorded every morning in a journal you keep immediately next to your bed. The more disciplined you are in recording your dreams daily, and the more detail you record them in, the more you will dream, the more you will remember of your dreams and the more intense your dreams will be. This begins a feedback loop where you begin to learn to control them. (Dreams can be controlled by focusing on a sigil designed to produce a specific dream while falling asleep.)

"Answers come in dreams." Dreams are the universally agreed-upon meeting place between humans and the gods across all cultures. It is through dreams that the progress of initiation is monitored and deeper levels of reality reveal themselves. Once you begin receiving direct lessons in sorcery in dreams, and enacting them within waking life, then you've seriously got something good going.

The hypnagogic or liminal state between waking and sleep can produce particularly lucid and oddly relevant visions. Salvador Dalí's "Paranoiac-Critical" method for retrieving information from this state was to slowly drift to sleep in a comfortable chair while holding a rock in his hand, which he dangled over the arm of the chair and above a steel plate on the floor. Right as unconsciousness began to set it, his hand would relax, dropping the rock on the steel plate, making a loud bang, and waking him up, at which point he would immediately write down the last thing he saw. I've actually never tried this for some reason, and should...

Astral travel beyond the dreaming state is not something I can regularly retain awareness of in my waking state, outside of the beginning stages of separation, easily induced through deep breathing, and spontaneous out-of-body experiences, which I can induce via eroto-comatose lucidity.[3] This is something that remains for me to make a concerted practice of. There are numerous modern books and in-depth training courses available on this subject which are probably better turned to than reading traditional sources, which are notoriously vague. If you want a short-cut, I hear Ketamine will do it; Salvia can also push one outside the body to some degree. N,N-DMT will take you directly to the punchline before dropping you back in your mortal frame.

Scrying is traditionally done in a black mirror or crystal ball. This puts me into a receptive and visionary internal state but does not produce anything but vague visions in the mirror. The industrial strength Brion Gysin method of staring in a wall-size mirror for up to thirty hours while smoking dope I have not attempted. Wall-size mirrors are hard to come by...

The Golden Dawn method of scrying and clairvoyance involves investigating various Qabalistic realms by projecting through the appropriate sigils (by drawing them in their complementary colors and then staring at them until burned into the retina, afterwards closing the eyes so the image is seen in the proper colors behind the eyelids, and then passing through the image) and rigorously testing any entities encountered by various Qabalistic formalities (it seems a little weird to me to assume that all spirits would know

Qabalah). This I have had some success with, and find it very inspiring. Crowley liked to throw nitrous oxide into the mix to liven up the proceedings. This I have not tried.

On a side-note, Stanislav Grof's Holotropic Breathwork (sometimes known as Vivation or connected breathing) can get one into very strange and meaningful states (it was developed to facilitate the types of breakthroughs garnered through using LSD in a therapeutic setting after LSD was made illegal). This is often used within the framework of unlocking buried traumas from muscle memory (Wilhelm Reich's critical concept of "character armoring") and processing and healing them by breathing "through" them. The technique isn't much more complex than lying on your back in the dark, on some blankets, and breathing heavily, deeply and very quickly without leaving any pause between the in-breath or out-breath, generally for around an hour. A good book/CD set on the subject is *Connect Your Breath* by Dave Lee.

Divination, Intuition and Omens

Divination generally works on the assumption that the universe is a hologram—that, like a hologram, the entirety is contained in every part, and that one can indeed see the universe in a grain of sand, or at least a deck of Tarot cards.

It is a good idea, especially when first starting, to divine on rituals before you do them in order to see if you should change your approach or ditch them altogether. One can learn some serious lessons in style this way, especially if working with the *I Ching*. I tend to consult the *I Ching* when I have questions about my own life or magic; as those who have worked with it even in small doses will know, it can be frighteningly direct and accurate. The Richard Wilhelm translation, by the way, is widely regarded as the best. (Many occultists go on serious *I Ching* benders, often to the exclusion of any other magick. By the time Crowley was in his thirties, his practice had been narrowed down almost exclusively to throwing hexagrams and O.T.O. sex magick, i.e. Wanking for Cash.)

I use the Tarot when doing readings for other people. At one point I was making a (meager) living this way before going on unemployment (ah, the glamour of the hard-boiled occult life). Learning Tarot takes forever, but as a nice side-effect, you end up learning the working mechanics and intricacies of the Qabalah and hence a gigantic underpinning structure of Western culture which may well begin to unlock enough wisdom and insight into reality to keep one merrily occupied for decades. The Golden Dawn method of reading the Tarot (also repeated in *The Book of Thoth*) is the best I have found.

One should literally be able to project one's reality into anything—clouds, tea leaves, dried rice, a television while channel surfing, an iPod on shuffle—and find one's answer therein, or recover information that gets you thinking about the problem in a completely new light.

Segueway for another story just because it's particularly amusing. During my freshman year of college, I was living in the dorms and had made fast friends with an exchange student from London named Matthew. He considered my interest in magick hilarious and silly, except when, in a moment of desperation, he asked me to do some for him to help him pass a test, which I did, although he didn't pass. Me, Matt and Matt's then-girlfriend Jessica spent a lot of time obsessing over obscuro indie bands and going through the bargain bins of local CD stores ad nauseum. I had a five-CD changer in my dorm room and one night, probably while stoned it must be admitted, I decided to turn the changer into a divination servitor. I created a bizarre gargoyle monster out of a stuffed jacket and a rolled-up blue towel for a head. It had condoms for eyes, a belt for an elephant-trunk like snout, and a pair of flaring wings made from a white sheet. This loomed over the CD changer. It somehow got the name "Hughbert Sibe." We would put in various CDs and then ask it questions, afterwards hitting the shuffle button and interpreting whatever song came up as the answer. It answered our questions dutifully and faithfully, if sometimes obliquely. There was a right-wing Christian girl on the floor I will call "Karen," the kind who comes to school with a long-distance boyfriend and keeps the poor bastard too, and of course never socializes with anybody else. She was suitably freaked out by Hughbert and refused to come near him, as he was deemed Satanic. Finally, after much cajoling, another girl in the dorm convinced Karen to talk to Hughbert, and hustled her into the room. Pressed for a question, she asked him "Hughbert, are you real?" and then hit shuffle. The changer immediately skipped to an Eminem song which starts:

"You know, a lot of people ask me stupid fucking questions."

She ran out of the room and we laughed our asses off.

Anyway. Moving on, at the next level is one's own sense of intuition. If you're a magician, you usually assume that walking around you're a bit more plugged in to the subtle levels of things than the people around you, what Eliphas Lévi called the "astral light." You get "feelings" from people and situations all the time. Sometimes those feelings have been right, but I can't count those as much as I can the times where it seems to have been my own anxieties, personal prejudices and internal monologue taking over and passing itself off as valid. Intuition and anxiety can be worryingly interchangeable for me at times, and it can be hard to untangle a genuine intuition from background noise.

Then there's omens. Like you're in the synchronicity slipstream and you're getting regular and direct messages to you from the universe. Now the more I grow up and the more I pay attention to these, the more I notice that they are often almost perfectly ambiguous. The universe never seems to come out and give you a direct "do this" or "don't do this" message. They are always ambiguous, sly winks more than anything else, that can be interpreted one way or the other. Maybe that's the sign that they come from a "higher level," where, er, "duality" doesn't apply. However, paying very close attention to them or even forcing it and running around interpreting numbers on street signs et. al. via gematria, impinging on Abyssal territory,[4] hasn't really got me anywhere. There are signposts but they don't seem to point anywhere in particular, and the next thing you know you're shitting yourself every time it's 3:33 on the clock.

I imagine all of these things are part of one faculty and one continuum. The question that's raised is: "What's communicating with you?"

Is it the consciousness/ego?

Is it the "transcendent self" or "Holy Guardian Angel"?

Is it a spirit or god, or "God"?

Is it a quote "demon"?

To what extent can spirits or gods (or even demons) be considered to be a part of the "transcendent self," anyway?

And what signs might one look for to distinguish between these? In some cases there are specific calling cards for specific spirits. Also, if something is completely "non-dual" or uninterpretable in a "do this" or "don't do this" sense, maybe that's a sign that you're at least communicating with something "above the Abyss" (the line between manifestation and Godhead)...?

What about "bad spirits" that might be trying to send messages to confuse or attack you? If, for instance, I find a flyer for a club night that is named after a Goetic demon while in heavy ecstasy at another club, how should I (as player of this video game) take that? That the club night advertised is a manifestation of the demon, drawing energy? That the flyer is just there to keep me on my toes? That it is a sign that the demon is active in my life? Or just that some club promoter thinks that the Goetia is like, hardcore, man? That is... are all "divine messages" necessarily benign?

At any rate, as one progresses, experience is gained, and the illusions of time, space and identity continue to melt, one begins to simply KNOW. There's really nothing else I can say, other than... follow your first instinct, and respect the reaction of *the body* over all else...

Banishing and Protection

Classic (Golden Dawn and Thelemic) theory on banishing rituals makes a clear distinction between banishing and invoking. This has been largely lost in the wake of chaos magic, and banishing rituals have been reduced to a formality to include at the beginning and ending of rituals, at worst a "signal to the unconscious that something magical is about to happen" or even a superstitious gesture somewhat akin to crossing oneself against the Evil Eye. Superstition can creep into magic incredibly easy and take the place of precision and clarity, but it should be banished whenever encountered. Every physical action taken during ritual as a matter of course is mirrored on the astral, whether the magician is fully conscious of this or not, and so nothing should be done haphazardly or on faith alone.

As far as basic banishing for protection, the simplest rituals are often the most effective. Simply visualizing an impenetrable sphere around oneself is a good example. Another is the Vajra mantra, in which the magician flings her right arm forward, simultaneously snapping her thumb against her index and middle fingers and shouting the mantra "Phat" (pronounced "pot"). This is given in all eight directions as well as up and down, clearing out any unwanted energy or information.

Beyond these rituals, it is important for the magician to pay close attention to protection and astral hygiene. Regular banishing will assist in creating an energetic blockade against intrusion, but any practice, magical or mundane, which assists in keeping clear personal boundaries is much to be desired. Keeping well-fed, as well as certain herbs and medications (some antidepressants, for instance) have also been observed to assist in preserving energetic boundaries.

Magick in general is a process of getting rid of unwanted crap in life. Banish everything which hurts you, wastes your time or which is unnecessary to your survival, happiness and/or self-realization. Invoke what supports that survival, happiness and self-realization. Have dominion over your own mind. Strive to only entertain positive and constructive thought processes, as nobody or thing has any right to make you feel or act any worse than your best. Thought and action fully focused on a single goal, without lust of result, persisting until the end, is one of the most effective magick powers of all.

Advanced Banishing and Protection

More complicated banishing and invoking rituals—i.e. the Lesser and Greater Rituals of the Pentagram and Hexagram—are shorthand for either inviting certain energies into your temple (i.e., your life and the universe you inhabit) or showing them the door. In practice they are used either for focusing consciousness on a specific energy, or completely clearing the decks so that the emptiness of mind necessary for meditation or further meditation can be facilitated. Think of it as sterilizing your instruments and laboratory before starting an experiment.

The Greater Hexagram is a Swiss Army knife for working with planetary energies and can on its own form the basis for countless ritual efforts. (Students of Tantra, especially the Tantra which stems from Mahendranath and is of somewhat Thelemic descent, will see immediate overlaps with the Body Yantra.)

The Greater Pentagram banishes or invokes the four elements, and the Greater Hexagram banishes and invokes the seven major planets; both can be easily expanded for working with the twelve signs of the zodiac. Planetarium software capable of pinpointing the location of any given planet in the sky at the time of working, as well as astrological software which can calculate the current ascendant sign, are exceedingly helpful (both are currently available as freeware products on the internet).[5]

Viewed from "above," these rituals interlock to create a simple, though versatile, map of the twenty-three cosmic forces most prevalently mirrored in the magician—as above, so below. (Other rituals exist for other important cosmic forces; Crowley's *Liber Reguli*, for instance, can be used for working with the energies of Sirius, the Dog Star.) This should be considered as akin to a yantra in Hinduism or a mandala in Buddhism. It is simply a map, but also a machine which can be used to potent effect. The Golden Dawn Lotus Wand unifies these forces into a single, simple and versatile ritual and mnemonic tool, which can be considered a three-dimensional yantra.

OK. So what? What does this really matter, and of what use could it possibly be to a citizen of the twenty-first century?

The most important truths of magic are often contained in the most clichéd sources and public stereotypes. (Stage magic, for instance, can provide serious insights into even the loftiest realms of the occult.) Take voodoo dolls. These work via the assumption that you can affect somebody by making a model of them and then including a piece of them (hair, nails, etc.)—and they do work. Similarly, in order to affect the universe, you would make a model of the universe (the banishing rituals as a whole) and include a piece of the universe (you). Performed properly, actions taken within this microcosm will then be mirrored in the macrocosm. One then has a diagnostic tool for analyzing and correcting imbalances in the energies in operation within one's own life (for instance, if in a depression, one could banish Saturn and invoke the Sun).

The symbols employed in these rituals are Medieval; however, they remain an accurate language for discussing energies at work on various levels. One should keep in mind that when an occult text says "Saturn," a huge range of things may be in discussion. The planet Saturn that hangs in the night sky is only one crystallization of an force mirrored, and personified, on both lower and higher levels.

The banishing rituals associated with chaos magic—the Gnostic Pentagram Ritual, Gnostic Thunderbolt and IAO Banishing—are effective as pre-ritual excitatory events which build energy, but are less effective than the traditional banishings at providing heavy protection.

The Thelemic banishings—the Star Ruby and Star Sapphire—align one with certain primal sexual energies (the Star Sapphire is also a codified sexual magick instruction). I have not used them during any type of heavy entity work and cannot vouch for their effectiveness.

There are two additional rituals which, though not technically banishings, are helpful precursors to further ritual work. The first is the Bornless Ritual in its many forms; the most advanced of which is the one given in Crowley's *Liber Samekh* (he designed this version for his student Frank Bennett). *Samekh* is technically an invocation of the Holy Guardian Angel, which is why its use is repeated at the beginning of other work in order to affirm divine provenance before colluding with other forces. While fairly complicated to learn, the ritual becomes easy and straightforward with repeated use; it raises a tremendous amount of "energy" (its use has been observed to kill street lamps and, on a separate occasion, blow out a sliding glass door; Marjorie Cameron had similarly unsettling experiences with it when Jack Parsons was regularly performing it in their house). The second is the Rosy Cross, a protective ritual to be performed after or even before any ritual work, which effectively draws a shroud of concealing mist around the magician's astral form, protecting her from unwanted attention, especially after doing heavy work, which may make her a target for energetic leeches. Consecrating the ritual chamber with water and fire, as in the Golden Dawn initiation ceremonies, produces this same concealing mist. Outside of invisibility strategies, Michael Bertiaux recommends in his *Voudon Gnostic Workbook* the adoption of utterly horrific forms on the astral in order to scare away any unwanted intruders, a practice similar to the use of godforms such as Mahakali and Bharaiva in Tantra. (Like everything else associated with Bertiaux and his work, I have personally found this to be counterproductive.)

On a more down-to-earth note, the recent book *Psychic Shield* by Caitlín Matthews is an *excellent* workbook of rituals for building up a rock-solid psychic foundation and boundaries. No fireworks or any of the cool "goth posing" of most occult texts, but this book alone, if one actually sincerely does the exercises, could get one very far indeed. If I were to recommend anybody a good starting book on magick these days, this would be it (as my friend Anastasia put it, "it's important to sit in mom's lap for a while before going off on one's own.")

Marsupials

I'm very tired of the word "sigil." It's all you ever freaking hear about when talking with occulty types. "I did a sigil for this, I did a sigil for that, yak yak yak, you don't know what a sigil is? Pish posh my good fellow, where have YOU been for the past decade? Sigil sigil sigil sigil sigil." For the purposes of this text I will replace the word "sigil" with the word "marsupial." At least it'll sound more exciting when you tell all your friends with the black band t-shirts and the nose rings that you jerked off over a marsupial designed to get you in bed with that chick who works at the retro clothing store downtown and *dude, it totally worked!*

Marsupials are symbols created to designate experiences you would like to have, and then sent down into the deepest levels of the mind through extreme focus and some method of trance which shuts down the conscious dialogue at least for a few moments, where it will then activate and produce the desired result, often with a wry sense of humor attached.

Marsupials can take any form—a symbol, a work of art, a series of tones, a mantra, a verbal trigger, a hand motion. They should be designed in such a way that you forget what their function is, and the intent remains hidden deep within the marsupial's pouch instead of out in the open. This often requires designing them well in advance of using them. Your body and your appearance are your strongest marsupial.

Almost all magic works on the marsupial principle, when viewed from a wide enough angle.

The Tetragrammaton

The Tetragrammaton or Four-Fold Name of God, YHVH, is the simplest formula of the Qabalah and one whose study can unlock much of the rest of the Tree of Life. It corresponds to the four elements, the four suits of the Tarot and the four major levels of manifestation of reality (Atziluth, Briah, Yetzirah and Assiah). Sparing you a digression into pages of Gematria and Qabalistic hoohums, I will give you my clearest understanding of this formula, which provides a direct method of ascension.

Y, Yod symbolizes the hand of divinity. H, He is a window, in this case a window on the world (a self). V, Vau is a nail, i.e. a principle joining two things together—in this case, manifest reality. The second half of the formula, VH, symbolizes subject and object, that is, you and the world you perceive. Both of these emanate simultaneously from a wholly separate entity, the first H, that which is symbolized by the phrase "the Holy Guardian Angel." This in turn is an emanation from Y, the non-local spark of divinity.

I.e., you are not in the world and the world is not separate from you. You and the world are two halves of one dream, as dreamt by a totally separate being. This should explain most magick, and definitely all synchronicity, nicely; there is no separation and hence *no causal relation* between subject and object.

The Alphabet

Magick drives materialists nuts because it's not about things that can be quantified or measured, it's about relationships and correspondences; it's about the spaces between things. This is why it usually makes immediate sense to artists.

If one has a set of symbols or letters which can represent the entirety of life, then this set of letters can both be used for random divination by selecting random sets of letters in response to a question and then assembling a story from the order in which they fall, or for sorcery by making purposeful arrangements and charging them by ritual. Divination can be enchantment (through self-fulfilling prophecy) and enchantment can be divination (a successful act of sorcery may only be a particularly good telepathic read of an event about to occur instead of its cause), but in this case they are both emanations of the representational system within which they operate. The medium is the message...

The Hebrew alphabet and the Runes are both examples of such "magical" alphabets. Austin Osman Spare designed his own and called it his "Alphabet of Desire."

Reality itself is an alphabet of symbols which are thrown randomly and assembled into new patterns every day. The House. The City. The Relationship. The Job. The Sun. The Moon. The President. The War.

Read the writing on the wall, and then cut it up.

You may also choose to consider, if you will, that it may not be human beings, but language which is the dominant species on this planet, as the most extreme interpretations of memetics suggest. Who do we die for, who are we enslaved for, what holds our identities together, what determines the boundaries of everything we perceive, what do we do meditation and magick to cut-up and overcome, what pre-existed and will outlive every human on this planet even though we think we control it, what do the smartest humans learn to evolve into...?

Rub out thee word forever.

The Holy Guardian Angel

A very problematic concept. Traditionally, attainment of Knowledge and Conversation of the Holy Guardian Angel is meant to be the first goal of the magician, before contact with other entities or realms is undertaken. In many ways, however, the Angel is something as undefinable as God or the path of magick itself. It is the beginning and end of the path. In yearning towards it we open side-avenue upon side-avenue of experience, though the straight shot of the arrow towards the sun may be the prescribed method.

The entire A.'. A.'. system of Aleister Crowley and George Cecil Jones is a multi-level approach to attaining Knowledge and Conversation.

My own Operation was kicked into gear by working with the Goetia in a sloppy and unhygienic manner. These demonic forces threatened to knock me out of equilibrium and I was pushed into the Operation as a matter of course. This coincided with leaving Santa Cruz, California for London and finding myself a complete stranger, having left my friends, family and girlfriend. This formed the first prerequisite, isolation. I was at the time living in a flat in Notting Hill which I rented following an outlandishly bizarre string of synchronicities involving Austin Osman Spare's artwork and some aristocratic warlocks. I embarked on the Operation as outlined in *The Sacred Magic of Abramelin the Mage* a month and a half after arriving in London, and partitioned temple space into my small room. This was laid out to specification as in the book, with the instructions followed as close to the letter as possible. Intense prayer, for several hours a day, beginning with one prayer per day and advancing to three, as well as prolonged study of the world's sacred texts, formed the second prerequisite: "Enflame thyself."

Beyond fervent prayer, the main form of magick used was traditional banishing as well as the vibration of God names and implantation of the Sephira in the body; for this I used the preliminary exercises in David Goddard's *The Tower of Alchemy.* The ritual soon encompassed my whole life and turned it into pure devotional energy. I also adopted the use of Crowley's *Liber Samekh* as well as personally created rituals and invocations. Chemognosis allowed for breakthroughs, though it did not carry me to the final stages; that I was left to do on my own. I also invoked other entities (specifically Typhon, as the serpent which squeezes the heart into a pure diamond, and hastens the heat-death of the Universe as described in *Liber LXV*) to accelerate and intensify my progress. The entire Operation was of the nature of raising and purifying energy through contact with a luminous and transcendent source. I was unprepared for the amount of energy raised and untrained in how to best harness it, and in some ways this contributed to much of my confusion and depression in the years following the Operation.

My awareness was expanding extremely rapidly during the Operation and my rational mind was struggling to keep up through massive intake of information, both from the Thelemic canon and the foundational texts of world religion. This made things problematic as I was not allowing the experience itself to take over; like Adam in the Garden of Eden I had an overwhelming need to name every facet of what I was experiencing, even if what I was experiencing was a pure chaos of sensation and intuitive perception.

The Angel manifests from the direction of Love, the divine key which simply and elegantly unifies all religion and magick. The grace and forgiveness I experienced during this time left me no way to react but to fall to my knees and weep.

My Operation lasted approximately five months in celibate, isolated prayer, after which I took the bold step of leaving the ritual chamber and assuming that my entire life was now the Oratory of the Operation. At this point everything around me began to take on the quality of direct communication from my Angel. I traveled Europe for a month and shortly thereafter found myself undergoing shamanic training in Nepal and then piecing my head back together in India before returning to New York, which marked the end of the Angelic Operation and the beginning of the demonic binding phase. As I raised myself towards the divine purity of the Angel, so did I raise Hell itself, which I would then have to wrestle with in the coming years. (In addition, the Angelic Operation appears to bend time and causality and can effect events occurring before the technical onset of the Operation; seeming to loop backward in time to lay the foundation for it to occur in the first place.)

In the course of the Operation the "center of consciousness" apparently (experientially) shifts from between the ears to the world outside of the magician's body. The barrier between self and other dissolves; in this state of heightened magical consciousness it seems that everything around you *is* you. Thoughts are immediately mirrored in the environment; direct messages are received leading one to higher consciousness; when people speak to you, you think that they *are* you and mistake their words for your thoughts, etc. This is a profoundly enlightening state, but also leaves one immensely open to outside influence. While in this state I became trusting of everything, with enough resultant faith and love that I could literally walk into a war zone (Nepal in Summer 2004) with no fear for my personal safety and immediately find myself in an angelic milieu. However, upon returning to New York, my sense of openness and trust was immediately compromised from every direction, and I had to learn (and continue to learn) proper grounding and personal boundaries. Comedown's a bitch.

I count this both as one of the loneliest and most profoundly beautiful times in my life. It marked the culmination of all of my magickal work up to that point and also a break from my previous life and entry into a more mature, if also much more complicated, phase. I truly believe that I entered into higher levels of perception at this time, and began to move in angelic currents running through mundane reality. At one point I breached directly, and physically, into the Aeon of Ma'at as previously identified by Charles Stansfeld Jones and NEMA, a reality running concurrently to, or on top of, our own.[6]

I now look back on this time with a profound love for the idealism, purity and naïveté of my younger self as well as through the lens of the bitter disillusionment of subsequently having had those ideals and purity taken advantage of. I have no final conclusions about the Holy Guardian Angel. Am I still in the Operation? Was I ever not?

Demonology

The term demon is here used to refer to any entity which perpetuates human misery in order to feed itself. This is a blanket, catch-all term for a particularly varied class of astral lifeform and in many cases it can be hard to distinguish demonic metaphor from demonic reality.

At the low end, the planet appears to be blanketed with an atmospheric level of unintelligent energetic parasites or larvae which congregate around easy marks (the severely emotionally damaged, psychotic, alcoholic, drug addicted, etc...) and certain areas, which subsequently become blighted. The fictional Yaqui shaman Don Juan referred to these as the "Predator" to Carlos Castaneda. Doing magic and raising energy without proper banishing and attention to boundaries is like taping a giant "free meal" sign to your back on the astral. There are numerous "human" beings who follow identical behavioral patterns (and have entered mythology as incubi, succubae and vampires). As long as you take regular precautions and stay conscious, these are best laughed off.

Progressing from this, the traditional Abramelin operation lists a total of 328 demons which are ranked in a hierarchy. The four Princes at the top of the hierarchy are akin to elemental forces and are the inverse or per-verse of the Tetragrammaton. The eight sub-princes are individual intelligences which preside over different areas of demonic operations in the human sphere, while the remaining servitors of the sub-princes are unintelligent drones with specific and singular tasks to perform. While in some cases the servitors have anthropomorphic or zoomorphic form, in others they form hive-minds or the demonic equivalent of bacterial colonies. Once one achieves Knowledge & Conversation, the next task of the initiate is to name and thereby master these negative aspects of the "soul." The images of each demon will likely vary from individual to individual. While some of mine seemed unrelated to my mundane personality and took the form of more universal archetypes, others had been at least partially shaped or given outward form by my individual experience and traumas, as well as my cultural context.

The 328 Abramelin demons added to the host body—man, the microcosm, the pentagram, 5—add to 333, Choronzon, the entity which dwells in the Abyss or Ring-Pass-Not which separates the individual intelligence from non-local consciousness or Godhead.[7] In one sense all individual traits and movements of the mind are demonic, as they are what muddy the waters between the divine spark in man (Kia) and the source from which it emanates.[8] Choronzon also formulates the gateway to Universe "B," the world of the Qliphoth or forces of nonexistence. These occult concepts can be explained in one sense by stating that as one progressively stills the mind through spiritual discipline, the mind kicks back by producing more and more resistance. Choronzon, the "Soma Swami," is the chaos of the "I" stretched to its absolute breaking point and the final resort of a sense of individuality which refuses to die, the sentinel which stands between us and Godmind—an entity of supreme power as it exists to facilitate our survival in the mundane world by keeping shut the doors of perception.

As the individual microcosm reflects at a lower octave the universal macrocosm, the demons which exist within the individual (i.e. "my personal demons") mirror and overlap with the demonic forces within the world. Because of this—and this two-way communication marks all high magick—it may be that each magician who masters their own demons contributes to the general condition of the world.

It is crucial to approach these areas with an initiated, i.e. holographic, perspective. On one level of manifestation a demon can be a negative personality trait or harmful thought loop; on another it can be an entity feeding on one's aura or occluding one from divine consciousness; on another it can be a person or condition within one's life; on yet another it can be a force at work in the world. An understanding of the Four Worlds of the Qabalah can help in grasping and logically categorizing this. As always, *as above, so below* holds true in all aspects of magick.

It can be easy to conceptualize all human misery as the work of malevolent and/or parasitic spirits (this being, of course, the belief structure of shamanism and spiritism as well as more modern "religions" like Scientology). If this is accepted it is then easy and, in some cases, useful to recognize and categorize these spirits, as by naming and giving them symbolic form, it is quite possible to control them, at least within one's own life.

The visions of the demons' forms and natures were garnered through working with a large black mirror[9]; they were called over the traditional three-day period more than a year and a half after the conclusion of my Operation, after I felt I had processed the demonic binding through my mundane life. I am uncertain that this was the best course of action. Each of the 328 demons was compelled to touch the Rod of Almond I used in the Operation (locating an almond tree in London and snapping off a branch when nobody was looking was an interesting exercise), brought under conscious control and then sent forth to build my Temple as in the Solomonic model.[10] The four demonic Princes of Abramelin's system were revealed to me in the following forms:

Satan, the reverse of Fire and the Archangel Michael, is a loathsome, simian creature, the archetypal "monkey on the back," whispering words which produce addiction to despair in all its permutations.

Lucifer, the reverse of Air and the Archangel Raphael, is a beautiful and light-bringing creature, the most human-appearing of the Princes. He is man's intellectual arrogance, presumption, pride—the pride which precipitates a fall.

Belial, the reverse of Water and the Archangel Gabriel, is corruption incarnate, a thick, black astral slime which infects the planet—pollution, filth, disease—a black miasma proceeding from physical manifestations such as chemical spills into Belial's screaming face astrally condensed deep within the Earth, vomiting forth black slime to corrode the world.[11]

Leviathan, the reverse of Earth and the Archangel Michael, is the hateful and hurtful aspect of physicality itself, all the oppression inherent in being physically incarnate, all that which is struggled against in the process of day-to-day survival. It was astrally perceived as expanses of broken concrete buildings; pavement cracked by writhing larvae and worms erupting from the Earth.

These were shown to me in a dream recently to essentially be layers in the psychic atmosphere blanketing the earth, which are stacked one on top of the other, and exist above the layer of the "Predators." In the dream there were multiple layers existing above the demonic Princes. These seemed to be the Gnostic Archons (the prison wardens of the planet, the "World Preset Guardians") or something similar. The chain seems to form a kind of demonic Tarot.

The *Goetia*, the first part of the *Lesser Key of Solomon the King* and the most famous (and generally used) of the Solomonic grimoires still in circulation lists seventy-two demons or daemons which were later assigned to the Shemhamphorash and the Decanates of the Zodiac. Methods for working with each of these entities are given. Goetia means "howling" and is a general term applied to the low end of Western magick, that is, making pacts with spirits in a situation where you are approaching them on their level, or a lower position from them, without having the spiritual dispensation to bind and control demons that comes with Knowledge and Conversation (a.ka. theurgy). Mainstream Thelema substitutes the seventy-two Goetic demons for the demons listed in the traditional Abramelin work in the demonic binding phase of the Holy Guardian Angel operation. In practice this is erroneous. The Goetic demons seem to be closer to the djinn of Arabic lore. They are mischievous, hard to control and often destructive, but evil seems an overstatement. Linda Falorio has suggested that the Goetic entities are alien emanations from various quadrants of the galaxy (i.e. the Decanates); Steve Savedow suggests they are of Atlantean origin. Wherever they come from, centuries of torture by would-be magicians appears to have left them with the behavioral patterns of abused children. Approached with respect and compassion they react in accordance. Breached boundaries—i.e. getting out of the circle or into the triangle—have been observed to cause physical respiratory damage in multiple instances. One wonders if this quality of certain spirit contact experiences has anything to do with the pandemic levels of asthma found in magicians both as a condition that is developed or one present congenitally (alteration of the breath, as those who have practiced pranayama or similar techniques know, will alter reality). When evoked to visible appearance, these entities appear as strange bendings of light, minute rainbow-colored streaks through the air, or will change your perception of your surroundings so that they take on the appearance of the demon's face or other form (much like how the suitably-named *Magic Eye* pictures work).

This is usually accompanied by a much more vivid internal representation of the demon's form, and telepathic communication with it. Working with the Goetia was once described to me as "the cocaine of results magic" and this is an apt description of my experience and the alterations working with these spirits made to my character at the time.

In addition to the above bestiary, the Angel has its own shadow counterpart, who seems related to but not necessarily identical to Choronzon, and is closer to the death instinct identified by Freud; it is the magician's longing for death and disincarnation, to be liberated from the strain of the world and the extreme pressures and responsibilities of the Great Work. It has its own Operation, which may activate of its own accord after the Angel of Light has been summoned. In my case this (apparently involuntary) Operation lasted between March and September 2006, after my experience with Enochian described below. Lust and spiritual arrogance led me to an absolutely brutal self-implosion in which I exiled myself to Vancouver, Canada and found myself once again in isolation and enflamed, this time with absolute suffering. This experience is analogous to the Adeptus Minor initiations in the Golden Dawn and the Fall of Adam. This is the lens through which I finally came to understand my experience, but it is a cross-cultural experience that runs throughout many traditions.

It also partook very vividly of the character of *Liber Cheth*, in which BABALON, the Scarlet Woman, takes away literally everything the magician has built up to this point.[12] During this period I was at times unable to properly take care of or feed myself, and for a solid few months could do little else but hide underneath the covers silently screaming in my own mind that I needed an ambulance, either to a mental asylum or a monastery, a situation requiring me to be medicated by a psychiatrist before I could begin to slowly walk the road to recovery (and back to New York). My energetic field was frayed and shattered and I became host to multiple parasitic entities "from beyond," as I was later informed by an energetic healer. The Buddhist practice of Tonglen was also crucial in turning myself around during this period. During this dark night of the soul the A.'.A.'., or whatever one wants to call it, dispatched two emissaries—one overt and one covert—to protect, re-orient and begin to heal me, which I am grateful for and immensely humbled by.

The visions of the Holy Guardian Angel and the Dark Angel (for lack of better terms) are identical experiences, viewed through different angles (heh); John Lilly expresses these eloquently as the +3 and -3 states of consciousness in *The Center of the Cyclone*. The Thelemic canon—specifically *Liber Tzaddi*—encourages the magician to unite with both. In my case, I had not achieved any modicum of spiritual maturity until taking tours of both heaven and hell, the abysses of height and depth, though doing so nearly killed me.

On a final note, two quotes bear repeating:

I know that God lives in everybody's souls
And the only devil in your world
Lives in the human heart
So now ask yourself
What is human? And what is truth?
Ask yourself
Whose voice is it? That whispers unto you?
Who is it?
That turns your blood into spirit and your spirit into blood
Who is it?
That can reach down from above and set your souls ablaze with Love
Or fill you with the insanity of violence and its brother: lust
Who is it?
Whose words have been twisted beyond recognition
In order to build your planet Earth's religions?
Oh children, you've still got a lot to fucking learn
The only path to heaven is via hell.
– The The, "Good Morning Beautiful"

O thou that hast beheld the City of the Pyramids, how shouldst thou behold the House of the Juggler? For he is wisdom, and by wisdom hath he made the Worlds, and from that wisdom issue judgments 70 by 4, that are the 4 eyes of the double-headed one; that are the 4 devils, Satan, Lucifer, Leviathan, Belial, that are the great princes of the evil of the world. And Satan is worshipped by men under the name of Jesus; and Lucifer is worshipped by men under the name of Brahma; and Leviathan is worshipped by men under the name of Allah; and Belial is worshipped by men under the name of Buddha.
– Aleister Crowley, "The Cry of the 3rd Aethyr" in *Liber 418*

Enochian

The Enochian language and system are an exceedingly complex set of tools transmitted by "the Angels" to John Dee and Edward Kelly in the sixteenth century. Since these same Angels allegedly gave Dee the idea of a British Empire and hence began the imperial age, there was certainly some heavy stuff being tapped here. Enochian is meant to be the original language of mankind, spoken before the fall of the Tower of Babel. Many people, including friends of mine, have reported seeing alien or angelic languages on psychedelics; perhaps Enochian comes from a similar zone deeply rooted within DNA. Dee and Kelly never actually used the Enochian system; it was later incorporated into the rituals of the Golden Dawn (although the version they used is fairly dumbed-down; much more accurate and exhaustive resources are currently available for those who wish to delve into this system). Crowley worked with Enochian along with Victor Neuberg in the Algerian desert in 1907, where by means of sexual magick they opened each of the thirty Aethyrs (only a small part of the whole system), one per day, producing visionary experiences leading Crowley further and further into the magical landscape. Depending on how one looks at the model, each Aethyr (beginning with 30, TEX and ending with 1, LIL) allows one to astrally ascend one step further to God, who dwells in LIL; or (and this is my view) each Aethyr is another layer of an onion successively peeled away from normal consciousness inward into the core center of the mind (Kia in Spare's parlance). *Liber Chanokh* by Crowley bulletpoints the necessary information.[13]

I picked up a bit of Enochian and did some minor experimentation with it in 2004, mostly making initial forays into scrying the first few Aethyrs; I had a few experiences where my visions seemed to overlap with those of others (including one conducted in a large workshop, in which myself and several other people garnered similar imagery with no prior knowledge of the territory). I also did some experimentation with the first and second Enochian calls (these are wholly different from the Aethyrs, all thirty of which are opened by modifying the nineteenth call for each). According to the late Enochian magician Benjamin Rowe, the first and second calls form a relay between spirit and matter, respectively, and can be used to hedge one's reality towards either. The first time I tried this, I gave the first call in the morning, and proceeded to go to work where I found a large and unexpected Christmas bonus waiting for me, as well as a package from a man I had never met in England containing a first edition of Peter Carroll's *Liber Null*, which he evidentally sent just because he thought I was cool. Did this mean that matter had become less tangible and thereby easier to favorably manipulate? Who knows, but it was certainly a lucrative day! After this I made a practice of using the first call before any group ritual work (regardless of system used) to hedge into spirit, and the second call after group work, to hedge back into matter.

I progressed through the thirty Aethyrs in October 2005 with a working group of six people, including myself. It is a poignant story, and not one, unfortunately, that I could fully recount here without naming names or revealing exceedingly personal information about myself and others; I will instead have to talk about it in vagaries, very frustrating to my deep-set emotional need for constant confessional.

The Aethyrs subsume all of the symbolism of the Western Esoteric Tradition and use that collected mass as a diving board into a very, very deep pool. In my experience the Enochian "universe" is a territory wholly outside that of either mundane reality or even the heightened reality revealed by traditional magical ritual. Western magic is the vehicle; Enochian is the destination.

The Enochian universe is one marked by extremely high frequencies, galaxy-spanning entities (as an example, one of the first I encountered was a flock of birds that made up manifest reality itself; others resembled high-voltage beings of pure information, interspatial or interdimensional rifts and portals, or supercomputer exoskeletons overlaying baby galaxies and the like).

Our working group proceeded by taking turns calling each successive Aethyr and then meditating in silence for about half an hour, each letting our visions play out. Group cohesion was still being built at this point. Roles were silently chosen—narrator, manipulator, guardian, comic relief. One group member took on the quality of a silently overseeing Tibetan master, from a slightly Western slant, as if in a T. Lobsang Rampa novel or a Nicholas Roërich painting. The atmosphere was light and humorous at the beginning; at one point I decided that a garishly colored painting of a cat named "Squirt" which I had bought at the Salvation Army and hung on my wall as a joke was actually a gateway to LAM, an archetypal Grey alien consciousness as painted by Crowley towards the end of his life. We also, at one point, decided that the Qa'aba, the holy meteorite in the center of Mecca, was actually a bonsai kitten,[14] information which we jokingly decided would end reality as we know it if leaked to the Internet. It made sense at the time.

After this things began to take on a darker edge; a mix between one of Grimm's more malevolent fairy tales and far-future nanopunk. As the Enochian took further hold, we began to notice a real tension building; as if working a siphon, we had to struggle to get it going at first, but when it got going, it got going, and there was a strong sense that we had to finish it. Our attention was at this point drawn towards a large, very bright neon, slightly icky-feeling polyester frog in the corner that I had picked up on a whim from a thrift store during a lunch break a week earlier (my decorative sense at this time in my life was High Stuffed Animal). At this point one of my friends picked up the frog, shoved it in my face and said, in a very tinny and weird voice I have never heard him use before or since, "I am the one thing that has fucked up every great magician, the one thing that they never conquer, themselves! I am the ego! I am CHORONZON!" (This sounds laughable out of context, but at the time it quickly became terrifying.) With each Aethyr successively called (we were at around 20 at this point), magical reality deepened, our actions became less our own, and the frog gained strength. Around this time my friend picked up the frog again and had it say "Wait till you see my belly full of WHORES!"

The next few hours of the working became a silent struggle with the ego, at least for myself. At this point I assumed that everybody in the room was experiencing the same thing, but later found that this wasn't really the case—everybody was in their own zone. Yet I was experiencing everything people were saying to me and doing around me as direct contact with another reality, and that after this point everybody in the room had been overshadowed by the Enochian system itself and were perfectly and precisely acting out parts in an initiatory drama designed to snuff out my individual ego forever.

I was slumped in my chair in the corner; the rest of the people in the room were sprawled out on the bed or the floor. I thought of myself as a dying king, ancient and unable to move, with the frog as my loyal vizier at my side whispering horrid nothings into my ear. I suddenly became convinced that everybody around me wanted to kill me, that they thought I had put myself above them by putting my picture on the back of *Generation Hex* and that now they wanted to tear me down and rip me apart. I closed my eyes and went into the interior landscape, endless waves of witchy, cybernetic landscapes spinning through infinity. As each Aethyr continued to be called I realized that this was the fabric of my ego, and that as I was rushing forward to grab it, like a snake trying to swallow its own tail, it was rushing away from me twice as fast. This continued in tripped-out la-la land for a while. The witch vibe increased; the fabric of the egoic landscape curled into a robotic, hyper-real wyrd-ring which seemed to take on the character of all occultism at all times, and which was outside of time in a zone visited during the Witch's Sabbath in all times and places. I opened my eyes, looked around at the people in the room with me, and thought, *This is how covens are formed...*

By this time we were about an hour away from dawn, and not even halfway through. Somebody grabbed the copy of *Gems From the Equinox* that we were using and began to quickly read through the Aethyrs one after the other. I was back on the bed at this point and began to go into Samadhi, tuning everything out and beginning to ascend towards the light. As this happened everybody in the room began to mock and cut me down in various ways, telling me I would never be able to silence the frog. This got progressively more intense until the cry of ZAX, the 10th Aethyr, was given, and all fell silent.

ZAX corresponds with Da'ath and the Abyss; it is the Cave of Choronzon. My memory of what transpired in this Aethyr is conspicuously blank. It picks up again finding myself staring at the stuffed frog, its head crushed in my right hand, squeezed so tightly around it that my knuckles were white and shaking. Somebody was still whispering out the Aethyrs in the corner. I began to feel an incandescent white light beginning to settle all around, subtly at first. As the ritual progressed I went fully into Samadhi and essentially catatonic, my fist clenched in a deathgrip on the frog. My eyes glazed over, staring blankly into the ceiling, and my body went completely still. Meanwhile everybody around me continued (though it was slowing) to do things to tempt me out of this state and let go of the frog. During this time I was still seeing the fabric of my ego, but now it was drawing inward, becoming circular, like a hurricane slowly shrinking into its central eye. Around the 6th Aethyr they started expressing concern about the health of my situation and whether or not I had gone into some kind of place I couldn't get back from. I did not relent. Around Aethyr 5, figuring it was now or never, I stood up from the bed, walked over to my altar, and crucified the frog above it. I hammered long screws into its palms and a third through its feet. I wasn't strong enough to get them through the wall myself, and one of my friends stood up and drove the screws home. (This was the most touching moment of the night.) In some ways this was terrifying, as we had just performed a group scapegoat ritual. I flashed that this frog was every scapegoated person or group in history, and it was totally arbitrary. It was just a stuffed frog. This is how wars start... a crown of thorns was placed on its head, made of leather, part of somebody's Halloween costume from earlier.[15]

I returned to the bed, closed my eyes and folded my hands as if in silent prayer. After this everybody around me became Angelic. They were at the bottom of the bed, putting rings on my toes, saying "Ring him with jewels, crown him, send him to heaven in a flight of angels..." Everything was becoming white and phosphorescent. Everything began to take on the character of a wedding ceremony, and I realized that during the course of the ritual I had fallen in love with one of the women in the room, now laying on the bed next to me. We appeared ringed with shining gold jewelry and finery and rose petals began to fall on us from the ceiling. In the third Aethyr I realized that I now had to give her up if I wanted to progress (this was seen as something that would have to happen in the future, presumed to be at the end of our lives after we spent them happily ever after). This was the most painful moment of all, but I turned my head away from her and closed my eyes, symbolically relinquishing her. At this point my ego wrapped up into a perfect and unbreakable wheel, perhaps the Philosopher's Stone or the "Alpha Ovule" of Mahendranath. By the 2nd Aethyr this became a giant spinning Aleph, the "Road Ends" marker on the Qabalistic superhighway, in imagery and detail more vivid than anything I had seen in waking or dreaming life, pure divinity. And then I merged into the light and I was it and it was me.

Finally, one of the people in the group read the call of the 1st Aethyr, LIL, with the voice of a forty-year-old Brooklyn single mother and phone sex operator. And we were right back to reality, right back to where we had started.

I was pure, I was whole. That was it. I'd won the game. No more magick, no more nothing. Just life. As we walked out of the room the sun had fully risen and my housemate, a music journalist, was quietly tapping away at an article (God knows what he had made of the noises coming out of my room). He had his iTunes on, and was listening to a song by The Books, built around a sample of Crowley reading the Call of the 1st Aethyr. (My housemate was the most un-occult person imaginable.) Um. Right.

Everybody went out for a cigarette again, except the woman I had fallen in love with and myself. I was sitting on the couch staring at the brick wall outside my window, in awe of everything. She came out of the room and bitchily and crankily asked for a towel, and I thought, is that what it's going to be? Is that going to be the rest of our life together? Domestic crabbiness and fighting over the bathroom and stretch marks and paunches and arguing about money, just like everybody else? Isn't that what I want?

After she showered I went in and took mine, still in ecstasy. Yet there was an anxiety beginning to tighten in my chest and grow. I tried to ignore it. It got stronger. I dried myself off and looked at myself in the mirror. Still there. I picked up my toothbrush and began to put toothpaste on it, and there was Choronzon again, right back inside me. And it said, I've always been here. I'll always be here. I was here watching when you were four years old, brushing your teeth. I am you. And then I remembered, that frog had something inside it. That frog was full of whores. And we never looked. And that's what I was feeling inside me.

I came out and sat next to her on the couch. I tried to kiss her and she backed away, and so I tried to play it off. And then I told her, we have a choice. We can leave what we've done as it is. We can leave it all wrapped up, the snake's tail in its mouth, all finished, and go and live our lives, in which case we'll be just like everybody else. There won't be any mysteries left, and magicians can't exist without mystery, so we won't be magicians any more. Or we can cut open that frog and let out the whores. Because the whores are the Qliphoth. And they're the only thing left to explore because they don't actually exist.

And then I left the decision with her. And she chose the Qliphoth. And when everybody else came back we went back in the room and she knifed its belly open and tore out its insides, and gave everybody a handful of cotton. "And some whores for you, and some whores for you, and some whores for you..." And so it began...

We drove out to the Bronx to retrieve some stuff and the entire cycle replayed for me during the drive. Everywhere I looked outside the window, there were street signs and shop names mirroring exactly what I happened to be thinking. There were some referencing higher intelligences at work on the planet, like a shop we passed called Sothis that I had never seen before. This is my temple, I thought, and furthermore, it *is* me, the universe *is* me. This is all me. Everything is me, I just forgot.

That night we went to a Thai restaurant and on the way we opened the first Tunnel of Set, Azapheme.[16] The first thing that happened after we sat down was that a man opened the door and walked directly up to us (we were sitting at the back of the restaurant). He had some kind of congenital bone disease where he looked smashed and hunched, cutting only 3/4 of a usual profile from the side, like somebody had shaved off the front of his skeleton. Saying nothing, he looked at all of us knowingly, held up a nickel, and then walked out again. And so it continued...

On the way back from the restaurant, and only after opening the Tunnels, I confessed my love, and it was reciprocated. And a voice somewhere, the echo of generations of failed magicians past, said, oh go on then. Have your own broken relationships. See how it feels. And so began the worst year of my life.

My completion of the ritual, as a punctuation mark at the end of the cycle of work begun by my Angelic Operation, was the opening of the grade of Master of the Temple, in which I was shown the state of consciousness in which there is no separation between self and universe and each mirrors the other perfectly and constantly. This demarcates the line where humanity ends and Godhood begins. This does not mean that I claimed the grade of Master of the Temple, since to do so would mean permanently stabilizing consciousness in, and then passing beyond, that state. However, that level of my self was activated and awakened, at least for a short period, and I was given a glimpse.

At any rate, at this point I was definitely feeling like I had attained the grade of Master of the Freaking Universe. I had a book out; I had just been on stage at Alex Grey's Chapel of Sacred Mirrors speaking to a packed house of two hundred people who all seemed to want to hear what I had to say; women everywhere wanted me; I had just fallen madly in love with somebody I was convinced was the woman of my dreams and, on top of that, was now convinced that I had touched Godhead. Aaah yasss, I had finally arrived, and my life was better than I had ever imagined it could be. All that hard work and toiling and paying my dues and humility (which I could surely dispense with now, I mean, just a little bit, right?) had paid off. What else could I ask for? What new wonders might life have in store?

The answer, of course, was that I was about to get slapped the fuck down and have all of it ripped away until I was crawling on the floor and begging for my life. "Don't be an Icarus," an ex-girlfriend had warned me after returning from India. Whoops...

It is worth noting that Paul Foster Case considered Enochian inherently detrimental to those who use it, and banned it from his order (Builders of the Adytum). Donald Tyson believes its use to hasten global apocalypse. My life did fall apart after going through the Aethyrs, and I did experience a personal apocalypse of sorts, but then again I was working with so much stuff at this time that could have done the same thing that it's impossible to come to any conclusions.[17] A few months after this I went back and read *The Vision and the Voice*, Crowley's record of working the Aethyrs, which I had not read more than a few chapters of, and was surprised to find many of the same experiences I had had, albeit filtered through a very different nervous system.

The Qliphoth

The Choronzon entity composed of the totality of the individual personality, in Thelemic and Typhonian Qabalah, provides a gateway to the reverse of the Tree of Life, the World of Shells, Universe "B"—the Qliphoth and Tunnels of Set. It is tempting, especially for those from a Judeo-Christian background, to identify this as "hell" or the source of evil or demons. The (un)reality is much more complicated and dangerous, as "evil" and demons are facets of normal existence and a necessary component of the divine plan. The Qliphotic Tree is the rotting afterbirth of that divine creation. Each Tunnel, when first accessed through astral exploration or freeform shamanic experiment, is an utter perversion and mockery of one of the Paths on the Tree of Life (symbolized on the Dayside by the 22 Tarot Trumps). These "masks" and their attendant experiences and "god"-forms quickly disintegrate into (im) pure Qliphotic energy, which cannot be described as anything but the energy which unravels Creation. As the Qliphoth proceed into density and form a pattern of descent and dissolution instead of ascension, they are marked by an overwhelming feeling of gravity—the gravity of the situation, smashing one into nonexistence until death, insanity or worse occurs. Everything about the Qliphoth is utterly wrong. They do not confer any power or benefit to those exploring them to my knowledge and experience. They do, however, provide a gateway to the alternate reality referred to as Universe "B" by Kenneth Grant and Michael Bertiaux—an utterly bleak and mechanized universe devoid of human presence or compassion.[18]

Perhaps, as astrophysicists have surmised that one may pass through the negating and smashing force of a black hole to emerge in another universe, so it is with the false Sephira Da'ath and Choronzon. Yet why one would want to take their vacation there when they could be on a package deal on a beach somewhere is beyond me. Even Florida would be better.

Sigils for each of the Tunnels of Set (along with for the dayside paths) are given by Crowley in *Liber 231*; Kenneth Grant expanded on this information immensely in his *Nightside of Eden*, providing correspondences and sonic keys which unlock each Tunnel. Linda Falorio's *The Shadow Tarot* provides a more practical manual for working with these forces. My own method for opening the Tunnels was to work with a (female) sexual partner; the character of each Tunnel suggests a sexual method (for instance, A'ano'nin, the inverse of the Devil, suggests ritualized anal sex; Yamatu, the Hermit, suggests mutual masturbation; and Amprodias, the Fool, suggests auto-erotic asphyxiation). Sexual role-play and the resultant perverse psychodrama, combined with the sonic keys, sigils drawn on the body of either participant in appropriate colors, and appropriate psychoactive substances if particularly daring, can be used to produce the energy necessary to activate each Tunnel. Once put into effect, the Tunnel will work itself out through role-play, visions, interpersonal drama and the environment over the next few hours. If not properly banished (and the best way to banish is simply to ignore the Tunnels, as they are non-existant), the energy will linger in the life of the magician. Having one's life utterly fall apart on all levels is only to be expected as a result. It would not be an exaggeration to state that one could literally murder one's own "soul" in this fashion.

After initial forays, I created a set of twenty-two seashells of equal size (all retrieved from a beach in Mexico), each with the sigil of a Tunnel painted on it in the garish color scheme given by Grant in *Nightside of Eden*. These were subsequently used to catch the commingled sexual fluids produced by each ritualized copulation, thereby activating the sigil as in the IX° OTO sexual magick system.

My specific experiences with the Tunnels are too harrowing, heartbreaking and upsetting, and still too fresh in memory, to discuss here, nor would doing so be appropriate. I credit Frater X. with pulling me out of these workings before it was too late, and saving my ass yet again, for which (as well as for many other reasons) he has my love and respect.

As the Dayside of the Tree can be ascended in one fashion (and element, that of Air or intellect) by giving the Calls of the Thirty Aethyrs in Enochian, so can the Nightside be spanned and descended by the use of the Formulas of HORIZON, developed by Frater Elijah before the turn of the Millennium. I do not have practical experience with these.

The initiates of the Golden Dawn put it best: "Stoop not down into that darkly splendid world."

Sex Magick

The control and direction of sexual energy is a critical point in magick. When dealing with sexuality we are dealing with the very essence of what it means to be alive. How, with who, how often and in what context you have orgasms is one of the most powerful factors in determining what your life looks like. It should then be no surprise that when used with the intent of effecting conscious change, sex can become sex magick and have a dramatic effect upon reality.

Sex magick and sexual identity form a gigantic spectrum of manifestation and contact with not only exalted (or debased) states of consciousness but also with non-human entities. Human beings are at the their most psychically sensitive and, er, "turned on" while having sex; even the slightest movements of energy and intent can have vast ramifications and nearly all traditional ceremonial forms of magick can be re-interpreted as sexual instructions, one of Crowley's big projects. The traditional assumption about "tantric sex" is that it involves having sex for godly long periods of time and, yes, this is certainly very fun, but the question then becomes what one uses the overloads of orgone energy for. The traditional aims of magick are all on the menu but the options are unlimited. Two or more psychically sensitive and properly trained partners can generate and broadcast any frequency into manifestation through sex and symbolic actions taken within a sexual context. Take, for instance, the protective and loving field generated in healthy families versus the chaos produced, and reflected into the children, by sexualy unhealthy or violent families. When correctly approached, sex is the gateway through which we become our most human, our most divine, our happiest. (The work of Wilhelm Reich on sexuality is overwhelmingly important on this subject, and to our health as a species.)

It should be noted that the practice of magick very often has the effect of dissolving the comfortable boundaries we place around gender and sexual identity, and begins to evolve us towards a state symbolized by the alchemical hermaphrodite or Rebis, Eliphas Lévi's depiction of Baphomet or the Pandrogyne creation of Genesis and Lady Jaye Breyer P-Orridge. I am consistently amazed at how central sex is to our sense of self, and the extent to which any given sexual experience can effect change to one's personality and energy flow. If deconditioning is one of your goals in magick—and it should be one of the central ones—then sexual experimentation and modification becomes *de rigeur*.

Sex magick is an area that needs to be massively re-examined and re-assessed, not in the least because much of the current writing available on it either reflects old and one-sided attitudes towards sexuality (i.e. Crowley, Parsons, etc.) or comes out of the "American" school of "tantric sex" which has no clue how to direct sexual energy past the second "chakra" and quickly produces the burn-out types that are pandemic on the New Age scene. (This is such a gigantic topic, however, that instead of trying to assess it here in full there could be an entire work dedicated to it—for historical comprehensiveness's sake, traditional forms of Western sex magick are summarized below for the moment.)

The Solomonic grimoires, as well as nearly all religions, insist upon celibacy as a prerequisite for entering higher consciousness. Total celibacy over long periods of time can build an immense sense of focus, clarity and willpower (as somebody who tends to look at life as a bunch of tedious crap you have to put up with in between having orgasms—or being creative, which is basically the same thing—I find this exceedingly challenging); so it makes sense that one might want to engage in this for long periods of time before, say, working with Goetic demons, who are notorious for taking advantage of any slip in focus, clarity or willpower.

The idea that sexual energy can be raised and directed towards marsupials is fairly common now, the simplest method of this being to visualize a marsupial while orgasming in order to deeply imprint it (taken from the work of Paschal Beverly Randolph). In the O.T.O. system, every sexual act produces a child; if not a physical one, then one on the astral; these can be consciously created and directed or they can be ignored, in which case the theory goes that they kind of hang around leeching off your energy, or incarnating as human succubae and incubi, especially if you're a magician who's used sex magick in the past and is now not paying attention to Orgasming With Intent.

The sexual magick system of the O.T.O., which I have minor experience with but have not made an extended or disciplined practice of, is a form of solar-phallic worship in which it is explained that there is only ONE god, and that all others are either symbols pointing to this god or are graven images. This god is reflected as the sun in the macrocosm and the phallus in the microcosm.[19] It then progresses to various forms of sex used for magic which can be interpreted on many levels, especially taking on the form of gods and goddesses while having sex (as in Tantra), producing children on the astral, charging talismans with sexual fluid, and an alchemical process in which during a male/female copulation, the male ejaculates into the vagina, lets it "stew," and then licks the commingled fluid out. This is then shared by the man and woman in their mouths and absorbed sublingually. Repeated over long periods of time, this is meant to greatly facilitate health and can also form the secret of "immortality" as it is meant to empower the astral body to the point that it is strong enough to maintain conscious existence after the death of the physical body.[23] At this point it should be able to forcibly eject somebody's consciousness from their body and take over. There are Tibetan Buddhist tantras for doing the same. The IX° O.T.O. also gives instructions for either incarnating a god in human form (the Moonchild rite) or implanting one's departing consciousness into an unborn baby. This is very weird.

Many aspects of the magick practiced by the O.T.O. and Crowley take on board Victorian superstitions (surprise surprise); mainly the obsession with the retention of sperm and that loss of sperm was akin to loss of physical, mental and spiritual health. (In addition, the Moonchild rite takes on board the nineteenth century European superstition that whatever stimuli a pregnant woman was subjected to would influence the later personality of the unborn child.) This is an ancient tribal superstition prevalent in many cultures. Modern dudes, however, seem to be endlessly obsessed with finding new things to do with their sperm and new places to put it, and try to spread it as far and wide as possible, often while videotaping themselves doing so for posterity on our camera phones, and find this so endlessly entertaining that through the miracle of video, DVD and the internet they spend countless hours watching other men do it, too, especially if they are B-rate celebrities. Never in history have so many men been so queer for each other.

In addition to the "traditional" sex magick system as practiced by the Caliphate O.T.O., Kenneth Grant has developed a sexual magick system revolving around the sixteen kalas or secretions of the vagina, which runs throughout his books; Frater Elijah has developed a battery of homosexual sex magick operations which were published online in PDF format as *Chaos Kung-Fu*.

It is very important for us as a species that we evolve sex for uses beyond just reproduction, which in its current form is ecologically suicidal, or pleasure, which is great but ultimately can only take one so far. As *typically* practiced, I see breeding as a kind of slow holocaust of cellulite and Barney videos. Then again, as I write this my friends from school seem to be getting married and settled down; my best friend from high school is married, owns an apartment and is in law school. His wife puts on an apron and bakes apple tarts for guests. Meanwhile I'm sitting here typing instructions on how to do WIKKED MAYJIKK SPELZZ to some unknown audience I assume understands or even cares. My my isn't life funny sometimes...

"Energy"

"Energy" is central to a lot of New Age thought. It always struck me as a lazy concept. I mean, what kind of energy? Where does it come from? What do you mean? The whole idea of kundalini and chakras also struck me as silly wishful thinking, beyond that, I rejected it out of hand because it is a de facto New Age dogma and its acceptance is enforced in almost all magical systems which are culturally sanctioned. At the same time, white-lighters, yoga chicks and alternative therapy obsessives, at least the ones who aren't fraudulent leeches, have a whole lot to teach us.

In doing work with the "energy" body I adopted the use of the ten Sephira and the Divine Names of God instead of the chakra system. I have found the vibration of the Divine Names one of the most potent techniques in beginning to melt reality at my disposal. As far as chakras, I have nothing terribly elucidating to say. Phil Hine once related the very interesting point to me that our current understanding of the chakras is a Western gloss which goes back only as far as Theosophy and, specifically, C. W. Leadbeater; the original meaning of chakra was a social unit or circle of gods, though there had never been a fixed meaning.

My "kundalini" (whatever that is) was activated in early 2006 by an Irish guru named Derek O'Neill, who I found in some ways profoundly insightful, moving and tangibly powerful, and in other ways fairly dodgy. This was done via reiki in a day-long group initiation and reduced me to tears. Regardless of any doubts about the validity of the guru, this experience deeply affected me and my attitude towards magic. During the hell I went through after this, the memory remained a symbol of hope.

In mid-2006 I did a tremendous amount of work in purifying and cleansing my "energy," which had become the psychic equivalent of a demilitarized zone. This was done by re-hitting the Hermetics and going back to working with the systems of Franz Bardon and David Goddard as well as the usual Golden Dawn techniques. I slowly began to be able to achieve immediate sorcery via conscious manipulation of the "energy" that it appears the entire universe, or the entire human perception of that universe, is made of, albeit in different vibrations and gradients of density. This worked well for immediate manifestation tricks. This "energy" appeared to me as something very akin to the "Magic Mirror" five-dimensional mirror liquid which features prominently in *The Invisibles* as well as in Terence McKenna's *True Hallucinations*.

While in Olympia, Washington in September 2006, when it was clear that my relationship was over and it felt like I had nowhere left to go in the world, that I was a broken man and would remain a broken man forever, and that any remaining hope had been snuffed out into the outer darkness, I hit a critical mass point where I found myself alone in a motel room contemplating the failure of my life, the lack of hope for the human race and the bad situations some of my friends were in. I was editing a book at this point and opened my iTunes, which picked up on somebody's shared files somewhere on the wireless network in the building. I proceeded to page through the names of dozens of rape, bestiality and child pornography videos and at this point something fractured. I found myself in the bathroom screaming silently into the mirror, rocking back and forth and drooling catatonically, horrible noises beginning to escape from my throat, until my face was an utterly unrecognizable gargoyle of inhuman misery.

At this point my reality broke completely, and suddenly everything was fine. A huge influx of something hit me and I could see my energetic body in the mirror, pulsing with my breath, radiating out an inch or two from my skin. I suddenly looked completely composed and beautiful and felt as if my entire body were breathing, a fully somadelic influx of pulsing, humming bodily bliss. I felt GREAT and over the next few hours continued exploring this.

The next day I was walking around the city and the woods in Olympia and found that I could continue to consciously intake energy from the universe in this manner. I noticed that people were reacting differently around me and that I could catch people's attention from several yards away when consciously directing it, even if they had not previously seen me, or that I could control how people were physically behaving around me if they got close.

In drawing energy in, I then pegged that the best way to do it was to draw energy from the center of the earth and from the sky at the same time. It then hit me that these were the Heaven and Earth of the *I Ching* and that each of the sixty-four hexagrams had to indicate a type of energetic state or interchange between each of these poles and, in total, form a map of how states change.

A few weeks later, after being kicked out of Canada by the border patrol,

I was staying with a family friend who just "happened" to be a student of Qi Gong. We ended up in a conversation about it and I told her about my experience. She immediately became overjoyed and said that that was exactly it, that I had activated what she called the "Ring of Truth," and also confirmed my theories about the *I Ching* and energy influx. Later, after doing some Qi Gong exercises with me and being very surprised at how sensitive I was to picking up subtle currents, she discussed my situation with her Qi Gong teacher, an highly credentialed Chinese master with a Ph.D. in Western medicine, who also became overjoyed and confirmed the validity of my experience, the beginning of a very positive and life-affirming line of inquiry.

A technical point about the Holy Guardian Angel. The magician is the center of her circle. The circle is her reality. Energy is drawn in from heaven and earth. This forms a ladder of the ascent or descent of consciousness into more exalted or debased vibratory states. However, the Holy Guardian Angel is not a higher level of one's self which is drawing you up along this central axis towards a higher state, as is easy to assume. It is a completely separate entity which moves outside of one's circle, like a shepherd, leading and shaping your experience. This is the initiated conception of the "witch's familiar." This transpersonal entity, once reached out for, can and will use anything and everything in your life to lead you to it and structure your growth.

The Tarot

A map of the life cycle. Here's one interpretation:

0. The Fool; 1. The Magician: Egg and Sperm; conception.
2. The High Priestess: Birth (passage through the birth canal).
3. The Empress: The Mother's influence.
4. The Emperor: The Father's influence.
5. The Hierophant: Education and Culturalization. Language.
6. The Lovers: Socialization, reaching out for others beyond family. Choice of type of person to become.
7. The Chariot: Beginnings of ethical and spiritual awakening. Realization of passage of time and the reality of death.
8. Lust: Adolescence, hormonal surge, beginnings of sexuality.
9. The Hermit: Awakening of full sense of isolate individuality. "I am."
10. Wheel of Fortune: Going out into the world; seeking one's fortune.
11. Justice: Slotting into a social role. Society exercises control over "free" individual.

[Most people stop here and play out their assigned role until death.]
12. The Hanged Man: Beginnings of inward journey, quest for inner truth.
13. Death: Realization of falseness of, and shattering of, constructed identity.
14. Art: The Holy Guardian Angel Operation (in whatever form). Connection established with transcendent self.
15. The Devil: Demonic binding. Exercise of control over previously uncontrolled facets of self and life. Struggle with material world post-Operation.
16. The Tower: Pinnacle of initiation reached; life appears to have been mastered. Pride precipitates a fall; the constructed world is demolished. Dark night of the soul.
17. The Star: Beginning glimpses of "eternal" truth beyond the limited ego. Connection with A.'.A.'.
18. The Moon: Unification with eternal feminine.
19. The Sun: Unification with eternal masculine.
20. The Aeon: Unification with time.
21. The Universe: Unification with space.

Would you like to run it backward or forward this time around?

Secret Societies

There are, and always have been, numerous occult orders and mystery religions in operation on the planet. They have to remain secret because the majority of people find nothing so pleasing and comforting as dragging everything down to their level. All occult orders on the "outer" have different nuances of character and style. All of them can socialize you into being comfortable with the theory and practice of magic. None of them can teach you magic, though in the best cases they can form a safe space for you to teach yourself. They are all training wheels. You do not need to join an occult order to get your training wheels. Everybody who needs them gets them. When the student is ready, the master appears.

There is at least one "superordinary," non-physical order in operation both on this planet and plane of existence and on others. Crowley called it the A.'.A.'., others the Great White Brotherhood, among other names. I consider Crowley a journalist who mapped some of the territory and wrote it down in the language available to him. That does not mean that the A.'.A.'. has anything to do with Crowley or that his writings are the only way in; far from it. The physical A.'.A.'. organizations that exist on the planet are distractions. This order is in all likelihood not maintained by human beings.

Its agenda is inscrutable. Talking about it is talking about an abstraction on the level of God, truth or the existence of the Abominable Snowman. (*The Process* by Brion Gysin is recommended, however.)

The A.'.A.'. system that Crowley left in written form, in which one proceeds through ten grades leading one from man to God, each of which subsumes various tasks drawn from both Eastern and Western magick and mysticism, is an excellent device for patching together training in an immense number of systems from various cultures. The Thelemic religious angle I can give or take; it is the technology itself that I'm interested in. Everybody who works through this should, to my mind, completely demolish it and replace each set of tasks in each Sephira and path with the best and most modern resources to hand. I.e. don't follow Crowley's instructions on yoga; go to a freaking yoga class. The A.'.A.'. system as given is only one man's map of the road that one man took. While the system may look cut-and-dry on paper, it is hardly so; I did not take the "grades" in an kind of a linear fashion and in some ways unfolded in all of them simultaneously, warped backwards and forwards across the Abyss, and so on. Crowley himself unfolded across the Tree in a fashion nothing like the printed system. The major hint I have to give is... pay close attention to the people who are most central to your life.

The best way to relate my understanding of what the A.'.A.'. "is" is to get all *Wonder Years* and relate yet another story from my childhood.

When I was in second grade I went to a primary school that was on the end of my street. Shortly after entering school my teachers pegged that I was a weird cat and too smart for them to keep docile in a "normal" classroom. So I was tagged as a "gifted" student and placed in GATE, Gifted and Talented Education, a program designed in the sixties to keep smart kids from killing themselves by putting them with other "gifted" students, which basically had the effect of making them even more eccentric and weird and improperly socialized (bless them, bless them all!). This meant that I had to be bussed all the way across town to a new school with a better GATE program which, because of public school funding laws requiring the most money go to the least privileged areas, was in "da ghetto," where people liked to drive-by and riddle the school with bullets at night, syringes would mysteriously appear on the playground, fifth grade girls got raped walking home from school and where I at one point became involved in some particularly degenerate gang warfare in which I was roped into a gigantic rock-throwing melee against a huge posse of Ethiopian kids.

Anyway, this actually turned out to be quite a positive experience for me, BUT prior to this, eight-year-old, second-grade me seriously rebelled against the concept of having to be bussed to some new school. The main reason was that I knew that if I stayed at the school on my block, I would be put in the third-grade classroom where they played this very strange game called "Wizards" every year. This was a game meant to teach spelling skills and which was played on a very large game board on a wall of the classroom over several months. I became obsessed with the idea of this game. OBSESSED. But eventually my parents persuaded me to go to the new school, and I relented, much to my chagrin, knowing I would now never get to find out about this mysterious game that I heard all of the third-grade students bragging they got to play.

So I ended up getting through third and fourth grade at the new school and began preparing for fifth, which was the final grade taught at the school. All along I had been hearing stories about the fifth grade GATE teacher, Mr. White, who was meant to be the supreme fount of wisdom and higher education. The fifth graders in his class seemed like Adults to us wee ones (why, many of the girls had just gotten their first hormone surges and now seemed twice as tall as the average fourth-grader, and some even—wonder of wonders—had things that vaguely looked like breasts!) They were no longer Of Us. They had moved on. Why, we heard he was even teaching them algebra... Meanwhile I was stuck in the fourth grade, still entertaining myself by carrying around a container of garlic salt from my parents' cupboard and trying to convince other kids I would turn into a vampire if I didn't keep licking it, when I could be learning algebra with this Mr. White. I mean, what gave?

Finally the year ended, and after summer vacation, I was put in Mr. White's class. This dude was seriously intense. He was an Irish guy in his forties, with thinning white hair and skin that would light up bright red whenever he got angry, which was often. He kind of looked like a burlier Timothy Leary, in retrospect. His idea of educating us was, wonder of wonders, to let us learn at our own pace, and he would give us cards with a set list of things to learn and tasks to do. As soon as we were done with one, we were given another, and of course it turned into a race to see who could get to the highest one. He would have us doing all kinds of weird things, like building transistor radios from scratch and having contests to see who could build the best marshmallow catapult using the laws of physics or, in my case, drawing comics, since I wanted to be a comic book artist at the time. We were in awe of him. Of course, he could totally fly off the handle as well (I have one particularly vivid memory of him screaming at me in front of the whole class and battering my desk with a large hammer because I had made a joke about ejaculation which I thought he couldn't hear... whoops...).

Anyways, a few months into the year, he announced that we were going to be playing a game called "Wizards." I went apeshit. And then it turned out that not only were we going to be playing "Wizards," but that Mr. White was actually the guy who had invented it, in the freewheeling seventies (in retrospect, it all seems so much more clear...)

In the structure of the game, each student in the class took on the role of some form of wizard, sorcerer or spell-caster, which were represented on a giant map of a fantasy landscape with small Velcro figures. Each week we would have various adventures and encounters with monsters which were meant to help teach us grammar and spelling (Get it? Spelling? If you don't, then you don't yet understand one of the critical secrets of "real magick" either...). Every week we would take a class spelling test, and whoever passed the test was raised a grade. There were ten grades to Wizardry in the game, and each time you advanced a grade your wizard became more powerful. Everybody in the class was in a fierce race to see who could make it to the end. By the time the game finished, only two people had made it to the supreme tenth grade, and I was one of them. Mr. White (of the Great White Brotherhood?) then informed me that the other person who had achieved the tenth grade wasn't as naturally gifted at spelling as me, so my achievement actually mattered less than his. Hah hah, take that! But then, after achieving the top grade, he allowed me to progress to making up new rules for the game and adding my own personality to it.

Take that story for what you will, if anything at all.

Skipping ahead a bit and passing over most of an oh-so-tormented and black nail-polish drenched adolescence filled with a lot of Joy Division and Vertigo comic books, during the last seven years I have climbed the ten-grade structure of the A.'.A.'. to the supreme level of Ipsissimus. This was essentially play-acting and a trial run in which I gained familiarity with the map. The map is not the territory (no duh). At present I consider this to have been only my Probationer period in the Order and [at the time I wrote this, in late 2006] was working through the Neophyte Grade. The experiences attendant upon this grade activated immediately and of their own accord; I did not have to "fake it till I made it." I also consider this all arbitrary nonsense.

During my trial run, as outlined in this document, I progressed quickly through the lower grades by gaining in-depth experience with magick, meditation, Qabalah and devotion to the Order, which was exercised through my life. In the Adeptus Minor (outer) grade I performed the Angelic Operation and then in the inner grade entered into a completely revamped reality apparently in contact with transcendent forces, and progressed from there. In the Adeptus Exemptus grade, I published a book summarizing my understanding of the universe (*Generation Hex*) and became the leader of a school of thought (the "Indigo Children" in this case). Via Enochian I then entered the Abyss and proceeded through its Qliphotic nightmare energy and was stripped of everything, via BABALON, and apparently abandoned by my Holy Guardian Angel. I then became nothing but a pile of dust in the City of Pyramids in the Master of the Temple grade, and became NEMO, nobody, a broken man, alone and anonymous in a foreign land and town (Vancouver, where Frater Achad had the same experiences in the 1930s).

From here I progressed to the grade of Magus and uttered my Word, ULTRACULTURE, which altered the fabric of the "occult dialogue," relinquishing the fruit of my labor up to that point to the wider world in a series of public acts and uttering truth so that all could be "enslaved" by it as is the Curse of the Magus; along with my own life this was offered as my sacrifice to God. And then all the light and all the darkness collapsed into each other and exploded and an endless and fertile CHAOS was born in the ringing tone that is AOM.

And then I passed unto Kether and the grade of Ipsissimus, the loftiest grade that it is possible to obtain by the Brethren of the Order A.'.A.'. while still incarnate, the trance of Nerodha-Samapatti, the very Crown of creation itself, which holds within its corona of light the very Kingdom, just as the Kingdom containeth the Crown, and Nirvana is Samsara as surely as Samsara is Nirvana.

And in this grade there was no longer any magic. There was nobody to pray to. There was nowhere to go. There were no longer any gods. There was no path. There was no Process. There was no A.'.A.'. There was no God. There was only one place to turn to get myself out of the fine mess I was in. There was only one Angel to guard me and keep me safe. There was only one person to pray to. And that was me. I that am I. And, in that sense, by default, I was God. And the final secret of magic was:

You're alive, jackass!

And then I died. And da fat bitch sang. And that person is now dead. And what it is that continues in this body, and what purpose it will serve, remains to be seen.

And so what?

Fuck it, fuck all of it. I have nothing to say other than they always told me that role-playing games and comic books and rock music would lead to the occult, and by golly by gumdrop, they were right, the fuckers.

Heaven (+3)

I love you, you love me, I am you, you are me. Grace and love are the only reality. This is the Garden of Eden. Earth is a school from which all graduate into light sooner or later. Everything is running perfectly and even apparent misery is part of the divine plan (to balance karma / purify matter into spirit / teach lessons / etc etc). Individuality is illusion and we are aware of this and hence liberated. We have free will, but all paths lead to the Source. Love forever.

Hell (-3)

Everything suffers all the time period the end. Earth is a prison planet; a torture device designed to produce the maximum yield of misery possible. The darkness is occasionally and temporarily illuminated by the false hopes of love, religion, family, success, all dangled in front of our eyes like the bioluminescent lure of a beast-toothed angler fish. Human beings are a crop seeded by some other form of entity and our agony is their food. "We teach all hearts to break." All of them. Individuality is illusion but our only respite from it is to be devoured. We have free will in order to make our suffering more poignant, and all paths lead to more suffering. All avenues of escape are covered. We have one alternative, which is to have compassion and forgiveness for everything in existence, in which case we win "the game"—but we still suffer.

Exit Strategy

In my current understanding [October 2006], taken from Sufism, the above two conditions (both of which I have experienced as "absolute truth" at different points in my life) are equally valid options. As long as we are physically incarnate, we are liable to be ping-ponging between one or the other, or hovering in some gradient in between, or in a different zone altogether. As long as we have a body, we can change the frequency we are receiving and transmitting on. Once the body and mind die, we're stuck at whatever frequency we've cultivated up to that point and re-absorbed at that vibrational level, without change, outside of time and space. The Great Work then becomes to cultivate the best state possible, in preparation for death. Heavy psychedelic and spiritual experiences can give us a small taste of death so that we see the importance of this. Choose wisely.

Vodou / Santeria

My experiences with Haitian vodou fall completely outside of my normal territory and do not fit anywhere into my constructed map of the invisible landscape. On this matter I have nothing to say, other than "children should *not* play with dead things."

Bön / Jhankri

The indigenous shamanism of Nepal and Tibet. I trained in Jhankri witchcraft for two weeks in Kathmandu, near Mount Everest, the story of which is related in "How I Spent My Summer Vacation" in *Generation Hex* (also in the English "high weirdness" journal *Strange Attractor*, No. 2). It involved a lot of drumming, and a lot of chickens died; I would say it more closely resembled traditional vodou than the Amazonian psychedelia commonly associated with the word shamanism in the wake of Terence McKenna. I made some progress but had the path re-sealed upon leaving Nepal. The major side-effect of this has been to deepen my ability to go into trance and let other beings overshadow me during invocation.

The Lizard People

They like to appear that they run the world. See the books of David Icke. As they fulfill a function very similar to the Demiurge or Iadabaoloth in Gnosticism, they can be anyone or anywhere. I'm not sure if I buy the physical shapeshifter angle, but I find it quite plausible, and seemingly borne out by my own experience, that these baaaad spirits can completely overshadow and inhabit outwardly human bodies. While many may run in family lines, I also suspect that these, or similar, entities can be implanted in human bodies in moments of severe sexual and/or physical abuse, which may or may not be ritually conducted, after which the entity then struggles with the human soul over time before overpowering and supplanting it (e.g. Skull & Bones Society). This is purely theoretical and starts getting into uncomfortable territory. I do not believe in the existence of organized Satanic abuse cults (a fiction mainstream society has been using as a way to smash pagan groups since Epiphanius of Salamis accused the Borborite Gnostic sect of ritually impregnating women, aborting the fetuses and then eating them in the fourth century, the exact same thing that Genesis P-Orridge and TOPY were accused of by Scotland Yard in the Enlightened and Rational Year of Our Lord 1992). I do believe, however, that Satanic abuse is a good metaphor for some of the modes of operation that such negative forces (and power elites) take.

> *"Who's your boss?"*
> *"Mr. Lizard."*
> *"And who's his boss?"*
> *"Another Missssterr Lizzzarddd...."*
> – Chris Morris, *Jam*

The Black Brothers

These rather humorously-named individuals are not the same as black magicians. So-called "black magicians" are usually fundamentally stupid, have little insight and operate at such a low level that they are hardly worth noticing, and generally so marginalized that they are invisible to society at large. Black magicians in this sense are usually engaged in making pacts with demonic spirits (instead of binding them), cursing, energetic or sexual vampirism in their many forms, animal torture for energy yield or capturing and torturing the spirits of the recently deceased. Sometimes magicians start out slinging around bad juju because they think they'll get away with it before they realize that they can't, "repent," get some higher insight and then get on the right track; some may even become saintly figures (the Buddhist sage Milarepa is a classic example). Otherwise black magicians tend not to live very long as their bodies seem to rebel against them and become riddled with (often undiagnosable) diseases; on top of that they often move in social circles where they become involved in hard drugs and the criminal underworld (drug dealers and the mob are sometimes known to employ such individuals for magically aiding and abetting various operations, as well as occult assassination—the Palo Mayombe community in New York, a major problem for NYPD, is a case in point), neither of which support a healthy, productive or long life. I have on multiple occasions hedged into "bad magick" when my back was severely to the wall or, in a few cases, when deeply hurt by somebody and absolutely overcome with hatred and a need for revenge; I have paid for this dearly every time.

Black Brothers, on the other hand, are an altogether more noxious phenomena (in my current understanding of the term). These are people who make it up to the highest levels of initiation possible before they must give up their ego, and everything that can be called "I," to progress—and then refuse to do so. They then get stuck in Da'ath and stop evolving, which means they're cut off from the magical current, never learn anything new, and end up having to support their twisted and fundamentally terrified egos by vampirizing the "souls" of others in large quantities. They have, however, probably accumulated enough potency by this point to really fuck things up for everyone else with their little games and paranoid power plays, at least for a short while. Leaders of cults or vampiric "religions" are often good examples of this phenomenon.

On a side note, I do recognize that there is a whole spectrum of Left-Hand Path spirituality which people take very seriously and sincerely (note that what is called "Left-Hand" in the West is very different from what that term connotes in Eastern religions). This usually involves the cultivation of extreme individualism, misanthropy, toxicity and anti-social behavior. While this might seem noble at first, and I have spent periods of my life isolating myself and spurning all others in the name of inner wisdom, I have to agree with the very astute Frater Haquan, who has pointed out that human beings are hard-wired to be social animals, and that this kind of behavior can precipitate a general collapse of both the functionality of the brain and the immune system (*The Lucifer Principle* by Howard Bloom is also very lucid on this point). Beyond this, I see the "true" adherents of the Left-Hand Path as those who have climbed or are attempting to climb the corporate, political, media, religious and other structures of this world and obtain true power by manipulating and controlling others and making the human sacrifice of their own conscience to the dark god that is their ambition. And those are just a bunch of fucking assholes, plain and simple, and they can all fuck off back to the country club or their lacy lairs of seduction or whatever puckered and sore-covered hole they were shat out from, 'cause they're not gonna get nothing from me.

2012

Well, we'll just have to wait and see, won't we...

Miscellaneous Quotes to Make Me Sound Cultured and Deep

"Often one has the feeling of climbing a mountain, for weeks, months, years; later one finds it was only a molehill. One was crawling along the level ground; the steep slope was only imagined. One was creating the steep slope. The mountain was one's own imaginings, one's own work-directives. We make work of our life to seem virtuous to ourself; blaming others and circumstances of money and of culture. One's pride, vanity, and the precious opinion of what one is and of what one is becoming, through mountain-climbing, creates the mountain slope. 'Look at me—look at how far I've climbed up the mountain! I'm higher than you are. If you're higher than I am, I started lower than you did and have really climbed further. My mountain is steepest.' TO SEE THAT ALL MOUNTAINS ARE SMALL MOLEHILLS, THAT ALL HUMAN CLIMBING IS THE DELUSION OF A DREAM, MOVE INTO PLANETARY ORBIT, AND LOOKING DOWN, SEE THAT ALL MOUNTAINS ARE MOLEHILLS."
– John C. Lilly, *The Center of the Cyclone*

"Fire and wind come from the sky, from the gods of the sky. But Crom is your God. Crom, and he lives in the earth. Once giants lived in the earth, Conan. And in the darkness of chaos, they fooled Crom, and they took from him the enigma of steel. Crom was angered, and the earth shook. And fire and wind struck down these giants and threw their bodies into the waters. But in their rage, the gods forgot the secret of steel and left it on the battlefield. And we who found it are just men. Not gods, not giants. Just men. And the secret of steel has always carried with it a mystery. You must learn its riddle, Conan. You must learn its discipline. For no-one, no-one in this world can you trust. Not men, not women, not beasts. This you can trust."
– Conan the Barbarian

"If you have ghosts, then you have everything. You can say anything you want. You can do anything you want..."
– Roky Erickson

"There is magic. And really there's no magic."
– The Go-Betweens

"Even the gods deserve their pain."
– The Lady's Law

[A Final Note: As of early 2007, very little of the above reflects my current practices or opinions, as I have given up Western magick; it is preserved here as a museum piece, though hopefully still of use to somebody. Special thanks to Shivanath for working with me intensively over the course of three weeks to decondition myself from the negative systems and patterns I had dug myself into in my practice, while staying on my couch en route to speaking with the US Government in D.C.—though patiently enduring his lumberjack-like snoring should be thanks enough.]

[A Final Final Note: Oh fine, here's the whole of Western magick in a nutshell, Probationer to Ipsissimus in twenty-six seconds:

1. First you get a witch's familiar (the Holy Guardian Angel).

2. Then you're the witch's familiar. (Having let go of the Choronzon Complex one's ego lies purring in the lap of the boundless divinity of the Source, safe, protected, at ease, attained.)

Bring your own Bedknobs and Broomsticks.]

Multiple Choice Test

Circle one (1) answer for each question.

1) Who did it?
a. God
b. The Sirian A.'.A.'.
c. The Pleiadian A.'.A.'.
d. That bastard / Those bastards
e. Me

2) What is it?
a. A spooky quantum effect
b. A giant space vagina
c. Inanimate matter
d. A bunch of horseshit
e. Me

3) Where is it?
a. Floating in a higher fluid
b. Brion Gysin let the mice in
c. All in my mind
d. Non-local
e. Me

4) When is it?
a. Up
b. Down
c. Yes
d. No
e. Me

5) How did it happen?
a.
b.
c.
d.
e.

[1] *Liber MMM* consists of basic instruction in meditation, banishing and sigils. *Liber KKK* is a graduated series of twenty-five areas of magick to develop one's own methods and rituals within, with general guidelines given.

[2] It is worthwhile to note that no matter how many times I convinced myself I had died and been reborn, I still appeared exactly the same to the people around me, with no change having occurred—this held true up until I underwent the experience broadly described as the Adeptus Minor initiation in the Golden Dawn tradition, which radically altered my personality to a noticeable degree.

[3] Experiment: Around three or four in the afternoon, have a really satisfying orgasm either with a partner or two or with yourself, and immediately go to sleep while lying on your back. I often find this puts me into a state where I do not have an astral body per se, but can remote-view the room I am in with as perfect clarity as if I was standing there looking at it, and sometimes from multiple angles at once.

[4] The Oath of the Abyss is a particularly demented aspect of the Thelemic system, in which the magician aspires to wipe out their lower personality and cross the chasm to divinity by swearing an oath to interpret everything as a direct message to them from God. A comic / tragic record of one man's attempt at this is Frater Achad's *Liber 31*.

[5] For those who care, the use of Vedic or Sidereal astrology in calculating the ascendant sign for the time of working, or for any other reason, is technically preferable to the use of Western astrology, as it factors for the Precession of the Equinoxes and therefore remains accurate.

[6] Michael Staley describes the connection between the Operation and the Aeon of Ma'at in his article "Supping at the Angel and Feathers." See Peter-R. Koenig's "O.T.O. Phenomenon" website

[7] I also associate the pentagram in this equation with the five kleshas or fetters in Tantra: ego, ignorance, revulsion, attachment and clinging to life. The

inclusion of ego here turns Choronzon into a flower of ego blooming from a tiny seed of ego... a reminder of constant vigilance...

[8] The numeration of Choronzon as 333 suggests the three faculties of the mind—symbolized as Salt, Sulfur and Mercury in Alchemy and Rajas, Tejas and Sattva in Raja Yoga, or Hegel's thesis / antithesis / synthesis—spinning wildly and out of any possibility of control outside of enforced mental silence.

[9] Black mirrors can be easily and cheaply made by coating the back of any piece of clear plastic or glass with black enamel spraypaint.

[10] Solomon is designated as one of the twenty-seven prophets of Islam. Presumably each of these prophets had/has their own method of ascent to the source. Solomon's is/was ceremonial magick.

[11] It is interesting to note that suffering is often symbolized as black smoke in Eastern systems—in the Tonglen rite of Mahayana Buddhism, for instance, where the intrepid meditator endeavors to purify this global bile or Belial through compassion.

[12] This is the experience attendant upon crossing the Abyss in Thelema. As George Holochwost put it to me, I crossed an Abyss, but not the Abyss. We are again dealing with the fact that things symbolically reflect on multiple levels and at different octaves. More specifically: "It is even said that to every Neophyte of the Order of A.'.A.'. appeareth a demon in the form of a woman to pervert him; within Our own knowledge have not less than nine brethren been utterly cast out thereby." – Crowley, *Of the Secret Marriages of Gods With Men*

[13] Unfortunately, Crowley does not include information about God's wise-cracking sidekick, teenage rap wonder LIL' ZAX.

[14] An Internet hoax from around 2000, in which a webpage carried instructions on how to place a newly-born kitten into a glass cube and feed it intravenously so that it filled the container as it grew and became cube-shaped. The site is still up: http://www.bonsaikitten.com

[15] A story from my childhood which bears repeating in connection with this. When I was twelve I was sent to camp for a week on Mount Palomar, as the San Diego public school system did to all sixth-graders at this time. At one point I found a small frog with its legs broken slowly dying in a cold stream. Feeling horrible for the frog, I put it in a plastic bag and showed it to a camp counselor. At this age I had an aquarium with two bull-frogs in it in my room who I regularly fed and cared for, I told the camp counselor that I wanted to bring the frog home and nurse it back to health. The counselor decided to take it upon himself to teach me a lesson about "the way things really are" and made me put it back in the stream to die, as is "the course of nature." This began to compound my already growing hatred of authority figures. When I went home, already heartbroken, I found that in my absence one of my own pet frogs had gotten itself smashed in between a large rock and the edge of the aquarium and gutted itself (a pet snake had also died). Later, when I was seventeen, I bought a copy of *Paranoia* magazine with an article about Jack Parsons in it, which included the rather stunning factoid that Jack Parsons and the Agape Lodge of the O.T.O. had crucified a frog on Mount Palomar in the Forties (Crowley's "Cross of the Frog" ritual).

[16] A Tunnel designed by Frater Elijah based on his own work with the Qliphoth and designed to collapse all of the other Tunnels into it and then simulate their effects without any lasting harm or damage, sent to me and a few others in private correspondence.

[17] For an immensely insightful look into a working Enochian group which went completely and utterly south, see the fascinating "Black Lodge of Santa Cruz" supplement to Joel Biroco's *Kaos 14*, which had the Caliphate O.T.O. threatening a lawsuit but which is still available online as a free PDF.

[18] In my initial encounter with this nightside dimension I was shown images of abandoned skyscrapers, nanotech-laded cumulus clouds, underground freeways; absolute technological precision beyond the need for human involvement. This only made sense several months later, in retrospect—all of man's creations and habitations without man are the shell of humanity, like a dried and polished snail-shell found in undergrowth.

[19] Kenneth Grant adds another angle to this in *The Magical Revival* by saying that the sun in our solar system is just a reflection of Sirius, the Dog Star,

home of DOGON FISHMAAAAN, which is interesting in this connection if one considers the fish symbolism inherent in many religions, especially Catholicism and definitely in connection with the Mass of Communion, which according to Crowley is a perversion of the use of sexual fluids for magick.

NOTES OF AN ALCHEMIST

IRA COHEN

On the eve of my forty-eighth birthday
February 2, 1983

Dreams of Aquarian splendor,
pain of mundane newspaper reality
in the subway of time
Sitting in the Silver People Gallery
about to meet Lionel Ziprin in front
of the Rene Crevel painting on East 87th Street
in the building of his current psychiatrist,
DR. JUSTMAN
I see it as a diamond, that time in the late
sixties, with Lionel, Angus, Snyder & myself
as four points of the inner square, 4 magicians
covered in carbon.
Caroline in flame colored clothing
glistening with lurex and light,
the spirit of today's transformation,
presiding angel of future possibilities,
selling postcards on 8th Street.
Lionel has been victimized by servants,
he says. He just fired the Latvian nurse
who broke a $3,000 lamp & has replaced her
with a Lady from Trinidad.
But I was really thinking of the past,
the time I first heard about John Dee's
magic mirror. It was the same day that
Marlene Dietrich discovered the Beatles
in the Cave in Hamburg
From there the El Dorado shed its beams.
There are only 9 men who know how to open
the locks of the main mint,
there where the gold is stacked underground
in truncated pyramids.
Sufi means I-END if you consider the Hebrew,
like in Am Soph, without END. And sophos is
wisdom in Greek. Am Keseph are the Silver

People. The Rabbis regard silver as more
precious
than gold. Reverse the time thread
in the concordance of desire. John Dee's
magic mirror is in the British Museum &
is Aztec obsidian. Lionel tells a story
about a prostitute who sits on a golden
stair above six steps of solid silver.
It is an esoteric story, he says, and on
the seventh step the initiate must refuse
her.
It was like sunlight on glass,
the sterling silver company of Grand Street.
How many times did we pass the 15,000
shining silver objects before Lionel bought
five trays, passing up the silver umbrella —
Of course we are all Lone Rangers looking
for Silverheels. it looked like Time froze
over,
the day the Luftwaffe invented amphetamine
& discovered a piece of the philosopher's
stone in the ashes of Auschwitz.
Now she sits in the desert & looks 15,000
years old. It's difficult to disentangle
the lines of the story, but it started in the
Mother's house near the silver store.
When Lionel saw *The Invasion of Thunderbolt*
Pagoda
it was upside down. It was then that he told
me that the images should be sent to Jerusalem
for safekeeping.
That was before they smashed the dollar and
sent the yen soaring. After 19 days
with no sleep, all the bankers of Europe
appeared at the door of rags & brought an
invitation to the secret city, from the
Eastern Wing of the Great American Seal —
Recently Lionel suggested a 7 year tax sabbatical
across the board/ After all Benjamin Franklin
got his turkey though the bald eagle was stamped

as tender. We woriy about the dross of gold,
the unclean side of metals, poisoning the
atmosphere with noxious gases.
The old man (John D. — Rockefeller, that is)
had a gold stomach & lived only on mother's milk.
Then the visitations began & patriotic solutions
were resolved in the colonial room.
In the end we can say that no human flesh has ever
touched the moon, not even excreta.
The moon has been touched, not by us, but by our
space suits. Silver is reflected light.
In total darkness we would never see it.
Lionel ordered a green hat from Lincoln, Nebraska
for $6. We must create the proper conditions
to induce precipitation, the strength of solvents
& rates of flow, the cyanide process. Omar Khayyam's
silver thread, the umbilical cord, the astral journey.
Enough slime has been smelted to build the sanctuary,
but still we are indebted to the marshals of seizure.
There are two courts here which should not be confused.
Now we are speaking of gold.
Yamantaka, the demonslayer, is in a box
reflecting no light. Lionel managed to save it
from the amphetamine heads who wanted to steal it
with winglights and high handlebars.
Thru the lens it all looks different, the profile
of the image with the light overhead.
If you weren't actually there how could you tell
the story of our uprising?
It was professional & matter of fact as stated
by the hero who survived.
He knew how hollow it was inside, yet recognizable
as the real thing. That was knowledge born of coming
out.
Alvin, the Negro Jew, was arrested coming out of the
St. Regis Hotel with a vacuum cleaner.
No fast movie here, but Barzel which means iron.
The moonfaced Chinese magician is conducting
rituals in front of the building/ New masters
are appearing all the time, even in Lionel's garden

as seen from the window, but that's a different
story now that Sheba is falling down & the telephone
keeps ringing in his dream.
A voice calls my name twice.
Stimulated by opposition, we sought our position in
time. The Silver People followed everywhere we went,
even into the Restaurant. It was a joumey containing
our history. Contact was never a mistake, nor did it
ever seem that the door of the city would one day be
closed.
"It was always this way," she said.
Lying on the couch having visions of the vessels
he materialized five dollars for cabfare and started
the search, that was not the first time, but it set
the stage for a beginning where the drama unfolded
in the foyer of pink thoughts.
A safari of stuff. Amazing, the consecration of the
connection. A dynamo of silver in a room of gold.
In the magic shop full of angels from every time &
every place she had to bring a flashlight. It was
before the advent of the curious toys.
Now he sets the price of gold on the market, acting
on behalf of the 5 Nations. He has to get up early
every day in order to avoid being murdered by the
errand boy —
Then he sets the standard for the golden mean in the
houses of finance.
I'd love to spoon in the light of the silvery moon,
sings a strange voice.
This is not a phonetic transcription, but says that
I've been to the store, that elementals come to visit,
that even clouds make promises which are hard to keep.

February 3, 1983

Even Moses could not pass the 50th gate.
Parked on 48th west of Madison.
The building on my right is called Religious
Science
& in letters of sculpted metal it proclaims,

WHAT MIND CAN CONCEIVE MAN CAN ACHIEVE
From Texas appeared the Mano Poderosa (Ronnie Burk)
In front of me three stanchions of iron & concrete
united by a fluorescent orange tape blowing in the
wind. Colonel Custer comes out of Cooks Travel
Agency
with his coat hanging on his shoulders
and we continue downtown looking for the lawyer
who will draw up papers for the Ganeshian Follies.
we pass up the bargain teddy bears being sold
from the back of a truck. It's a day scripted by
the No Nonsense Dada Kid. The lawyer is out &
we're on another wild goose chase.
Duke describes the great rotunda in the Motor
Vehicles Division, a 30-foot stained glass window
covered with tarpaper. Eight million dollars
in cash flow thru only one working window and the
fat woman said, "Thank you, I'm glad somebody noticed."
How he managed to hold his temper after eight hours
of waiting on lines, we'll never know.
And now the foundry has blown the statue of Mark Twain.
Candy Store Punks Kill Mom of Three and the socalled
wolf fears it is the night that corrupts.
After all we knew guys who were so spaced they could
walk down the street on their elbows.
Believe me it didn't end with Charlie Parker.
It's a question of overlapping soundtracks and mixing
the cuts until one scene suddenly pops out & changes
the electrical atmosphere in the room like a three
stage air purifier. We want it to make a big difference,
especially under the bed.
Now we are talking about feedback & freedom. Then we
learned how to fly. What is the ratio between hope &
violation?
The back of civilization turned to itself.
THE REPLICA ROOM IS NOT IN ROME, HE SAID.
We are trying to make it manifest on the plane of reality.
It's the State of the Art & we have made the connection
to interlock. Finally it was my own face I saw in John
Dee's mirror wearing pink plastic shades, trying to prepare

myself for the future I saw already forming in the
darkness. We went from the Magic Shop to the Assyrian Room
& then to the Egyptian Room. Now we see the sun hitting the
crystal & it illumines the New York Subway sending shafts
of light down the tunnels of the city
all the way from Pushkar. Nobody was conscious
of the recording, yet the voices of the women
uplifted our hearts.

ETERNALICIOUS

SHIVANATH

The following work is an amalgamation of several essays on meditation, tantra and magick.

DETONATING THE MIND BOMB

We've talked extensively about the nature of language and how it shapes our reality, how the definition of a word like "justice" varies so much that people can barely communicate about what is just, and what is unjust.

We've also talked about escapes from verbal reality: sigils, drugs, thoughtlessness at orgasm, all of that stuff. How magic often happens in wordless states.

Well, fuck it, it's time to pony up boys and girls: kill the killer. Destroy your minds.

You want out of the verbal trap? Take a shotgun and blow your mind away. And I don't mean for an hour, or a weekend, I mean permanently. Plot your escape from Verbal Reality and run, flee, into the mystical silence that produces stillness and the practice of the presence of god.

Yes, dears, we're going to talk about meditation, the ultimate act of rebellion against society, "the system" and all of those other illusory things. Meditation is not just social action: meditation is revolution. To become free—by any means necessary! This is not some crummy "meditate so you'll be nicer to people" post. This isn't "meditate so you'll be calmer" post. This is "meditate so you can escape verbal confinement and roam free in the universe."

Meditation as revolutionary politics, as anarchy, as Will and Life and Freedom. You know that your mind is a cage: that other people wrote the language you think in, that your conceptual frameworks were molded first by your parents, then by your schools, then by Aleister Crowley, Bill Burroughs and Swami Sivananda. Everything in words is garbage, ever-more confining and sophisticated traps to keep you in the realm of experience to which words can meaningfully refer.

Understand? Even the people who seek to set you free in words are liars and thieves, polluting the human race's cognitive sphere yet further. All I can do with this trap is to clearly label it: "This is a trap because it adds words to your world."

If language is a virus from outer space, it's time you cured yourself. Destroy all thought.

This is not meaningless radical bullshit. Or, if it is, it's at least real meaningless radical bullshit. About twelve years ago I broke out of the mental trap, cut through the skein of thoughts and escaped into internal silence—a persistent state in which, if I am not actively thinking about something, there is only a silent light inside of my head, or an occasional AUM.

I credit that experience with saving my life. Without the constant grinding down of language, the chatter, the psychic radio, the roaring evil nonsense which passes for our consciousness most of the time, it is possible to see things differently: life is beautiful, people are by-and-large kind and most suffering is brief or something people can accommodate to. To recharge, one simply sits along and plays with the experience of being alive, makes some tea, has a snack, goes for a walk, plays with a puppy. Without a mind there to spoil every experience with its constant stream of definition, doubt, negativity, appreciation, discussion—without the constant jump into meta-psychosis where every experience is rendered meaningless by being assigned an arbitrary "meaning"—why, then, life is profoundly good. All of it.

Do you understand what I'm saying? Your mind has most likely trapped you, unless you're one of the free, and magic is not going to save you. At least, not the kind of magic you're most likely doing right now.

Setting Goals: Will and Purpose in Meditation

If you meditate to feel nice, odds are you will succeed. Ditto for becoming calmer, less reactive, wholer. All of those are good, worthwhile goals. By all means, feel free to deploy the nuclear weapon to dig trenches or whatever.

Real meditation is about liberation. First target: the tyrant of inner interruption. Let me make this clear: Inside of you, there is a "seer"—something, which is at the moment implicitly "you," receives or has your experiences. You prick your finger with a pin, this "you" is what is aware that there is a feeling of pain. However, this "you" does not really have any idea of what it is, because it has been surrounded by a constant chaos for years.

Imagine growing up for your whole life in a room with blaring disco music, bright flashing lights and food which is randomly flavored with curry spices, Tabasco sauce and cloves. Imagine growing up in that room from the moment of birth, never knowing stillness, quiet or nature.

That's what it's like to be your soul, born into a body in the culture of language and, worse, the culture of constant interruption and entertainment. There is no space to breathe, to be, unless you still (or kill) the mind that is the Psychic DJ, spinning records of self-deprication, alienation and analysis. This is key: because that damn disco track has been playing since you were aware of being you, you think it is you. That's "introjection" in Gestalt terms—confusing parts of the environment with parts of yourSELF because they are constant, and you are also constant. Imagine a world in which every person slaps themselves in the face, hard, midway through every word of every sentence. Imagine the level of discourse, of understanding, in such a world.

That, my friends, is the world of the untamed mind, and unless you are liberated from it, this will sound insane.

Stop, right now. Do you have clear, unbroken awareness of what it is within you which receives all of your experiences: the five senses, the mind, the energy body, the chakras—what it is that turns all of that stuff into a sense of self, a sense of being? Can you look at the YOU within all of these things? Can you put your attention squarely on the Seer inside? The odds are not. If not, and you want to fix it, here's how.

Sit. Dark, quiet room or, better, a sensory deprivation tank. You'll see a marked drop-off in sensory phenomena. Sitting still (try yoga as a preparation) is even better. Just sit. Now begin to catalog *everything* in your awareness.

> *My right leg hurts. I'm thinking about my girlfriend.*
> *I'm wondering what this exercise will produce.*
> *What does he mean by "trap"?*
> *There doesn't seem to be anything happening.*
> *I hope my roomies don't come back yet.*
> *This doesn't seem very much like a disco, or constantly slapping myself.*

What you are seeing is the torrent of distractions which hides your true nature from you, and makes you a slave to what distracts you. This constant stream of stuff is *not you,* any more than your hair is you. If you cut your hair, or dye it purple, something about you changes, but you are still you. So it is with the mind: if you shave it off to two millimeters long, people will see something has changed, but you will still be you—but rather than staring at the world through a tangle of foot-long fringe caked in mud and shit, you'll see the world clearly. You can cut your hair. You can change its style, and remain you. Remember that in this next bit.

In the same way that your visual field becomes quiet when you close your eyes in a darkened room, you can cause your mind to become quiet. Combining lowered sensory inputs with lowered mind inputs can provide an environment suitable for coming to understand the basis of identity and perception, in the process becoming free.

But first, let's kill the mind, shall we? Tame the lion, bring the beast under control, sit firmly on the dragon seat.

Stopping the Mind

What if the voices in your head—not the spirit guides, but the ones you think of as "you"—simply stopped talking? Think about that for a second (paradox noted). No internal dialogue. No stream of critique. Nothing. You close your eyes, you put your fingers in your ears, and suddenly there's nothing. Stillness, darkness, silence, light. Resting serene within yourself, with no distractions. No sense of the passage of time, just pure being. The only thing between this and you is your goddamned mind.

Now, do you want to talk about freedom and liberation by killing it?

(Rolls up sleeves.)

OK, let's talk tactics.

This mind thing, it's just a bad habit?

Yes.

Try an experiment: poke yourself with something like a pencil, sharp enough to hurt, but not draw blood. Feel the sensation, then take a short break and think about how it felt, get some details. Now try the same thing again, but in response to the pain, mentally (inwardly) chant "ow ow ow ow ow ow ow ow ow" or some other verbalization of pain. "OW OW OW OW OW." Most likely you'll notice that the sensation of pain is less bad when your mind is filled with a symbol for the pain: by removing experience to the symbolic level, the intensity of the actual negative experience is reduced. That's the aetiology of the "mind syndrome." We form a layer between us and our experiences, negative first, but later all of them, and we call that defensive mechanism "the mind" and identify with it so completely that we mistake it for us. The noisy room with the flashing disco lights? We built it to get away from the negative experiences of childhood, of being a baby, of not having control, of being slaves to the whims of our parents, however well intentioned.

The mind forms as a defensive layer against real experience.

OK? Now let's try an orgasm. Watch it really closely: odds are that as you come, you'll enter an entirely non-verbal space for a short time. Nitrous oxide can do much the same thing.

That's non-verbal experience. Now, imagine being in that state—the no-internal-chatter experience of life—all of the time, without that goofy grin and the thrashing about, or the anesthetic effect on the brain. Note that you are still you at the point of orgasm, or on nitrous. There's continuity of identity, "little death" or not. Meditation is a way of permanently delivering yourself into this wordless state of being.

So, what's the fastest way of getting past a defense mechanism? Some people will try, endlessly, to pick the locks—dismantle it a layer at a time, understand it, etc. Workable, but slow. Why not just do what you're afraid of, realize it's not so bad, and then allow the defensive mechanism to fall off like a scab or a suit you no longer wear? A lusty virgin plays all kinds of games, dancing on the threshold of experience, and perhaps if the programming is bad enough (think: Catholic schoolgirls) becomes partly defined by defensive mechanisms built around not getting what you actually want out of life. It's a lot like that too: once you're having sex, you wonder what on earth you were waiting for, or at least many people do. Even if the first experience ain't great, crossing the abyss is useful in its own right. "The Mind" exists to attenuate our experience of being alive. Getting rid of "The Mind" is done fastest by allowing ourselves to acclimatize to having full-strength experiences, removing the fear which produces "The Mind."

Lose the mind, become more alive. Become more alive, lose the mind.

As a magician, this is the angle to work. Slip into the gap between thoughts.

As a last aside, before we discuss practical technique, let's just note that between these words, there is a space. If you read them aloud, there is a gap between words. You could make a silent track, a *4'33"*, by taking an audio recording of speech and recording all the silence between the words. That's true for your mind too: there's an implicit gap between the words in the stream of thought. The normal experience is that the words are "figure" and the silence is "ground"—if this position is inverted, so that you are aware of silence as the primary experience, and words as the secondary experience, you're already most of the way there, even if there's still a lot of verbal junk.

The Three-Point Exploding Head Technique

Three practices combined will produce faster, better results than any one alone.

The first is mantra meditation: you can read a book about this, but in a nutshell, pick a word (like "calm") and say it over and over again in your mind, to the exclusion of all other thoughts and phenomena. You'll find that things keep pulling you off course, so you're like "calm calm calm calm calm where's my cat? is that it throwing up? calm calm" and so on. This practice does two things:

1. It builds the "muscle" of returning your awareness to the place you want it: the mantra.

2. It builds the awareness of how your awareness is not under your control: you feel the pull towards distractions. You get to know it.

The second technique is: you just sit. With your thoughts. With your emotions. It's like mantra meditation without the mantra. Just sit and have awareness of what is going on.

A typical interplay between these two techniques is thus:

"badger badger badger badger badger badger badger badger badger badger mushroom mushroom SNAAKE SNAAAAAKE" (see http://www.badgerbadgerbadger.com/)

"I keep having these thoughts, and they're all in the emotional register of anxiety. I think I'd better take a look at that!"

(Long period of sitting with pure awareness of the anxiety.)

[Insight: Perhaps this isn't so important after all? Remember, things like Holotropic Breathing can help trigger these insights too; indeed, that's why they exist—you can do this quiet awareness thing while doing techniques like that and it works really well.]

"badger badger"

This approach—switching periodically to directly face obstacles to your mind's annihilation—appears to work much better and faster than straight mantra meditation in terms of really getting to the core of the issue. It won't make you placid and peaceful as quickly, but it'll expose you to what the hell is really going on inside of you a hell of a lot faster. Try at least fifteen solid minutes of mantras before switching over and doing just-sitting. Then try flipping back and forth. Eventually, just drop the mantras completely. It's tough going if you're doing it right!

The third technique is sensory focus: sitting, or doing an activity, and treating your entire sensory field as a single unit. See, hear, feel, smell, taste, feel your muscles and skeleton, the pressure of the seat, all of it. A simple way to get started is to sit and try to broaden your visual focus so you are aware of your entire visual field as a single piece, at once. Like having all peripheral vision, without the focal point darting from object to object. This kind of sensory broadening can be carried right across the senses too: first the whole visual field, then visual and audio as a single system, then take in the body too. But start with your strongest sense, either sight or sound for most people, usually sight. Or try and feel your whole body at once. Get away from the discrete and into the continuous.

These three approaches, taken together and practiced in cycles, can rapidly result in access to breaks from the stream of thought, resulting in periods of internal silence, free from the yattering of the mind. The big breakthrough: when your sense of identity shifts from the stream of words

("I am my thoughts") to the internal perceiver, the silent indweller ("I hear my thoughts sometimes").

Let me know if you get there.

How long, and how much effort this takes or is worth is an individual thing. I had not yet discovered Just Sitting when I made this transition, and my primary working tools were psychotherapy, Gestalt psychology and mantra meditation. It took about six years of an hour a day, and the final insight was made during a full-out acid ritual. That insight—"talking is the volume control on my reality"—resulted in a permanent transition to the wordless state, and that has been durable ever since. Your milage may vary: I think with better technique, and a pre-existing magical practice, as little as six months to two years of work ought to produce some really tangible results, with every step along that path resulting in a greater understanding of self, greater freedom from personal emotional problems, greater responsiveness. The process itself is valuable, but don't think there is a quick fix for the human condition. This is work, and looks like it!

BEYOND DUALITY: ***Tantra, Equanimity and the Stability of Mind***

Meditation: Why?

Before meditating, one should know exactly why one is sitting. This seems like a simple requirement, but is not. Are you sitting to stop suffering? That implies a belief that suffering can cease! That's a major claim and may align one with a religious tradition like Buddhism or Hinduism. How do we verify if those claims about the cessation of suffering are true? Is faith in other people's results appropriate? How do we know?

To generalize, are you sitting with the expectation of a result or benefit of some kind? If so, be explicit about why you think that meditation can produce that result. Similarly, if you are sitting to learn something about yourself, or your mind, or the world, know exactly why you think meditation can teach you that particular thing.

Knowing why you are sitting is the first step to dismantling the mental framework we build around the spiritual experiences we have. It clears the way to experiencing meditation directly, without constantly being focused on a perceived goal.

Meditation: How?

There are many forms of meditation—nearly as many as there are forms of physical exercise. Different forms appear to produce startlingly different results in the early stages, and claims that they all wind up in the same place have to be verified personally or taken on faith.

Furthermore, it is very difficult (or perhaps impossible!) to tell what a silent, non-moving person is doing with their mind. Although people may describe the experience they are having, and the technique they are using, exactly the same way, how can we know for sure that they are actually doing exactly the same thing? As an example, take mantra meditation. Two people might do this exercise, one hearing the mantra in their own voice, the other hearing it in the booming voice of a cosmic being thundering the mantra into their ears! Will these two meditations have the same effect? How can we know? What about more subtle differences: hearing the mantra as if in the center of your skull and in your own voice, versus hearing it as if you were speaking very quietly? How can we know for sure that these differences are significant or not?

The technique we will be using is called "Nath Sitting." This name is arbitrary: the technique exists in many cultures and under many names. I have seen an exact description of this technique called "contemplation" by Christian mystics, but other Christian mystics use the word "contemplation" to mean an entirely different process; comparison of meditation techniques in language is difficult.

Nath Sitting is done as so: one sits in a comfortable enough position, preferably with the spine reasonably straight, and attempts to have a relaxed awareness of all of the contents of the mind and sense organs simultaneously.

Now, here are the two distinctions from just sitting in an armchair vegging out.

1. One does not think about anything if possible. If you notice you are thinking, try and return to a relaxed awareness: Watching your self thinking is relaxed awareness. So is watching yourself not think. Trying to think about something is not relaxed awareness. If you are thinking, let it happen, but try and observe with relaxed awareness. If you are feeling, let it happen, do not interfere, and observe your feelings with relaxed awareness. Don't try to stop thinking or feeling: that effort is not relaxed awareness. Just sit.

2. One does not process sensory stimuli if possible. If there are background noises, do not go off on mental riffs about them and their meanings. Just let there be noises. Try not to fall into studying individual sensations as objects of meditation, simply let the whole sensorium wash over your mind.

Compared to other meditation techniques, this approach may seem to be only very slightly different from simply sitting there. This is because in the Nath philosophy, enlightened awareness is only very slightly different from just sitting there, if there is any difference at all. A very gentle tool is used to investigate a very subtle, or perhaps nonexistent, distinction between the two states of "enlightened" and "unenlightened" awareness. A few minutes of this technique will have some effect but things really begin to get started after a few months of a solid hour or two a day. This may seem like a large investment of time compared to the more frequently recommended fifteen minutes morning and evening, and it is.

Meditation: What?

So what, exactly, is sitting there not doing anything other than having relaxed awareness of your senses, mind and body going to achieve? What is the point of such an exercise, and why will it (eventually, perhaps) improve the quality of our lives?

The answer is that it is nearly impossible to do the exercise as described.

Achieving a simple, relaxed awareness of all of our senses and our minds turns out to be very hard. Usually the first realization is that our "minds" are in fact dominated by a constant stream of thoughts forming an "internal dialogue" or "stream of consciousness." Not everybody has this constant internal radio station of mental static, but most people do.

Another dominant phenomena is repressed emotions: we're on the go all the time, then we simply stop and find ourselves weeping as the sadness or pain we are staying busy to avoid come crashing home. Just sitting doing nothing is actually a fairly active process because it gives time and space for lots of mental phenomena which are usually dammed up behind activities like work and recreation time to come to the foreground. Old flashes of memory, distracting thoughts we never normally have time to be distracted by, wild speculations... All of this stuff comes up, and simply clearing the backlog of "deferred maintenance" on the mind can take literally months of steady meditation. Nothing happens other than watching a stream of mental junk.

Eventually, the stream clears, and we begin to enter the territory.

Meditation: The Territory

The territory is where meditation begins to teach us things we did not already know about ourselves and the universe. There are some basic truths ("sitting being with myself is hard and upsetting sometimes") which come almost universally, and quickly. However, "The Territory" is defined by four experiences.

1. Internal Silence

The "gap between thoughts"—the tiny moment of silence between the end of one mental word and the beginning of the next one—begins to be regularly glimpsed, or even enjoyed. Inner silence becomes a phenomena that one can produce at will with a little effort, or even an effortless state of mind and being.

2. Energy Awareness

Meditation brings to awareness input from senses other than the regular five or six, and you begin to sense your aura, the aura of other people around you, your chakras or energy flows, blockages in the energy flow in your own body or similar phenomena.

3. Spiritual Communication

Deep insights seemingly from beyond the human plane enter your awareness and begin to change your life. Perhaps you even see mental pictures of beings trying to communicate with you.

4. Emotional Catharsis

You notice patterns of feeling and thought which are usually hidden to you, such as repressed grief around the death of a parent or frustration with a career you thought was satisfying. You feel compelled to change. Note that all of these phenomena are fairly common aspects of daily life which are simply magnified by putting awareness on them for long periods of time. Nothing new is being produced, but existing truths are being made more visible by holding relaxed awareness. Most or all of these things are experienced occasionally in flashes by many people: a premonition about the future, or a brief glimpse of halos of energy around trees... a moment of rapture at orgasm when the mind is stilled... meditation simply takes these phenomena and brings them closer to our daily awareness by a gradual process.

The Aura

The human aura is a fairly widely accepted piece of energy anatomy: a series of roughly spherical shells which surround the human body, each composed of more and more subtle matter, or substances like "prana" or "chi." The objective existence of the aura appears hard to prove at this time, but enough people have the experience of one (going back thousands of years) that it seems reasonable to use the term without further justification.

It is my experience that meditation changes our relationship with the aura. Long spiritual practice of any kind tends to build an awareness of the aura, and a rapid integration of the body and the energy field, resulting in increased physical capabilities, better health and many other side benefits. For whatever reason, constant mental noise seems to interfere greatly with the perception of the aura and integration of the aura and the physical body, and meditation cures those problems. Many people, particularly those with strong hatha yoga practices, are only a small step from a high level awareness of the integrated mind/energy/body, and often sitting meditation is the missing next step to that state.

Both the Golden Dawn (a Victorian occult society) and the ancients who worshiped Mithras identified the zodiacal wheel strongly with the human aura. Not all schools of thought agree with this mapping, but I do. In the old images of Mithras, a muscular god is seen emerging from a "cosmic egg" which is inscribed with the symbols of the zodiac.

In high energy environments, such as a retreat setting, a magical circle, or a gathering of adepts, the level of the aura which corresponds to the zodiac can be seen and felt. It serves as a receptor for planetary influences (and therefore is the real basis for astrology) and also governs the expression of a lot of "fate" or "karma."

I cannot speak much more for this experience and its uses at this time, but drawing a zodiacal circle around you while you meditate, facing towards the position of your natal sun (i.e. your sun sign, but please be more precise if you can) can be a smooth and rapid method of extending your awareness in radical new directions.

The Fullness (and Emptiness) of Being

The human condition in its full reality is neither complex nor simple. Saints and sages from many traditions proclaim "you are god" or "you are pure awareness" in many different variations. Meditation is one key to beginning to tread the path to the discovery that in your current life this is already true. Discovering the reality of your aura is important, because it breaks the cultural belief system which is so prevalent in the West: that you are your body, that the mind is a product of the brain and that death is as permanent for the self as it is for the body. Furthermore, the aura corresponds closely to the "soul" and (in my experience) contains much of the "shadow"—those parts of us which are potential, but not manifest. If we are male, our aura will tend to be female, and vice versa. Similarly, if we are young or old, the aura or soul contains the potential for the traits we had in youth, or will in old age. It is the well from which we draw our beings.

Tantra provides a set of approaches to integrating the new phenomena that meditation reveals rapidly and easily relative to meditation alone. The creation of circumstances and contexts which facilitate insight and integration is the core of tantra. We are already our aura, our chakras, our souls, but we realize it not. We are narrowed and limited to a certain set of frequencies and experiences, and tantra provides tools to reverse this. The awareness created by Nath Sitting or other forms of meditation can be brought into ritual circumstances to quickly ripen understanding of what already is. This is the process of magic or ritual: creating circumstances which quickly allow initiation and insight into the real condition of our being! The stable mind, relatively deconditioned by sitting practice, can quickly see, understand and assimilate new phenomena which are made visible by unusual circumstances like visits to a shrine, a puja celebration and other places where energy is focussed on enlightenment. This dynamic, meditative awareness brought to ritual activities like worship of murtis or sacred dance produces rapid transformation. All of this is tantra. Furthermore, the stable mind, trained not to flinch or distract itself, begins to see the roots of being-ness: what it is to be alive, what it is to be an individual, what in the self is eternal, and what is passing. All of this is eternally present, but our focus is narrowed to obscure it, creating the limited sense of self we so typically experience. Samarasa ("equanimity") is the quality of self which comes from the realization of what the self is, and is not.

At the start, we asked "why meditate"—and this is basically why. Meditation reveals our life as it is by reducing the distractions and changing how we process sensory data. It gives glimpses, and perhaps full visions, of the Self, the Divine Indweller and the Soul. All of these are notional phenomena unless and until one experiences one, after which they become obvious: always was there, always will be.

All of that is here already, and meditation is how we learn to recognize it. No more, no less. You stare at being with an open mind until you realize what you are seeing.

The final wall—the "fourth wall," if you like—is between us and other people. We live our entire lives behind the screen which separates self from other, and it, too, is illusion. We are all one, all co-create each other through a continuous dance of perception, of karma, of gain and loss. Meditation reveals the dance of interbeing in a new light, one which reveals the entire play as a grand pleasure, an adventure, a game fit for god itself. I myself struggle to hold that view, having stabilized many of the earlier ones through my own practice, but I know that continued practice will make it possible.

Meditation is observation of what is. What is is only god. Meditation is observation of god being god. All perception has that quality, but meditation is special in its intention: to see what is true, beneath the great divine drama, and eventually to live as a conscious participant in creation, right alongside all the other god.

To enjoy the bliss of the creation as the creator entering into his and her own works. Some call it living from the divine source: I call it truth and wisdom.

I don't know why things are as they are. I do know that we suffer and die only in some part, and in other parts of our being we are eternally free, joyful, hopeful and optimistic. Meditation is one way to bring the wholeness of your soul to your attention and to experience that joy and bliss.

But don't take my word for it, or anybody else's. If you believe other people's assumptions, it is hard to discover your own inner spiritual authority, your own kernel-of-truth bullshit detector, your own will in the world. I've painted a picture based on my own experience, written words to try and communicate how I think the meditative experience works, but only the part which you verify for yourself is reality. All else is hearsay.

Study your own experience and be your own authority. Nothing is real beyond your own experience.

SHIVANATH'S NICKEL GUIDE TO TANTRA

In which Shivanath takes a quick stroll through the understructures of tantra with particular focus on stripping away the delusions which have built up around tantra, sex, Orientalism and Buddhism.

I'm a Nath. I'd been a practicing tantric sorcerer for about ten years before I became one, and I can't say that it changed very much in my outlook, but that's my lineage.

Almost all of the available material on tantra is bunk. Most of the translations were done by non-sorcerers who were incapable of picking apart metaphor from literal description, were not deeply enough versed in

Indian psychological and magical models, and were influenced by the early translations which miscast the entire field of study.

First, let's deal with the basics.

Tantra in Cultural Context

Tantra is a branch of Hinduism. Tantric Buddhism is more or less Hinduism with a gloss of Buddhism added. Vajrayana Buddhism is a grossly sexist form of tantra which really doesn't seem to offer female adepts any social roles, and is nearly entirely staffed by male teachers, which should make you suspicious right there.

Tantra therefore operates in the general framework of esoteric Hinduism: reincarnation, karma, the notion of the individual soul seeking a better relationship with the soul of the universe, chakras, energy bodies, gurus and the rest of the system. Tantra is "antinomian"—believing that there are no laws. However, it is not undisciplined, and any tantric adept with addictions, or who can be controlled by other people, is not an adept. The discipline is self-imposed, but it is ruthless and absolute.

A Brief Overview on the Practical Business of Tantra

Tantra can be divided into technique, philosophy, practice and action. Much of the technique is standard magical stuff found anywhere: banishings, invocations, etc. I've found it works a little better to use Indian-style banishings, etc., in a tantric context than, say, the LBRP, but the difference is fairly small most of the time. YMMV.

Philosophy is very simple in essence: whatever "enlightenment" is, it is visible right here and right now if you're willing to look there. It can't come and go—it must already be here. Now, how to notice it? This philosophy winds up in some strange practices: doing things which are supposed to be distracting or grounding, and not being distracted or grounded. Sex, eating meat, getting drunk, working a day job, having low or high social status etc. Implicit within this is the idea of reaching enlightenment while still having active karma. This is an explosive idea: normally enlightenment is said to be reached by exhausting one's karma. Finish the game, get to zero credit, zero debit and walk off the board into Samadhi.

Tantra suggests that one can be enlightened while still having karma—still having a social role, obligations, even desires. It simply requires one to be master of that karma—able to destroy it at will, able to control its expressions. One must still master karma, but does not have to annihilate it to do so. In this respect, tantra is about taming and domesticating the experience of the universe, rather than destroying it. The steps are still the steps of yoga, but the goals are a little different at an aesthetic and therefore technical level. This philosophy is often paraphrased as "learning to enjoy the created universe in the same way which god enjoys it," and I don't know of a better expression of the heart of the matter than that.

Practice is simple. Start with meditation. Learn how to "surf" the emotions—to feel the discomfort and emotional pressure which meditation brings up, but rather than hiding out in the white light and the roaring stillness, camp out in your anger and your pleasure and your pain. You sit, you feel rage at your parents, you sit with it. You don't judge it, you don't try and get away from it, you don't try and mask it.

You don't ask it to leave. You just be there with whatever it is. You do this for everything: bliss and horror. If you're not feeling the horror, you've either cleared all your repressed emotions, or you haven't hit them yet.

It's in there, trust me.

Meditation is Goalless. NO ALTERED STATES!!!

One simply sits and watches. Once the mind is solidly established in that practice and has stopped trying to censor things at a gross level, so you can watch, say, a curious thought about incest or rape or theft or murder and not really be upset to see that your karma includes such ideas, then you can begin to take it out into the world. You can begin to hold the same kind of awareness of "stuff just is what it is" while performing activities.

Action taken from this perspective—of just being what you are—can be insanely and destructively dangerous. Here's why. Most people are a finely counterbalanced network of drives and repressions. Dismantling the repressions without dismantling the drives can easily produce monsters. Here's the key: the fundamental drives are not bad. Sex, food, good work, nice friends and so on—all that stuff is great. But the drives get twisted: your parents say "sex is evil," so you wind up with a block, and behind the block builds anger.

Vent the anger at its target—your parents and their beliefs about sexuality—and you're golden. Vent it at your spouse or your sex partner, and you're an asshole. The skill and grace of tantric practice is knowing how clean you are accurately—what you can express purely, as-it-is, and what you're still tied up in self-destructive knots about. There are arts to this too: what to vent, what to burn, what to contain for future expression. You learn to "smell" material which is ready to blow, and to find safe ways of doing it.

Without that skill and discretion, tantra of any significant depth is a cheap and easy way to destroy your life.

I believe, although I have no first hand evidence to support this, that once there is essentially nothing left which has not been opened up in this way, one enters a "superconducting" state—zero internal resistance—at which point one simply exists and acts.

Sounds a bit like Zen, doesn't it?

Shortcuts

Tantra includes a set of practices which help people get to a frictionless state. Being pure divine consciousness in the bodies of hairless apes, we have a lot of issues related to the ape body. Apes are afraid of death, obsessed with sex and status, terrified of losing and so on. Full library of monkey problems! The consciousness learns to flinch away from the ape. "No, I'm PURE MIND!" Tantra therefore gets people back into the habit of just being what they are—divine consciousness incarnate as an ape. This involves cutting through culture. One cannot understand what a thing is, if one already knows what it is.

Sex, for example. What is it, really?

Strip away the cultural context of sex. Put some apes in a room, and give them license to do what they please. Retain the awareness which was built through the meditation—see the desires as they are, not as you would like them to be. Fairly soon, inspite of all the fun and games, it becomes apparent that the SEX thing is actually fairly simple: it's about reproduction, tribal bonding, power and, buried deep within, there's a spirit of companionship, of god-as-ape taking pleasure in the simple joy of fucking.

Strip off the culture and there's something rather touching underneath.

Cut a little deeper, and the reproductive aspect comes into focus: sex contains the antidote to death! Reproduction for the body is a shot at immortality! This is the beginning of unmaking the distinction between the goals of the body, and the goals of the soul—if the body understands that it, too, is pure consciousness.

Again, I haven't gone far in that direction. But Goraknath—codifier of Hatha Yoga and inventor of Laya Yoga and Kundalini Yoga, we're told—is said to be physically immortal and living in a cave somewhere in India. There are a lot of short cuts. Most of them boil down to "if you're obsessed with something, why not put it in a lab context, study the hell out of it, and then figure out what it really is and why you want it." Most desires drop away when examined that way. Disassemble a complex aggregate desire which has been hard to satisfy into the three or four primal desires which compose it.

Satisfy or release each individually. The few which do not go are typically very worthy and easy to satisfy.

It's the process which produces the apparent madness, the antinomian indulgence in the depths of human nature, the eating of feces and liking it. All of that stuff is just ways of seeing forbidden desires in a ritual context which allows them to be denuded of the glitter of being forbidden.

Nothing is forbidden. Do you really want to fuck a nun in the ass while a cardinal watches? Or did you just want to reclaim your sexuality and experience it on your own terms, not the terms of the Catholic Church? OK, very good, now go back to your house, buy the wife some long-stemmed red roses, and have a good night. That's the real spirit of the thing right there: most of the basic material is very clean and very loving.

It's the repression that produces the anomalies and the fearsome perversions.

Bliss

One side effect of all of this is bliss. It usually starts around the process of realizing that one is both male and female, and that the two can be unified in a variety of fun and interesting manners, but it can start around food, or love, or a bunch of other ways. It's basically a realization that you can be blissful regardless of what you are doing or feeling. It's pretty cool, but not that informative.

I wouldn't give it up for the world, mind you.

It's a great gift. Afterwards, everything is sort of pleasant, even the stuff which really sucks. However, it's easy to mistake this feeling of well-being, which is still rooted in the physical body, with the BLISS OF CONSCIOUSNESS which is a much deeper thing. Or is it?

There's only one way to find out—spending a lot of time in bliss. Poking around at it, turning it one way and the other, trying to see what it is and where it comes from.

To study bliss by being blissful is a high tantra. One comes around again to eating, drinking, sleeping, fucking and all the other arts and parts of life, but enjoys them so much more because the seeds of suffering are largely toasted and sterile and discarded. If you don't make yourself suffer, it's remarkable how little suffering there is in the world around you.

It's not a perfect world. But the world is much, much closer to perfect than the crappy self-image—self-myth—we start out with. Perhaps it is a perfect world... and a little more bliss... will show me... how to see that...

It's important to remember that you can still fry at every stage. Bliss is wonderful—but if you're an asshole, it can collapse. You can blow it by creating hatred in your own being. You can blow it by lusting and hurting people who are drawn to your balance. You can do all kinds of stuff which creates bad ripples in the force which kick you out of paradise.

Just don't! Basic goodness, basic goodness. All of that Vajrayana mayhem? Advanced practitioners. Stabilize the bliss and study it and, if you find that to maintain it, you have to bend the rules of the world a little, please do it with grace and love. That's the tantric way.

Blood Sacrifice, Death Cults, etc.

If death disturbs your consciousness, if you shy away from it, buy a rabbit and a book on skinning rabbits.

Kill it, skin it, cook it, eat it, wear it. If that wasn't enough, do it again.

Do it too often, one day you'll be the rabbit, seeing the experience from the inside.

Better to pray to Kali and ask her, if you dare, to help you with your problems around death, ask to be allowed to live happily and well, because your meditation is teaching you all you need to know at a fast enough rate.

Right? Do you see the model? The universe brings whatever you need to learn from, or you reach out for it yourself. The more you learn in meditation, the less in manifestation. It's critically important to understand why all of the darkness and death worship and orgies and the like exist: rapid ways of puncturing the garbage bags of the unconscious, spreading the junk all over the floor, picking out the useful stuff and burning the rest to nothingness.

Why Bother?

The core of tantra is the theological understanding that the universe was created by intelligent entities which want us to have fun in it. All the conditioning and the karma and all the rest of that stuff can be let go of, just as you can allow your mother to tidy your room, if you don't care about the lego models on the floor.

Your life is nothing but a hill of little yellow plastic bricks that you dance around as if it was the Goddess. If you're willing to let Her sweep it away, and put herself in the center, she will. It may still look like yellow plastic bricks to everybody else, but you'll know. Oh yes, my precious, you'll know.

Magic is a bad word. Nearly everything associated with the word "magic" leads to misunderstandings of the subject: parlor tricks, guys in funny robes muttering in strange languages, Aleister Crowley and the Golden Dawn. All these things are instances of magic, but magic is a great country. To understand magic by these fragments is like understanding France through pastries and the Eiffel tower.

Partly to cut through this baggage, I will be using the term "sorcery" frequently, mostly to refer to "getting something done by non-ordinary means." You can read it all as "magic" if you like.

The Social Construction of Words

A dog is only called a dog because we all agree that it is a dog, and that it is called that. In some cultures, a lot of the things we call dogs—Paris Hilton's carpet slipper, for example—might not be recognized as such. In other cultures, our definition of dogs as pets rather than food animals would be similarly puzzling. Both the boundaries of the object, and the definition of that object, are both socially constructed. We say "this is a dog" but they say "no, dogs are larger and brown and aggressive." We see the carpet slipper and the feral hound as two examples of one species, and they see two entirely different animals. Who's right? We might argue that it's *Canis lupus familiaris*, but we're appealing to Science, which also has some socially constructed aspects. Those words mean only what other people from our social group construe them to mean, regardless of the objectivity of the phenomena to which the words refer. There is no way out of this maze: even if phenomena are objective (which they are not!) words are completely relative.

"When I use a word it means just what I choose it to mean, neither more nor less." (H. Dumpty)

There's a need for this kind of pop-pomo linguistics because without it, magic will revert to being defined by a series of examples, which one person can define one way ("that's magic") and another defines another way ("that's just a coincidence"). While (nearly) all magic is subject to attack-by-denial-of-agency in this way, a properly constructed definition of magic is proof against this predation by petty tinkerers.

What is Magic?

Magic is whatever everybody involved in the conversation agrees magic is.

Now, this is a remarkably obvious and unhelpful definition in all cases except the practical one: this definition works. If I perform some act, and I say "I did this by Sorcery," and you say "No, that's just Chance!" then we are in two different universes of meaning: in my universe, there is pattern and causality, and in yours, only lowly chaos, unordered events open to any interpretation. This argument will not be resolved without new evidence!

I'd like to point that out again: the assignment of causality between two events, like "smallpox is caused by an organism" versus "smallpox is caused by invisible hobgoblins" is purely a personal choice and only rarely in magical practice is there enough available evidence to be completely sure.

If we all agree "smallpox will not touch us if we get rid of all the hobgoblins" and then we get rid of them, and nobody gets sick, this is the best case of practical magic: we make a plan, we act on the plan, the plan works, and we assign our success to magic. "We" is the social group which performed or knew about the magical act. We is the tribe, and almost all magic is performed relative to a tribe. If the tribe rules "magic" then it is magic. If not, it's just coincidence.

This is the big key to understanding the fuss-and-nonsense about "magic"—each different tribe has a local definition, ranging from the Western Rationalist perspective ("stuff and nonsense, except for Science") through to, say, African Shamanism ("that car goes fast because of the strong spirits!"). When these local, tribal definitions are not in harmony you get "reality wars"—places where conversation and narrative communication break down because of clashing definitions of words and cause-and-effect relationships. It is hard to talk coherently with a person who has a different model of cause-and-effect to your own: their narratives make no sense at all!

This is the first good diagnostic for detecting sorcery: localized breakdowns in cause-and-effect relationships which make communication and storytelling with people outside the tribe difficult. This indicates that something transpired which is only "real" inside the tribal group: local reality has diverged far enough from cultural norms to be called magical reality.

Baby Steps in Sorcery

To a baby, the entire world seems very god-filled and mysterious and beautiful and terrible. Enormous beings of unlimited power are responsible for every part of your survival and experience: your parents are god and goddess, lords of creation, makers of you. This is the universal imprint to which magic returns again and again and again: children playing in a reality they do not understand, overseen by enormous forces they do not control which they hope and pray are benevolent. To be a magician is to stay a child, living in the unknown, learning more each day about a universe it seems like you will never understand.

The cheese of Televised Consensus Reality is Swiss, shot full of holes: the New Age, the Snake Handlers, the Scientologists, the Hindu and Buddhist nations, Islam, Fundamentalist Christianity. Everybody who appeals to a higher power, to a notion of reality above and beyond the level of Fox News is a magician of one sort or another with an alternative model of reality, and access to alternative models of cause-and-effect.

"This Happened Because Baby Jesus Is Angry With Your Sorry Ass" is a magical narrative, ascientific, heinously heretical, arbitrary and childish. This is magical thinking in the raw: vile blasphemies against common sense and good reason in the name of a god who would almost certainly disavow all interest in the situation.

That quality—"this makes no fucking sense and is completely wrong by all reasonable reference points"—is a second good diagnostic for detecting sorcery. Anybody who lives in a world like that, even for a short while, is a magician of some kind, hacking cause-and-effect if only in their own minds. Magic is about redefining reality around your goals, your desires, your needs, your dreams, your ideas.

Sorcery is about getting your way in the world.

"I did it MY way" is the cry of the solitary magician. "WE do it OUR way" is the cry of the magical tribe. My house. My rules. Be the parent of your own magical self!

Brass Tacks: Bell, Book and Candle

Much of the stuff of sorcery is siddhis—minor powers which are developed by spiritual practice and meditation. If you can see auras and feel other people's chakras, you can sometimes detect when someone is lying, or foretell short term events, or get little visits from spirit guides (your own and others'). You can communicate with astral beings by telepathy and ask for favors, sometimes push luck and happenstance by will alone, and so on. Humans all have all kinds of capabilities, and mostly spend their lives with almost all of their capabilities fully absorbed in the material game we all play. When you begin to break away from that game, powers of various kinds just come. The New Age scene is full of people with minor capabilities which would be totally unremarkable in any shamanic culture, but stick out like sore thumbs here.

None of that shit really matters. You can develop it all in a few years of hard work if you want it, and it'll probably just come to anybody who's serious about living their life.

No. Real magic starts when you get ready to slide sideways in reality, crossing over from one form of existence to another. When you are ready to allow your core definitions of reality be redefined according to your own will and the will of god, you're ready to be a real magician, a sorcerer. The magic circle, that most potent archetype, is completely real. It represents the personal reality of the sorcerer, the human aura's projective surface on which reality-as-we-know-it is shone. The Magic Circle is Plato's Cave, and we, that chained-down god, amused into captivity by the show on TV in our open-doored prison cell.

Sorcery is the remote control on reality, the game controller on life. Punch in the cheat codes and the game changes. But at every step, you find yourself surrounded by peers, others playing the same game as you, like-meeting-like on the open field.

On Angels, Demons and Other Beings

From time immemorial magicians have conjured demons: creatures of darkness, evil, hatred, below-bestial lust, delighting in the murder of hope. Why?

Similarly, consorting with Angels and Gods is an ancient sport among mages. Why?

None of these creatures is different in basic structure from you or I at an essential level: each is a created entity, just like a horse or a dog or a person. They may reside primarily in the same place you go when you have a dream, a vision or a nightmare, but rest assured that you are as unreal to them as they are to you: one can approach the reality of nearly any being if one has the skill and agility. If you have a recurring dream of kissing an angel or being groped by a demon, night after night after night, that it is only a dream matters little: it is "real enough" to transform your life.

Whether seen with the mind's eye, in dreams, in visions, in dark glass mirrors or as apparitions, it matters no more than talking to a person face-to-face, by e-mail, phone, fax or postal mail: communication with real entities occurs. They are as real to you as you are to them, and you can usually decide how "real" you want to make those kinds of phenomena. If you can experience telepathic connections with other human beings, why not non-human beings, creatures from other planes and so on?

Obviously, care and discretion must be exercised. You don't want, by and large, to hang out with crack-dealing, gun-toting hoodlums to whom you are a wallet on legs—but if you want to buy crack, that's where you go. You're sick, you see a doctor. You're soulsick? Go see an angel, by whatever means necessary.

The reality you are in is already magical reality to beings other than you: your talents, your mind, your body—those things are magical. It is your familiarity, your accumulated habituation to being yourself which produces the illusion of the mundane world you live in. Because the inside of your aura has the same basic properties every day, you assume that this is the "real world," and because the surrounding culture tells you the "real world" is non-magical, you believe them. However, the upper chakras or sephirot (energy centers) control the parts of the psychic body which shape the aura and the reality projected within it. As one gains conscious control of those energy centers, it becomes possible (nay, easy) to simply decide that reality will change its flow and events will happen themselves into a different pattern—and it will soon seem normal, too.

This interim phase: the gap between the decision, and that new reality becoming normalized, is magic. It's the shifting, the crossing, that is magical. When you die, it's possible "you" will incarnate on a different plane of existence: perhaps a world where you (and everybody else) can fly, or manifest food from thin air. Those worlds exist, or at least are written about very often. Somewhere within your soul, there is the ability to exist and manifest in a world that works in such magical ways.

Sorcery, in essence, is finding out how your soul could operate in such a world, and then opening a bubble of that reality in your present environment, so that you can start exercising those unusual-for-this-place capabilities.

This is the Hack: to use the full powers of your awakened, expanded soul in a way which revolves around opening bubbles of alternate reality around yourself and perhaps your magical tribe: giving reality permission to soften, be changed and harden again. To shift local reality in the direction in which your desires are possible, then to experience them. Note that order: first move reality such that it is possible, or inevitable... then experience it. Manifesting things directly in mundane reality is possible, but very, very hard...

If you stay in that place of new potentials indefinitely, however, it is no longer magical. It's just normal again: a higher level normal. It's the shifting which is magical—the understanding that local reality is defined by consensus, and can be affected profoundly by your own intentions and the intentions of those people around you.

As you shift your sense of reality, you will tend to attract and be attracted to people and places with compatible realities: what starts as an individual decision about the nature of reality rapidly takes on the appearance of a "hard reality" as you find yourself surrounded by others with those beliefs. This is "planar travel"—moving between different tribes with different normative realities, or being drawn across the globe to places that are resonant with the reality you want to feel. Not everybody exists in the same world, and although we do seem to share the same physical space, countless billions of people will simply never meet.

Secrecy, Boundaries and Magical Orders

The separation between one consensus reality and another is maintained on many planes of existence simultaneously. The "causal" level is most notable: cause-and-effect explanations do not travel well between realities. One group will say "it was the Holy Spirit that brought us together," while another will say "well, it was just one of those parties." It might be the same phenomena, but the local conventions, names and narrative styles form a divisive "hull" on that worldview. The linguistic level is an easy way to see boundaries between realities. There are also often energy membranes that reflect the emotional and psychic levels of those same divisions.

Secrecy is another powerful way of partitioning reality: "To Know, To Will, To Dare and To Keep Silent," goes the old magician's saying. Silence has many purposes, but one of the primary ones is to partition the local reality of the magician fiercely: if one simply never speaks of magic, then essentially one's magical tribe is a tribe of one. This approach gave people a great sense of power and importance but at some cost in sanity and balance: it matters little how much you can bend and warp reality in the privacy of your own temple. It's taking your show out on the road that counts.

A "magical order" or society of magicians is typically defined by a large body of shared secrets that construe the "hull"—the boundary—of the Order. Within that hull, reality often has radically different properties—when all present are members, and the door is locked, consensus reality can be drawn far, far back without seeming ill effects. Anybody involved in such a group should realize, however, that the fluidity of reality is a product of the agreement of all present that it should be so, and the relative rigidity of reality outside of the temples of the order likewise: we are all god, and all of equal "power."

This is key: even the most pig-headed being is also god. Their wishes for reality have equal weight to yours, from the god's eye perspective. All divine children are loved and respected equally by their cosmic parents, perhaps with some exceptions for the exceptionally ill-behaved. Just because you get to fly around on the astral plane or make bubble worlds where nearly all the confining laws are gone, don't start thinking of yourself as qualitatively better than other people. You are not. They have collectively willed the mundane world into existence for reasons we may not even be able to guess at, and we exist within or alongside that creation.

Only a fool would think that we are lords and masters, and they are slaves and servants.

Of Technique and Purpose

The odds are very strong that you incarnated in this life for a definite reason. The most fundamental reason to do magic is to attain the goals and objectives that drew you to incarnate in the first place. The shock of incarnation is huge: the pain of birth, the limitation of infancy, the stress of childhood disappointment, the drag of age, gravity, the passage of time. The upside of incarnation is pretty fantastic too, but using magic to cushion the shocks of the world is no bad thing in the general case. If you came to be an artist, a performer and a healer, keeping yourself in tip-top shape by living in a reality in which your body is almost always fabulously well is no bad thing unless there are specific reasons not to do it. Magic to that effect might be symbolized as a high energy yoga practice, a special diet, an amulet, a practice like herbal baths, or just an attitude towards your body. The creation is of a field of intention, and beyond that, a field of definition. That is magical in and of itself.

Tactical magic tends to be a bit more concrete, rather like the difference between interior decor and jewelry. A small local magical act to fix a specific problem is only a focus, a concentration, of a more general understanding of reality: a tiny body decoration rather than an ambient environment. If you need NOT to get another parking ticket until the next grant check appears, a little shamanic work to get that end is only an aspect of a more general "everything here is going well" field.

But the techniques, whatever they might be, really are just that: they're triggers, ways of harnessing the innate power of an individual human being's manifestation engine, incarnation engine, life engine. Ways of tapping into what we all do all the time unconsciously to co-create the world we live in. There are some exceptions: invocations in angelic languages, for example, tend to work not so much because the magician thinks they will, but because angels hear their names, read intentions and can choose to respond... one of the few cases in which magic is rather more objective than subjective.

Magic is nothing less than the creation of reality at will. We are all doing it all the time, but the reality we choose to create most of the time is defined to be concordant with the ambient reality of the planet, the nation and the social group we are in. Taking responsibility for tuning your own reality for the effect and lifestyle you choose is a big step, but that's really all there is to magic. True magic, or sorcery, is in realizing that we have this capability, that we use it all the time to create the "normal" world, and that we can optionally become conscious and capable of action on those levels of reality, redefining our world at will and pleasure.

This is my understanding of the Nath Way, the Nath Sampradaya. It is a society of beings who, understanding that they are in some sense god, and fully vested members of the cosmic family, choose to live as they will, using intention, will, ritual, magic and every other aspect of life as means to the end: enjoying the universe that god created with us.

ENTERING BLISS (*Through Integrating Male and Female*)

So the male/female integration was fairly simple and technical. I was just attracted again and again and again to these crazy Libra/Scorpio women, and those are some damn annoying female manifestations—hot, but totally unable to commit to anything, even a date, or make their mind up. Powerful sexual desire from the Scorpio, but undirected and afraid of taking any form—that being a fundamental Libra quality. It was, bluntly, driving me nuts. So I'd read my Jung, and had some tantric technique, and I'd studied psychotherapy as both art and science, so I figured that I'd just, well, manifest whatever I was looking for from these girls internally within myself. I figured it couldn't just be sex, or I'd be drawn towards people who I was more likely to get laid by—it had to be something fundamental in their energy that I was looking to use to fill some kind of lack.

Alchemy, right? Solve et Coagula. But I needed something to solve. So I went looking for the aspect of myself which was those women: some facet which was wild and unbridled and sexual and indecisive and neurotic and insane and open and friendly and welcoming. But mainly hot. And I discovered that I did have that aspect of me, very strongly: it was who I had often been in past lives as a woman.

I was attempting to have sex with myself.

So I did: I started to become that aspect of me, in private, in my meditations. Tried to remember what it had been like, to feel that energy in myself. With some practice, it became possible to have both that energy, that wild-female-power, and my own somewhat repressed but strong male energy in my body at the same time.

It took a while, about a year and a half, but using this system in my masturbatory fantasies eventually balanced the two energies. I became equally comfortable with either set as "me," but remained as myself in daily life. Then one day, I began to realize that I could produce an essentially sexual bliss at will simply by allowing energy transfer to occur between the two.

I didn't have to be masturbating, or doing the visualizations. It just was there, any time I wanted it, as much as I would allow! That changed things!

Wow! That Changed Things!

I could not just feel like a hot girl when I wanted to, but actually feel like I was both having sex with a hot girl, and feel like I was a hot girl having sex. Sexual bliss on a plate. To be honest I was pretty careful not to do too much of the infinite-orgasms thing: I was more-or-less certain that there would be side effects, I just didn't know them at the time. I experimented some, but chose not to experience that as my default state of consciousness.

Instead, I merged them, this male and female, into an old, settled, married couple: removed the tension of separation and the bliss of union and allowed a basically independent state to emerge, one where I no longer needed anybody else's sexual energy as an input to my own, as is so often the motivation for sex, not just the pleasure, but a direct energetic rebalancing—young men and women, so strong on one side or the other of the force, need it to remain psychologically balanced—not just for pleasure, but to balance the kundalini. So I kinda took myself out of the game. Girls were still interesting as people, as friends, but I didn't really need sex any more. I still had relationships, still had sex and enjoyed it a lot, but my tolerance for BS had dropped way down because I was no longer psychically dependent on external sources of feminine energy.

Then I noticed I could catalyze the state in other people, and this made them a lot more fun to sleep with, because, well... if I went into the internal bliss, and they did the same thing, then you had these two bliss being bodies... well... It Was a Good Thing.

However, without really heavy prior practices, people didn't seem to be able to hold it, so that again was a relatively shortlived experimental phase. These days I tend to keep the energy down to the point where I feel a little better than I would without it running, and don't get entangled in relationships I don't want to, am not "thunderstruck by these tissues" and am comfortable and happy. I just don't really have the context to really let loose, and I'm not sure that anybody really does: the celibate, or householder, path really does seem to be more common than wild tantric orgies, and with good reason. It's a lot easier to arrange.

I don't know why it's so hard to arrange the other one. It's a shame.

One thing I have noticed, over the years, is that there's a lot of moral responsibility in being sexually integrated. The ego still has desires which it projects or which really are inherently in other people ("really" in ego speak, as it were.) Perhaps I botched the integration and it should have taken care of a lot more of my emotional needs, or perhaps those required other integrations which I'm still working out. Who knows? But being able to generate internal sexual rapture, or manifest very strong, but internally balanced male or female energy at will, can make one a hell of a manipulator.

If I walk around with the rapture even slightly on, girls take notice in a way which is both appealing and frightening. Appealing because, well, it's nice to be noticed, to be wanted. As a guy, being able to draw looks from stunning women was a massive ego boost. Frightening because, from my perspective, they're moths drawn to a flame which will certainly not help them much, and quite possibly do them some harm. They're certainly not going to do the integration practices, and contact with integrated energy is at that point basically heroin. Da Free John style addictive sexuality heroin, possibly. Here, honey, get a lot of my bliss field!!! Now drop 'em.

I just never go there. Not even once, thank god.

I think I'd be opening up a lot of temptation for very little reward: there's an ego need—residual self-esteem issues from my teenage years—but no actual sexual need. I'd be using sex with out-of-my-class women to salve a twenty-year-old wound. Not healing, but only damaging excess, would lie in that direction. Be aware that the internal sexual integration doesn't automatically free one from all forms of sexual conditioning, and that those other forms can still be woefully dangerous!

STAYING HIGH: *On the Longevity of Psychedelic Consciousness*

The problem is stabilizing the energy.

College works because it's a relatively value-free space: four years, external sources of money, little decision making beyond which courses you do, and massive, huge, incredible social license. Plus the school administration giving your life a basic shape and purpose.

With all that stuff as energy inputs, lots of people are capable of being wonderful. Then they get out into the real world and fall back on the coping skills and patterns of their parents, and the wonderful game falls apart. People gradually go offline without some form of strong spiritual practice, be it meditation or psychedelics.

But psychedelics cause damage. Not much damage, not significant, but over the years, unless people know how to stay psychically healthy, they begin to pick up more and more scars and bruises. Burned-in bits of trip memory, or wounds that got opened up and never quite closed. Stuff like that. It's hard to stay fully healthy as a longterm user of psychedelics, and most of the brightest, shiniest people seem to trip only rarely past about thirty, with certain incredibly obvious and powerful exceptions.

"Getting the magic back" requires raising energy. Spiritual energy, you know... juice. The kind of openness to god, to each-other's hearts, etc., which is easy, oh-so-easy, as youngsters, but is so much more difficult and complex when relationships begin to presage babies, and mortgages make more sense than renting. How do you love everybody when you've got this kid who's so much more important to you than the rest of the world combined, really, when it comes right down to it?

I'm not saying that it can't be done, but I am saying that the main obstacles are spiritual, not material or even emotional. Extraordinary power and circumstances need to combine to keep that kind of openness to the world going in large communities which aren't made up entirely of mid-20s or younger folks.

The actual dynamics I've had described to me in some detail by veterans of the 1960s consciousness movement. They basically suggested to me that there's a curve: time on one axis, state of awareness on the other. In the early stages, the drugs rapidly lift you to a plateaux. People can stay there with occasional psychedelic refreshers for about five years, maybe six or even ten in some cases.

After that period people begin to Come Down. Usually the process is extremely painful as the personality re-hardens, the drugs no longer provide any "lift." You still get high, but there's no spiritual opening, no sense of being liberated. Afterwards you're the same person you were before and the walls begin to close in. The personality stops changing much under psychedelic influences. The growth stops.

At that point, a lot of people slide over on to heroin or, these days, ketamine. The anesthetics kill the spiritual pain caused by both the re-hardening of the personality and the spiritual damage—bruises and little cuts—that psychedelics cause. I want to stress that spiritual damage from psychedelics is not minor in some cases—people can really break their "legs"—but that severe injuries on the spiritual level are the exception and not the rule. You can go hiking drunk a lot of times before you slip and shatter your leg, and so it is with spiritual work and tripping.

But still, the damage accumulates a little at a time, and most people have no tools to heal the myriad little rents and gaps that open in the subtle bodies as one zooms around.

The other part of that curve, the one which leads to a better life, is to smoothly transition on to a real spiritual practice before the end of the plateaux. Meditation, yoga, psychotherapy of a depth and power not commonly found, martial arts like Aikido or T'ai Chi Ch'üan, even Christianity in its more esoteric and applied forms, will all work. The form is unimportant as long as it solidifies one's awareness of the "energy body" or "aura"—that is to say, the thing most commonly written about as the "human soul."

Psychedelics extend the "plastic" phase of adolescence. They allow people to keep "growing" at an accelerated pace well into their middle years, and beyond. But there are prices to be paid for that plasticity: a certain lostness in the face of the conventional world, a mystification and distance from mainstream society. People of all spiritual traditions often feel like adults in a world run by children with enormous material power, playing obsessive games with money and power.

Real spirituality provides tools to keep that growth going long, long into one's old age. The "Old Boy" (Lao Tzu can apparently be translated as such) archetype, of the sage with the eyes of a child, represents what comes after the temporary softening-and-hardening propagated by psychedelics: the enlightenment of being as fluid as water or as hard as stone as the situation demands, or as your own pleasure chooses.

This isn't to speak against psychedelics or their place in our culture, nor to indicate that psychedelic shamanism is not a fully developed spiritual path—but if we would stop going down there to talk to those guys about the drugs, they might be willing to spend the time telling us about the rest of their spiritual lives, which I imagine are clearly a lot more complex, complete and compelling than most of the western Ayahuasceros realize. Given the choice, I think we may be having the wrong conversation with those chaps.

So back to Psychedelic Community. Groups of rapidly developing souls—people in deep flux—are often incredibly warm, open, supportive and loving. People going through changes together are like that, almost regardless of the context. Childhood, university, a workshop setting, a trip, Burning Man. Growth and lovingness and openness go together. The ossification of the nine-to-five world kills people.

All spiritual communities have a hellish melodrama side, just like college. People play out their heightened emotions, have sexual feelings more deeply and outside of conventional roles, push forward deeper into their potential and are filled with a sense of possibility, of excitement, of "anything could happen!" It is the "Fountain of Youth"—to live continually in the zone of life where being is becoming.

To seek to do this is to seek to be forever young, forever rich, filled with spirit. To be a fountain of possibility and life into the world around. To seek to share that experience in a group, to joyously voyage through life as a tribe of happy heathens filled with the joy of being alive is the highest hope most people can conceive of. Pure heaven and hell on the path beyond paths.

What I'm saying here is that "psychedelic" is a form of spiritual. This "psychedelic" community of which you speak is spiritual community. Expect all the trauma, chaos and mayhem that comes with that. Talk to some veterans.

Does this make sense? It's not an unheard-of thesis—that psychedelic practice is spiritual practice. But extended into community, it's clear that we haven't thought this through much as a culture. Similarly, I've watched a few people over the years start spiritual exploration by psychedelic means, not transition on to less stressful ways of staying high, and slowly harden into shells of themselves.

It's about the ugliest thing I've ever seen: people who've had recurrent brushes with the light fall into darkness with great struggle.

Think it through. There's a lot more to winning this game than the right people, the right place, and the right circumstances. There's an entire historical library of other people facing the same challenges, proposing their own plans, ways and solutions. People have been trying to get high and stay high forever. Community is part of the puzzle, but there's a whole other leg: sustainable routes to higher consciousness.

I speak from experience. I spent a good chunk of my early 20s as a serious student of shamanism in its most direct and applied forms. I went there—deep into the hinterlands of consciousness—over and over again by a variety of means. But I also had a solid meditation practice predating my shamanic experiences by a number of years, and as time passed and that practice matured, I slowly and smoothly transitioned from being primarily a shaman to primarily a yogi. The chaos and melodrama are not all that different, the constant change and opening and growth open out into life in a similar form—perhaps more slowly and manageably, but not always.

The people with practices, whatever they are, do better in the long term than the people without them. Building "psychedelic" community without having some kind of transition plan to help people survive the end of their psychedelic careers is asking to have a refuge for aging heroin addicts. On the Height, which was as much of a spiritual as a psychedelic scene, heroin had killed most of the brightest stars by the early seventies. The most beautiful and conscious faded away the fastest as the scene fell apart, largely (according to my contacts) because people were so burned out and damaged and didn't know how make it work without damaging themselves further. People had burned their resources.

To live well requires a plan. The drugs may carry you now, and may be an occasional option always, but there has to be something else to eat. Soma is part of a pattern, part of a way of life, and the rest of the picture has to be there for people to survive.

A community has to face these issues, to understand the natural life-span of a psychedelics user is only five to ten years, at which point they become a burnout or a spiritual practitioner of some other kind. It's a harsh truth, but it's the biggest obstacle to these kinds of endeavors—how do you make a good, grounded life with a group of people whose basic approaches to being alive are only good for a handful of years?

Think about it. Then start your Yoga, or your T'ai Chi, or your meditation, or your prayer.

ETERNALICIOUS

The Holy Fire of Eternal Liberty

Thee Ritual Manual of the New Naths

The Preliminary Invocation

Om Goom Guru Ganapati-Ganesh

Who Guides Our Art

The Unfailing

The Intractable

The Victorious

Who Flys the Banner of Heaven

Over the Ramparts

Of the Fortresses

Of the Earth

There is no Guru or Guide other than God Itself.

So Begins Eternalicious—The Holy Fire of Eternal Liberty—Thee Ritual Manual of the New Naths.

This manual is called *Eternalicious* as a gesture of faith and hope. We are all stuck in eternity. Until such time as we either choose the spiritual suicide of Nirvana or find some other form of conventional enlightenment, here we will stay.

I hope you enjoy your eternity as much as possible, and that you find freedom to live as you will, love as you will and die as you will.

The First Triad—Angelic Magic

Introduction: Our Standing With the Angels

Because we are operating in the West, and for the most part in America, angelic magic is the prerequisite of all other forms. Without a solid grasp of the local system and its technologies it is entirely too difficult and dangerous to explore.

America has an unusually strong psychic immune system, perhaps dating back to the ritual work and other actions of the Founding Brothers of America—the magicians and Masons who laid down the infrastructure of the nation on a spiritual, psychic, intellectual and magical level. We, their heirs, have improperly maintained and cared for the political system they left us, but the psychic defense network of the American continent is as strong and ferocious as it ever was.

This psychic defense network will, to put this politely, fuck your shit up royally if you start importing magic from other continents and practicing it openly. To prevent this immune reaction from taking you and your group out, usually by astral encapsulation or mysterious accident, you should consider three agreements as mandatory for further work.

The Three Agreements

1. The First Agreement: Respect

I will be on good terms with the angelic realms, regarding them as the local guardian spirits and guides, and respecting them as much as I would wish to respect, say, the guardian spirits of a Native American reservation were I a visitor there.

2. The Second Agreement: Shielding

I will erect suitable shielding and protection to prevent the foreign magics of the Naths from fucking up the local American psychic ecosystem like predatory fish in the Everglades.

3. The Third Agreement: Cooperation

I will attempt to follow all local regulations and traffic laws, and will take the hint from the angelic forces if they try to tell me that I'm doing something wrong, fucking up their plans or am otherwise in the way, out of line, or impolite.

You can absolutely ignore the angels and their realm and its ways and, in return, they can absolutely drop thousand-pound bombs all over you, your operations, your group, its environment and nearly anything else they choose. They are immensely powerful, real spiritual forces, in many cases the equals of what we call Gods in other cultures, and you are in their land and turf. Respect beings who were capable of manifesting things like hydrogen bombs and the scientific method. Or they'll kill you.

In practical terms, this first Triad is entirely about mastering enough angelic magic to be able to operate the rest of the system without violating the second agreement: Shielding.

It takes a fair amount of skill to be able to create and maintain a bubble of an absolutely foreign and independent reality (in turn supporting and manifesting a foreign magical and spiritual system) within the wider culture of the West, and not get in the face of something which is designed to stop other forces like predatory ghosts, faeries-of-the-unkind-kind and so on from preying on the relatively defenseless local population.

You are, in many ways, in the position of the Pakistani immigrant who buys a goat and then slaughters it in the street outside of his apartment as he would do in Karachi: police come and explain the local rules. If he keeps slaughtering goats, police come and take him away. On a magical level, the police are rarely physical police, and the warnings are rarely as simple as a knock on the door, given the problems with getting accurate information across the planes of experience. But, if you are doing the magical equivalent of what our poor immigrant is, be sure that action will be taken and consequences will come.

In short: slaughter your goats inside. Much of the rest of this document is dedicated to learning how to create private magical space. Once you can create, own, control and close subdomains within the wider world, you can begin to create and experience the Nath reality.

These subdomains, these "bubbles," are Magical Temporary Autonomous Zones, and the angelic guardians will leave them alone as long as they obey five conditions.

The Five Conditions

1. Honest

Nothing which other people need is taken into the Zone and destroyed, traded away into another dimension, or otherwise lost.

2. Benign

Nothing noxious or toxic is emitted from the Zone or brought from other planes into the reality outside of the Zone. Noxious things can be brought from elsewhere into the Zone, dealt with, experimented on, and then returned to the place they came or some other appropriate place, or Angelic Forces can be invoked to help clean up, but nothing bad must leave the warded region. This is where most magic goes wrong, resulting in punitive reprisals.

3. Beneficial

Everybody who enters the Subdomain leaves in better condition than they entered, and certainly not worse. No infections, astral or physical or psychic, no poisons, no rape-and-pillage, nothing.

This does not mean that people cannot get injured doing magic, and then healed before leaving the space: accidents or wars can happen. But the bubbles are only allowed to exist so long as beings enter in one condition, and leave in a better one. Any breach of this rule will show up on the radar of the angels who watch over the common people and swiftly result in harm-mitigation measures (read: Astral B-52s) being dispatched.

If you doubt the force of these beings, consider the fate of poor Chögyam Trungpa.

4. Non-Alchemical

Although the net effect of these bubbles has to be positive because the effect on each individual present must be positive, it is forbidden from the angelic perspective to simply pull resources from other planes of existence into this plane through these bubbles. No turning lead into gold or channeling lots of million-dollar-ideas! It causes game balance issues. Clever variations on these themes may be permitted: for example, taking payment for processing toxic waste, psychically pulling it into another dimension where one can process it cleanly using more advanced technology, then bringing it back clean. But these deals must be negotiated consciously.

5. Moderated

Moderate discontinuous change. It is possible—in fact, remarkably easy once one has the knack—to take a group of people into a state of being where a great deal of "reality" is withdrawn. In these states, people can change radically and dramatically with no "cause" other than "healing happened" or "inspiration was received." This kind of change is frequently acausal from the perspective of non-participants in the ritual: people change in dramatic ways, and nobody knows why. This confusion forms a "wake" rather like that left behind a speed boat, and the wake can cause confusion and harm to bystanders in a variety of subtle ways analogous to knocking them off their windsurfers. Discontinuous change should be moderated.

Wake effects are not the only reason to moderate discontinuous change, but they are the easiest to English. As your capabilities and experience grow, be sure to stay in tight contact with the angelic forces who watch over you to discuss and negotiate around effects which may be obvious to them, but quite invisible to you. Be aware that as a flesh monkey it is very hard to understand what is going on in enough detail to control the effects of your actions accurately, and help from the angels is often mandatory.

The Three Agreements (respect, shielding, cooperation) and the Five Conditions (honest, benign, beneficial, non-alchemical, moderated) form a provisional covenant between the Angelic Powers of North America (as we have experienced them), and the founders of the New Nath Movements. These agreements took a year of intense spiritual work, a lot of risk, error and mistake, and have held up reasonably well. However, it is important to understand that they are not final or complete. They are mutable and delicate and will only continue to operate with continued good will from all parties: this is a deal sheet, not a contract. If you, as a Nath, abuse the angelic powers, it is Game Over for all of us.

Play nice, or don't play at all is the Angelic Way—and never forget that we are in their turf, their world:

Magicians in the Rational Domains.

LVX, kids, LVX. Love.

First Practice: The Pentagram

The Lesser Banishing Ritual of the Pentagram comes to us from the Golden Dawn (an English magical group of the nineteenth century). Benjamin Rowe's "The Essential Skills of Magick" is a standard introductory text on this work and is widely available on the internet.

The LBRP is an elemental banishing. That is to say, it banishes energies typically called air, earth, fire and water, and associated elementals, energies in those frequencies and other matter. The space it leaves behind is often described as "suffused with spirit," that being the fifth element in the Western conception.

Importantly, the LBRP is well-understood by the angelic world as a standard magical exercise, and when they see it done, they encapsulate the area in a protective field. Within this initial protective field, additional rituals can be done to create additional levels of shielding, and this Russian dolls approach is critical to performing Nath magic safely: we construct a complex system of layered protection so that at no point does our energy directly leak into the North American Malkuth ("Kingdom" in Hebrew; used to mean "World").

Second Practice: The Hexagram

The Lesser Banishing Ritual of the Hexagram is also from the Golden Dawn. It banishes at a much higher level, extending to the planetary and astrological influences, depending on the exact variant of the ritual undertaken. The LBRH is four or five times as powerful as the LBRP and also serves to channel enormous quantities of angelic light and heat into the local magical environment. It is extremely good, powerful magic.

Donald Michael Kraig, a Nath of the Mahendranath lineage, wrote a book called *Modern Magick* which provides an excellent overview of the Western Magical Tradition. It provides a good version of the hexagram ritual, and much additional information on the Golden Dawn and its ways. I recommend avoiding entirely the evocation, talismanic magic, demonology and "identify, objectify and banish" rituals, and anything else that seems a bit fishy, because much of the material in the book stems from Medieval sources, and times were different back then. Some of it simply no longer functions cleanly or appropriately, being the magical equivalent of a horse-drawn cart.

However, at this time, the LBRP and LBRH are unsurpassed, and much of the other material in the book is of similar quality.

One clear issue with the hexagram ritual is its intensely Christian focus: INRI, the Light of the Cross, etc. are key phrases. It also incorporates some Egyptian material ("Isis, Aphophis, Osiris"), which was probably designed to cover up some aspects of the S.R.I.A. material which was not appropriate for public viewing in the Golden Dawn. At present, the best I can suggest is "deal with it as it is."

Third Practice: The Heptagram

The rituals of the heptagram are not in common circulation and are basically unnecessary for common practice. However, it is formally necessary to "do the heptagram" in an abbreviated form before opening the Nath Circle. This is part of our agreement with the angelic forces.

The Abbreviated Banishing Ritual of the Heptagram

The heptagram has no compass-and-square edge construction. One is therefore not constructing a heptagram, but a human-approximation of the heptagram, unlike the hexagram rituals which could, in theory, be mathematically precise. The heptagram is in some sense beyond human understanding. Or at least that's what my sources say. Preface this ritual with the Banishing Ritual of the Hexagram, and finish with either the Banishing Ritual of the Pentagram, or the Banishing Ritual of the Hexagram.

1. Inscribe a heptagon (seven-sided figure) on the ground of your working area.

2. Stand in the center of the heptagon and say "I stand within the confines of the Mysterious Kingdom of God. I always Have and Always Will remain within the Palace of the King of All Worlds."

3. Now draw a heptagram (seven-sided star) on the ground of your working area. There are two possible stars: one joins points opposite on the circle and is sharp and pointed (masculine), the other is more rounded (feminine). You should draw the pointed one. You remain in the center of the heptagram as it is drawn.

4. Stand in the center of the heptagram and say "God above and world below, Kether and Malkuth, are One."

5. Now draw the feminine seven sided star, the other heptagram, which is made by joining alternate points of the heptagon. You remain in the center of the space.

6. Declare boldly "I am the Child of God. I am the Son of the Mother and the Daughter of the Father."

This abbreviated ritual does only a small part of what more advanced and complete Hepagram rituals will do, but serves our purposes.

Study Guide

Read Kraig's *Modern Magick.*

Read Rowe's "Essential Skills of Magick."

Practice the LBRP daily for at least six months until you have the hang of it: see the standard texts (*Modern Magick, The Golden Dawn,* etc.) for more details on how Hermetic magic is typically learned.

Consider yourself a student of this tradition also.

After the LBRP seems to be fluid, natural and powerful, move up to the LBRH. For some people that may take only a few weeks. Do the LBRH at least three times a week, but be careful of the "it blew me on my ass" factor.

If it's knocking you about too much, either moderate the frequency of your practice, or step back to the LBRP for a bit.

These rituals are violently powerful when done with that intent and force.

After a solid month of doing the LBRH daily, start to experiment with the ABRH7. Try it once, wait a week; if nothing bad has happened, try it again. You may not be aware of much as the ritual is somewhat "over the top of the head." Or it may be very dramatic. Your Milage Varies.

In short, study to become at least a competent, and preferably excellent, ritual magician in the Western Magical Tradition. Their technology works very well, is time tested, and is an important part of being able to operate as a magical being in America, which is our goal.

The Second Triad—Opening the Nath Circle

First Practice: Invoking the Nath Circle of Kali

The Nath Circle of Kali is the first of three levels of "opening" Nathspace. In the same way that each of the pentagram, hexagram and heptagram rituals opens increasingly deep levels of the Hermetic/Angelic space, each of the Nath rituals opens a deeper level of the Nath reality. It is important to remember to always open with the Angelic rituals to create a box inside which the Nath ritual energy can be contained: even the energy which forms the boundary of the Nath circle is enough to stimulate an immune response!

Opening the Nath Circle of Kali is disturbingly simple. Draw an equilateral triangle in the air at shoulder height, point down, around three feet on a side, starting at the bottom point. Then trace upwards from the bottom point of the triangle about halfway up. This design—the triangle with the line—is representative of the Yoni of the Goddess. See light pour forth.

Then, touch the line and draw a line of light from the upper right corner of the triangle in a circle around you and your group, finishing at the upper left corner. As you draw the line, chant "Om Kali Om Kali Om Kali."

Second Practice: Invoking Shiva, Consciousness Within

The Goddess represents everything other than awareness: all phenomena, all matter, all energy. The polarization between Shiva-consciousness and Shakti-everything can be increased, making it easier to see that you are pure consciousness embedded in pure energy.

To invoke Shiva sit in the center of the Kali Circle in lotus position, or at least cross legged, and visualize yourself as Shiva, lord of Yoga, king of Yogis. Visualize a beam of light cascading down from the third eye of the Cosmic Lord of Yoga at Mount Kaliash and entering the Nath Circle through the Yoni of the Circle and penetrating your own third eye, revealing the Shiva consciousness within.

Third Practice: Unification of Shiva and Shakti

With the Nath Circle of Kali open, and all participants having made identification with Shiva (even women should identify with Shiva in his male form at the opening) it is possible to begin to experiment with gender as a symbol of matter and consciousness: male symbolizing awareness, and female symbolizing the universe.

To start, let those who wish to represent the female move to the Yoni of the Goddess and manifest in their most powerfully female forms. Then spread out to the edge of the circle, or circumnambulate. Those representing Shiva, maleness as a symbol of awareness, should remain in the center of the circle. The first polarity is that of seeing and being seen: those in the center should attempt to be without form or attributed, pure desireless awareness, while those at the edge of the circle should attempt to be pure energy, pure desire, pure potentiality.

The extreme changes of consciousness which this practice can produce are to be taken as indicators of the true nature of all beings, rather than insight into the particular nature of a given individual. Anybody who mis-identifies with one extreme or the other, mistakenly thinking "I am Shiva" or "I am Shakti" has misunderstood in the same way that a scientist would if they claimed "I am Water" or "I am Carbon." We are constructed of both Shiva-awareness and Shakti-phenomena and contain both properties.

These basic polarities should become well-established in the space, and in the individuals present, before moving to the next state.

To proceed, let those acting as Shiva rise and move towards the Goddess Center of the Circle. This operation is quite tricky at first because, although the material movements required are simple and obvious, the energetic and magical effects those actions produce are subtle. Here is the motion: those in the center of the circle move towards the edge of the circle, retaining Shiva-awareness as they go. Those at the edge of the circle move to the center, retaining Shakti-energy as they go. The result is the inversion of the polarities in the space; now Shiva-awareness is at the edge, and Shakti-phenomena is at the center. This state of reversed-polarities should not be held for more than a few minutes (at most) before proceeding: it is a transitional-state only.

The stable working form of this space is stabilized when the Shivas and the Shaktis all gather in the center of the space again, unifying the Shiva and Shakti consciousness by merging together into a group mind awareness of unity. The intense energy of the deep opening of magical space, followed by the polarization into consciousness and energy, inversion of the space and reunification in the center, has many parallels to alchemy and other forms of tantra, but some qualities all of its own. Once energy has equilibrated between those manifesting as Shiva and those manifesting as Shakti (holding hands in a small huddle and Oming can help!) the entire group should move into a profound bliss state in which male and female properties can be manifested at will by those of either biological gender, and profound openness and love are found. This state should be understood to be as real-and-unreal as drug insights: do not assume the person you see clearly as an incarnated goddess now is one outside of this magical space, or that you yourself are anything other than who you are in the ordinary world when you return to it. These spaces show us what potentials lie within us, the deep well of being which we could potentially draw from in our lives, but until we have manifested those realities outside of extremely intense ritual spaces, they are only potentials. To assume or expect to be able to maintain these states of awareness in your ordinary life without years of spiritual practices is exactly the same mistake as thinking that because you can breathe air, you should be able to breathe water: magical reality of the kind opened in these spaces is as different from ordinary reality as that metaphor suggests.

Study Guide

You should build up to the unification of Shiva and Shakti in a group context a little bit at a time. Firstly, work through these rituals on your own, walking around in the space, playing both or all parts. Work on your own gender integration. Then perhaps try the space out with a single partner, or two other people, gently understanding how the dynamics of these altered realities are affected by the mix of people you are working with, the size of the group, and many other factors: phase of the moon, time of day, physical state and condition of the participants, and so on.

In group practice, expect rocky comedowns for the first few cycles, until people begin to loosen their attachment to ecstatic states of consciousness. It can be very hard to go from these ecstatic states of insight back into the regular world. Finally, if you are having trouble generating the juice to get these rituals working, each step can be charged further by extensive use of mantras and other traditional ritual energy-gathering techniques: "Om

Kali," "Om Namah Shivaya" and so on can be chanted before, during and after each step.

The Third Triad—God and What Is

First Practice: Astrological Meditation

Inside of the unified space, energy is usually intensified to the point where exercises like Nath Sitting, while extremely effective, are not necessarily the *most* effective use of the space. The following approach to meditation is wholly ineffective except in the hands of very advanced practitioners in ordinary space, but in an open ritual field of the type described above, even those with only a few months of practice in the regular state of awareness may be able to shift a lot of ignorance very quickly.

First start by preparing a meditation seat. This seat should be a piece of cloth about four feet square inscribed with a copy of your birth chart. When in meditation, you sit in the middle of this chart, initially facing your Natal Sun. The precise orientation of the chart is unimportant, although you may wish to experiment with aligning the chart relative to various current astrological conditions.

The purpose of this chart is to reveal to you the precise shape and form of the parts of your energy body—your aura—which encode your natal astrological imprinting. Here is the procedure for basic astrological meditation.

1. Sit in the circle facing your natal sun.

2. Go around charging each one of the astrological signs, natal sun sign first. (Each sign is charged with the energy of that sign, of course.)

3. Go around charging each of the astrological houses: first house with Aries, second house with Taurus and so on.

4. Go around charging each of the planets—Sun first, then Mercury, Venus, Mars and so on.

5. This is a learned knack: interlock the imprints present in your energy body with the charged energies on the meditation seat. This can take a few hours of practice before you feel the "click," or longer for some people. When it happens, you will feel the symbols and energies represented on the cloth as if they are parts of your body like your hands or feet.

6. Feel for blank spots, blocks, tensions, interrelationships and all other phenomena, bringing your consciousness to every part of your astrological bodies.

This process is vital because it helps you to disidentify your self and its traits from your astrological imprinting. Without some approach to this disidentification, it is easy to go through life thinking "I'm an aggressive person!" because you have, say, Mars conjunct your Sun and Pluto in Aries. With that awareness, you can disidentify that energetic trait from your self and come to regard it as an aspect of your body, like having red hair or long legs.

Be careful with changing your astrological imprinting. Although it seems fairly easy to do, beware of unexpected side effects.

Second Practice: Burning Karma

Again, this practice is primarily a knack practice. Once you have it you will never forget it, but until you have the experience, it can seem completely opaque. I will try as best as I can to explain.

Fundamentally, karma is burned by awareness. A direct, clear insight into a pattern or a stuck, buried emotion will often clear them, and this is a simple form of burning one level of karma. Often a cyclical behavior (say, brief relationships which end over suspicions of infidelity) can be cleared by re-experiencing the underlying emotions (betrayal of trust) and identifying the imprint which is being replayed (betrayal of trust by an earlier partner).

Burning karma in this magical space can be approached in a yet-more-direct sense: one can directly access and claim the energy at a chakratic level and pull it up the central vertical axis of the body into the crown chakra where it is consumed into nothing by your own potential for enlightened awareness.

For example, in the above example, the energy driving the pattern might be stuck in the second, third and fourth chakras, like a black wire running through each chakra, with a tied knot in the fourth chakra. One would feel the energy phenomena clearly, feeling the pain and stuckness, then visualize taking hold of the wire and pulling it up into the seventh chakra through the clear light of the open spinal channel. Once in the clear light of the spinal channel, the energy form can be moved safely to the crown chakra (which should, of course, be opened before beginning this exercise!) and consumed into nothingness.

This meditation uses the chakras as a metaphor for a much more profound, but autonomic, process: the causal body clearing out the deep imprints it can carry using the physical body as a laboratory bench to work on these processes.

This practice should be approached cautiously, as it can cause disorienting changes in your personal identity.

Third Practice: Invoking the Guru

The inner Guru may or may not be a personal experience of an external entity. Some writers and teachers suggest it is a reflection of our own inner divinity, and others that the Guru is an external entity. My own feeling is that the Guru is an external entity which one accesses through one's own inner divinity, reflecting that even God is, in some sense, guided by God. This truth can be seen in the various Indian folk tales in which divine beings still have Guru-type relationships with other divine beings, for example the relationship between Ganesh and Shiva.

Invocation of the Guru has roughly the same relationship to the New Naths as "Knowledge and Conversation of the Holy Guardian Angel" has to conventional Western Esoteric Tradition practitioners, although the process and theological implications may, in practice, be entirely different. The Guru may or may not be an aspect of the soul and could, in fact, represent an external being with quite clear views and opinions. Furthermore, the Guru may turn out to be an astral aspect of a god, a living being, perhaps even a human teacher.

In short, invoking the Guru is no minor business: you should *want* to be involved in a guru-disciple relationship, even in your own head, before you try this.

1. Collect a set of Guru and/or God images: living teachers, saints, traditional and untraditional god images may all be suitable, but filter carefully for your own taste.

2. Look for commonalities in the eyes or energy of these teacher images: can you see a single light shining forth on each one? This is the Guru we seek to invoke.

3. Take a picture of yourself, and surround it by the Guru images you have the clearest relationship with, the ones you have less doubt about. Imagine the light you see in their eyes spreading into your own eyes, seeing yourself as a future-Guru. This represents the potential success of the Guru in enlightening you! It is a vision of a potential future state.

4. Meditate on the wish to be enlightened and the wish to enter the stream or process or relationship or phase of life/being which will bring you to that state. Feel the desire to understand what life is, who you truly are, and to have all knowledge revealed to you (or however you conceptualize the enlightened condition).

5. Repeat for the relationship with a physical teacher: feel your desire (or aversion!) for a physical guru-disciple relationship. Understand your preconceptions about this state of being, and where they fit into your life.

6. If this process reveals no "show stoppers"—reasons that you reject the Guru paradigm, personal issues which would make having a Guru intolerable or other issues, go ahead and broadcast the desire that the universe (or God) bring you a Guru experience.

This is a serious business: it makes the most intense love spell look lightweight in its implications. Be aware that this ritual should change your life now and in the future, possibly putting you in contact with a being you could form an eternal bond with. This ritual represents the final teaching of the *Eternalicious* text. Success! *[See the "Some Science Experiments to Try at Home" section for an appended ritual, the Macroscope.]*

GORAKSHNATH & SITANATH DISCUSS THE NATURE OF LIFE

This text is drawn from a much longer, partially channeled dialog between two Naths and Goraknath.

Shivanath. What I'm wondering is if the asskicking in any way, shape or form correlates to expanded consciousness or enlightenment or if it's more to do with equipping people to make changes in manifest reality by spiritual means, purification to wield power versus purification to get out of this mess. Could Ammachi just zap somebody: "You, you'll become happy now. You'll stay happy. You'll untangle your karmas and become enlightened, but every step will be pleasant and joyful." She's God so I have to assume the answer is Yes. It would seem easier that way...

Sitanath. That doesn't seem especially likely.... you make it sound like She'd be putting someone under a spell.....or the reverse.

Shivanath. "Reversal of reality is the job of Maya, reversal of the reversal is the job of the Guru." – Ganesh Baba. I'm literally asking, if (as we know) she can take a little pot of jam and make it feed 500, why doesn't she just immediately transform all of her devotees' karmas or instantly free them from all illusion? Clearly there's some kind of constraint: it doesn't seem to work, or ever to have worked that way. But, whatever that constraint is, it's becoming important.

Sitanath. She's said so many times that there are some karmas that can be taken away, some that can be partially mitigated, and some that we just have to endure.

Shivanath. In your ordinary life or mine, if something good we want can't happen, there's a limit somewhere. We don't have the money, or the right training, or the class is on the wrong side of town on the wrong night, or they just sold the last one and it's backordered. Our ability to get what we want is limited by circumstances. Amma or Goraknath's current form's desire for people to be happy clearly isn't limited by those kinds of constraints. Even though we're spared enormous trouble, we're not spared all trouble, yet it seems that's what they'd want, doesn't it? It seems like here's some kind of paradox, a more evolved version of "Can God make an object so heavy God can't lift it?" It sounds like a shallow question, and it is. But after a few years of serious work it is an important shallow question! What's the limit on divine action? Is it free will? Is it that we're only seeing a tiny snip of time, so they're doing what's best over eternity and that turns out to be a lot of hard work now, and a lot of cool stuff much, much later—either decades or lifetimes?

Sitanath. Sometimes it seems like our own readiness and capacity to receive it.

Shivanath. That always seems like the limit—but then, why don't they just magically redefine us to be more ready, like redefining the pot of jam? If my "identity" is limiting how much they can help me, or whatever, I'm absolutely willing to have whatever that bottleneck is cleared.

Sitanath. I wonder also about what we're supposed to do in the world? If that kind of magic in one place might detract in some other way.

Shivanath. There's no "opposition"—no counterforce—that can stand up to the Divine Will. Yet change seems slow and difficult.

Sitanath. Have you tried asking Goraknath's current form about this one?

Shivanath. God no. Do I look crazy?

Sitanath. [Grin.] Yes.

Shivanath. OK, no, let's give it a shot...?

[Shivanath begins to meditate and make psychic contact with Goraknath.]

Shivanath. Oi. He says that the creation is, in certain places in the universe, essentially out of control meaning, literally, that it cannot be controlled in total, even by him. It could be erased or broken but, short of that, it can only be tweaked and redefined.

Goraknath. "Even divine beings step into such tar pits gracefully."

Sitanath. [Grin.]

Shivanath. There's some sort of notion of interwoven complexity like you can darn holes in a blanket but you can't just pull out the red threads and replace them with green ones, or the Gordian Knot. It's Pizza Hut!

Sitanath. ?!?

Shivanath. There might be planets a little like this one all over the galaxy. But none of them have the particularity of Pizza Hut—the sea of forces which produce it—cheap plastic—crass commercialism—garlic—the Italian-American cultural context. It's attachment. The reason they don't simply evacuate the human population of the planet and redistribute them to sane planets which got over war aeons ago is that there are things here which people want, which are actually amazing experiences, but which people can't get anywhere else. So the trick, he's telling me, is to try and fix the horribly broken stuff, without killing Pizza Hut, or Burning Man, or the Sistine Chapel. If He or Amma generated the thought of "all people eat healthy food and lose their taste for unhealthy food" they could make it work, but it would be like trying to bleach the blue out of a blanket. Earth without cheesecake wouldn't quite be Earth. It's like art restoration and what I'm asking is basically "why don't we just paint over that and put up a nice NEW mural?" Yes, it'd be faster and easier but it's not the point.

Sitanath. Exactly. Do you have a sense of what is the point?

Shivanath. The point seems to be that there are things which make Earth very special but they're embedded in a lot of crap and search-and-replace style miracle fixes tend to horribly mar the good stuff or....

Goraknath. "Decontexualize it."

Sitanath. Why is the context important?

Shivanath. Michaelangelo's David wouldn't be what it is if it had been produced by a computer-controlled lathe. Part of what makes it what it is is that it was produced by raw brute consciousness. The miracle is that it was done by a spirit and hands.

Goraknath. "Not the object, but the process. You like the David, don't you? But would you want to be in a place where any school kid can produce one by pure thought? What makes it special is that it was done here, where it is hard. the object itself is nothing, a rock. But Michaelangelo's consciousness is everything, a jewel cutting against self-chosen limits."

Sitanath. Though [devil's advocate]... if everyone/thing is enlightened/ realized/God... why does that matter?

Shivanath. Art. People like looking at the pretty planets. Make some worlds. Make some beings to enjoy them. SimGod. That's textbook Vedic Hinduism right there, just updated with modern metaphors.

Sitanath. So, even if we're all enlightened, the *lila* continues...

Shivanath. He's only got one comment on that.

Goraknath. [Shows a picture of Almora Baba here. He appears as an unnaturally gorgeous young man of around twenty-five wearing a turban and a leopard skin jacket. He looks like sex on legs.]

Sitanath. [Laughing hysterically!!!!] HA HA HA HA HA!!!!!! [Grin.] That was so perfect!!!! ... Is there a reason why the lotus is continually sprouting from the navel of Brahman?

Goraknath. "I took that body because people enjoy it. If you were all knowing, all powerful, all seeing, all being, all knowing to the point where all futures were open to you, what would you choose? I chose to have a good time. To party in the creation, to teach yoga to the kids, to play in the sun on beaches as an anonymous surfer, to fly in the clouds as a condor, to grow in the grove as a tree. But many others choose simply not to exist, to fade into the infinite bliss/desire/wholeness of the uncreation, to serve as raw material for other's dreams. The greatest creations induce forgetting. Masks so perfect they hide god completely, leaving only Shiva or Amma. Or Frank or Harry or George. The real reason we do not simply redefine you to be happy is that you already are, and wear this mask because you choose to. It's none of our business."

Sitanath. Ha!

Goraknath. "What do you think it means when we say that 'we are inside every person'—the Atman inside me, or Ammachi, my 'sister,' is exactly as the Atman inside of you or Shivanath. You have exactly the same powers and choices we have but we remained awake outside of the game, while you played it endlessly. Little children will endlessly cry 'almost finished' when they are no such thing, so you only know the game is over when they come inside. We come when we hear crying, great suffering or torture—as a mother knows the difference between a hide-and-seek yell and a dog-bit-John yell. But we don't interfere in the games, and they are all games, apart from a few out-of-control worlds and, even on those, only a few out-of-control corners. God's business is not to patrol God, not to control God, but to simply observe and enjoy. We enjoy the company of our peers and equals greatly, and voyage through the universe for our own pleasure. Those who have finished the game may choose to join us, or play again, or dissolve."

Sitanath. Why does the game arise?

Goraknath. "The game arises out of many, many possible activities for God. Contemplation, meditation, silent pondering of the void, sex, etc. all produce very little form and little illusion of time or space. The Game of Life, this part of reality where there is breeding and life and death and experience, where things matter and beings forget, it is very dense, very hard, very durable. Once it arises, beings are drawn to it because it is so different from the uncreated state or 'seed consciousness'—the awareness of the individuated Atman without a being or a body to experience matter/time through. Many beings look at Life and simply slide straight by it. Others play and play and play and play until Brahman itself reabsorbs the entire playing field. But this is an aesthetic, not a moral preference. No soul is bound here, but the rules of the game strongly suggest that players should complete a round before leaving, for the benefit of the other players. Otherwise positive karmas accumulate in the system, gradually causing the illusion of matter and material being to fade out, as it did at the end of the *Mahabarata* when all parties involved simply swam into a river of light never to return. Mass readiness to exit occurs at great crescendos, but otherwise beings typically wile away their time in very pleasant places, paradise planets of the upper astral realms. Hard matter, like your conception of Earth (which actually contains many planes, of which yours is one of the lower material ones) is like hard drugs. A game for the young and the strong and the brave, with horrific casualties. But how do you stop a brave young girl from doing methamphetamines in a biker bar?"

Sitanath. !!!

Goraknath. "How can you deny the Soul the *Easy Rider* experience if it wishes to see the facet of the jewel represented by a physical body, a lot of speed and a large motorbike? The Atman is indestructible and all else is a child's crayon drawings for its own amusement. Watch children play and discover how much fun their experiences of monsters are. So comes war, and soldiers, and dragons and other entities—games of Hide and Seek where a player becomes Smaug for the other players' Hobbits."

Shivanath. (Yes, he's using metaphors easy to find in my brain. Sorry.)

Goraknath. "There is no sense of non-equal in the creation as we understand it, any more than an actor's shoe size is changed by the roles they have played on the screen. The Atman is unaffected by the experiences of this great game."

Goraknath. "'But it sucks,' you say! 'Argh, ow, stop eating my leg!'"

Goraknath. "But there is no leg. From an outsider's perspective it seems as curious and quaint as somebody sitting over a computer game sobbing for the fate of their space invader. 'You guys are nuts' is basically how we view it."

Sitanath. Do we know before we enter that we'll forget who we are? and is the forgetting of importance to sustain the game? Is there a way to truly remember who we are and stay in the game?

Goraknath. "Those of us who re-enter the creation from time to time to perform housekeeping experiences for the other players are gods. Outside and above karma, beyond the system. But we do not create and destroy at will because we are here to improve the game, not to end it. Players who are done can leave at any time, and exits are clearly marked—anybody, at any time, can choose incarnation on a series of planets which will rapidly result in their reaching "enlightenment"—the full experience of Atman is Brahman—experiences for the other players are Gods. Outside and above karma, beyond the system. But we do not create and destroy at will because we are here to improve the game, not to end it. Players who are done can leave at any time, and exits are clearly marked—anybody, at any time, can choose incarnation on a series of planets which will rapidly result in their reaching "enlightenment"—the full experience of Atman is Brahman. Yukteswaraji, for example, has an open offer to the entire Earth which is still extant, and available to any who have heard of his disciple Yogananda's book. In short—yes, you yourself have entered the game, partially (partially!!!) forgotten your true nature, in the manner of a mother playing along with her children so as not to disturb them so much as she retrieves chocolate-cake-covered plates from their play area. By pretending to be a cowboy or an indian as she passes through, their games are undisturbed apart from necessary maintenance functions. This is the nature of most of the Divine Servants—souls who have realized Atman, but not Atman=Brahman. To realize Atman is to know you are God, immortal, indestructible. To realize Brahman is to know that all is God. To know Atman=Brahman is to realize that you are alone in a perfect universe, a point of light reflected back in infinite mirrors."

Sitanath. Why do we cling to the illusion when we know it's not real?

Goraknath. "Because it is better than 'reality'. Reality is limitless potential. We realize parts of that potential to create 'Maya'. There is no such thing as salt or sweet or hard. Until I made it, there was no yoga. Are paints more beautiful tidy in their tubes? Or as an image of God?"

Sitanath. How do we get to Atman=Brahman?

Goraknath. "Even the smallest being makes a *murti* of its life. How is not the relevant question—only why?"

Goraknath. "Are you done with this game? As a player, yes. But as a helper... as an assistant to the Divine Mother, as a shadow of her power and form, have you done all you came to do? Furthermore, is there no joy or triumph left in your soul? One day, do you want to be the one in the chair, radiating life to a million beings because it gives you joy? Or do you want to go home now?"

Goraknath. "'This world sucks.'"

Goraknath. "'Does not!'"

Goraknath. "'Does too!'"

Goraknath. "'Well, would it suck if there was enough to eat, peace everywhere and an end to all disease?'"

Goraknath. "'Hell no! That would rock!'"

Goraknath. "We really have conversations like these at the other level. When we feel like it, it is our pleasure to come to worlds like this and hand out gifts. Always mindful of the planetary balance, and the right of beings to enjoy the creation as they wish, even the stupid and ugly ones. Nobody has to be prey more than once. Once, you may have to do it simply so that you have had the experience and 'know' rather than 'guessing' what it is like. But after that, the Internal Atman can guide the soul in perfect safety. The point of the game is that people get the experiences they want. The 'rules of the game' are agreements between beings about things like money, sex, power, keeping score, which siddhis are manifestable on which planes and so on. Those rules are immutable and incontestable by democratic assent."

Goraknath. "This is a paradise world. Do not come here and make war."

Goraknath. "So the bodies on that world will literally not sustain the war energy. The binding agreements of incarnation prevent it. Such worlds are neither hard to find nor to enter. There are 'elitist swine' worlds where centuries of art and training are required to enter: 'Nobody may come into this theater who has not memorized Beethoven's entire works and can perform them to orchestral concert standards on any instrument in an 1850s orchestra.' But who wants to play that game, other than the kind of people who choose it? Life is the same on all levels, the little quirks of a personality can, in the wider scheme of things, collect with many similar souls to create almost any kind of rarified or specialized experiences. The 'Material Earth World' you are kind of in right now is a 'bad place'—a shithole corner in bad need of fixing. You are part of a work crew. I and Amma and other beings are 'Foremen' who direct the labor to turn it from a horror into a pleasant garden. It will take 200 years, after which you may do as you please here. The journey will not be easy, but the time is short and the tasks manageable. A few lifetimes of effort for endless centuries of margaritas and sunshine. Understand this. Gods enjoy the same pleasures as mortals. They do not labor, they do not argue, they fight for fun. The create offspring as art, rather than because their bodies drive them to it, and they do not wish ill on any being. The 'Burning Man' aesthetic of 'nothing is forbidden, but you could make us happier by doing that somewhere else' is very close to how the universe works. Enlightenment is a pipe dream of mortals. It exists but is not what almost anybody wants. Those who do want it proceed smoothly and directly on the indicated paths. But there are games around this 'Absolute Goal'. These games are lotteries. An Improbably Huge Good Karma is not the same as enlightenment. Enlightenment is simply the awareness of yourself as the Atman. All else is decided past that level and need concern nobody who has not attained that awareness. Atman awareness is not hard to master. But you must understand that you have mastered it endless times and the process is as natural to you as breathing. Lose the awareness, step into the games of the world, pick up the dishes from the birthday party for your children, slip into the kitchen, restore the Atman awareness, do the dishes. Then go out and watch the kids play from the next room, enjoying the pleasure you have enabled. A perfect family life is much of the Gods' own pleasure. Look at Ganesh or the other Children of the Gods. This is what we do for fun. Even the child must be understood to be two things: a body, which you create and maintain, and a soul which is God. The body of the child is art. It is the creation of a very flexible beautiful old-designed classical murti: Human Being. Can you open to create without fear at a canvas?"

SACRED DISCO: Saint Maurice Gibb and His Hymns to Lalita

Do What Thou Wilt Shall Be The Whole of the Law.

Cori Josias hints at his own initiation into the Tantric Mysteries in the disco classic "The Hills of Katmandu":

"The Hills of Kathmandu"

We can fly above the sky
in Katmandu
Peace of mind
we're gonna find in Katmandu

Peace of mind, also called "samarasa" or "one taste" or "the peace that surpasseth all understanding." Mystical peace!

Smoke-scented breeze fills the trees
and you drift away.
Slowly downstream
in a dream that goes on and on
on forever!

Compare with "The Inner Light" by the Beatles:

Turn off your mind, relax and float downstream
It is not dying

Both describe floating downstream in the eternal dream of life.

We do not know who initiated Mr. Josias, but by the time of this song the party is clearly over: His band name, "Tantra" is too above-board and open at that time to have concealed anything of note. By the time of this song, the early 1980s, Disco's tantric roots are out in the open and the show is over. We must go back, earlier in time, to discover the true masters of the tantric art of disco.

Saint Maurice Gibb, Guru of the Bee Gees, Saint of Disco and therefore the Paramguru of House Music, was most likely initiated into tantric practices in 1967, which was an auspicious year all around. Maurice had travelled with his brothers seeking spiritual wisdom and enlightenment from the masters of the East and West, visiting India, the Middle East and Sacred Cairo in a single voyage. Barry Gibb recalls the trip in a *Mojo* magazine interview:

"Despite the fact that their thirteenth single, 'Spicks and Specks,' was bulleting up the local charts, and despite having heard not one word from Epstein, the Bee Gees sailed for England on January 3, 1967.

"'We stopped off in India, the Middle East, Cairo, the Pyramids,' says Barry. 'And the things we discovered in back street bazaars!! You could buy bottles of Dexedrine, every kind of stimulant, no questions asked. We were on a ship, but we flew all the way.'"

("The Rogue Gene" by Johnny Black, *Mojo*, June 2001.)

Of course, Barry (who was not initiated until much later) was not going to reveal the real reason for his brother and Guru's journey in *Mojo*, but I think the itinerary makes Maurice's intentions quite clear: a magical passage to the centers of the Tantric and Hermetic magical worlds, India and Egypt. We can only guess at his linage, and perhaps this will become the topic for a future paper. Secretly carrying the secret wisdom secretly gathered from the secret masters on his very low profile journey, Saint Maurice Gibb, now known secretly as Swayambhunath Mahadevadas, begins the Great Work of disseminating the teachings to all of us through his music, and in the process lays the foundation for much of our own mystical progress. Thanks, Saint Maurice. Rather than dwelling further on the mundane biographical details of this tantric saint, let us look at the fruits and holy offerings of this great man: let us appreciate his songs, these holy hymns of the Divine Passage, the mystical journey of a man through the Womb of Creation into Eternal Love and Bliss in the vision of the Goddess Lalita, the Divine Mother in the form of the Playful Mother, playing hide-and-seek with her Eternal Children. When Lalita is seen clearly, all the phenomena of life are perceived as the joyful game between the Mother and the Child, in joy, bliss and peace. We will trace the journey of Saint Maurice by a close reading of four songs which reveal his mystical progress.

Let us begin with the first track, an "innocent tale of lust" to an untrained eye. I will be interspersing hints as to what is actually going on between the lines for those who have not practiced the art of reading the Twilight Language of the Tantric World by reading the works of Mahendranath or the Bauls of Bengal.

The first song describes Maurice's encounter with his Guru. It also gives us some notion of the nature of the student/teacher relationship, and the spiritual powers of this august and unknown personage!

"The Woman In You"—Meeting the Guru

The woman in you brings out
the man in me
It's the woman in you

The casual assumption here, of course, is that "the woman in you" is actually referring to a woman. This is naïve: why would the Woman in an actual woman seem so remarkable as to be remarked on twice? Rather, it is the female aspect of the (male) guru manifesting which is so remarkable.

And the finer parts of your anatomy

"Finer," in this case, referring to "less material"—this is a reference to the subtle body of the guru and its enlightening power. This subtle body is often female if the guru is male. See how this simple "song of lust" conceals the spiritual reality of a Guru who is both male and female and has mastered the subtle bodies. This is the Twilight Language at its finest.

But baby sharper than a knife
help me to know you
Show me the night to satisfy
A sinner with the flash of an eye
There'll never be another me

What more beautiful expression of the tantric insight is possible?

I never knew love could wind me up
I don't do my stuff
'Til you go walkin' by
And maybe old enough to try
I never knew anyone in between
The devil and the angel

"My adepts stand upright; their head above the heavens, their feet below the hells."
– *Liber Tzaddi vel Hamus Hermeticus*, via Aleister Crowley

All in one and maybe old

"ALL IN ONE"!!! The Guru is Everything in One Being.

Enough that I can ride
Your love let me burn
Let me slide down to your soul

!

You can pull me in
You can push me out
But your baby needs love
Somebody to hold

Maurice feels like a child next to the Guru, somebody who needs shelter and protection. The Guru creates and withdraws distance between them.

Show me what to do

"TEACH ME GURUDEV!"

The woman in you brings out
the man in me
It's the woman in you
And the finer parts of your anatomy
But baby, stronger than the wind burn
In the fire out of the night
I'll teach you how to tremble
If you give me the night

"Fire" meaning Sacred Dhuni. Tremble refers to Kriyas, purifying physical trembling and vibration often found in advanced yoga and meditation. These lines constitute an invitation to initiation into advanced yogas, in the night, sitting by the sacred fire. "Give me the night and I'll teach you Kriya."

There'll never be enough to me
I never knew I could find the best
But searchin' out the rest there
Is no doubt and maybe we can
Sweat it out

A true compliment to his Guru, "the best without a doubt!"

I never knew we could find
A way this crazy situation
Over me and we forget about
The world outside

Pratyahara—the fifth step of Yoga, withdrawal of the senses as we "forget about the world outside" and focus on the soul within.

My love in your eyes
There's no world
There is no time

Saint Maurice is recording and announcing his Samadhi, his fusion with the god within. This is marked by the end of the subjective experience of time, leaving him marooned in eternity.

You can hold me in

You can throw me down
But your baby needs love
Somebody to hold
Show me what to do
The woman in you brings out
The man in me
It's the woman in you
And the finer parts of your anatomy

Saint Maurice has reached the first level: he has understood that there is no world and no time, that the Guru is real, that Male and Female are only aspects of the soul and can be manifested at will, and that the Guru uses this subtle body's powers to teach. Maurice has made good progress on the Path! But now here he is: an indestructible soul in an impure and contaminated human body, struggling to integrate the truth that there is no death, that he is stuck in Eternal Life incarnating over and over again. What to do? What to do? Let us examine the next step!

"Stayin' Alive"—The Eternal Life of the Soul

Well, you can tell by the way I use my walk
I'm a woman's man: no time to talk

Clearly a reference, albeit heavily veiled, to male/female integration: the original may well have read: "You can tell by the way I use my walk I'm a Woman/Man, no time for talk"—only time for action!

Music loud and women warm
I've been kicked around
Since I was born.

The path of the tantric mystic is often a hard one, if leavened with joy and great parties.

And now it's all right. It's OK.
And you may look the other way.

Often we are beneath notice... or above it!

We can try to understand

The New York Times' *effect on man.*

???

Whether you're a brother or whether you're a mother,
You're stayin' alive, stayin' alive.
Feel the city breakin' and everybody shakin',
And we're stayin' alive, stayin' alive.
Ah, ha, ha, ha, stayin' alive, stayin' alive.
Ah, ha, ha, ha, stayin' alive.

Everybody, brothers or mothers, male or female alike, is going to live forever at the Soul level. We are all staying alive for eternity, whether we know it or not! In the next verse the tofu of the issue is presented: Samarasa presented for the first time in verse to the broadest Western audience possible. Samarasa means "equanimity" or "one taste," indicating that all phenomena, good or bad, are interpreted the same way: as life. This produces a very flat, even state of awareness which can be unpleasant at first.

Well now, I get low and I get high,
and if I can't get either, I really try.
Striving for the extremes of human experience.
Got the wings of heaven on my shoes.
I'm a dancin' man and I just can't lose.

Refers to the assumption of the God Form of Mercury or Hermes, indicating that Saint Maurice has not dropped his Hermetic magical practices at this point in his career.

You know it's all right. It's OK.
I'll live to see another day.

Because of the continuity of the soul, present events, no matter how bad, can be faced bravely. Taking the fear of death out of human experience begins the path of return.

We can try to understand
the New York Times' *effect on man.*

???

Whether you're a brother or whether you're a mother,
You're stayin' alive, stayin' alive.

"Stayin' Alive" is a universal experience. We are all eternal.

Feel the city breakin' and everybody shakin',
And we're stayin' alive, stayin' alive.
Ah, ha, ha, ha, stayin' alive, stayin' alive.
Ah, ha, ha, ha, stayin' alive.
Life goin' nowhere. Somebody help me.
Somebody help me, yeah.
Life goin' nowhere. Somebody help me.
Somebody help me, yeah. Stayin' alive.

A profound plea directed at anybody who may be able to take this mystic higher than his position of being in a state where nothing seems good or bad leading to the sensation of suspension in nothingness and aimlessness: we will see the Goddess Hymns as attempts to escape from this bland holding pattern! On the prayer, the request for divine aid, please compare Ganesh Baba's Ganeshian Prayer: "Oh God, if there is a God, please help me, if you can help me!" Faith is not an article of faith for tantrists.

Well, you can tell by the way I use my walk,
I'm a woman's man: no time to talk.
Music loud and women warm,
I've been kicked around since I was born.
And now it's all right. It's OK.
And you may look the other way.
We can try to understand
the New York Times' *effect on man.*

???

Whether you're a brother or whether you're a mother,
You're stayin' alive, stayin' alive.
Feel the city breakin' and everybody shakin',
And we're stayin' alive, stayin' alive.
Ah, ha, ha, ha, stayin' alive, stayin' alive.
Ah, ha, ha, ha, stayin' alive.
Life goin' nowhere. Somebody help me.

Somebody help me, yeah.
Life goin' nowhere. Somebody help me, yeah.
I'm stayin' alive.

Life is eternal. Saint Maurice knows that he will be here for a long, long time in whatever condition of consciousness he exists in. Help is required for one marooned in eternity! Saint Maurice knows what to do; he must appeal to the Divine Mother, the Creatrix of the Universe, God Herself, the Highest and the Lowest, the Virgin and the Whore, the Scorned and the Sacred: BABALON, or as we much prefer, Lalita. The difference between BABALON and Lalita is much the difference between a twelve-year-old Catholic school boy's fantasy lover, and that of a mature saint: BABALON represents the shadow of the Virgin Mary, where Lalita represents the absolute wholeness of the Universal Creator. Saint Maurice sings to the Divine Mother to bring her to his aid!

"More Than a Woman"—On Meeting the Goddess Lalita

Oh, girl I've known you very well
I've seen you growing every day,

Only from the perspective of one marooned in eternity can the Divine Mother begin to be appreciated. Although Saint Maurice's understanding has grows by degrees, as he has "seen Her growing every day" he has never really appreciated what he has seen.

I've never really looked before
But now you take my breath away.

Now the vision has unfolded and, indeed, the vision of Lalita is breathtaking. The "breathless state" is referred to Swami Yogananda in *Autobiography of a Yogi* and identified with Nirvikalpa Samadhi, a meditation in which the body becomes rigid like stone and breathing ceases as the soul voyages in divine bliss. Saint Maurice has penetrated into the deepest mystery and is honored with the fullest vision of the Divine!

Suddenly you're in my life,
Part of everything I do.

"He Has Attained"—he is with the Goddess, seeing all phenomena as the Divine Mother at all times. 8=3!

You've got me working day and night
Just trying to keep a hold on you.

However, this state still requires constant effort for Saint Maurice to maintain. He still hopes not to slip, therefore has further to go!

Here in your arms I found my paradise,
My only chance for happiness.

How true! Is there abiding happiness other than in the Lap of the Divine Mother? I think not!

And if I lose you now I think I would die.

A common misperception: certainly he would continue to exist as he has experienced the individual indestructibility of his soul, as recorded in "Stayin' Alive."

Oh say you'll always be my baby,
We can make it shine
We can take forever
Just a minute at a time.

Welcome to the New Eternity: not the individual soul lost in the universe, floating in space and time, but the individual soul (Atman) surrounded by Brahman—the creation and the creator falling into eternal love.

More than a woman, more than a woman to me
More than a woman, more than a woman to me.

Lalita is more than a woman, or a man, or any limited being or conception! Although women can express more of her sweetness than any other created material form can, and may indeed take on her attributes for lifetimes at a time, still Lalita is above and beyond all individual created beings, while simultaneously being all individual created beings!

There are stories old and true
People so in love like you and me
And I can see myself
Let history repeat itself!

Saint Maurice wishes to be part of the grand tradition of enlightened saints, in love with the divine, who made their state known in song and story: Mirabai or Kabir or Rumi are truely his forebears!

Reflecting how I feel for you
Thinking about those people then
I know that in a thousand years
I'd fall in love with you again.

Reflecting, that is to say meditating, on his feelings for Lalita, the Goddess, Saint Maurice realizes his future lives. In a thousand years, he will be reborn and live again as a mystic who falls in love with God all over again. The *Yoga Sutras of Patanjali* suggest this siddhi of knowing your future lives is attained by meditation on the throat chakra. Saint Maurice has now passed beyond the desire to take no further rebirths, and into the True State of Enlightened Humanity: a willing submission to the constraints of rebirth not as a sacrifice or an entrapped state, but a game between the Divine Mother and her Divine Children, swimming in and out of the waves of emptiness and bliss, playing in the sun in the eternal shore at the edge of existence and enlightenment. Saint Maurice has lost his attachment and aversion to future birth and future experience and returned home as a child of Her Who Is Everything and Everyone, Lalita!

This is the only way that we should fly
This is the only way to go

All other enlightened conditions may retain attachment and aversion to rebirth or scorch the seeds of the creation in the process of attempting to bake the cake of enlightened awareness.

And if I lose your love
I know I would die!

Oh, silly boy!

Oh say you'll always be my baby,
We can make it shine
We can take forever
Just a minute at a time.

Eternity eternity eternity! To live in the eternal present with the perception of Reality, of the Goddess all around as all-that-is and all- that-is-not... OM!

More than a woman, more than a woman to me
More than a woman, more than a woman to me

She is everything, all space, all time, all consciousness, all matter, conscious, aware and playful, overseeing the world with indescribable tenderness. Her love creates all phenomena, but only a true vision of her reveals why suffering appears to exist, why so many seem to live in bondage (not the good kind either.) We witness a modern tantric saint's union with the divine mother in her form as Lalita, voyaging endlessly through creation with his beloved, birth after birth. How far can this go? Let us turn to the next song to find out!

"How Deep is Your Love?"—The Final Hymn to Lalita

I know Your eyes in the morning sun
I feel You touch me in the pouring rain
All phenomena are Her, the Goddess

And the moment that You wander far from me
I wanna feel You in my arms again

No longer afraid of death when the goddess is not manifest to him, Saint Maurice simply longs to see her again.

And You come to me on a summer breeze
Keep me warm in Your love and You softly leave

Saint Maurice has become rather unattached even to Her, watching her come and go in his awareness. At peace at last, not detached from the creation, but no longer clinging, even to the Goddess herself!

And it's me You need to show
How deep is Your love?

The gentle chiding indicates great familiarity with this divine personage.

How deep is Your love?
How deep is Your love?

I really need to learn
'Cause we're living in a world of fools
Breaking us down when they all should let us be.

A mystery—why does such an enlightened person still think of the world as full of fools? Why this experience of being "broken down" by the outside world? Does this indicate a subtle duality remaining in Saint Maurice's awareness between the divine mother and her "world of fools?" Is not this "world of fools" also her, her creation and her body?

We belong to You and me!

Self-possession is a fundamental human right: you belong to yourself first, and other people may possess you only in as much as you give yourself to them, perhaps as a gift of love. See *Freedom is a Two-Edged Sword* by Jack Parsons, inventor of solid rocket fuel and lifelong student of Aleister Crowley.

I believe in You.
You know the door to my very soul.
You're the light in my deepest darkest hour.
You're my savior when I fall
And You may not think I care for You
When You know down inside that I really do
And it's me You need to show
How deep is Your love?

What a beautiful hymn!

How deep is Your love
How deep is Your love
I really mean to learn
'Cause we're living in a world of fools
Breaking us down when they all should let us be
We belong to You and me
Na na na na na, na na na na na
na na na na na, nana na na na
na na na na na

From the rhythm and intonation here it appears that a sanskrit mantra was removed from the release version of this song, leaving "na na na..." as a placeholder.

And You come to me on a summer breeze
Keep me warm in Your love
Then You softly leave
And it's me You need to show!
How deep is Your love?
How deep is Your love?
How deep is Your love?
I really mean to learn
'Cos we're living in a world of fools
Breaking us down
When they all should let us be
We belong to You and me
Na na na na na
How deep is Your love
How deep is Your love

And this, dear readers, is the question: Can you love all of it, all phenomena, Gandhi as much as Hitler? Because this is the tantra of the New Age, the New Aeon: for all people to see all phenomena, internal and external, as nothing more and nothing less than the action and the presence of god. This is the Way: no creator and no creation, but rather All Creator and All Creation. Break down the fourth wall between yourSelf and God. We are all equally It, all equally Her, all equally Him. And, by God, She Herself is out there somewhere too, waiting for us to make enough noise for her to come down here and see what the party is...

Love is the Law, Love under Will.

AN INTERVIEW WITH MONICA DECHEN GYALMO

PRINCE CHARMING

One day in the early XIVth century a lone warrior dolphin (pod of one) named Prince Charming, the author of this narrative, whilst offering his amateur massage services to various non-insect-nymphs at the Astral Pulse Island wet bar, after taking one too many sips of goldschlager, suddenly blacked out and awoke floating on a bed of wasabi aioli and papaya-chili sourkraut in a giant conch-shell-shaped potato cheese pierogi at the Wooden Eagle, Hamtramick, Michigan's Polish pleasure palace. He found in his pocket a notebook filled with love poetry, music notation (of an unknown Archaic Eastern Indo-European tablature) naughtynaughtynaughtynaughtynaughty charcoal sketches and a diary detailing sexual experimentation of increasing perversion. I, Prince Charming, had been initiated into the tantrik cult of MONICA DECHEN GYALMO.

Among the great female adepts of Tibetan Tantra, MONICA DECHEN GYALMO is foremost. She is an eighth century Saturnalian princess who became the tantric consort of Tibet's Great Guru Padmasambhavavavavavavavoom. Her exemplary life story describes the ideal path of a yogini (a female practitioner) in so far as it provides a blueprint for every Saturnalian woman who aspires to Buddhahood. She is the first Saturnalian woman to achieve Buddhahood and has had numerous incarnations and emanations in Hamtramick, Tibet and the other Himalayan countries. As a young woman, Tibetan King Trisong Detsen offered her as "present" to his teacher Guru Rinpochemon, a Dharma-offering for his empowernment. From then on she became the main companion (sangyumyum) and pupil of Guru Rinpochemon. She received all of Guru Rinpochemon's teachings. Through her practice she reached the highest realization. Together they hid illegal fireworks all over Tibet and elsewhere. Monica is frequently spotted sporting around town in deified form as the Queen of Great Bliss as a red mambo dancing figure with a damaru (double-sided bongo drum) raised in her right hand and a curved knife held to the ground with her left. It was on one such excursion our UC security strike force was able to corner MONICA DECHEN GYALMO at an ATM and extract this telepathic interview.

Prince Charming: O Monica, splendor of perfect whirlpool, sweeter than either ambrosia #5 or Kern's nectar. I'll get straight to the point: Is doggy-style Tantrik sex? Or when my girlfriend is on her period? What if I fantasize about lady celebrities or sports stars during sex? What is Tantrik sex?

Monica Dechen Gyalmo: First, you must find yourself as a whole being—separate of all worlds but your own. Once you are alone in YOUR place, you can reach out to the contributing body—your sexual partner. Here, in this perfect cerebral union, you can create the 10,000-mile bridge. This bridge is the lasting foundation for lasting sexual ecstasy. It can be traveled for many hours, many days, many months. Even a lifetime. In my experience, this is the essence of the Tantric: the will to last and to endure. It is commune and coitus. Union above union.

Your fantasies about sports stars and celebrities are natural. But if these fantasies break into your Tantric motions, be aware—and beware. For the flowers blooming under your Tantric actions may wilt. Reserve your fantasies for when you are alone. Besides, one's partner can always sense when the other's thoughts are drifting.

Prince Charming: O Monica, the righteous, vigorous, triple-tongue'd phoenix of learningz, whose body is the command: So how did your yoga work begin and where did the Tantric sex figure in that?

Monica Dechen Gyalmo: Yoga called out to me. It was a sun fixed in a constant yellow-gloried sunrise. It was in me since birth. Since birth in me was it, like a curious monkey and a ferocious tiger. Tantric sex is merely an extension of the practice. A long arm made of flowers.

Prince Charming: O Monica, the ever-wakeful, whose word is true: tell me about your Tantrik money purification ceremony.

Monica Dechen Gyalmo: Sometimes my thoughts grow tired of fiscal matters. Money is both filth and purity. When it is acquired (in the tangible form of currency), I neatly fold it into bundles, lay it in the Hantonic Ancient Box, and hoist it to the ceiling. A small, paper-based flame is burned beneath this elevated box for six minutes and thirty seconds. The flame is then choked with an acolyte staff. The box is lowered onto the ashes. Purity comes when the smoke diminishes from the room. It would be wise to send me your money and have it purified. It is, of course, tax deductible.

Prince Charming: O Monika, ornament of nature, the darling of the world, mistrix of the fiery diadems, your initiated name is Swami [untranslatable sigil]. Your first scroll, *Psychosexualized Yogatronixxx*, was published in 1142 B.C. At that time there was very little interest in the spirituality of Hamtramick, although now it's exploding like the plague. Why do you think the popularity of Ashram Mishra Tantra, Kaula Tantra, Samaja Tantra and other physics-based LSD "cult of ecstasy" experiences have grown over the past 4,000 years?

Monica Dechen Gyalmo: Some phenomena simply cannot be explained.

Prince Charming: O Monica, fair of form, victorious, radiant, glorious, eternal, omniscient, world-promoting, merciful, forgiver, loving, mighty, wise, holy: Wow! What's the biggest hurdle that you face, Monica, in your work to visualize the pre-Aryan, Indus Valley deity in the act of sexual union with a human aboriginal consort?

Monica Dechen Gyalmo: You have uttered the sacred word: "Wow!" It is this word that lunges my being headlong, with strength and commitment, into the many faces of adversity. It is such a positive word. I use it sparingly to intensify its significance. Now, in terms of hurdles, they change each day. The universe changes each day. So does our body. And so we face each thing as if it were the first and last to be faced. I visualize nothing unless it is in front of me. This does not answer your question. Nothing will.

Prince Charming: O Monica, here deep in the soft grass under the singing sugarbirds: Are the 666 Hamtramick Srutis parallel to, or intertwined with, the 92 Srutis of traditional Vedic Kaula Tantra?

Monica Dechen Gyalmo: Ah, but the singing sugarbird song is intoxicating. So intoxicating that my focus goes elsewhere. How can I possibly commit to the thought of Royaltane Fixture of Godcrew Nathan and his cronies in the 666 Hamtramck Srutis when there is such beauty to emphasize? The aforementioned clan produces an ugly head. So sick is the thought that I must go elsewhere in thought.

Prince Charming: O Monica, the sorceress and enchantresses of uncontrollable passions: What occupational performance enhancing therapies do you recommend for firefighters? What sort of ritual aroma therapy work would you recommend to an impotent firefighter?

Monica Dechen Gyalmo: Again, you can send me any tax deductible contributions if you are a firefighter and I can perform my services to help with work related injury. As far as impotence, seek the flower of the blossoming lemon tree. Soak this blossom in the milk of a fertile goat on the new moon and repeat the sacred purification chant.

TANTRIC PICNIC

HANS PLOMP

Everywhere around Kathmandu small posters glued on walls invite people who are interested to take part in Sri Bhan's Tantric picnics. Participants will be initiated into the secret love techniques of the Orient. A curious friend of mine has attended one. She tells me: "He has great powers. After we'd talked a few moments, he knew exactly what was wrong with me. Then he pressed a certain spot in my neck with his fingers and I think I left my body. The next thing I knew Mr. Bhan was massaging me and I was crying with happiness." She stops speaking, a dreamy look in her eyes.

"And then what happened?" I encourage her.

"That's when I arrived," says Tom, her friend and traveling companion who's not very happy about it all. "I felt uneasy about this picnic stuff, so I followed her to his house. It turned out to be a private teaching: just him and Elke. At first they were sitting in the back garden, but then they went inside. I decided to hang around and after a while I thought I heard Elke crying. So I rushed in and found her lying on a sofa with the guy bent over her, stroking her. When he noticed me he gave me such a mean glance that I decided to intervene."

"I didn't notice anything mean about him," Elke protests.

"You couldn't see anything because you were crying. Anyway, I picked her up and took her out, as this guy was hissing at me: 'You are abducting my patient during a medical treatment. All her problems are your fault!' He's a dangerous creep, this Mr. Bhan."

"But he does have special powers," Elke insists. There's a fanatical tone to her voice, promising stiff resistance.

I'm sitting in a modest chai shop enjoying an advertisement for tinned milk:

Here I stand, tin of milk in my hand.
No teat to pull, no hay to pitch,
just knock a hole in the son of a bitch.

Tom enters and, chuckling, I read the text out to him. But he won't be cheered.

"Please help me," he says.

"What's the matter?"

"Elke has been seeing that creep again," he says.

"Where is she?"

"In our room. She can hardly walk but she wants me to take her to him."

I accompany him to their hotel. Elke sits in a chair, her face pained, her legs somewhat spread apart.

"The creep applied vaginal acupressure yesterday," Tom explains, "because of her supposed penetration fear."

I have to suppress a smile. This problem needs a serious approach.

"Sri Bhan has pushed a magical pellet up my vagina. When it dissolves my problems will have dissolved with it," Elke says. "I have to see him today for a check-up. These are my own problems and my own body, you know."

"But angel, the guy is taking advantage of you," says Tom.

"Listen who says so," she says, glaring.

It's more complicated than I've realized. I take Tom aside and offer to accompany him to Sri Bhan's place. Sri Bhan is a thin, oily man with golden teeth, well into his forties. Tom tells him the treatment of his wife must be stopped immediately because she's ill. They are returning to Germany as quickly as possible.

"They cannot do anything for her in Germany. It is very dangerous to break off my treatment." In a threatening voice he adds: "I am the only one who can help her."

"Our decision has been made," says Tom.

Suddenly Sri Bhan becomes amiable. "Very well then, you must decide for yourself, of course. Are the two of you married?"

"Not officially, but that's none of your business."

"I see," says Sri Bhan pensively. "When are you planning to leave Kathmandu?"

"Preferably tomorrow."

"In that case I wish you all the best. I'll send someone to the hotel tonight with my bill."

"I'll pay right now," Tom protests.

"No, no, tonight is fine. I have no time to make up the bill right now," says Sri Bhan.

That very afternoon Tom and Elke leave Kathmandu. The next day I hear that an American professor and his wife have been arrested. Coincidentally, they have checked into the room Tom and Elke just left.

Some days later I meet the unfortunate couple in a restaurant. She is a beautiful Japanese woman who doesn't speak much English. The professor indignantly tells his story to whoever will listen: "A couple of hours after we arrived at the hotel the police burst into our room and arrested me for possessing counterfeit dollars. They must have brought those themselves. I've never even seen a counterfeit dollar! We were very lucky that a certain Sri Bhan passed by the police-station. He negotiated our release and explained to me it was all a case of mistaken identity. It seems some criminals had been staying in the room we just rented."

"The notorious Sri Bhan!" I exclaim.

"Do you know him?" the professor asks. "He seems to be a very influential gentleman. He is an initiate of certain secret tantric techniques and has offered to share his knowledge with us."

"I can imagine he did," I say emphatically, glancing at the Japanese beauty. They already seem so enchanted by Sri Bhan that I refrain from further comment.

About a week later I meet the couple again. Like me, they are cycling in the valley and I ride with them a while.

"Have you been to Sri Bhan's tantric picnic yet?" I venture.

"Oh no, that's for beginners," the professor laughs. "I'm a professor, you see, so we were allowed to take part in higher grade rituals."

"What are they?" I inquire.

He hesitates and looks at his wife, who approves with a beaming smile. "Well, Sri Bhan performs special tantric techniques with my wife." In an almost scientific voice he continues: "I have to watch them without getting an erection. It seems simple, but in fact it's quite hard."

"That must be difficult indeed," I say. "Is it an expensive course?"

"Oh yes, it's only for very advanced practitioners and is quite expensive. But he's giving us a handsome discount," the professor says without a trace of mistrust. "We're so proud the guru has accepted us as his pupils."

Tibetan Tongue Tip

Along the main street of the Goan sea resort cloths and garments from all corners of India are fluttering in the gentle winter breeze. Whole families have settled there, along with their businesses. Nomads from Rajasthan offer embroidered marriage garments. Kashmiries specialize in ornaments and small sculptures. Westerners try to sell cameras or sleeping bags. The Tibetan vendors offer both magical and religious artifacts from their homeland and plastic and nylon products in eye-searing colors.

Sandup is a Tibetan, yet he looks strikingly Western among the other market vendors. He has cut his hair short in military style and on the corner of the carpet on which he displays his wares rests a packet of American cigarettes. In the shade of his umbrella I see a family-size bottle of Coca Cola. When I sit down on a corner of his carpet, instead of the usual chai he offers me a cigarette and a coke.

I've bought things from Sandup on a few previous occasions and it has always struck me that this most westernized of all vendors should offer such extraordinary objects for sale. Among the most striking of the things he displays I find some splendid goblets made of human skulls and a collection of wind instruments manufactured from human thighbones. I'm fascinated by these artifacts, remnants of a culture that has been practically wiped out. Carefully I finger the instruments, some bare, some inlaid with silverwork.

"How do you play them?" I ask.

He shakes his head. "I'm not blowing these," he says. "They attract spirits. I'm a Buddhist."

Sandup doesn't speak much, but when he does he uses short sentences. Sometimes I don't see the connection between them.

"But these are instruments used in Tibetan Buddhism, aren't they?" I ask.

Again he shakes his head. "Bönpo," he says.

I know that Bön is the name of the original shamanistic religion of Tibet, the one that existed before Buddhism got its foothold on the roof of the world. These two religions have mixed to become the unique Tibetan strain of Buddhism where there's a place for roguish tricksters, smutty stories and divine madmen.

"I'd like to buy this bone trumpet; if I can play it," I tell Sandup.

He calls over his shoulder into the bushes behind his shop where his family stays in a tent. A young woman in traditional Tibetan dress appears. Generally one only sees Tibetan ladies wearing their hair in thick plaits, but this woman's long black hair hangs loose. She's an astonishing beauty.

"She knows more about Bönpo than I do," says Sandup lighting another cigarette.

I notice he doesn't inhale. He says something in Tibetan to the young woman. She smiles and squats beside me.

"I am Tsipa, Sandup's sister," she says in charming English. "Which kangling do you want to hear?"

I point at the instrument of my choice. She puts it to her lips, producing a long-drawn, serene tone. Then she hands it to me. "Try it," she says. "There is no danger."

It excites me to put my lips to the bone she has just blown. I try, but produce only a pathetic squeak.

"Well, never mind," I bear up bravely. "I'll exercise at home."

Tsipa fascinates me. In India it's a rare occasion to meet a young woman who will converse so directly with a stranger.

"Why do you blow the kangling, but Sandup doesn't?" I ask.

She laughs mockingly as her brother looks away, slightly annoyed. "He's afraid," she says. "He knows all about America, but he's scared of spirits."

"Aren't you?" I ask.

"Not at all!" she says. "I've gotten to know them and have overcome my fear."

"On what occasions is the kangling used?" I ask.

"At the ritual of Chöd in cemeteries and terrible places," she says. "An aspiring initiate has to spend many nights all alone in such a spot. He has to blow the kangling to call the demons. These will appear and tear open his belly before eating him hide and hair. The first times you will be terribly scared and feel hellish pains. Some go insane or die with fear. But after a few nights you begin to notice that the demons only attack you when you're scared of them. Then, gradually, you overcome your fear of evil spirits and of death itself. If all goes well you find yourself back in the body that has been devoured by the demons, and everything seems like a hallucination. But these experiences have an impact that is stronger than normal reality, a lasting effect. That's how one learns about different realities and dimensions and how to exist there. That's the aim of the Chöd initiation."

"Seems rather drastic to me," I say.

"It's one's own choice, it's voluntary," she replies. "There are other ways as well. In our religion we strive for harmony, even harmony between light and dark forces. Before the Chinese invasion of Tibet there was a monastery for vampire monks. These vampires were considered holy because they never sucked the blood of innocent people. They would feed themselves on people who were tired of living, who wanted to commit suicide. Buddhism frowns on suicide, so these suicidal folks would go to that monastery to feed the vampire monks. In such a way they did each other a service."

Sandup makes a derogatory noise. To him this is primitive paganism.

"Why are you so westernized, even though you're a Buddhist?" I ask him.

"When the iron bird flies east the Dharma will fly to the west," he recites, pensively observing me through the smoke of his cigarette.

Tsipa comes to my aid. "The iron bird is the airplane," she says. "It is an ancient Tibetan prophecy that came true. When airplanes came to Tibet the Buddhist teachings went to the west."

"And so will I," Sandup says. "I want to go to America."

I ask how much they want for the kangling and Tsipa looks at me in a peculiar way.

"You can have it only if you can play it," she says.

I strain, relaxing my lips in all possible ways, but no sound emerges from the thighbone.

Tsipa shakes her head with a roguish smile. "Sorry, you can't have it."

I feel rather embarrassed.

"But you may come back and try again," she says. "Only when you succeed in playing it, can you have it. For free. You see, this thighbone belonged to a member of our family."

I'm perplexed. Suddenly she shows me the tiny tip of her pink tongue.

"Come back tomorrow," she smiles.

My heart beats at double speed as she leaves me. I take leave of Sandup and walk to the seashore. Floating in the tropical ocean, I can't stop myself from dreaming of the tiny pink tip of her tongue.

Fear the Engine, Pain the Fuel

"The darkest hour is just before dawn. Do you know why?" My questioner looks at me intently, her eyes so dark I can hardly distinguish the iris from the pupil. Her small head is close-cropped and she wears the red maroon habit of a Buddhist nun. I reflect upon the question, trying to imagine the workings of her inner world.

In a second-class sleeper of an Indian train one travels in full contact with the other passengers in the compartment. We touch and smell each other, and it's quite normal to have your neighbor's head rest on your shoulder. I'm sitting opposite this slight nun, who after hours of complete silence has suddenly asked me this question.

"Maybe people only pray for help in their darkest hour, maybe the gods only come to our help when we pray," I endeavor.

She smiles somewhat disdainfully, at my ignorance I suppose. "There are no gods outside us, everything is within," she says, setting me right.

In the compartment, which officially seats ten persons, sixteen people have found places: two extras sit crammed on the benches and four others recline on the luggage racks. The nun looks around the compartment, requesting a better answer to her query.

"When the hour is darkest, one dies. That's the end of all problems," a student on one luggage rack remarks.

The nun shakes her head. "Death is no way out. It is merely a continuation of illusion, without a material body. Those who create hell in this world will find hell in the hereafter."

A dignified Sikh sardar translates the conversation into Hindi for the benefit of the passengers who don't understand English. The listeners' attentive eyes reflect the philosophical depth of this ancient culture. When no one else responds, the nun proceeds to answer: "A contented person will never change, but a person in great distress will. Fear is the engine. Pain is the fuel of transformation. Somebody who is in great pain may finally give up bad habits to lessen their suffering. That's why humans only develop through fear and pain. Those are our greatest teachers."

An urbanized young lady in tight jeans agrees: "You are right. It's the same when we are born. At first we are so comfortable in the womb, floating happily inside our mother. But as the time of delivery approaches the baby feels the first labor pains and a great fear takes hold of it. Suddenly the paradisiacal surroundings feel like a straightjacket. The baby has to leave the womb, but it doesn't know how. Then begins a titanic struggle to get out. Only one exit offers itself, but it is far too narrow. Yet the pain becomes so unbearable that the baby finally enters what seems like a tunnel of death. After a terrifying journey this turns out to be the birth channel."

The woman has kept everybody spellbound with her vivid description and I notice we all heave a sigh of relief when she finishes. Even the locomotive sighs, ejecting a cloud of hot soot which blows in through the windows. The sardar tries vainly to close them. Fortunately someone opens the door to the gangway so the draught can drive out the smoke. The nun claps her hands: "Now you see; now you see."

I don't understand what there is to see so the student on the luggage rack explains: "Because the smoke scared us, we had to change the situation to let it out."

"Are you a Buddhist as well?" I ask him.

"Oh no, thank God, I'm an atheist," he smiles. "I am a convinced Marxist. But in essence we use a similar principle as this Buddhist lady: people will only revolt to change their situation if it has become unbearable. In communism we call this *Verelendung*."

"That's a correct statement," the sardar remarks. "The difference is that the Buddhist aspires to spiritual transformation, whereas the communist aims at material change."

"Together they would make a perfect couple," another passenger quips.

He's a slim gentleman immaculately dressed in an utterly British dark suit. When he has our attention he carries on: "If everything is illusion, we should create an illusion which appeals most to us. As we create a garden out of wasteland."

This new approach is duly considered by all. The nun is the first to react. Like a snake she sways her head to and fro and says somewhat menacingly: "So you do not mind to live in an illusion?"

"Not in the least. As long as I feel good in it. If there is nothing but Maya, how can we ever live outside it?"

All are silent, slightly shocked by the bold statement of the gentleman. Only the nun mutters: "Transcend it, transcend it."

The sardar clears his throat: "Excuse me sir, but can you tell me from which religion this vision derives?"

A modest smile appears on the gentleman's lips as he answers: "Most certainly sir. This vision derives from my private convictions. I'm a philosopher, you see. I have created my own religion, so to say. To quote an ancient Sanskrit poet:

No one behind, no one ahead,
the path the ancients had cleared has grown over
and the other road, the wide one
that everybody follows, leads nowhere.
I am alone and go my way.

I observe a certain admiration among my fellow passengers for this well-phrased philosopher. The nun withdraws into meditation to protect herself against such profane statements. I decide to throw in a few words: "It is said that every child is born with a clean sheet, a tabula rasa. Some destroy their sheets, others create something beautiful. What would you do with your sheet?"

"It's really very simple," he answers. "Creation is beautiful, life is sacred, the universe is just and loving and we have eternal life. This is the illusion I cherish. It's a time-tested faith, which has served billions of people during their existence in this 'Valley of Tears,' as you Christians call our precious earth." He casts a meaningful glance toward me.

"I don't consider myself a Christian."

"Why not?" The sardar is surprised. "There is wisdom in every religion."

"That's why I'm not a Christian. I am a bit of everything. I gather my knowledge from all teachings and from my own experiences," I say somewhat ponderously.

"An eclectic Gnostic; definitely eclectic," the philosopher remarks.

The student makes a defiant sound and begins a small offensive: "What if there is absolutely nothing but our material world? What if we have only this life, as every sensible person knows? What if your splendid illusions are nothing but romantic fantasies to protect you from the grim realities of life?"

The philosopher is unperturbed by the attack. "If there is absolutely nothing but our material world, young man, I won't notice it when I pass away. For how can one notice something when there is nothing? Yet I have lived my life in a grand illusion. That's what I call serendipity."

At that moment a legless beggar, sliding across the floor on a piece of cardboard by pushing himself forward with his arms, appears in the doorway. He raises his hands in the eternal gesture of supplication.

"Now that's what I call grim reality," the student says almost triumphantly, pointing at the invalid man.

"So let's change his grim reality into a happy one," says the philosopher, taking a fifty-rupee note from his wallet.

Now the sardar peels a hundred-rupee note from his pocket and everybody starts to scramble for some money. The beggar is flabbergasted. He pushes his way into the compartment and proceeds to touch the feet of his benefactors. It's a habit I've never grown accustomed to, so I try to hide my feet. He notices my embarrassment and decides to thank me with a song: "Jay, jay, Lakshmi jay."

Some passengers begin to clap hands. Within a few moments the whole compartment is clapping along happily, including the nun, the student, and me.

I MARRIED MY-SELF

LAMDA

Though Man May Build
His Edifices
Though He
As an aspect of She
Shall Build and Number
And Restrict the Eternal
This is yet—
The Eternal
And Form is Dissolved
In Rapture

The Eternal Cosmic Dance
of Love
For there is Nothing else
but Love

Difference
Division
Love Bindeth them—
and Loose
Love Uniteth them—
and set Free

They—Dancing Partners
B

Multiform in Color
On a Checker-Board
Dance-floor
In Pythagorean Temples
In Temples of Pythagoras
Just for the sake of it
She Dances
Vain
And Glorious

Just for the Sake of it
She Dances
Victorious

No-Difference
Between Me and She
I see She
There is No Me
For I am She

I married Myself

It was a dream
That I-Was
Ever Not

ARE YOU A SKIN?

JOHNNY TEMPLAR

I once said we were once innocent. But I was wrong. I once said we were born in the heart of suns, made of star-stuff, come here as the lenses through which God looks upon his creation. I thought us One. But I was wrong. Did not recognize the dream I had woken into. Did not recognize it for what it was. Did not recognize you for what you are. And this. And.

And how do you sleep?

I cannot. This world. Sleeps. Asleep.

You are asleep. How do you sleep. Asleep.

I came here with love for you. Gave it to you. Opened my heart to you. And sleeping, you saw yourself. Tossing and turning in bed, wrestling with your own guilt, your shame, your self-hate, the thoughts that leech your brain at three a.m. You only saw yourself. I came here trusting you. Crawling into bed with you. Opening my arms to you, letting you lay your head upon my chest, letting you feel the safety of eternity in my arms.

And I taught you things. Secret words and hymns. Secret stories you had never heard before, stories in which you were hero and heroine. I kissed your wounds, lay my hands upon them and sealed them. Made you whole. How do you sleep? Asleep.

I told you of worlds within worlds. I made myself weak for you, opened my chest and let you see the memories in my soul. Weeping. I showed you truth. In trust. Truth is. It is. I raised my wrists to you in supplication. I told you I would heal you. And so you would know you could trust me I lay myself vulnerable before you, naked, a drop of influx. But a gift to the sleeping is never seen. The sleeping dream of other faces, other lands, other times. Never see what is. Never see the simple love that waits for them, acceptance, silent voices of family. Asleep.

And you had already been sold.

And they say that everything in this world is for sale. But not everything is. Some things can only be given. From parent to child, from teacher to student, from friend to friend, from lover to lover. And I wanted to give you everything.

But you. You had already sold yourself, paraded yourself at their slave auction, in front of their laughing, boiled mouths and lathered fists. For them to strip bare before all, laugh at, pinch a roll of fat to see your worth, squeeze your breast, run cracked fingernails across your teeth. And how slowly the bidding must have gone, for such a broken soul. You could have found salvation, healing, light, love but instead you chose the highest bidder. You chose to serve THEM. And all for a thimble of glamour, of magic dust, glittering in the wind briefly, a dazzling light show, and then gone forever. A moment's distraction, a magic show in a concentration camp.

I will splinter my chest. Cast my ribs at your feet, a single rune, plain to see. Screaming at night. Holding my face in my hands with my knees around my ears screaming till I gag with the weight of existence upon me, hiding under covers from the nightmare of the waking day. This world is burning, aflame with ghosts. The dead hate the living. This world cries out for release from its own weight. Once I wanted to see truth. I wanted to wake so I could come and tell you of what glories lay outside the bedroom I made with you. I stand at the sunrise with bleeding ducts. Back hunched. Shoulders broken. I gave you my heart. A diamond. A mirror. Girt with a serpent. Perfect. My heart knew love. It knew the world beyond this. There as a mirror to show others what they were, to show them what they could become, to whisper to them of man-yet-to-be and give them hope.

Nailed to the crossed wood in the tomb of our predecessor. The perfect man. Sagged and broken by gravity, hanging above the fresh earth. Melted like Icarus. And I cried out for you in my misery. You who I had given my heart to, who I had given my blood for, who I had given my name for, my future. And you came with knives. Sleepwalkers. Skinwalkers.

And I whispered to myself that it was a ritual of Becoming. In the cup of her fornication.

At time's altar I leave the sacrifice of my self. The human sacrifice that magick requires. Lost boy, a flicker running in the reeds of dawn, of the eternal. Slain at the foot of truth so I can go free. Safe from the demons who wear the skin of men, of women. The demons I see in my mirror, darkly. Walking wrapped with the skin of my dreams and my hopes and my love. Skinwalking into my arms to open the spaces between my ribs and lick at something human, something real, something you never were. Judas. Monster. Whore. You never wake. You always sleep.

I touched light once. And you, you who only spoke as if you had touched it, who never had, you thought to steal it, to adorn yourself with it, to thieve and absorb by association. So you spoke to me of the light, of love, of liberty, croaked a song you had only memorized the words to, could only make a passing rendition of. And I trusted you. Trusted your sincerity. And behind the rotting skin you wore you smiled to yourself and thought yourself clever.

Crawling along the floor, vertebrae broken, looking up from the ground's horizon, shivering, bleeding. This is what you call awake?

And you speak your babble. About new frontiers and new ways of being. What are you saying? This nonsense that falls from your mouth? Who are you? And can you hear yourself? And you think your theories mean anything? This world is burning. Sleep of reason. Sleep of compassion. And your cleverness will save you? Your brain is a waste. Your life is a waste. They eat us all. They teach all hearts to break. And you think you can serve them, that you can make up your face and smile at the beauty of your rotting costume in the mirror and go out and serve them, help them snuff out the light? You think on that day you will be rewarded? They will eat you all the same. You Judas.

I wanted to wake. And I woke into nightmare. I know why you choose to sleep. But I do not forgive you it.

We spoke of magic. I showed you to spell the words hope and love and silence in the sand. I showed you the secret glyphs, smuggled them across, under my breath. And what was magic to you?

A way to get what you want. A way to achieve your "goals." A way to push others out of the way on your sprint to the finish line on the road to the maw of Leviathan. A dress-up set, a way to hold yourself above others, to blind those around you with the radiance of Lucifer, that they might think themselves inadequate before your graven image, that they might bow at your feet. A fix, a hit in the mainline of dead souls, a hit of crystallized graveyard dust sparked with the blowtorch of your self-hatred, a darkly splendid world to fill the hole where light never lived, simian addiction dripping from the blunt, haired stinger of Satan. The black sickness of Belial to drink, to make yourself drunk on, that you might see nothing but your own ambition.

You think you raise yourself up? You think yourself wise, or talented, or diligent; you think yourself the light of your universe? You think yourself in control?

You are asleep. And you are worse than asleep. For you began to wake. And you only woke up enough to see THEM. And in your fear of your own weakness you thought to serve them.

Coward. Judas. Traitor. Whore. You should be kicked through the streets, shivering and bleating like a starving dog, marked for all to see.

For it is those like you who have made this world what it is. Who have reduced the promise of this human race to a stale lie. Your tongue darting across your lips. Your pinprick eyes, grey, cold-blooded, understanding nothing but devouring, fixing up your next meal.

And when the other foot drops, will you be able to buy your way out? With money, with souls, with your body? When the time comes to wake, what will you wake into? What will you see? What will be waiting for you?

I am whispering in your dreaming ear of what will be.

And soon I will shout the alarm.
Soon you will wake. As you must.
And you will see.
That underneath your skin
Is nothing
But the hand
Of your owner.

THE DAY I WENT TO FETCH THE ACIDS

JOEL BIROCO

There's a story I sometimes tell, that illustrates how times have changed since we entered the Age known as "The War on Terror," a feeble scared time when people are encouraged by propaganda to check their own actions constantly, lest they be engaged in something accidentally subversive. And certain activities are no longer deemed the actions of ordinary upstanding citizens, and certain books you haven't read but still have in a bag to go to the charity shop may be enough to put you away.

I was about fourteen; it was in the 70s, a gentle innocent time of failed hopes of parents seeking refuge in a mere two channels on the telly (BBC 2, though possessed, could not be watched, it was a class thing), a time of a bath always on a Friday before *The Virginian* and being allowed to stay up late to watch *The Invaders*. A time of not being able to figure out the huge white ball in *The Prisoner*. A time when one never realized bread also came unsliced.

I was into chemistry and had converted the shed into a laboratory. Put up shelves and lined them with bottle after bottle of chemicals I'd bought mail-order from a laboratory supplier in Birmingham. The chemicals and glassware would arrive in big boxes packed in shredded paper "straw." Even the red phosphorus had come through the post. I loved taking the top off and smelling it, there was something rich and inviting about that smell, a smell of seductive danger, and its beautiful crumbly texture; it was like chemical truffles. Even the antimony dust was delivered through the mail, which I later read Israel Regardie managed to poison himself with in one of his alchemical experiments.

These "vigilant" days it would be hard to obtain these things, and if you tried your name would be flagged up on a database as a danger to society, you'd be seen either as a terrorist or running an LSD factory. Honest curiosity about the elements of the earth and how they combine is no longer considered a reasonable pursuit for a private citizen. What normal person heats red-orange potassium dichromate crystals on a spoon over a burner in a shed? Would the explanation that "I just love the way it flares up and makes ten times as much stuff and green" stand up in court? Would the strips of magnesium raise eyebrows? I saw an old battered child's chemistry set in an antiques arcade the other day, the copper sulphate tube still full, and thought, it has gone the way of the golliwog. Not that there was ever anything much in a shop-bought chemistry set.

But back to the innocent 70s, when you could plot to your heart's content, just for fun. My final box for stocking my lab arrived, minus certain items. A note in shaky old person's handwriting explained that I would have to come and collect them from the supplier, as they couldn't send the concentrated acids, concentrated ammonia, caustic soda and the tub of phenol through the post. So I set off on my trek. Travelling to Birmingham on the train then seemed like something grown-ups did; it was an adventure involving a lot of responsibility. Buying the right ticket, having to make sure I was on the right train, all those platforms. I felt easily out of my depth. This was underscored by my mother's nagging to ensure I had the correct money for the bus and my A to Z of Birmingham. Never once did she seem at all concerned I was going to be bringing back about a gallon of stuff that could burn a hole through the train carriage floor and result in evacuation if the concentrated ammonia bottle smashed in a confined space. Well, I was careful not to mention such details. Though, oddly enough, I'm not sure it crossed my mind a great deal either. I knew what I was doing. I was just going to get some things. I told my parents it was important, I needed this stuff because I was going to be a forensic scientist when I grew up. Mum gave me her best shopping bag to put the bottles in.

It was a grey overcast day when I arrived in Birmingham. I eventually found the place in the back streets, great looming industrial chimneys, dirty walls, rats scampering by bins. It seemed to be some kind of warehouse, the only entrance was up an iron fire-escape upon which moss was growing, vivid green in the drizzle. I walked up the long and slippery iron staircase and into a small room with a seat and a serving counter in the wall. Behind I could see a cornucopia of chemical delights, long and wide shelves stacked with bottles and equipment. I dinged the bell and a very old man came to see me.

"I've come to collect these things you couldn't send through the post," I explained, handing him the note sent with my last order.

He took the pencil from behind his ear, licked the tip, and ticked them off. Then he went to fetch them.

"Is this your bag?" he said.

I unzipped mum's best shopping bag. He placed the bottles in one by one. They were litre bottles.

"That's the concentrated hydrochloric acid, this is the concentrated sulphuric acid…" Glass bottles. More followed, "Concentrated nitric acid, concentrated acetic acid." He crossed them off the list. Then he dragged over a ribbed amber-colored bottle, "Concentrated ammonia." He placed it at the other end and plonked in the middle a tub of phenol and a plastic bottle of sodium hydroxide pellets.

He tugged on the handles of mum's best shopping bag, the glass bottles clanking together like pints of milk, and said, "bit heavy, will you manage?"

"Yes," I said, "it'll be alright." I wanted this stuff bad.

Then he zipped up the bag for me and in a moment of wonderful grandfatherly concern, that grows more ludicrous each time I think about it, he said:

"Now you be careful with those."

CAUSAL COMOGENY AND COSMOLOGY

GANESH BABA

Creation and Evolution

(This essay is the first section of a longer piece called "Causal Cosmogeny and Cosmology, probably written in the 1970s.)

Creation is often confused with evolution. Actually, it is the reverse current of evolution—a sort of anti-creation in the manner of anti-matter of modern physics; or is even analogous to the pair of opposite currents in electronics—the current of electrons on one hand, and the opposite-directional counter-current of voltaic electrical flow, an elementary concept in electronics.

Creation proceeds from the Causal (karan), or Absolute plane of Infinity, via the subtle plane (susksma), to the plane of inorganic matter. Evolution, on the other hand, proceeds from the gross material plane via the subtle plane, i.e., the vital, mental, intellectual and spiritual planes, back to the Absolute, thus completing a full cycle. Though they are, as it were, concurrent or co-existent or even, co-lateral, their directions are evidently opposite directions. Of course, they are not at loggerheads with one another, not at cross-purposes, but in sympathetic and sychronous harmony. Between them they provide the gamut of the created and evolving universe: from the Unconditioned Absolute to the Conditioned relativistic cavalcade of the Created Cosmos, and back from that state through the integration of the parts to the evolution of the whole, the Absolute.

In so-called modern cosmology, what is construed as the current of creation—from energy to matter, matter to microbe, microbe to man, man to human, human (via the Darwinian ladder) to super-mental being—really constitutes the current of evolution. That construct is evidently fallacious from strictly terminological considerations, even in modern, scientific terms. Modern science conforms to the above analysis; but modern scientists, especially the physical scientists, who deal with the total picture of the phenomenal universe along with its ponderous panorama of ponderable matter, use, I am afraid, anachronous terms in this regard.

Yes, the creation of the material, inertial or even relativistic universe from molten matter (yelu or primordial plasma), or even the synthesis of the matrix of matter from its subtle elements, whatever they may be (it is first from the Unconditioned Absolute to the Conditioned Relativistic—thence, to the mechanistic), constitutes the correct course and career of the current of Creation. The opposite process, i.e., the emergence of organic matter from inorganic matter; then from organic matter to organic life; i.e, the emergence of the vital from the material, physical, or phenomenal—from life to mind; from mind to intelligence to the ego or individual vital-conscious unit; from atomic or individualistic to the universal and the Cosmic, and from the Cosmic to the Causal Absolute; constitutes, indeed, the eddy-current of evolution. From the grossest to the grosser; from the grosser to the subtle; from the subtle to the subtlest on the Absolute Unconditioned Causality, is, verily, the course of evolution, which is, indeed, a refining movement. Isn't the movement from inanimate to animate microbe and from microbe to man and man to the divine, indeed, subtilizing, refining?

Creation is a course of coarsening of the subtlest Causal Consciousness, the Absolute Spirit, to the sub-vital field and flux of matter; the grossest condition of the subtlest, the Causal Consciousness. Cosmic Consciousness is the first conditioned state of the Absolute Unconditioned Consciousness, the Subtlest of the subtle; which one cannot correctly conceive with lower planes of consciousness, such as life, mind, intelligence or ego unit. Absolute Causal Consciousness, through Its Imponderable (achintya) Differentiation (ved) and Integration (aved)—the philosophy of Achintya Veda—ved of Lord Chantaya's—becomes the Cosmic Consciousness, which guides both the concurrent course of Cosmic Creation and Evolution; and supertends to the twin currents, the twin brothers of Cosmic parentage, in their career in opposite directions—though their magnitudes must be matched to maintain the Cosmic Balance or Universal Equilibrium. Spirit is unitary simple. Matter is manifold complex. Creation courses from spirit to the matter; from simple to the less simple, and thence, to the complex, or even, sometimes, compound. As such, the making of physical meat, the main matrix of the body, the gross frame; from matter to microbe, thence, to the physical, or body-based man, the most complex physical formation—minus his/her vital, mental, intellectual and egoistic planes—constitutes, of course, the eddy-currents of creation, the organic creation. Meat is the grossest of all matter. Carrion (meat minus life—flesh minus the vital force, the biological animation) is the end-product of the eddy-current of creation; the flesh being the final physical fruit of creation from the simple cell to the complex tissues.

But, when the virus or "gene" became endowed with, or exhibited, a spark of organic vitality, a biological "life," the march from unicellular amoeba or microscopic microbe to the manifestation of man, the movement via the vital, the mental, the intellectual and the egoistic to the plane of the super-egoistic Cosmic Spirit or Divinized Man, indeed, constitutes the main stream of the evolutionary process. Thus the eddy-current of organic creation, through its psycho-somatic progression to the integral man constitutes the main stream of biological evolution from microbe to man.

Murder of or Muddling with the Masses

The heroics of the elegant elite may one day recoil on them like a boomerang. The mass may not for long allow the long rope it has so long allowed the wags to wag their tongues. They howl of spiritual crisis and start howling back when mention is made of the motto, "Spiritualize the secular." Well, by all means be secular, but do spiritualize. Otherwise, how do they propose to avert the spiritual crisis of which they themselves are crying about the most ferociously? Such an unscientific and irrational and illogical approach and contradictory conduct betrays the inherent hypocrisy of their pious professions and ardent advances and even admonitions against mass morale-failure. What other than the spiritual would sustain the morale of the mass, much less morality. Who cares for morality at the moment? Even the morality of the nation (which is more important to the man of the moment, than the morale) is flagging, faltering, fumbling and failing and the smug secularist is flying in the face of facts. But how long can he keep flying? He has to face facts, he has to come down to earth, he has to come to brass-tacks. There is no escape now!

The slumbering mass is waking up and cannot be long kept in the present semisomatic state. You know what happens when a hungry giant wakes up after a long nightmarish sleep. The demon will demand an inordinate volume of food to satisfy his long-lasting hunger in sleep. The trial of those who have used the rabble as the cannon fodder of mass destruction will now be demanded as the fodder of the hydra-headed giant: MASS! They have seen through the game; they have penetrated into the vanity and pretenses of the ailing class—the few selected few who hold the destiny of the mass in good and traditional first. The mass has mostly played his part of the game: but the custodians of his destiny have gone cocky and unplayed him. Under-paying has been the main weapon of under-playing and all deceptions of anti-social nature arise from that septic focus: the failure of the spiritual level of society of which they are the custodians. Who, for heaven's sake, is better suited to be held responsible for the deterioration of even bare morale and wide prevalence of low morale? They all stem from the old-secular attitude of the people in "power," who rule the roost.

The corruption, the jeopardy, by the follies of religionists of overzealous spiritualists are part of human history. But what is confounding to the cynics, the skeptics, the so-called secularists (-ve) is the uncanny capacity of the "church of spirit"—the invisible church of our culture—for self-renewal and self-resurrection.

Holy Ghost—the indwelling or Immanent Spirit

Paraclete—Hidden God

Failing faculties, the loneliness of menace, and fear of spiritual reckoning might find them bankrupt. God had chosen to men as "free" instrument for His divine plan. Prudence, playful preparation. Faces scored by age and intense expenses of power. The lost ones—the ones that would in darkness. Those who have lost served the Church and the faithful are those that have been closest to the people, who are the images of Christ. We are priests, preachers, prelates and pastors by virtue of an act of dedication to the people who are the flock of Christ.

Apostasy—The stronger the faith; the stronger the reason twice used. The projection of the tormented spirit into the arms of the Almighty.

The Light—Beginning of peace of Communion (the astral light of Kriya-initiation). Christ was a Kriyaban par excellence.

The Light is like a dawn seen from a high hill, flooding swiftly into a landscape—the landscape of the phenomenal universe.

One could trace in tragedies the promise of future mercies. "Some of them would keep a small light burning that one day might light a million torches." An Omnipotence working by a mighty evolution to an ultimate good.

Kriya—Ultimate absolution of a fathomless future.

Everywhere man has become aware of himself as a transient animal and is battling desperately to assert his right to the best of the world for the short time that he sojourns in it. Everyone is asserting his claim to identity and recognition, that may continue even after his exit from this passing show. Everyone has his ear for any prophet who can promise him One.

Revitalization by Sex

Sex is everybody's vital problem. The seekers of all ages tried to understand or explain it through religion, art, science and a number of other orthodox and unorthodox ancient and modern projects. Unfortunately, very many such attempts to understand it have almost proved a total failure. None except the Yogis and Tantrics, the spiritual bio-technologists, who have put it into practical use, especially on the psycho-spiritual plane, have come to grasp its real nature. Yet we are, almost all, more or less, practical sexologists both in our amours and in parenthood. All are agreed on its potent potentiality of effect on the biological or vital relations of our being.

Until now our knowledge of psychology has accepted sex as an important secondary human need. We should agree readily with Freud, that in the normal biological phase, sex is almost the primary mover of the biological or vital universe—reproduction and spiritualization both allow the biological being to live into eternity; both physically through reproduction, and spiritually by spiritual regeneration as Kundalini shakti or the potential power of the psycho-somatic, which all we biological beings are.

In my view, the only progress we could make in such studies is to accept sex as a subject of cosmology, mythology, biology and psychology, meaning a subject of the Psyche-somatic, a governor of our physiological functions, the satisfaction or dissatisfaction thereof determining a major measure of personality and also a major measure of energy, and to modify it by appropriate modulation, moderation or even immanation. There is nothing immoderate or immodest about frank discussion of sex. It is obsolete prudery to avoid or underestimate its open avowal and apt action for its appropriate utilization in all fields of human endeavor, especially in the psycho-somatic or bio-psychic fields. Sex is involved in biology and in psychology—body and mind. As sublimated, awakened Kundalini it can give terrific Cosmic Action Power or Kriya-shakti, transcending the most primordial relativist proclivity within the compass of our comprehension or reception. This relativistic proclivity of mind to gravitate towards the polar—to create counterpart or opposition between opposite and magnetic poles—must be overcome, before real romantic love between souls and souls' passion is equally defenseless and defeated.

Happiness and Contentment

Seek God—gain contentment!
Seek your Self out—gain God!
How to seek out the Self?
By meditating upon yourself.

How to seek God? God is a social concept, a product of society. Human civilization is a product of society. They are, therefore, connected as twins. So, if you cannot approach one of them directly, you may approach the one you do not know by approaching the one you know.

In your life, whether you first heard of human civilization or of God, with which one are you more familiar? With human civilization, of course. God, then, must be a product of the social search for the Self that we call "religion." Religion is our collective effort to find out the reality of existence: the Self. Human civilization is a product of human activities aimed at aiding that collective effort to find the core of human existence, in and on this planet, and our sense of wonderment, awe, inspiration and devotion to the things of our faith, fancy and pleasure.

So, to look for God, we can look at the present. Our present is a product of our past, and the future is governed by our present circumstances. Therefore, the future has its basis on the past. To build our future, we have to rebuild our past. But the question is, how to build the past, when the past is dead and gone? You must resurrect, or disinter, your past in your mind and see how best, or better, you could have built it.

To seek the Self, the body-mind machine must first be in optimal operating order (O3).

Meditation: Silent concentrated thinking. Gradually the mind takes a progressively decreasing part in the process, while intuition takes over. Intuition is the thought-process of super-mind, which is an involute of mind.

Yoga: The study of the mind by the mind. Yoga gives rationality to religion and reason to faith. The mind is a subtle organ of the body, like any other organ of the body, though they, of course, are gross.

To keep the body fit and healthy, one must undertake adequate physical exercise and follow other rules of health. This is a step toward making the mind healthy—for the mind and body are organically related—but more is needed for a perfectly healthy and strongly penetrating mind to be able to study itself. That can be done with an assault on the vagaries of mind. The speed and thrust of the assault is ultimately up to the leader of the assault.

The Self cannot be attained without development of body and mind because the Self is the field of the super-mind, which can only be reached either by the mind developing and blossoming forth into super-mind, or by complete transcendence of the psychic mind. When the psychic mind is annihilated, the super-mind rushes in. It is here that God resides and must be found, nowhere else but here.

The Sufi poet says, Grow thy garden inside and thy homes and gardens shall flourish.

Inside is heaven. So, can God be found inside thyself, in the silence of the resplendent inner garden.

To the degree that the devotee attunes himself to the will of the Lord (the Self)-awakened consciousness—to that degree does the Lord's grace flow out in his favor. Thus strengthened, the devotee finally merges his self into the flux of the Cosmic Self and becomes one with Him, in endless bliss. Only then does the will of the devotee become the Will of the Lord, for he cannot will anything which the Lord does not Will him to will; his will is His Will.

Love is an expression of happiness. Bliss is continuous, condensed happiness. Therefore intense love—devotion—is a product of bliss. Bliss being continuous and God being all-bliss, it is logical to conceive of God as Love.

Thus, only through devotion and sincere effort in the search of Self can true happiness and contentment be found.

THE SAYINGS OF GANESH BABA

These were gathered by American poet Ira Cohen at the Kumbha Mela held at Allahabad in 1977.

Beware of the non-psychedelic.

Wise men don't love wise men, wise men love fools. And you are such divine fools.

We are in the post-lunatic.

Anyone who does not do his duty by the mothers will be fucked by the Tantric forces.

Real saints are mad. In fact there are no saints but sinners. Real saints won't be declared.

One will have to have an uncanny sense of humor. Abandon your languages, especially the French, Dutch and Germans.

Somebody must write a book: "Kings With Straw Mats."

God is the supreme shopkeeper; his market is infinite.

Kriya-yoga is cosmic communion through cosmic action. Cosmic action is already going on within you.

It is all right to remain a stranger.

The beads of the rosary are inside your own body. God did this in order to impinge the inner rosary.

In Tantra, if one is a meat-eater, we give him so much meat he will ask for dal and chapati.

Reversal of reality is Maya's job. The reversal of that reversal is the guru's job.

You are the nearest to yourself.

Just as strong women want strong men, wicked witches desire great wizards.

Polar swingback: When you reach the highest point of positivity, you'll swing immediately into negativity.

Our natural state is eternity.

Without fucking we are fucked up.

Materialism is morbidity.

The soul is the only censor.

We must express the dignity of poverty.

Real yogis sleep by day and fuck the night.

There is food everywhere, I tell you.

Why is the Westerner coming here to dig our dust?

People who have not felt God do not know how cool is his laugh.

Let one mystery remain.

A non-psychedelic can never enlighten a psychedelic.

I am a Naga-hipster; we don't bother with petty formalities.

Whether they give us one blanket or two blankets, it doesn't matter much. You see we know this body will not last.

Don't count time if you want to evolve; if you count time you will revolve.

Ganesh Baba says he studied under Dale Carnegie: He was a great master, greater than those modern Indian phonies. He said, "Stop fucking. Start living."

On sex: We cannot be thunderstruck by these tissues.

Buck up or fuck up.

Once a psychedelic, always a psychedelic.

Sensation should not affect you but the principle behind the sensation.

Ram is the rest point of the mind or soul, not the man with bow and arrow.

What Marx called synthesis, Christ called God.

No sucking in our ashram.

If you have to pay five rupees to see Rajneesh, then you have to pay five rupees to see my doodoo.

I look upon you successively as a skeleton, then as a complementary circuit.

The history of India is a continuous stream of high hoax.

Beware of India. This is my last comment.

Another comment: India is OK. Beware of Indians.

The first lesson from India you can learn: We will all die.

I have died four or five times and I am still alive and kicking.

Don't cut the vegetables. Make them whole.

We will always fuck the mothers of the spiritual, three orgasms an hour, the older the better.

A fool laughs three times. The first time when others are laughing. The second time when they understand the joke. The third time when they wonder why they laughed when they didn't understand the joke.

Ganesh Baba on himself: He is not only the goofy Himalayan psychedelic yoga teacher but he was a student under Einstein, Schrödinger, Jung, Max Planck, not second or third hand but hot hand, asker of the most insidious questions under the sun. Only by asking silliest questions can you get wisest answers.

Ganesh Baba's guru said to Ganesh: "Sit with your back straight until you drop dead. Then you will be be sitting in my lap and I will be sitting in the lap of God." I believe him and I am still going that way.

Ganesh Baba says: All faiths pretend syruptitious information is divine knowledge.

There is no playboy, only dull-boy, I tell you. It is a quarter past twelve by my Playboy watch.

For the true psychedelic the nuptial bed becomes the surgical table.

Dharma can fuck everybody. If Dharma can't fuck there will be only goody-goodies.

Life is like a fruit. Any place it finds a gradient, that way it will go.

Fuck two hundred western women and nothing will happen. Fuck one Indian woman and she will suck you through and through. Beware of Indian women. One fuck will affect your grandmother in heaven.

Bhaktivedanta used to come and take bhang with me secretly. Now he wants to fuck the psychedelics.

I once had eighteen posh theatres, then I went to one of the theatres and I thought it was the bathroom.

On the Nagas: We are the oldest monks in the world. No one can compare with us in our phoniness. We will outshout you all the time. We are not ordinary monks but hipster monks.

Suggested prayer for Ganeshian Aspirants: Dear God, if there is a God, please help me, if you can help me.

Ganesh is Gnosis.

In our camp food is given only when starving. Then when you are fed, you are fed up.

Ask your guru. He reads the paper between the lines. (Read this at least twice before laughing. — I.C.)

I want to love people at a distance.

A man who does not know grammar cannot know God who is the most refined principle.

Do mirror-yoga.

The underbeard is a huge Ganeshian joke.

Let philosophies flourish or be demolished.

We wizards want witches to fuck.

The most powerful speaker, if he is not boring, is no speaker, I tell you. A very sweet boring to the center.

The body will die, the personal psyche will die, the cosmic psyche will die, but the cosmic spirit will never die.

We are sun worshippers; we live the simple life. Look, we have just one light and yet see these exhibition halls!

Live it light. Only a touch. It is all in here.

Ganeshian Psychedelic Message: Yankee, stop your hanky-panky. Don't be so swanky.

I want to forsake myself before the true image and to fuck the mother of the devil if need be.

For simple men God is spirit.

Ganesh Baba says he blew Winston Churchill's mind with slick English on horseback.

Bring my saffron-robe. Today I will match my color with everybody. (From Tagore)

In Indian poetry you don't have to ask who wrote the poem, it comes in a line.

I don't care what a man does or does not do, as long as he does well.

Remind me to tell you about extra-cerebral nostalgia.

As a wizard I have beaten your witch out. As a Baba I love you.

You are only mad. He is madder. I am maddest.

Last comment by Ira Cohen: OM is Home.

TRISHULS, TIBETANS AND TSUNAMIS

DAVE LOWE

Even Saddhus Need a Vacation: Kathmandu, Nepal

It took four circles over the Kathmandu valley for the Bangaldesh Biman pilot to find a gap large enough in the monsoon clouds to land his Fokker 70 from Dhaka. My nose was pressed against the window on the right hand side of the plane, looking for any sign of the snowcapped peaks Nepal was famous for, but all I saw was endless gray mist, swirling clouds and buckets of rain pouring off the wing.

When I stepped out of the deserted airport terminal, I split a cab with the only other passenger on the plane that had survived the hellish overnight transit stop in Dhaka, a retired fisherman from southern Japan who spoke just one English sentence.

"I am fish man from Japan," he told everyone. "Fish man."

Other than muffled grunts, his only gesture to the Nepalis at the taxi stand was to flash his passport like a necklace of garlic to ward off vampires.

"Nippon! Nippon!" the Fish Man snarled.

As we waited for the car to pull up, Fish Man was growing stranger by the minute, flicking his fingers at invisible mosquitoes, and on the ride into town he pulled out his disposable chopsticks, which had used to eat with during the flight, and began to mimic the Beethoven music coming out of the radio. As we swerved around police checkpoints, whom were searching trunks for Maoist bombs, random cows chewing newspapers and crashing trishaws ringing their bells, he laughed wickedly to himself at some private joke.

"Nippon, Nippon," Fish Man mumbled.

As we reached the downtown area, I was glad when Fish Man motioned with his chopsticks for the taxi driver to drop him off, nowhere near the place I had booked, just off Durbar Square in the old town. Fish Man stuffed his chopsticks back into his bag, hopped out, threw some bills onto the front passenger seat, strapped his tiny backpack on, and strode off into the traffic.

With just a week in Nepal, I only had enough time to explore the Katmandu valley, and I was glad of it: the day before I arrived in Nepal the mayor of Pokara had been shot dead by Maoists in broad daylight, the bus lines across the country were cut off, and one of the strongest monsoons in years was expected within days, reducing trekking routes to mush—the increasing reports of trekkers being first detained by Maoist rebels, lectured on their movement, coerced into giving a donation, and then being issued official "receipts" were also a put-off.

That afternoon, walking through the narrow Medieval lanes, packed with temples and scenic village life, nothing was more interesting than the numerous saddhus I passed, the holy men who covered their bodies in ash, and wandered the subcontinent in search of enlightenment. As we eyed each other as exotic creatures from opposite ends of the human spectrum, the saddhus smiled at me serenely, carrying their tridents and small satchels stuffed with clothes, leaving a cloud of hash smoke in their wake.

The next day I took taxis to nearby villages and temples scattered around the capital; the closest were Patan and Bhakatpur, where temple complexes draped in garlands of saffron marigold flowers and trays of flickering votive candles were filled with people at all times of day. Random monkeys scrounged for food left behind, leaping down from trees in the temple courtyards.

Walking though the quiet neighborhoods, I reached the edge of the city, walking off the beaten track into quiet rice fields where women tended to their crops and school children rode bikes home, ringing their bells.

With heavy rain and clouds each day it was muddy going, and every time the rain stopped I looked around to get a glimpse of the snowy Himalayas, but they were always hidden behind the mist. By day three I was getting sick of the thousands of postcards for sale all over the place with pictures of snow capped peaks framed against impossibly blue skies, scenes I had yet to see.

The most interesting place I went was Pashupatinath, a suburb of Kathmandu where the bodies of royalty and commoners are burned on ghats perched over a small river. When I was there, I watched four funerals take place: there was no family present, and no ceremonial speeches, or music, or tears. The bodies were offloaded from trucks, laid out in the open. They were then un-wrapped, face up, where flower petals were sprinkled on them. The bodies were then re-wrapped again, for the last time, before being laid out on a large stack of wooden logs that were already set alight.

It was an eye-opening experience to say the least, and a good preparation for Varanasi, that was made even more interesting due to the relaxed nature of the passer-bys, who walked by the burning ghats on the opposite side of the river on their way to school, the market, just stopping to watch the spectacle for a few moments before moving on, munching on snacks, talking on cell phones, and just watching the flames do their job. Death was just another part of life.

There were saddhus here too, watching the scene and trying to convince me, the lone Westerner there, that enlightenment was easy: just follow them up to their caves high up in the mountains.

When the bodies were sufficiently burned, the attendants took metal brooms and swept the burning debris into the river, where it went out with a huge boiling hiss of steam. The next stack of wood was already being put in place for the next body to be burned.

The old town, and especially Durbar Square, was the best place for people-watching: tailors sewed clothes out on the sidewalk, wrinkled women sold saffron garlands for the temples, and random cows had to be avoided as they blocked alleys of traffic. The ubiquitous sadhus were there too, muttering prayers to themselves as they wandered the cobblestone streets in the rain, their dreadlocks dripping water and their calves smeared with grey mud.

I bent down to tie my shoes, and a thumb suddenly flashed out of nowhere, slammed into the center of my forehead, leaving behind a bright orange mark. Stunned, I stood up to find a naked saddhu standing serenely before me, his dreadlocks wrapped expertly around his head, smiling at me. Then he bowed and said some prayer in Nepali. Unsure of what this was, I smiled and turned to go, but the saddhu leapt in front of me and tapped his bowl for a donation. I had heard of beggars being creative to get money, but I'd never thought saddhus had turned to drive-by-blessings to speed up a slow tourist season. I reached into my pocket, pulled out a small note, dropped it in the bowl and left the saddhu behind, to wait for more victims.

As I walked back to my hotel in the growing darkness that night, I passed a contingent of forty soldiers patrolling Durbar Square. Standing there watching the procession, I jumped when someone pulled my sleeve, expecting another random blessing from some impish saddhu. Instead, a well-dressed man in a business suit wordlessly handed me a business card, which read, "All Roads Lead to Everest Casino."

The last neighborhood I went to was Bodnath, a monastic complex built around a large stupa near the airport. After 1959, when Tibet was invaded by China, Katmandu has harbored one of the most vibrant Tibetan communities in the world. Here, elegant silk scarves from Tibet flapped in the breeze next to prayer flags, antique thankas, prayer wheels and conch shells fashioned into horns. It was like an authentic look at old Tibet. Or so I thought.

When I got to Bodnath, there were more tourists than pilgrims, and most of the people walking around clockwise, the Tibetan tradition, in the trademark burgundy red robes were foreigners, their heads shaved, discussing meditation in Australian accents, in German, in Russian. The whole neighborhood looked like a Tibetan Disneyland with Dalai Lama t-shirts, postcards and Potala Palace cafés serving banana pancakes and mango milkshakes.

When I found an internet café five blocks from the stupa, three bald, red-robed monks came in calmly and sat down chatting on cell phones while their friends sent e-mails and surfed Britney Spears websites.

Katmandu is one of those places some of your parents' friends probably went to in the late '60s and early '70s, heading between Turkey and Thailand on the great overland backpacker trail. While the vibe is gone for the most part, it does linger on in some ways, and nowhere moreso than the Snowman Café, around the corner from Freak Street.

Here, for fifty cents, chocolate cake, vanilla milkshakes and other comfort foods are served beneath psychedelic wall paintings and peace symbols dangling from lamps with Marley and Hendrix on the speaker system. Today most of the customers are young hip Nepalis, wearing tie-dyed T-shirts, smoking and sending SMS messages to their friends.

Out one afternoon waiting out a rainstorm, a sixtyish American man came in with his college-aged daughter. They took out their raincoats, grabbed a table by the window and ordered a piece of apple pie each.

"This is the place your father came when he traveled across Asia."

The man's daughter just sat there and stared out the window.

"Before I met your mother, before I started the restaurant, before your brother..." his voice trailed off as the Nepali waiter dropped off the cakes they had ordered. His daughter wasn't interested, just started eating.

Her father repeated the sentences in a louder voice. She just sat there and ate a few more bites, before her dad slammed his fist on the table, dropped some bills on the table and threw up his hands at his daughter's boredom. They left as fast as they had come.

I was sitting in Durbar Square when the thousandth person came up to me asking if I needed a guide. I shook my head and the guy sat down anyway, bored out of his mind. It was the four-month low season, during which even penniless saddhus, I learned, earned more money than he did.

To prove this he pointed to the nearest saddhu, dressed in ochre orange robes and carrying the trademark trident, sitting perched on a low wall accosting tourists as they walked past to take a photo. As we watched, a couple from Europe stopped. The woman smiled and posed by the saddhu, the man took the picture, and then the saddhu stuck out his hand and asked for 1,000 rupees, equivalent to thirteen dollars. The couple gasped, but paid up anyway and moved on.

"See," the tour guide said, "easy money."

On a good day, saddhus could earn five times what a tour guide could earn, so much so that young guides contemplated rolling in human ash and growing thick dreadlocks just to cash in on the Westerners' fascination with saddhus. He went on to say that most of the saddhus weren't here now, because it was low season. I told the guy the story of my drive-by-blessing, and he laughed.

"To see the real saddhu show, you have to come back in September, when the 'official' saddhu season is here."

"The saddhu season?"

"Yes, the saddhu season. They come here to make money from all the tourists here for trekking."

He went on to explain the flood of tourists in the fall, and how their hard currency kept these cool, possessionless holy men who wandered the world in search of enlightenment, rolling in enough cash, and hash, to last them till the next year.

"Where do they go?" I asked. "In the off season?"

"Goa," he said casually. "Techno music. Cheap hash. They hang out with the backpackers there, on vacation."

I guess even saddhus need a vacation, too.

How Well Do You Know Mother Ganges?: Varanasi, India

Nothing can prepare you for the maelstrom of chaos, confusion, cows, noise, dirt, touts, beggars, holy men, suicidal trishaw drivers and more that India sends at you from the moment you arrive.

The day I left Nepal there was a bombing in the Katmandu valley, and security was tight at the airport, with police dogs sniffing car bumpers and searching behind seat cushions for explosives. And with the Indian Airlines flight to Varanasi virtually empty, check in was quick, though six thorough body screenings and bag searches followed before we even boarded the Airbus 320.

After take-off, the cabin crew handed out customs forms. Ten minutes later the chief steward came through the cabin shaking his head and peeled off another form to replace the first, which his female colleagues had given out. Upon landing, the customs agents threw up their hands and issued us a third form to replace the second, which we filled out on the tarmac before being even let into the terminal. When we handed this form to their colleagues inside, they wordlessly handed us an even larger fourth form to replace them all. Welcome to India...

After being spit out of the sweaty terminal, the taxi ride into Varanasi was smooth for the first twenty kilometers as we sped through rural Indian villages, not unlike Vietnam or Kenya, and it seemed the stories of India were exaggerated—but they proved true the instant we plunged into rush hour traffic in Varanasi. While by no means a Mumbai or Calcutta, the streets were crammed with pedestrians, trishaws, cows, beggars, policemen, holy men and street vendors all pushing and shoving their way down to the river, where Sravana, the sacred month honoring the monsoon rains that are so essential to Indian farmers, was underway. Almost everyone was wearing aircraft orange clothes, and men were running around in a religious frenzy.

The crush was so violent that the taxi driver refused to let me out to find my hotel on my own, and called his assistant on his cell phone to come and guide me down the narrow, twisting paths of Varanasi's old city that lead to the sacred waters of the Ganges.

He was right: cud-chewing cows jammed intersections, flies buzzed in clouds so thick I mashed my lips together to avoid sucking one in, and I had to navigate around elderly holy men and women who staggered by, bent double with age, their hair matted into dreadlocks and with their entire worldly possessions carried in cotton sacks.

My room turned out to be a converted shrine that had alcoves for votive candles and arched whitewashed doorways that overlooked the Ganges. Sravana is a religious holiday celebrated each July, and the smell of incense smoke, monotonous chanting, crashing cymbals and celebratory roars from the crowds of devotees went on through the night, every night I was in Varanasi. Devotees carried shoulder poles decorated with cobras and balanced at each end with two ceramic pots that they filled with water they had dipped from the Ganges.

Of course, worshiping Shiva and the monsoon isn't the only Hindu activity in Varanasi, also known as Benares, "The City of Light." For Hindus, to be cremated here is to ensure salvation, and it is the dream of millions to be burned here, though most can't afford it. Here, the simple act of bathing in the river purifies the soul, and thousands come to the city to do just that.

At both ends of the city, large cremation ghats burned twenty four hours a day, seven days a week, smoking the horizon by day, and lighting up the sky at night. Cremating only Hindus at the south end, and all other religions at the north end, the ghats are operated only by the untouchables, who form the lowest caste of Indian society.

As I approached the ghats, the smells of burning hit first; then the silence of my footfalls: as I got closer, I found myself walking on thickly compacted ash and wood shavings from the firewood. Almost every person I passed reminded me not to take pictures.

"No photo, no photo, sir," they said over and over, and as I reached the railing, where no more than ten meters away a dead body was being reduced to ash, they looked into my eyes curiously, to see what my reaction would be, no doubt used to tourists being shocked by the spectacle.

Workers carried dead bodies down to the ghats constantly, where the bodies were prepared for the final sacred funeral rites. Chopped firewood was quickly stacked, and the fires were lit, and the body was then quickly consumed by the flames as onlookers, none of whom were even related to the deceased, looked on.

"No photo," they reminded me again as they staggered past.

The untouchables had grown immensely wealthy off the business of death, and the surrounding neighborhoods near the burning ghats had an otherworldly, alien feeling, completely disassociated even with India, or anything we come to accept as normal in the West. I wandered for hours there, talking to people, watching them work, taking in a scene people in some countries would pay not to see.

Even Indians, visiting the city for the first time, were in shock at the scenes on display everywhere.

"This is shocking, truly shocking, man," mumbled an IT professional as he videotaped the morning puja, where garbage and trash floated around people as they went about their bath.

A lot of time was spent walking along the ghats, as the stone steps leading to the river were exposed because of the low waters of the dry season. Watching people bathe, dogs fight and street vendors sell their wares to people sunning themselves on the steps went on from sun up to sun down.

At one ghat, I lingered longer than normal, snapping pictures, and a crazy man came out of nowhere and vigorously shook my hand up and down and said coldly, "Yes, shit. You take picture of shit. Shit river. Shit city. Come," he said, trying to pull me away by the arm, "I take you to my shit shop."

And each morning I rose before dawn and hired a boat to slip along the ghats to watch the morning puja ceremonies commence, where, all along the Ganges' expansive waterfront, facing the yellow rays of the rising sun, people of all ages and walks of life came to bathe, say prayers, wash clothes, fish, take a nap, consult with a holy man or just take in the scene. They never minded being watched; I sensed a feeling of pride from the people of all ages who went on doing what their ancestors had done for generations.

In the evenings, I would also hire a boat, and in a complete reversal of the dawn ceremonies, I watched people light small candles set in flowers that were set afloat in tiny boats. As it grew dark, large clusters of these candles floated downstream like ever-changing constellations, mirroring the real ones in the dark, vast sky above.

A lot of time in between was spent just dodging the predatory touts, who pecked you like vultures at a dead carcass, whereever you went, no matter what you said or did. Everyone had something to sell you, either reams of silk or a boat ride or a head massage or an internet connection, and despite your real name printed in your passport, forget it, because in Varanasi, it will change to:

"Hello, Hashish."

"Hello, Massage."

"Hello, Marijuana."

When a ten year old kid asked me my name, I replied casually, "Marijuana." When he wrinkled his nose, no more than ten seconds passed before a bleary-eyed tout wandered up and wheezed, "Hello, Marijuana."

The kid burst out laughing and whenever I passed by him or his friends they shouted, "Hello!! Marijuana!!! Hello!!" which earned me strange looks from the Western tourists wandering past.

With so much enlightenment and drugs everywhere, the place was bound to attract its fair share of crazies. And it has: all you have to do is walk down the ghats and you will see them: local saddhus smeared with human ash, comparing their dreadlocks with an equally bleary-eyed saddhu from Santa Cruz; groups of Japanese religious students, heads freshly shaven, bathe in the Ganges, urged on by a gnarled guru standing high and dry above them on the platform; a white saddhu, well known in both Kathmandu and Varanasi, wanders around carrying an umbrella in all weather, shouting at people in Swedish and saluting people as though in a military parade; while whole clusters of others crash out for days on the ghats sleeping off their latest hash binge; ignored by all except for the numerous stray dogs, the canines forgoing enlightenment and just curling up next to these convenient bodies for warmth to ward off the overnight chill.

When I stepped off the boat from my last trip down the Ganges, one such saddhu, lucid now as he awakened from yet another drug fest, eyed me coolly as I paid the boatman and stepped onto dry land.

"How well do you know Mother Ganges, the river that is sacred to all Indians?" he asked in perfect English with all the seriousness of a customs official.

"OK," I answered lamely, with a tired smile, as I walked away, hoping to avoid a lecture and the request for another donation.

Just when I thought I had escaped him, he swiveled his head around.

"How much?!" he thundered, smacking the concrete angrily with his hands for emphasis, sending molting pigeons and stray dogs scattering away from him in all directions.

McNirvana: Dharmsala

Was Dharmsala just another franchise of McNirvana, where people came from near and far to soak up and tank up on spiritualism and religion, and nothing more?

As I got off the bus from Amritsar, it seemed just that. As a town perched high on a spur of the lower Himalayas, it was decked out with the usual round of internet cafés, banana pancake breakfast joints, and bhang (marijuana) lassis on the menu. Everywhere I looked, flyers advertised Tibetan massage, Tibetan cooking, Tibetan meditation, Tibetan thanka painting and Tibetan enlightenment courses, offered to the crowds of pirate-pants wearing, Nepali-cotton-bag-toting members of The Tribe, the blurred international set of travelers that pounded the place's pavement, or lack thereof, in search of either spiritual sustenance or a natural high trekking in some of the world's tallest mountains.

Beyond The Tribe, I found the spirit of Dharmsala to be so much deeper: I lingered at steet corners, talking to friendly Tibetan monks eager to practice their English; I waved at lively Tibetan grandmothers who wore broad smiles at any time of the day, watched whole Tibetan families running shops and businesses and always ready to say hello, and, finally, saw His Holiness the Dalai Lama himself, who had lived here for forty-five years with his government-in-exile after being driven out of his homeland in 1959.

Over seventy years old, he kept a very active schedule of preaching and teaching, and I learned as soon as I checked into my hotel that there was a specially scheduled teaching going on while I was in Dharmasala.

Everywhere I went in the town, people were talking about it: The Teaching. Sixteen tour buses of Taiwanese Buddhists were in town, and after giving a hefty donation to the Tibetan cause, had been granted a ten-day lecture series by his Holiness. It was open to the public as well, the English translation of which was broadcast on local radio.

"Oh, I'm just waiting for my friend," a British woman told the waiter in the restaurant primly, as he tried to take her order. A few minutes later she checked her watch and stood up to go. "I'll be back, after the second Teaching," she said cryptically to the man who nodded his head in understanding, like in some spy movie.

"Do you know what time it is?" asked an Aussie girl, even though I wasn't wearing a watch.

"8:15," I told her, remembering the clock I had seen on the wall where I had just gotten breakfast.

"Oh," she slurred, "my holy man told me it was eleven o'clock." She laughed as though this was hysterical. Then she turned serious. "Are you here for The Teachings, too?"

As I walked to the temple, following the crowds down the hill, I saw a woman who had been on my bus from Amritsar walking along in front of me, conversing in rapid-fire Korean with the stray dogs that lived in the town. She was feeding them rice paper snacks that she tossed like birdseed from a bag in her backpack, but they refused to eat them, and they were getting more and more aggressive, looking for meat, anything more substantial than flimsy crackers. This made her furious, and she slapped her thighs in disgust, spitting out more angry Korean bursts that left the dogs more perplexed, wary of this mad woman, and still hungry.

"Oh, hello," she said to me kindly when she recognized my face. "You go to The Teachings, now?"

At 8:30 the lecture started, and though no one is allowed to see the Dalai Lama inside the temple, crowds gathered outside to listen, prostrating themselves on the floor in front of the monastery as they lifted their clasped hands to their heads, faces and hearts. It was eerie watching the monsoon clouds crash into the hills while his voice trailed off into the forest of pine trees behind the complex, thinking how much his people in Tibet would give for him to lecture directly from the Potala Palace, his ancestral home.

When the lecture was over, he made his way back to his residence. Suddenly the three hundred Tibetans, many of whom were dressed in traditional clothing and draped in chunky turquoise jewelry, sank to the ground as though in the presence of a King, and it was impossible not to be moved as the tears flowed down their cheeks and their hands clasped over their heads.

I was lucky to be standing right where he swept down the staircase, and was one of the few people he shook hands with before he stepped into his tan-colored Suzuki SUV. He smiled at me through the glass and pressed his hands together. I bent, smiled back, and briefly felt like Richard Gere.

The rest of the day I spent meeting some of the other residents of Dharmsala, all of whom had skipped The Teachings that day, perhaps because they didn't need any, or maybe because they had already had been filling their heads with enough Teachings of their own.

Some were posted on the walls:

"My Fellow Dharma Brothers and Sisters, I implore you to please read the Golden Light of Sutra 1,000 times in the next twenty-four hours, to alleviate the violence, pain and suffering in Iraq. Our positive energy flowing from India will therefore immediately reduce the suffering there."

"If anyone is catching the train to Delhi from Pathankot tomorrow, and wants to share a taxi to the train station, please contact Tenzin Chorghi, the (very tall) American nun formerly known as Sharon."

"Looking for someone who answers to the name of Xi. Of former British nationality, has been living in India for seven years. Please contact Rinpoche Smith at the Shangrila Hotel.'

The rest, however, were strictly off the wall.

"How long more will you be traveling in India?" I asked a French girl as we watched the parade of monks and nuns, after The Teachings, go back to their monasteries.

She scratched her head and said, "I dunno, my passport expired three months ago."

An Israeli grandmother of twelve had decided to stay in India forever.

"It will never change," she added happily, "and I will never leave," as she knitted a hideous purple scarf at the foot of a waterfall, just outside of Dharmsala. "Why should I go back, where my children can, how you Americans say, put me in a home?"

"But where do you plan to go?"

"Everywhere. Everything is possible in India. Look, even the Dalai Lama is here, who will be next?" as though she expected the Pope to relocate to the Subcontinent.

"Have you been to Kerala, the south?"

"No, not yet. I keep being distracted. I don't know, the spiritual energy keeps pulling me north," she said with a straight face, "like a magnet. I've never been south of Delhi."

A Spanish girl in a café leaned over to me and pointed to a word in her Ayurvedic massage handbook.

"What does this word mean?" she asked dreamily, as she pointed to the word "hibernate."

When I told her what it meant, she smiled, thanked me, and returned to her manual.

"How long have you been here?" I asked the blonde curly haired Dutch girl who sold me her bus ticket to Manali, because her hew Tibetan boyfriend was now taking her to Srinagar, Kashmir, for the Peace Festival there, and she was off the next morning to cling to the back of his motorbike for three days.

"Oh, about a month."

"You are here for studying?"

"Yes."

"Have you been to the Dalai Lama's for his Teachings each day?"

"I went, the first day, and it was very interesting, don't get me wrong, but once I'd seen him, well, that was enough." Her voice trailed off. "But since then, I've been... so busy."

"With what?"

"Classes," she said vaguely, as though she were trying to remember exactly what she had been in the classes for. "One was for Water Therapy," she said brightly. "We sat in circles, drinking water, for hours, and were told of the healing power it had on the body, the importance of drinking enough water each day, and the spiritual dangers of not drinking enough."

"I think that's called dehydration."

"Oh no, it was developed over thousands of years, this Water Therapy."

"How much was the course?"

"2,000 rupees..."

"Sod enlightenment and trekking, I'm here for the food," scoffed an Irishman and his mates on the terrace of a restaurant run entirely by twelve-year-old school kids on summer holiday. They were in India for nine months and couldn't stop dreaming of all the Western food they had eaten in Kathmandu.

A Canadian woman with long blonde hair was talking to an Aussie girl working at a Tibetan bookstore, perched in a pine forest high above Dharmsala, in the Tushita Meditation Center blessed by the Dalai Lama.

"Can you tell me the four noble truths?" she asked her new friend.

"Uhhh... no, not all of them," the Aussie girl replied sheepishly after she could remember just two, though she had been studying the religion for nine years and spoke nearly fluent Tibetan.

"Did you get The Teaching His Holiness gave yesterday?" the Canadian women went on, unperturbed.

"What, the one about women's bodies being disgusting?"

"Yes," the Canadian Girl sighed, running her hands through her hair in frustration. "I'm having so many conflicts here. I'm thinking I should go home, leave this place. I mean, it's no good to the other students in the class when I am so confused."

"I think it was a metaphor for male monks to reduce their desires," her new friend offered, hoping to calm her recently acquired, and increasingly agitated, friend.

Canadian Girl nodded her head violently. "I know, I know. I am, like, devoted to more than one species, in this lifetime, you know, and I don't know how the Dalai Lama, who doesn't have a vagina, can sit there and tell me, a woman, who has a vagina, that it's evil. I mean come on, women, with their cycles, are connected to the earth..."

Altitude Attitude: Leh, Ladakh

Leh, the capital of Ladakh, was once a stop along the vast Silk Road that stretched across Asia; a tiny, Buddhist, mud-walled town hiding in the shadow of the royal palace that clings to a rocky hill directly above the jumbled labyrinth of the Old City's narrow lanes. Ladakhi Gompas, Tibetan Buddhist monasteries, are perched even higher, with golden yellow curtains flapping against whitewashed walls where lines of prayer flags are stretched across the deep blue sky.

With the summer high season in full swing, the town's bazaar hummed with whole Argentinean families in trekking gear, blonde Swiss mountaineers, more stoned, stone-faced, and dread-locked Israelis than Manali, British social workers doing farm projects in Zanskar, and clusters of chainsmoking French package tourists, while the locals tried to go about their daily lives with dignity, snapped rudely in photographs if they wore any turquoise or were carrying prayer wheels—even school children walking home from school had to carry newspapers to cover their faces when tourists tried to take their photos.

"You!" a bearded man shouted at me in the main bazaar. "We met. Kabul Bazaar. Remember? You were traveling with the German puppeteer…?"

"I've never been to Kabul, sorry..."

"Kabul! We met in Kabul, last year. It was summer." He lifted his hands in frustration.

"I told you, I've never been to Afghanistan..."

"I'm sure of it. You bought a lapis lazuli necklace for her, and..."

No matter what I told the man while I was in Leh, he was convinced I was the guy who married the German puppeteer from Bremen, and every time he saw me he greeted me like some long lost friend.

"You! Kabul!" he shouted each time.

That experience summed up perfectly what Ladakh was like, because Leh was packed with people escaping the monsoons in the south, and hardly a day went by when some character you had seen on a train, bus or plane in India didn't walk past you in the bazaar: the crazy Frenchman from the Rajasthani train fistfight; the ditzy Australian from Dharmsala who had now divorced herself from her holy man; the Austrian couple that had gotten "more" in their food than they had paid for in Jaisalmer. Six Scots I had met in Agra, still decked out in their Pakistani wardrobe, made a brief appearance at a Tibetan restaurant one night, but left quickly when they couldn't get a table.

Even two anonymous travelers that had bailed out of my jeep trip to

Leh were found sitting in a corner table of an internet café, still smiling sheepishly after arriving from Srinagar, until the dagger-sharp looks from me and my travelling companions Brandon, Yael and Steven scared them away like vampires from daylight.

"The travel gods have yet to curse them," snarled Steven.

With the phones never working, the power always off more than it was on, and the internet eternally clogged, Leh was great for catching up on our individual Indian journeys, feasting on Tibetan and Indian food while watching the sun creep up the hills as it set behind the glacier capped mountains, and drinking mint tea and fresh apple juice from Kashmir.

"Hello, friend," said a tall blonde massage therapist from LA, (who I will call Phoebe), at my guesthouse the first morning I arrived, shattered from the two day slog from Manali. "Welcome."

She had just arrived in India, was here as a dedicated Spiritual Tourist and had not only done a three-week camel trek in Mali—during which she had completed a Native American rite of passage, where she meditated on a mat and only drank water for a week—she had also completed, she said with a smug smile, four ten-day Vipassana no-talking meditation courses in Big Sur, California.

Phoebe had only been here a week and was already an expert on where the best trekking company was and where the best vegetarian food was and where you could stay in a monastery for free if you didn't mind cold showers.

"Come to Summer Bounty, tonight, friend," Phoebe said slowly, referring to the veg/chill out restaurant on Fort Road. "There will be some groovy people there."

There were groovy people there that night, but it felt like the intergalactic bar in *Star Wars*, with practically every nationality represented, freaked out to the extreme. A poster on the wall announced a séance later in the week for channeling the "Great Spirit of Bob Barley," Janis Joplin was on the sound system, and even the Ladakhi waiters had dreads down to their knees.

A Swiss woman was warning her newfound friends of the bacterial dangers of sharing joints mouth-to-mouth, and was instructing them on how to stick it in their noses to inhale; a lone stray Yak had wandered into the restaurant and was eating the flower arrangements off an empty table, a Scot was telling all about the book he'd just read, claiming the Bush family were space aliens.

And when a German woman asked a man thought to be a native of her country "Where are you from?" the Caucasian man stared back at her and growled, "Goa."

The whole place was horizontal: people's bodies were scattered all over the carpeted floor, lying stretched out on pillows smoking chillums and talking in low voices. As soon as I walked in, I felt vertical, and self-consciously crouched down until I recognized Phoebe crashed out in the corner showing off her Masai warrior scar to some stringy haired Kiwi girl.

"Hello, friend," Phoebe said, introducing me to her "smoking buddies," who peered at me sagely through a haze of a thousand lifetimes' smoked hash. No one even acknowledged me, and even Phoebe went back to explaining the meaning of her scar/tattoo.

When the waiter took my order, a girl across from me blew pot smoke in my face and started to cackle like a witch. Maybe it was the altitude, or the choking incense, but before my drink, or food, even came, it was time to for Alex to leave the Rabbit Hole.

The altitude was fierce. The town sits at over 12,000 feet, and on my second day in Leh, I was crouched down for a few minutes buying some apricots. When I stood up, suddenly the world went black, spun around like a washing machine and I was falling through a tornado-hole in the ground... when I came to I was staring up at the sun, a Ladakhi grandmother was screaming in my face and fanning me with her silk hat, and my now-useless legs were blocking traffic, both bovine and vehicular: a huge cow and a massive army jeep loomed over my head and somehow I managed to crawl out of the way before being first trampled and then run over.

Though Leh won hands down over Manali for freakdom, as always in India, it was religions that defined the odd Masala mixture of the transient visitors to Leh: Islamic Kashmiris, always ready to strike a bargain for a pashmina shawl over bottomless cups of mint tea; Ladakhi Tibetan Buddhist monks, on pilgrimages visiting historic gompas in the Indus valley; Jewish Rabbis, flown in from Israel by their government to celebrate the Sabbath each week at the Leh Jewish House, to keep the newly discharged, and very disgruntled soldiers, Jewish; Catholic, cross-wearing Europeans, celebrating weekly masses at a different hotel; and even a few hardy naked saddhus that hung around the main square, looking for alms to fall into their hands. And day and night, all over Leh, on swirled the World's Finest Freak Show: free, weird, surreal, and always entertaining. "Whee!!!!" shouted some French girl as she spotted a stray cow chewing on some garbage. "Une vache sacre!!" she wailed to the night sky, bowing down before the bovine creature reverently as though she were in the presence of some great celestial being, as the cow, now wary of this mad woman, munched on.

Booked on an excursion arranged by Yael and Steven, we left one morning before dawn and caught a bus to the Tikse Gompa, seventeen kilometers from Leh, where the dawn puja, or cleansing, ceremony takes place in a musty room holding an enormous bronze Buddha statue, with walls painted with scenes from hell, amid the strong stench of rancid yak butter tea.

The Gompa complex covers an entire hillside, modeled on the Potala Palace in Lhasa, and has priceless views of the glacier covered mountains across the Indus river valley. With over one hundred and fifty monks in residence, they rise each day at dawn to the sound of two yellow Mohawk-hatted monks who blow bone-white conch shell horns encrusted with turquoise stones and silver work from the wooden roof, and they come in, one by one, smiling at each other and saying "Ju Le! Greetings!" before filling the rows of straw mat covered benches in descending lines of age, from eighty down to just eight years old. When the venerable Rinpoche of Tikse is seated, they strike a yak skin gong, and the chanting and meditation of the puja begins.

Slowly, as the daily ceremony gets underway, the monks begin to rock back and forth in their seats, eyes squeezed shut, hands at their sides as the Rinpoche, wearing the same yellow robes and seventies-esque John Denver-style sunglasses as the Dalai Lama, conducts the pitch and tone of the mantras and phrases repeated by all in attendance.

Except for two. The youngest monks sitting right in front of me whispered continuously back and forth so much that when a senior monk walked past he bashed their shaven heads with prayer books. The youngest, Problem Child, was the worst, and he acted as though the whole puja was just a joke and all the monks were there just for him to laugh at. Even more funny were the foreigners sitting with their backs to the walls, appropriately sitting as far away from the Buddha as possible, and directly beneath fierce portrayals of blue-headed demons smashing the skulls of the wicked and deceitful.

During the three-hour puja, Problem Child didn't close his eyes for a second. He just hummed some nonsense song that clashed with the monotone chanting, and in punishment got himself assigned to tea duty: he had to lug huge brass teapots around, filling all the senior monks' bowls with tea in penance, bowing to them deeply as they continued their mantras and chanting.

When it was finally over, the monks spilled out into the thin desert light and continued the chores they were meant to complete before the next puja at noon.

Problem Child took off down the stairs shrieking like it was the last day of school.

Perched high over the town, Shanti Stupa is Japanese-built and features a shiny round Buddha statue facing in the four sacred directions. With more staggering views over Leh and the Indus river valley, it's a favorite place to watch the sunset, and like everywhere in Leh during the high season, there was a battle to deal with the crowds of people jostling for space. Steven and Yael were leaving on the flight to Delhi the next morning, and we decided to brave the 600 steps at about 5:30 p.m. when the sun's fierce rays had finally died off. We took about fifteen steps and practically collapsed, gasping for air in the thin atmosphere as Ladakhi school children laughed at us, scampering up them as easily as if they were walking down, instead of up.

By the time we reached the top, the sun had slipped behind the mountains, and the valley floor, now darkened, stretched before us. We could see a Ladakhi polo match, we could hear the distant calls of prayer from the Kashmiri mosque in town (where a Pakistani flag fluttered, defiantly, most days) and watched great armadas of Indian Army trucks and vehicles trailing even greater dust clouds as they drove off to their distant army bases near the Chinese and Pakistani borders.

When we finally reached the platform in front of the Shanti Stupa, high and isolated in the most remote reaches of the Himalayas, it felt like Rome in August, awash with two camps: Cows and Meditators. The place reverberated with the usual Tower of Babel languages you hear everywhere from Angkor Wat to the Tower of London to Ipanema Beach.

As the only independent travelers there, we dropped our voices immediately—hard for Yael and Steven, who shouted most of the time—and crept around the lotus-seated foreigner meditators with care, watching out not to smash any fingers. We avoided the herds of Cows/Tourists, too, and their guides who looked at us contemptuously like we were army AWOLs without our "General" to tell us where to eat and what to see in their country. We used hand signals to communicate and found an empty place near the precipitous edge where we could shoot our photos without disturbing anyone, the Tourist/Cows or the Meditators. All around us was The Silence.

"Click," went Steven's camera, with the precision of a rifle.

"Hum," went Yael's, with the scream of an AK-47.

"Whine," went mine, as though magnified through loud speakers.

There was a murmur of disapproval from the Cows, and rustling of angst among the Meditators, and we exchanged glances and hand-motioned to cut the photos out.

It was too late. A tour guide snapped his fingers at us, and a tall blonde foreign woman went a step further, emerging from her bliss, swiveling her neck around like a Buddhist Exorcist, shooting us a look of pure hatred, and screaming, "Can you take your god damned cameras and jump off the mountain. Sod off!"

Most evenings in Leh, the power was dead, and the "nightlife" consisted of bakery-hopping, from the English to the Swiss to the German to the Dutch, and around again, sitting around before flickering candles, draped in our hideous purple and blue $2 wool Kashmiri shawls, talking travel and drinking the only, and most awful, beer available in Ladakh: Kingfisher, made by an Indian multimillionaire from the south who likened himself to Richard Branson, and was planning to start a low-cost airline in India the following year—his vision was to create a cross between Southwest Airlines and Hooters Air.

Sometimes Phoebe was there, with new friends in tow, other times it was clusters of Israelis who were friends of Steven and Yael, who drowned out English with Hebrew in the predominantly Israeli company that was all around us; other times it was travelers we met while visiting gompas, and others it was Nepalis and Sikkimese who had cornered the Bakery market in Ladakh and distributed every chocolate croissant, apple crumble, and peach cobbler to the highest bakeries in the world.

Into Thin Air: Little Tibet

No matter what time of year you come to Ladakh, there are always toothpaste-white glaciers hanging from anywhere you look in the mountains: outside your hotel window, perched behind some thousand year old village, or sliding down a ravine towards a seething river. The country is so high, and the air so thin, that they never melt. Snow and freak blizzards are also possible at any time of the year, especially in the mountain passes, which can be snowbound even in the middle of summer.

Surrounding Leh are three of the world's highest passes, where ancient trade routes from central Asia had no other choice but to climb over them to reach markets, and civilization. Kardung La was the highest, at 5,600 meters; followed by Tang Lang La, with 5,400 meters, and then there was Chang La, at 5,100 meters. With autumn fast approaching, snowflakes were already starting to settle on the higher elevations around Leh, and the mountains were turning silver and white overnight. Yet the human flakes in town had yet to be chased off to southern, warmer climates, and herds of them continued to gather in the main square of the town, chilling out, eating Nepali cakes and pastries, and also trying to arrange group trips over some of the world's highest roads to places off-limits just a few years ago: Nubra Valley, Pangong Lake, the Zanskar valley and Moriri Lake.

Posters carpeted the place with urgent requests to join jeeps to Kashmir, Manali, even Delhi, and to share costs for an eight to ten day camping trek. All the travelers seemed eager, responsible and reliable, but the reality one learned was that for whatever reason, the altitude, the heat or just something that was in seeping into the water, 90% of travelers flaked out, backed out and just plain disappeared.

"I could have strangled that Japanese girl, friend," said Phoebe in a rare show of anger one day at lunch, as she dug into her vegetarian Tibetan soup. "That girl simply vanished like a ghost."

At first I could hardly sympathize with her, having had just one nasty experience with the bad behavior of two travelers in Manali as proof of what she had already experienced. But once I began to arrange my own trips, the problems mounted like the mountains all around us, and by the time I left Ladakh, I swore I would never rely on another traveler again.

One of the closest places to go was Nubra Valley, the furthest north you can go in India, off limits for foreigners until just recently, where I went with Yael and Steven, another Israeli couple with shaven heads, a couple of Italian astronomers, two British guys from Manchester, two Polish social workers and two Swiss Italian chemists.

The main "religious" draw for travelers to Nubra was not the spiritual pull of Dharmsala, or the ashram that was Rishikesh; it was the cathedral-like mountains, icy blue rivers and lush green valleys that resembled the scenes of Afghanistan flooding the international news programs at the time.

The trip nearly collapsed when the four Israelis complained that the jeep they found that morning was not the "big jeep" they had been promised; and the trip was nearly called off as the travel agent desperately tried to explain that the "big jeep" was always the mode of transport for environmental reasons. The arguments flew back and forth in the office, discounts were promised, and the British barmen laughed at the "transvestites" that were causing the delay, and tried to remember the lyrics of the Eurovision song contest, won the previous year by an Israeli tranny. The trip finally left four hours late.

Kardung La Pass sits between the Nubra valley and Leh, and stands as the highest road in the world, just under 5,600 meters, or 18,300 feet.

Take two steps up there, and you're already gasping for breath, but the Sikh soldiers who were stationed at Kardung La, oblivious to the amazing so-close-you-could-touch-them view of the snow-swathed Karokorum mountain range just behind the pass, were playing a tense game of cricket in the thin air, the World's Highest Cricket Match.

A French film crew, smoking, of course, sucking even harder on their Gauloises in the high altitude, filmed away as some French mountaineers group hugged and cheered "Bravo!!", some Aussie rugby blokes were trying to chat up some wisp-thin Dutch girls on puttering Vespas and some dread-locked Japanese were posing, *Easy Rider* style, on their 500 cc Enfield motorbikes as their friends recorded it with their shiny Sony.

The scenery after Kardung La was a lot of "same same, but different": huge mountains, steep, stomach-churning drop-offs, bone-white glaciers and deep river valleys full of gleaming Buddhist stupas with Ladakhi settlements and their complex irrigation systems channeling cold, clear glacial melt water to their barley, potato field and apple orchards.

Ignoring the scenery, most of the people in the bus talked Europolitik with each other, trashing the Euro currency and bemoaning the impending addition of ten new states, which set off the Poles like a bucket of water dumped on a cat to defend their motherland and the honey pot of money they would get to build up their country.

The British guys, dressed in black track suits, sent poisonous looks at the Swiss and their perfect alpine gear and accessories, while the Italians had gone shopping before we left, expertly matching their new Indian Pashmina shawls with their dark brown leather shoes.

"Look," the British guys said sarcastically to the Italians when the driver pointed out a herd of Pashmina goats munching on some grass, "There crawls your next season's Pashmina!"

"Si," the Italians countered coldly, serene as monks behind their gold Dolce and Gabbana sunglasses, "Versace winter collection."

I was still firmly under the wings of Yael and Steven, and throughout the bumpy journey they lectured me sternly on the cheapest way to travel in Israel and introduced me to Hebrew food, including an Israeli-inspired dessert (not eaten in Israel), oddly called "Hello to the Queen," made of chocolate sauce covering a bowl full of chalk-dust-dry cookie crumbs and cashew nuts. They perfected my Hebrew pronunciation, which consisted of long sessions practicing hacking up an imaginary phlegm ball to get the special sound that I heard constantly in India.

"Indians can reproduce this sound as expertly as any Israeli," I said to them brightly, referring to the constant spitting and throat scouring that went on all day and night, in train stations, streets and other public places. They were not amused.

Our accommodation was in a Ladakhi farmhouse, large and rambling, with mud-brick construction and hay bales stored on the roof for the long, cold winter, where temperatures would soon plunge to -30° Celcius.

We all pitched in for dinner to make the dough for the Ladakhi momos, pasta shells stuffed with peas and spinach, and helped the matron of the house steam them over a fire lit in her tiny courtyard; her husband invited us inside afterwards, and happily sent round cup after cup of chang, fermented barley wine that tasted like watery, sour orange juice but was as strong as rubbing alcohol.

Tibetan food is bland and plain, and while it fills you up, you tire of it quickly.

"Where's the barmaid with my mead and victuals?" joked the Brits as they turned their noses up at the same food we had all eaten for weeks. The Poles lauded the cook for momos resembling the large plain dumplings they ate at home, while the Italians picked at their food, diva-like, and talked endlessly with the Swiss Italians about the swish fusion restaurants they missed from Milan. The Brits got pissed on some Kingfisher beer they had brought along in their backpacks, but had forgotten to pack a single shred of warm clothing.

After dinner, we walked to the dyke, where cold water gushed through sluices into the fields of barley that were already turning brown. The sun was gone, fallen behind the mountains, and great stretches of darkness crept across the land, erasing the deeper river gorges first, then the dark green settlements stretched along the river; then the Gompas higher in the hills, and the final act being the slow crawl up the mountains, the waning light tinging the tops pink and gold several hours after the sun had slipped behind the icy Himalayas. The temperature plunges immediately, and the stars that came out were so bright the sky was still light blue when they appeared, and even shooting stars were visible long before darkness fell.

Except for the Israelis, who quickly grabbed the entire indoor room set aside in the farmhouse for travelers, the rest of us went outside, under the brightest carpet of stars outside of the horn of Africa or outback Australia, and counted as many as three shooting stars per minute streaking simultaneously across the sky.

The voice of the river, which first put us to sleep, grew louder during the night, and as the Ladakhis' intricate network of canals and sluices sprung to life after midnight, with the opening of the floodgates to irrigate the land at dawn, the rush turned to a roar. When we woke up, the square patch of land we had slept on was now surrounded by large gurgling streams leading to the thirsty fields.

On our way back to Leh, we stopped off at dark sand dunes where double-humped Bactrian camels, left over from the ancient silk trade from China, still grazed on food in the valley floor, now harnessed by enterprising Kashmiris for rides.

With three quarters of its waters in Tibet, and only one quarter in India, Pangong Lake is as far east as you can go in Ladakh; a deep turquoise, Maldivian blue that stands shimmering, and calm, in front of 7,000 meter, permanently snow-bound mountains, you can actually see the beginning of the Dalai Lama's home country and even higher snowfields than those around Leh.

It's also a place where you need a permit to visit, and India's bureaucracy stretches even to the high Himalayas. Border guards snap to attention stiffly when your car approaches and each takes a copy of the permit, and a good look at your face, when you pass through: like Kashmir, border tensions exist with the Chinese, too.

My last trip got off to a bad start; two Israeli brothers, heirs to a Tel Aviv furniture fortune, claimed they had been told it was a strictly out and back trip, with no overnight camping involved, despite the posters stating it was a three day trip; Fabienne, the no nonsense, French-Algerian journalist from Radio France, who had been among the first teams to arrive in Kabul and Baghdad after they fell to the Americans, was adamant that camping was going to be part of her vacation, and having already lost three days waiting for other travelers to make up their minds, argued fiercely with me to convince the guys not to puss out and come along, camping along side us.

Arguments flew back and forth, and finally the trip was off. As a last-ditch effort, I huddled with Fabienne for one last time and convinced her we should let the guys come back alone, as we would brave hitch hiking or the local bus back to Leh. Fabienne agreed, and the trip was back on.

We left at seven the next day, and during the long drive and waits at checkpoints, Fabienne taught me volumes about the *Apocalypse Now* similarities of "Bush's Video Games" in the Middle East, how blue smoke was used to obscure American soldiers from Iraqi battalions as they were bombed to death, how cigar-chomping generals pushed back the journalists who had gathered, circus-like, watching the spectacle, and how the 300-strong CNN team was there to support just one on-camera host who actually stood in the window of his five-star hotel wearing a helmet and flak jacket despite there being no danger whatsoever; and how a Chicago news man refused to wash his face for fifteen days so his "viewers would know how hard he was working" at covering the war in Iraq.

The conversation then swerved towards Israel, and the Israelis bristled as she went on explaining how she had interviewed Arafat, and had been in Gaza and Ramullah dozens of times. One of the Israelis had been a soldier stationed there, and she asked him if he knew about the Grandmothers, retired Israeli women who cross-questioned soldiers who held up innocent

Palestinians without cause when crossing the checkpoints.

"No," he said coldly.

When the atmosphere became too tense, I swerved the conversation back to Iraq, and Fabienne went on, revealing tips on how she smuggled SAT phones past anti-French American generals, and got closer "access" to news stories by bribing eighteen-year-old American soldiers with free SAT phone calls to Iowa and Alaska, the best way to appear Afghani (hunch over, wear a burqa and shed the Nikes for safety), how to get access to former Taliban leaders in the hills above Kabul and how she had been reporting at Ground Zero hours after 9/11 because she was on vacation in New York at the time of the attacks.

"Oh, I'm dreaming of my Kabul," Fabienne said to me when we passed over Chang La, completely snow-covered and freezing cold as we waited to pass through yet another check point; when she saw the Indian soldiers wandering around brandishing weapons on the third highest pass in the world. Later she became even more Afghan homesick when she saw solitary road crews smashing rocks to make the roads that kept the Indian army running.

"Just like my Khandahar," she said dreamily, going on to explain how her colleagues, and good friends, were killed on that road in an ambush, and how the UN charged 2,000 American dollars for a flight that lasted less than twenty minutes.

The last hour of the road to Pangong was amazing; a deep, verdant green moss grew along the river valley, and we stopped to listen to our voices echo around the purple rocks and crags that rose above our heads.

In the afternoon, we laid, Cannes-style, on towels by the shimmering lake, watching the blues change with every passing cloud and watching the mesmerizing shadows creep and crawl across the rocky scree slopes that tumbled down from the glaciers.

When it was time to go back to Leh, the Israelis tried to convince us to go with them, but Fabienne and I stayed firm; the driver, eager to get home, told us a bus was leaving at 12:30, and that we couldn't buy a ticket until eleven the next day.

We said goodbye, and found a place in an abandoned field, outside of town, and pitched our tent as the sun set. As Fabienne read her book, I hiked up to a nearby gompa, built into a cave, chatted with some teenage villagers and watched the clouds turn to gold with young monks who said little but smiled a lot.

When Christine and I arrived at the bus station the next morning, just before ten, after collapsing our tents, we were white-faced to find that the bus was almost about to leave.

We hadn't even bought tickets, and were still on the roof of the Jammu & Kashmir (J & K) bus when the driver just lurched into gear and took off, with us hanging on like monkeys, frantically climbing up onto the pitching roof to tie down our bags, before crawling down the bus's shakey and cracked aluminum ladder and inched our way along the bumper to the back door, our teeth chattering wildly, where we slid inside to find the bus passengers packed inside like chicken feathers in a pillow.

Somehow, the conductor took pity on us, found us some seats by moving around some bundles and bags, right between five Indian soldiers carrying rusty AK-47s. They looked at my French companion with contempt and sat there smiling Cheshire cat-like at her as we bumped along, barely able to contain themselves.

Fabienne, tired of the male chauvinist "eve teasing" that she had experienced in India, where Indian men leer, sneer and make hissing noises at women, grabbed one of the guns, cocked it, and aimed out the window at a mountain, earning the respect of the soldiers, and also earning us a new seat next to the driver, who regaled us of stories fighting the Taliban factions in Kashmir that fled over the border after the Americans attacked, Fabienne told him stories of riding the Americans' "toys," the Black Hawk helicopters and Hummers in the Iraqi desert and how the first time she had met Arafat at a conference he had patted her head affectionately, like a puppy.

At our lunch break, at some lonely restaurant high in some pass, a friendly Tibetan monk behind me tapped me on the shoulder and handed me a heavy wedge of barley dough, that was raw, with a hunk of yak cheese in the middle.

Fabienne flatly refused, even though she hadn't eaten solid food for six days due to the altitude, and watched me, smirking, as I discovered that not only was the yak cheese runny, a generous amount of yak fur was mixed in with the dough. Happily waiting for me to swallow the Tibetan delicacy, Fabienne could hardly contain herself.

"Bon appetit," she said facetiously, pursing her lips together to stop from laughing.

Braver than I had been in the past, I picked off as many yak hairs as I could see, and tore off a piece; I took a deep breath and popped it in my mouth. It was not only as sour as the chang I had drunk in the Nubra valley, but there was way more yak fur that I thought inside, and as I swallowed, I almost dry heaved as the yak fur stuck in my throat. Fabienne came to the rescue and handed me her water bottle as she collapsed in laughter. The monk slapped me on the back, grinning, thinking that it was my enjoyment of his food that made me grimace so strongly. When we stopped for the next break, the yak-fur-sandwich went straight into the bottom of a ravenous stray dog's stomach sleeping by the side of the road, who inhaled the food like a furry vacuum cleaner.

Just after navigating the twisty roads, and as we were accelerating towards the straighter roads of the Indus Valley, a deafening explosion ripped through the bus, which we thought was a gas canister that had blown up on top of the roof. It was actually a tire blowout, and we nearly rolled off the cliff while the bus driver tried to control the lurching vehicle. It took thirty minutes to fix it, and then we were back on the road after the truck tire on the roof was dusted off and cinched into place.

Three hours later we pulled into Leh, passing the Israel brothers sipping strong apricot juice, but smiling weakly. The travel agent that had rented us the car grinned at us even more, relieved to see that we had come back in one piece.

Between trips to the far corners of Ladakh, I had short stays in Leh, where the Freak Wheel spun on: bearded Eurotrash walked bare-chested and barefoot through the town banging cymbals, their girlfriends trailing behind them twirling their hair; the Kashmiris patiently asking again and again for us to sit with them drinking a mint tea, hearing about the problems of their country and how buying a Pashmina for our dahlings would help solve them; French girls drew long drags on their Gauloises in cafés that oozed nothing but Parisian stink, not chic; and sunburned Brits came back from ten-day high altitude treks raving about the Premier League football matches they had missed on Sky Sports.

A notice was posted for a three-day trip to Moriri Lake, twenty kilometers from China, with a couple whose nationality, due to more bad behavior, will also remain anonymous. When I left for the Pangong trip, I met them, with a British traveler who was also keen to go, and they shook our hands, and promised to wait till I got back; reassured, we put the money down for the permits.

When I got back, the couple had disappeared, and taken their permit with them. With a bit of sleuthing, which wasn't hard, because Leh was a one-yak town, I found where they were staying, and discovered that not only had they told their landlady they were going to Moriri that morning, they had said nothing to me or the other traveler even though they knew we were waiting to share the car; not to mention the three agencies, who were waiting for them not only to confirm their plans but to pay for their previous trips.

Furious, I wrote them a carefully-crafted note, calling them on their treachery, and left, searching the town's notice boards for any and all trips to

Moriri, even calling in at the Israeli House where Shabbat was underway to see if some Israelis were going to Moriri; before I finally gave up. The British traveler was so mad she left the next day for Manali.

I had two days left, and as the flights to Delhi were packed, I was going to be stuck in Leh waiting for the next confirmed seat. Moriri was off, and I was livid, the fourth time a trip in Ladakh had come to grief because of other travelers.

Then I remembered my Nepali contacts in town who ran the bakery racquet, and knew everyone. It turned out there was a local guy heading to Moriri the next morning. Clutching my permit, I tracked him down, paid the deposit, found a tent, sleeping bag and mat, and instructed them to pick me up the next morning at seven.

Moriri was on.

I learned more about Ladakhi culture on those two days than in the previous weeks in the country; I heard about their witch doctors; the funeral rites; the Yeti myths and footprints that circled around the place; how his grandfather had traveled on the passes before there were roads. When we reached a chorten that was draped on prayer flags we circled it in the jeep three times, and the driver gave me a white silk scarf to tie around it for good luck on the rest of our journey.

While their devout Buddhist sensibilities ensured our safety on the twisting roads, their taste in music was nowhere near as inspired. The music swerved between acid trance from Goa (a gift from some Israelis), Tibetan monk chants (a cassette from his uncle), Lobo (including the classic "You, Me and a Dog Named Boo") and... Milli Vanilli (left behind by some sheepish German man's wife).

"My grandfather went to Tibet on his ass," Soman said with a straight face, referring to the convoys of donkeys that were used as transport. Later in the trip, I saw a group of trekkers, half French, half American; one American had obviously set his sights on the Isabelle Adjani look-alike on the trip. "Your ass is bigger than mine," he told her with a shy smile, talking about their transport, while she stepped away and struck up a conversation in French that he couldn't understand.

Along the way, we passed through a deep gorge carved by the Indus river, where solitary families were preparing for winter and hoisting hay on their roofs, and where rocks and boulders surrounded gompas and schools where red cheeked grandmothers walked home from classes with their grandkids.

The last hour, we entered a valley so broad and flat it felt like Mongolia, and then we passed little Moriri, a gem-like lake that reflected the clouds like a cool, blue mirror. Marmots stood up to greet us as we passed through the final barrier to the large lake, and when we descended to the valley floor, great gusts of wind blew mini tornadoes around the car, as Tartar horsemen drove their animals home, followed by dogs that looked like Alaskan malamutes. It was truly remote, truly Himalayan, and truly Ladakh.

That night I camped near the village in an open field where shadows from curve horned goats loomed on the walls of my tent, as they butted heads with rivals; and large packs of vicious, wild dogs sniffed around my tent looking for food as I shivered, remembering the Yeti myths.

During the night, I could not sleep, because the altitude was 4,600 meters, so high every time I drifted off to sleep, I woke up, gasping for air and breathing as deep as I could, starved for oxygen. Praying for daylight, the wind picked up so strongly that the tent nearly blew over, and by the time dawn came I was ready to leave for lower ground.

When the sun did come up, it was two hours before it cleared the mountains around Moriri, and I had enough time to get down to the shore, where the sun's rays flew over the top, illuminating the glaciers behind me in gold and pink; and it was so cold that the ground was solid ice, and each step was crunch-crunch-crunch in the thin air. Painted ducks from China were feeding in the shallows, where strange, crustacean-like brine shrimp cruised through the water, even though the ocean was hundreds of miles away and thousands of feet beneath me.

In my last few days in Leh, the seasons finally clicked. Summer was over, with fall, and the bitter winter, on its way: the Aspen trees had suddenly turned yellow overnight, frost covered the ground in the morning and, though the sky was clear, the sun's rays were now weak. Prayer flags that had flapped to the north now flapped to the south, as the chilly winds shifted from the warm Indian Ocean monsoon to the cold northern winds sweeping off the Mongolian plateau.

More than the physical seasons were changing in Ladakh, as Kashmir was off limits to tourism, and with Nepal's Maoist woes scaring off more and more tourists, Ladakh had become the center of the Himalayan trekking trade, and over 40,000 trekkers were expected in a country that had received just 3,000 people only two years before. The invasion has brought along with it the problems, and headaches, the country had long been free from.

For centuries the average Ladakhi bartered for everything, and no one went hungry or lived in slums. Now the young flocked to the cities to get jobs and garbage and crime were rising: a foreign girl had been raped in Leh in broad daylight, a group of German tourists had lost all their money from a trekking company when the employees, and their money, went missing, and even the most remote Gompas now had to padlock every room to avoid theft from not only the foreign tourists that flocked there, but from their own people.

All around town, the elders were preparing a mid-winter gathering to devise new restrictions for the next year's tourist season; bed taxes and flat minimum charges per day for trekking were to be implemented, and it seemed that 2004 was going to be the last year for unchecked tourist arrivals in Ladakh. The Israelis, having gotten wind of these developments, were already outraged, and desperately looked for other cheap places to crash in India.

On my last night in Leh, I rounded up people I had met there for a Freak Free dinner: no bland momos, no banana pancakes, just some of the best Indian food I had even tasted, at a restaurant ironically called Baba's Little Italy: some New Zealand travel agents, a group of Aussie surfers from Margaret River, a sociology couple from Stanford, a Thai classical dancer traveling with her American English teacher husband, two retired Israeli school teachers, two stockbrokers from London, a pair of Korean photographers traveling with their French Canadian English Lit teacher, and a Kiwi mother-daughter team traveling around the world. It was a mini-United Nations around the table, and not a Freak to be seen.

That was until Phoebe turned up, cool and distant now that her newly-minted relationship with her muscled, tattooed Lenny Kravitz look-alike Israeli boyfriend Shlomo had been sealed on a recent, and carnal, two day camping trip. She no longer called me "friend," and curtly told me that she too was following the seasons, and was off the next day to travel southward towards Goa, with Shlomo in tow, following the flocks of migrating club kids and hash heads south for the winter, away from Ladakh and the hauntingly beautiful Himalayas.

Ganesh Is My Co-Pilot: Bombay, India

"Sorry for the delay, sir, but the police are looking for terrorist bombs," said the taxi driver to me, a recent migrant from Kerala, as we waited in a monumental Bombay traffic jam just meters away from the Gateway to India, where exactly a year before, on August 25, two bombs had killed nearly sixty people, set off by people the police had yet to catch. Nervously he scanned the cabs around us, reminding me in a hushed tone that it was two cabs like his that had been packed with explosives and driven into crowds, then detonated.

Half an hour earlier, I had jumped off the overnight train from Delhi, and you know you're in a Westernized city when you see a McDonald's inside the station, the taxi driver is sending SMS messages, and more women on the sidewalk are wearing jeans than saris.

Policemen were walking car to car, screaming into walkie talkies, searching for suspicious packages in back seats and questioning random people. Sniffing dogs lunged at open windows, snarling and barking.

Despite the delay, and the air of danger, I was glad for the "fresh" air; the train compartment from Delhi was filled with champion farters and the noisiest, piggiest snorers I had ever heard, and I had hardly slept on the eighteen hour trip.

As we passed the last roadblock, the driver began weaving as fast as he could in the traffic, the bright blue Ganesh idol hanging from his mirrors jangling around and around, the elephant god's face frozen in a plastic smile, the cone of incense he had burning mixing with the car fumes, cigarette smoke, and a cocktail of other smells that seeped up from the monsoon-clogged drains.

When he lurched to a stop for a red light, we watched a woman with a pile of grass accept five rupees from passerbys to feed the massive, black cow that was sleeping beside her, who was happily chomping down on the free food.

"This city is full of rackets," the driver said ruefully as he furiously tapped more SMS messages in his cell phone, wrapped with a purple Ganesh plastic protective cover.

It was great to be back in a tropical country, with humidity and palm trees; in less than twenty-four hours I had gone from being breathless in the high Himalayas to the sweltering heat blowing off the Arabian Sea, and from what I saw cruising down from Victoria Terminus station, Bombay was an Indian Hong Kong, New York, Cairo and London combined: there was a container-freighter clogged harbor; high rise residential apartment buildings, hundreds of black and red taxis like in the Egyptian capital, and rusty double-decker red buses replacing the stinky auto rickshaws and bicycles Delhites used to get around.

And, once again in India, I had "changed" countries without crossing an international border: from the deserts of Arabian Nights Rajasthan; to Tibet in Ladakh; to the surrealismo of Varanasi and the blinding white stones of the Taj Mahal, each time you moved in India, whether it was stepping out of an overnight train, or a short plane ride, it felt like you were in some other country, something I had never experienced before.

When I reached my hotel in Colaba, the driver whistled when he heard the price and said, "I can get you a room for 500 rupees." I declined, knowing full well the high percentage of commission that price included, and how awful the budget accommodation was in Bombay: airless cells in firetraps.

"You need taxi now," he spluttered, instead of asking, hanging around in the lobby, still hammering away at his cell phone's keys.

"No," I told him wearily, and with a grunt, he still wouldn't go away.

"You stay Bombay for Ganesh festival?" his eyes lit up as he showed me his prize possession cell phone for the fifteenth time. "Very interesting, Chowpatty Beach, we give Ganesh a bath..."

"No, I only have two days here." His smile faded, he slammed his phone in his pocket, and was gone.

With a sea view, a huge marble bathroom, and with a view of the Gateway of India, I wasn't moving: no more power cuts like in Ladakh, and freezing cold rooms like in Manali, or touristy hotels with banana pancakes on the menu like in Rajasthan. I was looking forward to some satellite TV, room service and steady air conditioning.

That afternoon, I walked down the pirate DVD and software covered alleys, where Kashmiris sold dusty Rajasthani handicrafts, and the whips of Delhi were replaced with goat skinned-drums and huge Flintstones balloons; Nike shops competed with designer sari stores while many homeless slept, begged and sold their wares to the menagerie of wealthy Indians, Nigerian drug dealers, Chinese businessmen, Italian housewives and Sri Lankan cricket players who browsed and dug through the piles of fake goods sold by some of the most persistent salesmen I had seen in India, no doubt all degree holders from the Agra School for Touts.

And all along the alleys, hung up in corners, in windows, hung around necks, and decorating t-shirts, was the thick trunk-nosed Ganesh, holding his arms up and looking like a Buddha in need of a nose job. Bombay was definitely enamored with the Baby Elephant God, the one you hardly saw in Delhi.

"YESSSSS!!!!!!!" they cry as they watch you walk past, hands extended to shake your hand, "WHAT ARE YOUUUU LOOKING FOORRR??"

"FEEL ME!!!!" sleazed a salesman to a group of blonde Germans who he wanted to touch a Pashmina he held out to them. "VERRRY SOFTTTT!!!!!"

"I can get these in China for forty rupees," I told a DVD salesman who started screaming at me when he wanted 300 rupees for a single disc.

"YOU LIE!!!!" he screeched as I told him that was the retail price. "No wayyyy!" Then, when he realized I was telling the truth, dollar signs clouded his eyes and I became his new best friend.

"We go into business, you and I, please, leave me your e-mail, I want to know more about this..."

"I'm your friend!! Remember, your friend!!!" screamed another salesman after another woman, who was trying her best to just squeeze through the Hong Kong-like night market crowds, not interested in buying a mirrored bedspread.

"Why am I looking at shoes made in Vietnam when Nike is American?" shouted a South African with a six-person entourage in tow, at a salesman in Bombay's only Nike outlet, where I was sheepishly buying a pair of shoes to replace my pair that was shattered after two and a half months in India.

"Almost nothing in USA is made in USA," I said to him sarcastically.

The salesman nodded in agreement. "Indonesia. Vietnam. South Korea. India."

The South African shook his head angrily, and said, "I have AMERICAN MONEY to spend here, DOLLARS, and I want AMERICAN PRODUCTS. Show me your AMERICAN MADE SHOES!!!"

The salesman shook his head, and said, "I'm sorry sir, this is all we have..."

The South African huffed loudly, and stormed out, his entourage in tow.

"It's unbelievvvvabble..." screeched an Indian woman at an intersection across from Victoria Terminus, talking to her friend in a solid gold-colored sari. "Can you imaginnnneee living at home with such a mother in lawwww? Its positively crrriminallll what she's done to my sisterrrrr..."

Her gold-saried friend clicked her tongue in agreement. "Talk about a trageddyyy....Forcing her to cook and clean in this day and age, and she's been to America!!!!"

Negotiating Saigon-like traffic system, where crosswalks and crossing lights were nonexistent, and where street signs had either been stolen or completely missing, made it even harder to get around the twisting streets that were fringed with Gothic cathedrals, British Railway stations and colonial buildings; Bombay's soul may have been Indian, but its skeleton was British, bone white, brittle, and ancient, and decorated with gargoyles, Queen Victoria statues and rusting signs for Cadbury's and Guinness. And it was this contrast that stretched to the people that lived there, too.

"I've never seen such a city's newspapers so different from the reality of the streets," said an Indian woman who was living in Princeton, visiting home with her husband and kids for the first time after ten years, as we watched the Bombay skyline grow larger after our three hour trip to Elephanta Island.

She was right. The *Bombay Times* was so stuffed with Bollywood blockbuster news, model movements and fashionista articles that it was hard to believe it was the hometown paper of a city where thirty percent of the population lived and died on the streets. Nothing was even mentioned of the plight of these people, only the news of the rich and connected, with advertisements for the launch of the new "Manhattan" credit card; printed with skyscrapers and yellow cabs to remind one of what Bombayites dreamed their city could be. And all day long the tables at Barista, India's knockoff Starbucks, were full of college students drinking fake frappacinos as street kids hovered at the exit, looking for pens and any loose change.

In India, where wealth and poverty went hand in hand in most towns and cities, the disparity was especially magnified in Bombay, where, the greater the wealth, the greater the poverty, and everywhere you walked, especially at night, it was around rows of sleeping bodies, whole families cooking in the gutters, taxi drivers sleeping in their cars, and stray dogs and cats yowling at each other in the darkness, and above them, the shiny billboards for Air India flights to Los Angeles, and bright photos of luxury apartments more costly than London or Hong Kong.

When I took a taxi to get to Chowpatty Beach, the scene of the following week's Ganesh Festival, the driver thought I was mad to miss the festivities, which would bring thousands of pilgrims to the beach carrying their favorite god on their shoulders to dip in the sea for good luck.

"He gives us EVERYTHING..." the driver went on, pointing to the faded and peeling photo of Ganesh on the dashboard, where most cab drivers have their own photo to identify themselves. In India, most likely it will be their favorite deity, and in most Bombay cabs, elephants greatly outnumbered Krishna.

"Are you SURE you can't stay for our Ganesh?" asked salesmen and hotel bellboys and more taxi drivers and random people on the streets.

The night before I left the city, I went out with a Chilean lawyer living in Auckland, two British exchange students living in Chengdu, and a couple from Delhi who were here, as wide eyed as we were at the spectacle and speed at which Bombay moved compared to sedate and dour Delhi.

We hit some bars in Colaba. It was a Saturday night, and we climbed dank stairwells to places dimly lit and so full of people it seemed a fire marshall's nightmare, and squeezed in past mini-skirted girls and guys wearing Travolta hair swept back severely with Brylcream, after struggling to make sense of the common door policy where single men were barred, but single women were allowed in without question.

"In China, the women are kept out in droves, especially in Shanghai, where most are pros," screamed the British over the noise.

I nodded, reminded of the tight-jeaned Vietnamese girls who hung around *Apocalypse Now* bar in Saigon, and the ghostly white faces that you saw after dark, waiting in dark shadows for prey.

Here in India, it was eve-teasing that kept the men out, and to protect the dignity of women, not only were they given free access to bars and clubs, they had women's-only train cars on suburban rail lines, and even a line of taxis for women.

The streets of Bombay may be 1920s Victorian, but inside the bars and clubs, the atmosphere was very 80s, with Depeche Mode and vintage Madonna on the sound system, and there was even a breakdancing contest going on at one place. We hadn't been at one bar for five minutes when a business-suited guy handed us all his business cards to act in some Bollywood movie being filmed the next day.

"It's got Miss Universe in it," he shouted, but none of us were going to be around, and gladly told him no thanks.

On my last morning in Bombay, it was Sunday, and Colaba's roads were deserted of traffic; the street sellers were setting up their stalls, and even at this early hour they were eager to make a deal.

"YESSSSSS!!!!!" a man shouted at me from thirty meters away, wanting me to buy his chess set made of coral.

I ignored him, but it didn't matter, because all his neighbors who were still setting up got into the act, and a chorus of "YESSSSS!s" followed me for four blocks.

As I ducked down a small alley to take a shortcut back to my hotel, to get away from the noise, the hawkers and the traffic, I stopped to cross the street. A tugging at my shorts made me think it was a child or some leper, and I shook my head. But when I looked down, it turned out to be a blue-eyed goat, about to make breakfast out of a chunk of my shorts.

The lights changed, and I lept out of the way of the animal's jaws before it tore off a piece.

Freaks to Geeks and the End of India: Goa, Bangalore and Kaniyakumari

The flight from Bombay to Goa took off from the main airport, passing over luxury condominiums and swathes of slum areas that went straight to the horizon. Seconds after rotation we slammed into monsoon turbulence, and as we ascended, and during the hour flight, it was a nonstop roller coaster of lurches and stomach-churning plunges that suspended cabin service and kept the seat belt sign permanently on. Our cruising altitude was 16,000 feet; no less than three days earlier, I had been standing on solid ground 3,000 feet higher in Ladakh.

On landing at Goa, once again, it was like you had stamped your passport into another country: now it was like a mixture of northeast Brazil and Mexico, with red roofed colonial villas, whitewashed churches straight out of Europe, and beaches and scenery straight out of Cuba.

Like everywhere else in India, cars and taxis became showcases for religions, and Goa was no different: the Bombay taxi driver's Ganesh statue had now been replaced with ivory rosaries that jangled from the mirror, and Virgin Mary statues, too (glow in the dark, the driver told me) on the dashboard, her arms outstretched and her head tilted to one side. And not only dashboards were spouting religion, because all along the roads were signs:

JESUS LOVES YOU
SIN IS NOT IN
MARY'S VIRGINITY IS PURE

I stayed in the Fontainhas area of Panjim, on the river where I got a room filled with a dark four poster bed and huge creaking cabinets set next to lace curtains that opened onto a small latticed balcony; it felt like Florence, or Spain, but sacred cows and chai wallahs calling out and walking down the street below were reminders that I was, in fact, still in India.

I took a local bus to Old Goa, where churches and cathedrals sit on a muddy river surrounded by lush coconut plantations. St. Francis Xavier is buried in one of them, and the gold decorated naves, crypts and altars remind one of the ornate churches of Innsbruck or Vienna.

That evening, I wandered down a cobbled lane, following the golden light, rays from the setting sun that struck the colonial and art deco houses, churches, and government buildings in the town, watching women hanging washing, artisans paint tiles in outdoor studios on streets with names like Rua Sao Tome and Rua Vasco De Gama and Rua San Jacinto, crowded with glassed in art galleries selling water-colored paintings straight out of Mykonos or Provence while kids in the street played cricket and football as nuns in starched white smocks walked school kids home in the gathering dusk.

The next day I boarded another Air Deccan ATR 42 and arrived in darkness at India's own Silicon Valley: the IT center of Bangalore.

Instead of Krishna, Ganesh or Jesus, it was Larry Ellison and Bill Gates who ruled this town. All along the streets were sellers hawking books on:

HOW TO GET RICH—NOW!
RELEASE YOUR INNER MANAGER
BE A CEO, FOR LIFE

There were no books on Buddhism, no Krishna kitsch, no Hindu Holy Men begging. The streets were filled only with business-suited locals, yakking into cell phones, mostly in English, and mostly with people twelve time zones away.

The newspapers were full of ads for self-fulfillment seminars and business networking functions and software job fairs and three-step processes to getting a US resident visa and how to immigrate to Canada with 25,000 US dollars.

And all over the city, empty walls were plastered not with spiritual gods, but with the gods of the IT generation, geeky Bill and sneering Larry, both looking like heads of state in three-piece suits and looking very out of place in the steamy, Indian heat.

But they weren't the only ones out of place: everywhere you went, mixed in with crowds of locals, you passed khaki-wearing American IT professionals bragging to their Indian colleagues about nightlife in Atlanta; expat wives bored to tears in Barista reading battered fashion magazines, tech kids from San Francisco wearing Craig's List T-shirts and skateboarding down rutted roads, and polo-shirted ad execs from Chicago, wide eyed at the cows munching leaves from overhanging tree branches at bus stands.

And all around were Yahoo and IBM campuses and Singaporean tech parks and high rises that were taller and plusher than anything you can see in Delhi or even Bombay; and shiny shopping malls that had popped up everywhere selling more self-fulfillment and get-rich-quick books than you could read in one hundred lifetimes.

I never saw a religious building, or any sort of begging, in Bangalore, not a single Indian saddhu, but I did see Western saddhus, a.k.a. "management consultants," handing out resumes at street corners, looking for jobs, and, even weirder, a white beggar sitting on the sidewalk sticking his hand out at passerbys. Even the auto rickshaw drivers had photos of Bill and Larry in their mobile cabs, and one was even taking HTML classes in his free time.

My last journey aboard Indian Railways was an overnight train from Bangalore to Trivandrum. At the Trivandrum train station a white Toyota sedan was waiting. The driver got out and loaded all my luggage into the back seat. There were no more train, plane or bus journeys in front of me: it was my last day in India, and my final destination before my afternoon flight to the Maldives was Kanniyakumari, the very tip of India where the Bay of Bengal, the Arabian Sea and Indian Ocean mixed. It seemed like an apt place to end my Indian journey: having stood at the end of the road in Hundur, in the Nubra Valley, as high geographically, and physically, as you could get in India, now, less than two weeks later, I was at the tropical, polar opposite.

The eighty-six kilometer drive was, once again, another passport stamp change: this time it felt like Sri Lanka, but even more so, like Vietnam: as the only communist state in India, it was no surprise to see many hammer and sickles painted on walls, and red flags fluttering in front of police stations. The lush, palm tree-studded countryside was reminiscent of the Mekong Delta, and when we passed a line of Chinese fishing nets, imported from North Asia by sea traders and adopted by locals to catch bait fish, Stalin, my driver, asked me if I was amazed by this spectacle: I told him we had the same things in Vietnam and he brightened.

"You know Vietnam?"

"Yes, for several years."

"Then you are a communist then?" Stalin asked happily, taking his eyes completely off the road as he lit his cigarette.

"Oh no, I'm not a communist."

"Are you sure? I am a communist! My mother is one! My brother is too! My father is dead, but he was one too!!"

I nodded my head and then Stalin rambled on, changing topics, telling me how the book *The God of Small Things*, by Arundhati Roy, was a sham, and a bad reflection on the good people of his home state.

"We don't like this book," he said, shaking his head angrily. The next minute, he was talking about David Beckham; the minute after that, the outlook for the Indian economy after the poor 2004 monsoon season.

On and on the conversation swerved, as the car lurched around cows, random bicyclists and school children, between the corruption of Tamil Nadu politics, Bollywood films (which Keralans didn't watch, because of the language barrier), the truth to the virginity of Britney Spears and the treachery of President Bush.

When we reached Kanyikumari, the sea was roiling with huge breakers that rolled in and smashed themselves on the rocks; the sun was high in the sky, so brightly reflecting off the sea you had to squint to look at the water, young and old Indian women in bright saris were bathing in the sea, an informal football match was being played on the beach, and dozens of young couples and families were sitting along the battered sea wall, eating grilled peanuts and drinking chai from tiny earthenware cups emptied then crushed underfoot in the sand.

"You did it!!!" screamed Stalin as he joined me in the shallow waters for a dip. He lifted my arm above my head as though I was Rocky. "You've been from end to end of my country!!!!"

We laughed and said yes when some people wanted a photo with a foreigner, and we happily smiled and hammed it up for the camera as the waves crashed in, the sky burned with strong equatorial light, and the smells of Indian tea, curry, charcoal smoke and incense swirled all around us.

It was a fitting ending indeed.

Paradise Found, Paradise Drowned: The Republic of the Maldives

With 1,200 islands, ninety resorts, 99.6% water, 0.4% land and all less than two meters above sea level, the Maldives is not your average country: five star is the norm there, and with daily rates rising from $500 plus per person per day, to the sky's-the-limit resorts where the room alone costs $10,000 per night, plus service charge, most independent travelers would be bankrupted within hours of arrival and sent packing on the next flight to Sri Lanka.

However, if you are able to afford the sticker shock of the accommodation, the country is one of the most unique on the planet. As a completely independent archipelago, the country has its own language and culture; the Maldives is where the concept of shell money was invented.

It is the only place I have ever been where the photos in brochures simply fall short of the reality: there are no roads or highways here, and there is so much water and open space that you have to get almost everywhere by seaplane. Gone is a horizon interrupted by mountains because the sky comes straight down to the sea on all directions, similar in a sense to a blue desert rippled with waves. The country's airport is an aircraft-shaped island with water on all sides, and an aborted takeoff here would mean a dunk in the Indian Ocean.

On the surface, the Maldives is paradise, in the classic sense; Robinson Crusoe excursions visit sandbanks with exactly one palm tree on it; water bungalows have retractable glass floors to feed the colorful fish, buffets serve mountains of seafood and fresh fruit three times a day, and water temperatures are a perfect 29° C every day of the year. A "cold" day is one where the air temp drops by more than four degrees.

But there is a side to the Maldives that guests don't see: the water in the sink and in your glass is desalinated, and even the Coca-Cola bottling plant here uses seawater to make soda. All trash has to be removed on time each day to avoid burying the island; sand is pumped from the lagoon to preserve the sugar-white sands from the rising sea levels; and every food item from Dom Perignon champagne to sea salt has to be imported.

The biggest danger is getting hit by a coconut; in fact, it's the leading cause of death in the Maldives.

The reefs are full of fish, manta rays and even whale sharks, so common in some places that encounters can be guaranteed year round. Diving each day before breakfast, we surfaced in water so calm and clear it felt like bobbing in the middle of an alpine lake. Frequent night dives at unnamed reefs were punctuated with flashes of lightning spreading out from massive, anvil-shaped thunderheads, passing overhead like antique clipper ships.

In between the diving were visits to the many luxury resorts scattered across the country. Perfectly manicured pathways, gracious staff, luxury water villas and blinding white beaches were strange oases in the deep blue ocean, morgue-like and quiet on the expensive ones, (Soneva Fushi, Banyan Tree) and rowdy and boozy on the cheaper ones (Club Med, Fun Island).

Even the staff was weird. Most at the expensive ones went about their jobs with the efficiency of those staff at a villian's lair in a James Bond film, dressed in head to toe in flowing space-station robes, or black silk jumpsuits that swished as they walked, a vacant yet brochure-perfect smile spread across their lips. Nothing was too large, or too small, a request. Towels scented with peppermint were pressed into your palms as soon as you stepped off the speedboat, and a frangipani flower, wrapped in a silk ribbon, was handed over to you like it was the Hope diamond. Everywhere you went, wide smiles, polite nods and patronizing words followed you like a fragrance; each staff you passed offered the same, note-perfect "good morning, sir," and you began to wonder if the Stepford Wives had expanded into the hotel industry.

But all was not quiet in the staff quarters, and more than one were quietly questioning their workplace, which offered them no escape: they lived, ate with, and drank with their work colleagues. That could be heaven or hell, depending on how well you got along with them.

"Can you believe the hotel handbook actually has a chapter about the ban on sexual relations not only between guests and staff, but between staff and other staff?" whispered a Japanese girl with rose-red lips at one resort, her eyes wild from months of forced abstinence. She confided in me that she was planning to quit and go back to Osaka, but she couldn't.

"All staff must hand over their passport when they arrive," she said. "The GM won't let me go until they find a replacement who speaks Japanese, and for three months now, no one. This place is a golden prison for staff, but heaven for guests."

Life for staff at the cheaper resorts swerved to the opposite end of the spectrum. Sex with guests, or staff, went on without any reprimand from management, and with all staff HIV negative—because a positive result of an AIDS test would have been followed by a speedboat to the airport, where they would have been kicked out of the country—meant that unlike at home, STD risk was literally written across potential sexual partner's forehead, or at least in their HR file. More than one GM had been sent packing after rumors of orgies and three-ways with couples were picked up by the resort's owners.

Truthfully, the release was necessary: cast adrift in the Indian Ocean with little contact with civilization for months on end, staff was imported along with the food and the furniture. While many I talked to moaned about being far from home, for some it was precisely this that attracted some to the Maldives in the first place, including a London party girl at one high-end resort. She needed some distance from her pushy coke dealer.

"Lots of sand around but none to snort," she said ruefully as she tucked into her dinner one night while everyone looked away uncomfortably.

Many of the staff in the Maldives were rumored to be on the run from something: ex-wives, debtors, the police, the Mafia, ex-business partners, Interpol and more. If so, it was the perfect place to do it. Water separated each island as perfectly as a bottomless canyon.

"Shipwrecked," whispered John, a French guest, at one resort, as we drank at the bar, watching the staff dance underneath a pulsating strobe light. He pointed his finger at them again and whispered, "Shipwrecked."

The antidotes to the resorts were the local islands, where dive liveaboards stocked up on essentials and gave their guests some time to get off the boat. Completely off-limits to overnight stays for foreigners, it was only on these islands where one could experience the country's culture that, unlike almost any other, is tucked away behind a veil, some sort of tourist apartheid.

Often ignored by the luxury resorts, where a weekly Bodu Beru drum performance was the closest guests got to the people, life on the local islands was as fragile as the coral reefs themselves: over hundreds of years, the Maldivians had learned to survive with meager vegetation, water and animals; learning how to use coconuts for food, shelter and even clothing, they had learned to tap toddy, go fishing for marlin with just a hook attached to coconut rope, or navigate their elegantly decorated dhonis at night just by the position of the stars.

The locals were always willing to teach you how they built their traditional dhonis without plans, saws or even nails; and I couldn't believe that two weeks before, I was telling bewildered Ladakhis what it was like to swim in the ocean, and now I was explaining the concept of a mountain to people that have never seen snow, a hill, a cow, a skyscraper or even a dog, because canines were banned throughout the country.

Most of the guests and many of the staff turned their noses up about the local islands, which they thought were breeding grounds for witchcraft and superstition, choosing to spend their days off at the pool rather than taking time to get to learn another culture or language.

And it was out there, inbetween visits to the resort and the local islands, in all that blue emptiness, where the experiences and memories from India came flooding out, so much so that more than once I left people slackjawed at my blabbering, my mumbling and ramblings. Finally, after months of India, the lessons were sinking in.

With tourism less than three decades old in the Maldives, many locals derided the young people who knew more about hip-hop than traditional fishing, leaving in droves for Male and jobs with hotels there. Despite these fears, the Maldives was now threatened with extinction by a far more sinister force than package tourists. It was threatened by the very sea itself.

The Maldives is famous for being a country that won't exist in less than one hundred years. Even though the unthinkable is decades away, the sunken future of the Maldives has already arrived: a few weeks before Christmas, a strong tropical storm arrived during the highest tides ever recorded in the country, waves and wind heavily eroded beaches, leaving resorts with washed-away coconut trees and collapsed water bungalows. Sand pumps worked overtime to repair the damage.

The work was finished quickly, and the white-sand, blue-water paradise that attracts 700,000 people each year was quickly restored. But the damage to the fragile islands prompted one German girl to ask me one night in the bar, "Dave, what would happen if there was a wave in the Maldives?"

I looked at her as my blood ran cold, and said, simply, "We would be drowned like rats."

It starts with ear-splitting screams, pounding footsteps and the sound of splintering wood; and, more ominously, with a distant roar that sounds like a line of approaching 747 jets flying low. More screams. And the roar only grows louder.

It's 10:30 a.m., the day after Christmas, and we're still reeling from our hangovers from a late night drinking in the bar. Cold, dirty seawater starts pouring in under the door. In seconds there are sparks popping out of the power outlets, and then they explode. I leap for the exit, but I can't get it open, there's too much water pouring against it. The roar continues growing louder, along with the screams. Using all my strength, I smash it open, and by now the water is knee deep, freezing cold and surging faster and faster, like a washing machine gone mad.

"The children! The children!" a staff member is screaming, and I join him to ferry kids who are drifting past us in the rushing water that is pouring over the island. As I run to the beach, I look out at the ocean to see that, clean to the horizon, it has turned a dishwater grey, with whitecaps like a stormy

North Sea. The Maldives blue has completely disappeared.

With the last child off the beach, I run to the opposite side of the narrow island, and see water surging towards me; I turn and see the island is now completely submerged. Champagne bubbles dribble up from the sand beneath my feet. For a split second, I think the island is sinking; the ocean is rising so steadily that it seems we're dropping down, and fast. I look around, and see people standing like wax figures, frozen in stone.

The first wave sweeps in, and smashes me against the wall. I'm gasping for breath, barely breathing, tasting gasoline and raw sewage mixed in with the salt. Another wave slams into me, and I'm smashed against the wall again. I grab a pole for support.

I frantically swim for the reception area, where staff and guests are screaming for God, Allah and Buddha. Surrounding me are televisions and computers that are tumbling over and over; in front of me, a wall of glass implodes, sucking desk chairs and office equipment underneath into the swirling currents. Deckchairs, mattresses and lamps fly past.

Seconds later the main wave hits, and blackness replaces the bright sunlight; surging, boiling white water rapids swallow me, and an interminable amount of time passes. Another wall collapses, and I see a huge palm tree hit the ground in a silent crash.

When I come to, I'm gasping for air, and the sound of water is rushing through my ears. A huge piece of wooden deck is smashing into the poles holding up the roof, and it seems determined to crush its way through the island. I squeeze my eyes again, and wait.

Suddenly, it's as if someone has flushed a toilet; the water is gone, the wave has passed, but it's sucked the ocean out along with it. Tropical fish are flopping frantically in the sand. I run to the beach and see that thirty meters of vertical ocean have disappeared; if time had stopped, I could have walked along the rim of the atoll.

In the confusion of screaming guests, distraught mothers and overwhelmed staff, another wave smashes into the island, surging in from the opposite direction, full of furniture and debris.

When it's gone, only silence is left behind, but in the quiet, injured people come hobbling in from all directions, bleeding and mumbling incoherently; staff begin to count heads, but there is no dry paper, no electricity, no radio, no telephone, no cell phone coverage, no contact with the outside world. We have no idea what's happened, or what is to come, but when another train of waves approaches, and the hissing, roaring sound that none of us will ever forget is back again, people begin to use the word *tsunami*.

A group of Japanese have somehow found some lifejackets, which they quickly pull over their heads, form a circle, and run around, yelling, "Tsunami! Tsunami! Tsunami!" until an Australian snaps at them, "Shut the fuck up!"

As I struggle to put my sluggish brain into gear, revolving through my brain, as if on some vicious merry-go-round, is the Bee Gees' song "Stayin' Alive," which the DJ had accidentally played twice the previous night. We plunge ahead to help the injured, keeping a nervous eye at the sea, where gigantic whirlpools form, eddies and currents from a sea that has gone completely mad, swaying back and forth like a huge bathtub.

It's early that afternoon, after hours of uncertainty, rumors, tears and monotony, all under the burning sun, after more waves, when people begin to start checking out of the hotel—mentally speaking, that is. A man salvages a briefcase, and a random cell phone, and sits staring out to sea; a staff member finds a tin of lip balm and is running around yelling at people that they need it; and a young receptionist shrieks in Dhivehi, then faints right in front of me.

Then, a French woman, hands at her throat, starts yelling at no one in particular.

"Mes bijoux, mes bijoux!" she cried, pointing to her room, now gone.

And then an Austrian is demanding where her plane is. And an Italian woman wants a refund. Immediately. The staff point to where the buildings once stood, decimated by the waves.

"Wait," says one as he stalks off, disgusted.

The hysteria gets worse: it's the end of the world, moans one lady; we're now going to starve to death, screams another. On and on it goes. The little civilization that existed on the island has been wiped clean in an instant, and the terrifying void is now filled with rumors and speculations that swirl on and on, out of control, more ominous than a wall of water.

That night, the moon is as full as I've ever seen it, illuminating the horizon with a silvery, mercurial light. We're grateful: more waves are predicted, and no one wants to be caught off guard.

Not taking our eyes off the horizon for a second, we count our losses in the darkness. Cameras. Cell phones. Clothes. Money. Books. Heirlooms. Jewelry.

"The reef," murmurs a French dive instructor, hoarse after so much screaming, who was in the water when the tsunami struck, and had completed her first emergency ascent in her fifteen year career, "saved your lives."

She's right. We don't have time to lament our losses, or sleep: we have to keep our eyes on the horizon.

The next day is long and hot. As the sea slowly returns to normal, the tides return, and when it goes out, we pass the long hours salvaging for our things. Passports, clothes, shoes, suitcases, books and resort debris are mixed with smashed wood, doors, television sets, air conditioners and more. Every once in a while there is a sharp cry as someone finds things that belonged to them.

A DJ, flown in to perform on Christmas Eve, has lost 2,000 CDs, from ten years of work. An American woman is looking for her wedding ring, and a German man is looking for his cameras.

It's sometime that afternoon when screaming starts again, and people begin to run.

"A wave! A wave!" someone shouts. Heart in my throat, I bolt for a tree, and climb it, heart racing, barely breathing, acting like a shell-shocked soldier after hearing an innocent firecracker explode. It's time to go home, but beneath the relentless equatorial sun, stomachs rumbling from hunger and tongues swollen from thirst, we have no idea when that will be.

The second night is longer, and darker, than the first, and not just from the fact that the moon is gone, making it almost impossible to see the waves: I remember the story that John, a French guest, had told me, of the three spirits dressed in jewelry that had visited him in the middle of the night, warning him sharply of some impending danger, right before the tsunami.

By day three, morale is low, and we settle in listlessly for more waiting. All of the sudden a buzzing seaplane circles the island. It lands, taxies and the cabin door pops open. The Canadian pilots are stunned at the damage, and one snaps pictures as though he is on holiday.

"Get us off this godforsaken island," snarls a Sri Lankan chef.

And in a carefully choreographed convoy, seaplane after seaplane takes everyone back to the capital, where we are dropped off, barefoot, sunburned, exhausted and starving, where locals run up to us and ask us where we've come from. When we say the name of the island, they gasp.

"We heard everyone was dead there," one woman says, shaking her head.

The next day, I board a Singapore Airlines 777. As it lifts off, the cabin is full of people quietly sobbing. The crew looks at each other in bewilderment. Clearly, their training has covered serving drinks and food. It has not covered how to handle this.

During my short transit stop, where I watch fireworks burst on New Year's Eve, I terrify a young sales girl at a shopping center where I greedily snap up underwear and socks and fling them onto the counter, happy to wear some clean clothes at last.

"What happened to you?" she says, carefully checking my signature with the back of my credit card, to see that she isn't helping some wanted criminal steal underwear. When I tell her, she bursts into tears.

On a bright New Year's Day, I boarded a brand new Airbus A340 that lifted off gracefully from the runway at Changi airport for the long flight to New York. I was seated in the last row, between an American couple, whose driver saved their lives in Sri Lanka when he drove their taxi into the hills as soon as the sea withdrew; and another American, who had tossed a coin to choose where to spend Christmas: Koh Samui or Phi Phi. The coin landed on Samui, and he and his friends were spared a hell that tens of thousands of others hadn't been. Despite our ordeal, and lots to talk about, we quickly slipped into silence, the weight of what we'd experienced finally sinking in.

It was some time after we soared north of Japan on that long eighteen-hour flight that memories from India resurfaced: the colors, the smiles, the faith, the devotion and reverence for gods large and small that I had witnessed in that country rose up within me and began acting like a soothing balm to the pain of the previous four days.

In the airport at Newark, New Jersey, I went through customs with suitcases leaking seawater that a startled customs agent unzipped, releasing a gasoline smell into the terminal.

"Welcome home," he stammered, waving me on after I told him where, and what, I'd come from.

The next morning, walking the cold, crowded streets of Manhattan, people kept asking me if I was all right. Surely I was shaken up, traumatized, damaged, unable to sleep. I'm OK, I nodded, saying I was sleeping OK, that things were fine. I kept ignoring that nagging feeling deep inside me that something was different. It wasn't until hours later, when I turned a corner and was slammed by the neon, noise and nutcases of Times Square, that I realized what it was.

New York City felt small.

S/HE IS HER/E: POEMS FOR THEE MAJESTY

GENESIS BREYER P-ORRIDGE

A Debris ov Murder

This is the time we make noises
Playing a game of mixing
And we are contrived to play this
It is a painful thing to be alone
But more painful still to be polite
More painful still to have to be so,
So polite
So… kind
And…
Well I don't want to seem
Ungrateful
Though I am obliged in a way
And then again
Is obligation enough?
Is pain so bad when one believes
In nothing?
To have ideas
To have a philosophy that seems to
Be proven correct by one's
Experience
One's L-if-E
One's er…
Loves and emotions
Yet it still gets destroyed
Mutilated
It is so easy to destroy
To amputate our destiny
You probably think I am trying to
Justify events to feel less pain
Painkiller
Killer of pain
Painkiller
Killer of pain

You probably think
That's thee game
That's OK
But I see you as a beautiful gift
That gave me the only happiness I
Ever felt
And I taught you alchemy
And sacrifice
And like my child
You
Left home
Where is home now?
Who are your new famille?
Are they good?
Will you develop and grow?
Yes love's never lost
She said to me
KNOW
But
I replied to her
It is sometimes stolen
And I mailed it to her...
Trivial you may say
But no more trivial than being
Alive
At last the innocents
Have
Finally slaughtered the
Innocents
It's all very simple of course
And all makes sense
Or so it is said
Who are your new famille?
Where are you now?
Will you develop and grow?
Are they good?
This is the tree bending
This is the last straw
And no one can change
What may never occur

Naturally we can all argue about
Anything
And we do
Oh yes!
We most certainly do my dear
Everyone has felt this pain except
For those human animals
I will keep my dog thank you and
Remain here to make a decision on
Behalf of us all
Is that what you want to hear?
My dear…
We were sentimental and quite
Capable of finding laughter
Not French
Will you develop and grow?
Are they good?
Who are your new famille?
Where is home now?
Perdurabo
Perturbed
All ways easy to choose
Up
Like talking to the dead
Agree and do nothing
I have seen my lover grow up and
Die
Of cancer he said
Of a kidney disease
He said
I have grown up and seen my lover
Die too
She replied
I am here now
Watching him die every day with a
Smile on his face and death inside
His body
Injection corruption every night
With your body my dear
Dear new lover

Inject me with fear
Teach me
And erase all that is coumfortable
It makes life seem easy now
My dear…

THIS IS ME
THAT'S ME
THIS IS ME
THAT'S ME

This is me
A little boy who says his prayers
Yes… every night
A shining arbor
Beneath the covers
Concealing a world of demons
Perturbed Perdurabo
One is revealed
One is removed
One is returned
One is destroyed
This story is a problem too
And a trail of love
Like talking to the dead
Agree and do
Dealing now
So one removed
Will remove the problem
Unless we see one
Four then will be ONE
Loyalty is now a failed commodity
And memories
Are made of the same money as
Paper
Reverse
THE RUSH

S/He is Her/E….

All Beauty is Our Enemy

Ah, my friends
These are needfully sadistic times
Pettiness rules each day
And blatant corruption is emblazoned in
The highest places
Corruption is seen as
Quite forgiveably virtuous
The charmed live empty lives
And the replete live charmingly

And is this not all dreadfully appropriate?
Brutally entertaining?
In those mythical quagmires of morbid
Ocean, so long ago, I would sooner
Concur that it was a molecular ugliness
That parasitized carbon and gave it
Pretension.
Indeed, it was molecular ugliness that made
You and I.
For is not water and carbon not the source
Of these "flesh vehicles" we so stupidly
Protect?

No splendor of random lightning
Nor angelic creatures with an impossible
Fervor for defeatism
Created us. No! We are mere accidents of
Nature and nature has no intention, no
Morality, no sentiment, no love.
Nature is merely accident, and if you were in
The accident,
God help you.

These laughable dreams uphold beauty as a
Quintessential golden thread in a maze of
Weak nobility.
Nature is their mother
Suckling us as pure untainted infants in a

Perfect garden.
Spoiled only by the errors of a few.
Empowered by our mysterious flaw.
Our destiny, to find our way back
To the light and escape the ugly demon
So unspeakably hideous at the

Black center of our beginnings.
God.

Yeah! Right!
I don't think so…!
I don't think so.

Oh, thin insipid lullabies of compliance!
Do we not see the ripping flesh
Of countless pretty creatures
As they become sustenance for the
Grotesque lust all bodies require
As an indefatigable right?

I don't think so.
I don't think so.

There is no beauty here
No higher purpose
Than limitless devouring
And mutilation
The program dear blinkered friends
If program there is
Is
Survival
The program.

Survival by assimilation
Survival by annihilation
Survival by abomination
This is our lot

Survival by assimilation

Survival by annihilation
Survival by abomination
This is our lot.

Our mortality wounded
Blind endeavor
There is no dignity here
No honor in this grotesque carnal
Craving
There is no dignity here.

Ah yes! But wait! Tell me quick!
You are here to save us all
God
You are our priest, our light
God. Our conscience
God. Our eyes
The selfless creator of beauty culled

Beautiful things
God. You say. God.
God you say, God.

Survival by assimilation
Survival by annihilation
Survival by abomination
Survival by ejaculation

This is our lot

Ah yes! See beauty in everything you say
God
Stop! Right there God
Let me remind you of that you would exhale.
God.
God. Those who find beautiful meanings,
God.
In ugly things are corrupt God
Without charming God
They are pathetic God

God. This is a fault. God.

Survival by assimiliation
Survival by annihilation
Survival by abomination
Survival by ejaculation

This is our lot

These mediocrities
God they are our down fall
God.

At Last…

At last
At last
You ask
At last

At last, at last, you ask
I've been waiting so long
I've been looking so long
And now
At this time
At last at last
You ask

At last
At last
You gasp
Time's up

Simply dancing duet, weaving, spinning, regret
With you, yes-you.
At last
At last

If we were everywhere,
Return to stand and care
Yes-you
Yes-you

Did I surround you, yes-you
Could I confound you, my profound you
Yes-you
Yes-you
At last
Except

I was twinning with you, yes I.T.'s swimmingly true
Yes-you
At last
At last

TIME'S UP!

There were mentions of this
Crafted spell—binding kiss
Dissolution to bliss
For you, yes-you
Yes-you

At last
At last
At last
We gasp
TIME'S UP

And I'm ready to know
And I'm willing to go

At last
At last
At last
At last

Angel with iron wings

I see you walking slowly in the deep blue
Of a silver lip twilight
I hear only the murmer of crushed grass
And the broken crystal noise
Of your
Wings
Splitting the sky
Into little flat pieces
Words of blood
Have lost their pictures
Separated

At last
At last

Life offered you a golden mask
At heart
You play with stars
Display so perfectly my secrets
By gentle movements of your hands
Now speak to me in four voices
Each with its own tongue
And hungry hushed gasp
Giving lips
Splitting the sky

In reverie you chose to flex
Space rolls
Grinding
Huge
Malformed porcelain splinters
Cracked desire
Broken blood
Hull
Skull
The engine never ends its humming
Splitting the sky

And it is true

IT IS
IT IS

Imaginary time
Divine intervention
Penury
At last
At last
Angel with iron wings
Whose presence
Turns
Vertebrae to snow
Accept my life as water
That it might flow
Everywhere it sings
Splitting the sky

AT LAST!
AT LAST!

Might I be blessed to tell
Replenish space
And purged with fire
Swim through the well
Retrieve my answer
My spiritual desire
Splitting the sky

At last!
ATLAS

This golden mask
No son
Not you
Yes you
Knot you
Y'Eshu

Yes-you
Yes-you

Eshu it's you
Yes you
Y'Eshu
Atlas

May play with stars
May say this scars

At last
At last

Time's up!

Door one: Send up flare
Door two: See who's there
Door three: Is this me?
Door four: Open the door…

I AM THE DOORMAN

Door number one: And there's no fear

Door number two: And there's no maybe

Door number three: And there's no doubt

Door number four: And there's no pain

I am the doorman
Living near the beach
And it's safe

Door one: Send up flare

Door two: See who's here

Door three: Is this me?

Door four: Open the door…

I AM THE DOORMAN

Door number one: And there's no fear

Door number two: And there's no maybe

Door number three: And there's no doubt

Door number four: And there's no pain

I AM THE DOORMAN
LIVING NEAR THE BEACH
AND IT'S SAFE

Source Are Rare

Each day we WILL embrace the Holy
Each day we will embrace the Holy

Blessed are the mad
For they shall touch the Holy
Blessed are the mad,
For the shall touch
Each other.

What can I say?
What CAN I say?

Your needs are blocked
Your dreams and your rights to dream
They are
STOLEN
You are being re-POSSESSED
You are being disguised
Disguised for ease of location and
Suffocation
Your breath, the breath of young joy
The breath of BEAUTIFUL bodies

Well
This holy breath
This breath of your enthusiasm
Is being asphyxiated
Because you tried
You tried to discover nature
Of the material of your own mind
You do have a mind
Don't you?
You do think a little tiny bit
Don't you?

You are slightly awake
Are you not?

Oh I'm sorry, my mistake
I was assuming you understood what I was saying
But
Hey!
We all make mistakes don't we?
And after all
The Holy breath of your enthusiasm well,
That's the material of your own mind not mind
Remember
It's no mind
And
Er
Well
You're forgiven
I think
Oh and er
As you now re-MIND your SELF
Your very OWN self
Er, as you learn to OWN your SELF
As you own your MIND
Your body
Your body
In fact sometimes your MYSTERY
Very suffocated,

YES.
I'm not sure you're thinking at all
But your breath
Your breath is being diluted, polluted,
Poisoned and
Fragmented by

FEAR

FEAR!
Not YOUR fear, no, not
Your
FEAR
But the manipulating
Self-seeking
Twisted and depraved
Ummm…. Suburban fear
The fear of old, alien brooding
And
Heartless hunters
Now, are you sure?
Are you sure as you now remind yourself
Your very OWN self
As you learn to OWN yourself
As you own your MIND
As you RE-MIND your SELF
Your BODY

Sometimes even your mystery gets
Suffocated

I was watching you know
I was
And
I saw what you did
I didn't say anything I
Didn't think it was really my business
But I was watching and I saw
And I thought you were pretty disgusting
In fact

I could even argue
That you were a
Blasphemous kind of demon but I
Am not judgmental
I don't try and push my opinions
On people like you
But I'm watching
And I'm sure
What I saw
Was what was going on

DO YOU REMEMBER?

I saw you paid with forty pieces of silver
(Maybe even fool's gold)
But you were paid
You were paid by cowering wretches
Who hide away in perverse churches
Of so-called
POWER!
And
As we all know
POWER
Is often,
Very quiet.

These infinitely grey corridors of power
Where vampires of this "Game"
Screech emotional,
Physical
And
Sexual abuse,
These corridors of power wear
Feigned
Outrage at their own VILE reflection
In the pockets of the rich
In the pouches of those who
NO the "GAME"
These corridors
Where sport

Is dead and steals
And enjoys its devotion to secrets
To sexual lineage and bloodlines

I've seen you THERE
And I didn't really like what I saw
But it's not MY place to say ANYTHING
Anymore.

These people
Whose depravity is
As pleasant as emasculating
YOUR
Sexual power and potence
These people
These addicts
Remain impoverished weaklings
Who shrivel
And are deformed in the LIGHT
These corridors are like a funhouse
That leads me to see everything and
SPEAK
NOT
AT
ALL.

Bee Honey

If you could
Just
Bee
Honey
Bee sweetly stick
Honey
Sticking pointing
A whey
Curdled warm
Honey

Cat
Like fish
Like milk
If k-new should
Must
Could would will can
Should just
Bee
Honey
Money
Merely twist
Snake a-way
Like sin
Singing a wish
To just bee
Swarm
Warm away
A whey honey
To ore from
Form gold
You would
Bee golden wood
Nest
Wheat of thieves
Eat
Breaking inn
Drin-king men
And queen
Four roads wind
Lead
To gold
Blow nowhere away
Fast honey
Cold sold
So old
Laughing
Mouth
Making
Making anything
Something specific

Specify
You tell me
Bee
Specific
Bee honey
A tool
Use fool
Laughable
Able too
Yet not
Use
But made by
Mouth formed
Stamped
Out
Destroyed
Shaped
Solid as a car
Millions
Mewling lions
Devour
Yours truly, own
Mouth maker
Ache scream lose
Loose
Drifting
Sometimes
Just finally buzz (saw)
Us
Sting die
Cast
Agen as tool
Stool
Split would
Break down
Down falling
To earth
Only if you
Could just
Honey

Bee
Honey
Make
Take
honey
bee
one lie
only
one fast
last
time
honey
just
alone
with
me
beeeeeeeeeee

BLACK MASS

Jason Louv

M'blese, m'pa wè san mwen. (I'm wounded, but I don't see my blood.)
– Haitian song for Sen Jak Majè

For no known reason, I tremble, I quake. This, so they tell me, is the voice of Ghoul and Ghoul is the Djinn of the Desert, Keeper of the Land of Fear.
– Brion Gysin, *The Process*

I know you. You specialize in war news. You supply the ink, the soldiers supply the blood.
– Captain Nemo, *Mysterious Island*

(This is part one of a serialized novella. Though fiction, it is, in one sense, a record of undergoing the psychic ordeal known in the Western Esoteric Tradition as Crossing the Abyss—or, rather, An Abyss.)

With a gun at my head I am focused. They've stripped the bag off of my head and they've got me facing into the camera. They've got a knife at my throat and they're shouting at me. They start the camera and the knife presses down.

"My name is John Nemo," I say. "I'm a photographer for the Associated Press. I am being held by operatives of Al Qaeda and I am meant to beg for my life. My captors have called for the destruction of the State of Israel and they feel that this is the best way to send you the message."

My hands are bound behind me in the chair; they've had me like this for the last sixteen hours. The headless body of a U.S. military contractor is hunched over in the chair to my left. My gray work shirt is soaked; I'm leaking sweat from my forehead and chest and it's pooling behind me at my bonds. I'm told that in situations like this it is quite common to develop an illogical empathy or compassion for one's captors. This is not something that I am experiencing.

I know they're going to behead me now. The giant bearded and masked man on my left, the one called ibn Fasid who has been playing cards and smoking Russian cigarettes with his two compatriots for the last several hours while I have been bound and bagged, has sunk the serrated knife into my flesh and I can feel a trickle of blood. They're going to cut my throat for the camera and nothing will change because of it and this world will continue. They're going to stop halfway through so that they can show me trying to breathe through an opened windpipe. And then they're going to finish it. God seems very far away. My life does not flash before my eyes.

I am already a nameless and faceless man, a symbol for money, for crimes commited by men I have never met and never supported, a symbol for centuries of tangled history, stories long forgotten and confused by the process of time. They are going to waste my life. I don't feel God but I can see Miranda's face. I wonder when she'll hear about this. What her reaction will be. But God is missing; the reason for this, the invisible culprit.

I feel I'm beginning to lose my head.

Further back a bit. I'm in a hotel in Dubai. I'm twenty-nine years old and the assault on Fallujah has been underway for exactly two days. I'm back from my first assignment in Iraq, in a semi-operational hospital on the north side of Baghdad, photographing the deformed bodies of infants whose mothers had been exposed to the depleted uranium rounds used by the United States military. It's a lot for a young man to take in. I've been drinking too much. I upload the contents of the three digital flashcards I've used to the AP office and I'm informed that the photos are too extreme to be of much marketable use. I'm paid a kill fee and I stare at the sum in my bank account for over an hour. Then I send the photos to every progressive blog I can find. The children are the best evidence I've seen that the universe is run by chaos alone. Distended faces locked in frozen and, worst of all, lucid and knowing screams. Children with fingers where their faces should be. Bloated, massive bellies and leaking brains. At night I dream of the noises they made and how they moved in their slicked cots. Their faces plead with me, asking silently—And what will you do? What will you do for us?

I've been sitting in the hotel bar watching CNN with the rest of the journalists who are using this building as a waypoint. We watch the rhetoric and we watch the tanks, the US stormtroopers crawling through the sand-blown alleys looking for insurgents. All I see is waste. We smoke cigarettes and discuss the war. Some think it will end after a few key offensives are undertaken against remaining insurgent strongholds. Most think it will never end, not now, not when Bush has just won his second term, when profits are high and strategy has been completely lost.

It's too hot to go outside with anything less than an air-conditioned car waiting for you right outside the hotel door, but there's an observation floor with tinted windows at the top of the building. I spend my time away from e-mail and the bar there, watching the sun go down most nights. That's the first time I see Miranda. I've got my headphones on and I can't hear her when she floats into my field of vision and asks me a question. She's about my height, tanned, with the creases around her eyes characteristic of people who have spent a lot of time in the desert, dark blonde hair tied behind her head in a bun. I take out the headphones and look up at her with a questioning gaze.

"I asked you, what wire service are you working for?"

The best photographers I know are profoundly empty and distant people. Mediocre photographers always use their cameras as social crutches, to get themselves into and document situations that they would not normally have the social skills to negotiate. The best ones, though, are blank, invisible people who do their best to completely remove themselves from the situations they document, who are easily forgotten, assuming they're ever noticed at all. I'd spent my entire career as a photojournalist aspring to the latter, with mixed results, though I had never had problems being a cipher or removing myself from the pain of relating to my fellow humans. Hence this woman's abrupt interruption of my life carries with it a certain tinge of inexcusable violence that catches my attention and will, eventually, do the same to my heart.

Miranda's a correspondent for the *Guardian* assigned to cover the plight of refugee children in the Kurdistani border. She's French, lives in London sporadically. She tells me about her experiences with children living in subhuman conditions, the walking wounded and the particular horror of the child that is forced to shoulder the sins of a world they are yet too young to have any culpability in. In her estimation, some of these children will go on to great things. Those who survive atrocity have two choices. They can reject violence, and realize the fundamental sorrow and uselessness of it, on all sides. Or they can seek revenge, and continue the violence in one way or the other. She tells me she did her best to inspire the first in the bandaged and traumatized children that she spoke with, knowing that the latter was close to inevitable.

We talk for hours, and I tell her of my own experience with the children in the Baghdad hospital. Something is communicated, if anything else the shared guilt of voyeurs of misery. We sit on plastic chairs watching the city lights until we're the last ones in the room. She speaks of a Spanish boyfriend of uncertain status, travelling in North Africa, who she has not seen in seven months. Past midnight she rises to retire. "Well John. I'm going to bed now," she says. I nod and when she walks by me her skirt brushes my hand. I try to think of something to say. I look around at the ferns decorating the lounge, the unattended and locked miniature bar, the long shadows, and wonder if she wants me to follow her. I run her final comments in my mind over and over again. She's already gone, though. I watch the blinking lights of Dubai, the playground of the Middle East, for half an hour before I retire to my own bed. It's another hour before I finally sleep, the hum of the air conditioner keeping me awake and tossing in my coffin of a room.

It's another week before I see her again, a week spent with the nonstop barrage of CNN and pack after pack of Gauloises while I wait for another assignment. I keep thinking about her but she's nowhere to be seen. There's a big Scot named Orson who takes a liking to me, and our conversations over as much Stella Artois as we can afford get more and more involved. When he asks me where I'm from and I say California he laughs and asks what could have ever possibly inspired me to end up in a neon hellhole like this. I don't have a good answer for him. My American-ness is a constant butt of his jokes.

"You people fucked it all up. Bad fucking karma mate. Bad karma. You had it all on a plate and you threw it all away."

I look at him blankly.

"Think about it," he says. "America got sold to the wrong gang of bastards. You can take the century leading up to this miserable war as a competition between two families for dominance of the country, the Kennedys and the Bushes. Both of them started by glorified drug dealers, Prescott Bush and John Kennedy, who made their money running booze during Prohibition. For a while it looked like the lace curtain Irish Catholics had it made. You had John Kennedy in office, so cranked on speed that he was coming up with bizarre plans for human betterment like space travel and desegregation because he was the golden boy and he didn't have anybody telling him no. Think what would have happened had he lived. He'd already turned on to LSD via some connections with Timothy Leary. He could have led us all into a new age. Space travel, acid, Martin Luther King, social justice. We could have won the game right then and there. Bullet in the head is what you get for shit like that. Then they iced Bobby and MLK. Big hole in the heart of America to let the darkness in. Couple of decades of the government flooding the ghettoes with nightmare drugs and genetically engineered AIDS; dirty little wars and fuck the poor until it all comes right back around on us and they blow up those two towers. Assuming Dick Cheney didn't arrange that one himself. Very likely, that. And right then and there America had the whole world on its side again. You could have done anything. Anything. And you fucked it up again. Dark forces, mate."

Orson sees me as an American, and hence the problem. Ignorant of history and just about everything else, with eyes just a little too close together. American devil. The English I've met tend to feel the same way but with the Scots they've got less of a sense of culpability, more of the moral righteousness of being a bit closer to the stepped-on side of the world equation. I'm patient with it, but not too patient. The more I drink the more I tune it out. I see the faces of those children again. We keep drinking.

After one all-night session I find myself on the floor of the bathroom in my room. A bunch of journos from the bar are in my suite arguing and drinking with the TV on. I look down and I've got track pants on and a t-shirt with Felix the Cat on it with crazy, drugged-out hypnotic eyes that I've had since college. There are cockroaches running past me on the floor. I think I've been vomiting but I can't remember. Those children come back to me. My body's useless, and I've got the relaxed ease that comes from physical failure. Jesus, I think, I've never believed in you but I need your help. I'm a Crusader and a Templar and I'm in the desert and I need God on my side 'cause I'm dying, I'm dying. I'm twenty-nine years old and I'm dying. I think of Miranda and my mind turns and rends itself to pieces. A woman you only met once. To pin your hopes on that. For shame.

I feel very far away from home, and far away from myself. I've forgotten who I am. I think back to my childhood. Playing in the long grass with my trucks. I don't understand it. I think of my teenage years, hours with my first camera, learning to develop my own photos. College; parties and studying and girlfriends. It doesn't make sense at all. It bears no overlap with the person on the floor and unable to move. I see a child with liquified flesh and a hair-covered scab for a face. What the fuck, I think. What the fuck. What the fuck.

My name is John Nemo, I think to myself. I'm a photographer. I'm here as a witness, that's all. And what I'm witnessing is the loss of the last bit of good in the world. I think I'm going crazy, I think. I think I'm losing my head.

In my room Orson's yelling at the television. "Fucking Americans! Fucking cowboys!" I can hear the destruction of Fallujah, rockets and running commentary. "Like it's a video game!" I stumble onto the bed; the room's spinning. The mattress is already occupied by a Senegalese drug dealer friend of Orson. When I collapse next to him he looks at me and says "You look in a very bad sort friend. You look not good at all. You look like a corpse, man." I look up at him. "Hollow eyes, sunken cheeks. You look like a fucking ghoul, American. You look like you wanna feast on the dead." They're all laughing.

Jesus Christ, I don't care if you're the reason we got into this, you still gotta help me. You gotta help me, man.

I was born the year we pulled out of Vietnam. My parents were peace activists. They marched against the war, lived in a co-op throughout most of the sixties, ran a leftist bookshop in Los Angeles for a while. My dad escaped the draft as a conscientious objector, something he was always proud of. The first thing they taught me was that there was only one truly dirty word in the English language, and that was War. They wouldn't even let me touch toy guns, no matter how much I begged them.

I got my first camera when I was twelve. The totemic power it had accumulated in the half a year of asking for one constantly was not diminished in the receiving. I remember its light brown leather case and its single glass eye. My parents had me do odd jobs for film money; it was a present that came with stern warnings and responsibilities. In a way it was a signifier of the onrush of manhood, something that I was entrusted with the care of, and a way to express my own developing individuality.

I began with birds. Birds were a challenge; they were something to approach delicately and with grace, a test of the photographer's mannerisms. Birds taught me the photographer's instinct: How to walk, how to approach difficult subjects, how to handle the camera without startling the subject, how to maintain appropriate distance when capturing a fleeting moment of beauty in its natural environment. Starlings and goshawks were my mentors in my chosen art, and they were often harsh ones, forcing me to learn patience and humility, leaving me to wait silently for hours in silent places in the woods for three seconds of opportunity for a snapshot, three seconds that one mistake could ruin, leaving a day wasted.

My days in the woods with my camera were spent with a certain sense of presence, of being together with the vegetable intelligence of the woods. The woods had their own lessons for me, in simply existing, and allowing me to compare the turmoil of my young mind with them. As I sat and waited to see a bird I would imagine manhood. Manhood was a quiet strength, broad shoulders, a knowing and confident smile. It was having a woman on your arm, and having a job to do. It was the smell of smoke and aftershave. It was being trusted and respected by other men and, most of all, it was freedom. I would wait for the birds for hours, listening to the rustling of the foliage, tiny and not-so tiny animals burrowing through the underbrush, the trickle of a stream in the distance. I learned to push away the desire to see birds, and in that I learned the most important lesson of all. I began to learn that time, like mind, was a substance that could be touched.

Time starts to change when you're twelve, along with your body. For most it is the first awareness of death, of the frightening permanence inherent in the idea that you're changing and will never go back to the way you were again. The slow realization that your childhood, and innocence, are over. You watch your parents' weary complaints at the dinner table and you begin to suspect that something very special is about to be taken from you. You stop sleeping well, staring at the ceiling in fright, as new chemicals flood your body and cause new sensations. The realization that your parents will be dead one day, even more frightening than the idea that you will be dead, too abstract of a concept to fully comprehend. More upsetting is the idea of aloneness, of losing your safety, of losing your family. The idea that you will be called soon to the test of life, and that you may well fail.

I remember a profound sense of sorrow from that time; the name of the sorrow was the passage of time. A speeding car that one knows will crash, that one is unable to escape from. Time could be touched but time could not be stopped, and I knew that it would take everything.

When time put on a face and showed itself, it was called Death. Death made only infrequent appearances in my young life. There were the childhood cataclysms of dead pets. There was the day I returned from school to find both of my parents home from work, and to be informed that my grandmother, who had languished in the hospital for months, had died in the night. My major emotional reaction to that was the shame of not having much of an emotional reaction. I remember sitting with my parents for hours and putting my face down on my arm as if to pretend I was grieving, when in fact I was only waiting to escape the situation, feeling obligated to express grief. At one point I heard my father emit a single sob, one of the only times I ever heard him cry, and a needle of terror twisted sideways in my chest.

The guilt I felt at my lack of ability to express emotion in this situation compounded in my head and I began to compensate by expressing even less emotion. The passage to the new state of manhood was marked by a parallel passage, one to a state of distance, of emotions that became more dulled with each year. This was how one became a man.

I remember the last night of my childhood, when I met Death for real. I had driven across town with my mother on an errand, and we had stopped at the old house, where I had been born and lived until I was ten years old. It was a tiny cottage barely big enough for the family of four that we had become, in an old part of the town. The new occupants had painted it white, instead of the schoolhouse red it had been; they had replanted the garden and made modifications and extensions to the house so that it was unrecognizable from its previous state. I felt a numb sense of dread and mortality, and pushed them away, turning from them so that I need not see them. We walked down the street that my mother had walked me up and down in my stroller, to the small park at the end of the lane. The park had been a cemetary at the turn of the century; sometime in the Sixties the bodies had been exhumed and discarded, and the gravestones removed so that it could be converted into a park; the only reminder of its previous function a single row of tombstones in a far corner.

That single row of tombstones had been my refuge as a child, a refuge from the frivolous talk and casual brutality of other children. Across from the tombstones was a small playground, with swings and a slide, and a large metal caterpillar made for children to climb on. The land of the just-born and the land of the long-dead, side by side; maybe those are the two human states that have the most in common, the most to say to each other.

When we came upon the park again, the playground that I remembered, that I had learned how to be a social being at, was gone; the old metal equipment had been discarded and replaced with garish, bright plastic equipment, with no sharp edges or rust, nothing that could conceivably hurt a child, and no soul either. It was a tiny thing but it was as if I had been slapped, humiliated. When we returned home I cried in my mother's arms for two hours. She was confused and frightened by my behavior; I couldn't express how I was feeling to her, only my sorrow, a pattern I would in the future repeat numerous times with women, looking for love only in the saddest of moments. When I finished crying I was no longer a child; neither was I an adult.

From then on, it was the camera. It was my need to prove to my parents that I could in fact be an adult, with the camera. Though birds were my major subject, I began to explore the larger world, taking photos of cityscapes at night, road signs, landscapes. I didn't take pictures of people. I kept my camera hidden, refused to bring it out at family functions no matter how much I was cajoled. Being caught taking photographs was like being caught masturbating. It was mine alone.

That began to change in high school, where I joined the photography club. I was a gangly and awkward teenager, always dressed improperly in too-high jeans and faded button-up shirts, with long, greasy hair and acne that ravaged my face. I learned to hide behind the camera, use it as a prop. As an adult I would come to understand that this is an almost universal experience with professional photographers. It's the first stage of the art. I began to take snapshots for the school newspaper, of the school basketball and football games, of the student elections, of anything else that needed it. I wore the camera around my neck constantly.

When I was sixteen, at lunch, I witnessed a spontaneous fight between two skinheads, boys who were constantly walking the line of expulsion. They were like a blister suddenly raised and burst at once, a tangle of punches; they were grabbing each other by the lapels and smashing each other's faces, which were swelling up immediately, until the smaller of the two went down, to be kicked savagely until a big teacher arrived to pull the victorious boy off. I stood there at the periphery with my camera, mouth open, and slowly raised it to my eye to take a picture of the boy on the floor. His bald head was gashed; his mouth and eyes purple and swollen. The shutter clicked. He spit a single tooth out in a black spray.

It was the first time I had been close to real violence. I couldn't take my eyes away from the boy on the ground. Finally the school security arrived, and cleared us away. An ambulance arrived shortly thereafter, and I took more pictures as they lifted him into the back on a stretcher. I was transfixed.

Developing those pictures in the school darkroom was a secret shame. I was irrationally terrified that somebody would find them, as if I was somehow complicit in a violence much greater than the one I had been witness to. The secret thrill of the voyeur ran through me.

That was the year that the first Gulf War broke out, after Iraqi troops crossed the border into Kuwait. I watched the war on television with my father, the computerized missle strike simulations and the grand spectacle of CNN.

"That's not war," he would tell me. "That's a commercial for a chicken dinner. They know better than to show the reality of war now. If they hadn't been showing American boys in bodybags on television in the Sixties, they never would have had the trouble with protesters, with us, that they had. They've learned not to upset the middle class."

My parents, bless them, returned to marching. The marches in our town were tiny, overwhelmingly futile and punctated by harassment and screams from passing trucks. I could never bear to go with them. I was too shy and awkward; scared that I might be seen, photographed. Anyways, I was a nobody; who was I to raise my voice? I only wanted to stay in the woods, to be alone. I didn't want to express how I felt. I didn't have the right.

Such a disappointment, I would think, looking in the mirror. Scared of other people, scared of yourself, scared to go out and face the world. Awkward and babbling around girls; only mediocre at schoolwork; terrible at sports. Scared to come out from behind your camera, your security blanket, your only salvation. Ugly and scabby.

America was long gone by then.

The hotel in Dubai's the crossroads of the worlds. Dubai's like Las Vegas; big, gaudy and, in Muslim terms, lawless. It's where the whole Middle East goes to get their money laundered; hence nobody ever tries to blow it up. The heat's unbearable.

It's another week before I see Miranda again. She's been in Kurdistan on another assignment. I spend the week making a circuit between checking my e-mail and laying in cold water in the bath; the hotel's air conditioner is undergoing sporadic bouts of malfunction. I try feeding myself from room service constantly to keep the fatigue away. AP picks up some of the tab, but hardly enough. I hit that state of emotional overload where focus becomes impossible, and days become blurs of habitual tasks incorrectly performed. Keys lost, toes stubbed, can't think, can't communicate; I stop making an effort to remind the outside world of my existence.

I sit at my computer and chain-smoke, reading the constant updates and blog commentary on the Fallujah offensive.

"Like the rest of this war," one blog reports, "this isn't about anything except vengeance and has nothing to do with sound (heh) military strategy. And they call it 'Operation Phantom Fury,' the latest blockbuster for an audience that has long become too jaded to take notice. Seven private contractors are killed and we have to level this relatively unimportant town like we did Hue City in the Tet Offensive in Vietnam. The brutality here is hard to convey or offer any kind of casual commentary on in something as frivolous as an online journal. Have the flag-wavers and hawks so quickly forgotten what we did to Al Fallujah in the first Gulf War, when we tried to bomb a bridge over the Euphrates and 'missed,' hitting markets and killing over two hundred civilians; or when the English 'missed' and dropped laser-guided bombs on another market, killing another hundred and fifty or more? They try to sell us the doctrine of 'collateral damage,' but when does it stop being a 'necessary' by-product of war and become pure negligence and absolute barbarity? And yet seven military contractors are killed and we level this violence. Nobody's driving the bus here, that should have been clear long ago. How much collateral damage can the world accept as a 'necessary' by-product of a war that was founded on lies and corporate greed, and hardly 'necessary' for any reason other than to give jobs to men like the very contractors who were killed on March 31?"

I can't pull myself away from the computer, and when I do, I'm underwater in the bath or in front of CNN downstairs again. My moments of realization that I'm in a horrific tunnel of my own creation are fleeting. You're making this, I tell myself. You came here for a reason. You're choosing to dwell in horror. You don't have to stay here. This isn't the only face the world has to show you. You're choosing this—Then something that sounds like my conscience, but only leads to my own dissolution, takes over, and says: Coward. How dare you try to look away. How dare you turn your back. And there are those children again, and they say—What will you do?

I find a website where U.S. soldiers trade digital snapshots of slaughtered insurgents for pornography. There are pictures of bodies demolished from bunker-buster shells; a single pair of boots in an array of gore with fragments of bone and meat protruding from them; bodies with gaping headwounds piled at the side of a city street that looks not terribly different from a suburban lane in America. At the bottom of the page I find a picture of an Iraqi combatant's face that has been sliced cleanly off and placed in a steel bowl full of blood. The face has been there too long and is covered with green mold and rot.

"The enemy has a face," says Colonel Gary Brandl in article I find on the Scotland Today site. "It is Satan's. He is in Fallujah, and we are going to destroy him."

Then there's the chess set made from severed fingers. I think of the image from Vietnam of the boy with the necklace of ears harvested from Viet Cong. I think of all those scalped Indians. I think of Max von Sydow in *The Seventh Seal*, playing chess with Death by the seaside, and the Dance of Death at the end, when Death leads him and his followers over the hill, that most potent of Medieval images that has somehow not lost its potency in this, the most Medieval of all modern times.

"What do you mean you don't have any work for me?" I shout at my editor over the phone. "This is the heaviest fighting since the beginning of the war!"

"You're not qualified to go into combat zones, John, and right now the papers belong to those who are."

I put down the phone exactly as the call to prayer begins. I think of the opening scene of *The Exorcist*. Max von Sydow again.

I'm back at the bar when Miranda shows up again. She's with another man and I try not to show a reaction, but I can feel the acid of jealous rage rising up in my stomach. Relax, I tell myself. This is why there's wars in the first place and you hardly know this woman. Don't be a child. I casually say hello when they appear. She introduces me to her companion, a photographer that the *Guardian* has assigned to be her partner for a story. I calm down, and then I think, oh. Another photographer. Competition most foul? I order three Heinekens.

"We were in Basra," she told me. "It's a broken city; the scars of what the Americans and English did to it are everywhere. The *Guardian* wanted us to do a story on Shi'ite extremists, how they're coming up against the secular population and causing friction. You have to be careful with stories like that so that they don't become propaganda. I don't want to assist in a 'divide and rule' policy. We travelled to the city in a ten-ton UN supply truck. We hopped off along the Shatt al-Arab waterway. Five minutes later the truck rounded a corner too fast to avoid a riot, lost traction and fell onto its side. Eleven people died."

The man's name is David. As I ease into his presence a bit more, he begins to strike me as a nice kid. He's got a sport fleece on, short hair and wire-rimmed glasses; he looks relatively inexperienced but has a well-meaning glow about him. The way his body language is around Miranda, and the way he defers to her and watches her expectantly while she's speaking suggest a kind of cowed awe, that he looks up to her as a mentor figure and seems uncomfortable with his own youth and inexperience. I remember that not-fully-comfortable-in-your-own skin feeling all to well, when you're still trying to figure out the natural arising social boundaries and hierarchies of the world. He's drinking his Heineken a lot faster than we are. Must be tough growing up in the middle of a war. I hope, for his sake, that he doesn't have the same voice in the back of his head that I had in mine, the one saying, This'll make a man out of you. In my case, regular exposure to horror did make a man out of me, a very scared and confused man, and it burned the bridge it took me across.

Miranda, on the other hand, is displaying the same casual ease that left me reeling on our first encounter. She's wearing the same desert khakis, dark blond hair pulled back, sunglasses on a cord around her neck. When she smiles the crow's feet at the corners turn up, her face radiating kindness. I catch myself staring; there's something about her that calls to a fundamental need in me that makes me uncomfortable. It's not a need for sex, or companionship, or even nurturing; it's a need to know that good still exists. And then I catch myself again, and tell myself that I'm projecting an ideal, the last thing you ever, ever want to do with a woman. And then I catch my own suspicion of women by its tail and look at the beast called fear and self-doubt. And by then I've finished my second beer, and lost my train of thought, and I'm still doing my best not to stare.

There's a kind of casual ease between us, a familiarity that I know she's feeling as well, though there is little trace of the suggestiveness of our first meeting. I begin to wonder if I had imagined it completely, mistaken simple friendliness for sexual interest. David's talking about the sectarian violence in Basra. "The fundamental feeling I got from these people is that they're tired. They don't want to be fighting each other. But they're living in chaos and the nightmare of the occupation, the tension is huge. A mosque gets bombed and then there has to be retaliation, and then retaliation for that, and so one, and sense is lost. It's crowd dynamics. A lot of people seem to think that the Americans are engineering it..."

"Of course they are," Miranda replies. "They've engineered excuse after excuse for the occupation and this is one more of them. They'll do everything they can to paint these people as animals and fanatics, who can't run their own lives and who need iron rule, and if that includes 'dividing and ruling' by instigating violence between the Sunnis and Shi'ites then that's what they'll do. And if the support for the war begins to fade they'll do it even more. They'll create violence to justify violence, blow those mosques up themselves and blame it on whoever they want."

"Same old story," I added.

"Yes. It's the return of the counterinsurgency in El Salvador. They'll train death squads to hit both sides until the entire country is destabilized and devolves into complete civil war. Then the U.S. won't have to waste taxpayer money on ammunition to do the job that the Iraqis will do themselves. Same tactic they used in El Salvador, and Vietnam, and Indonesia. Same tactic they use in the ghettoes of their own country."

I restrain the need to counter with a jab about English gunboat diplomacy. As an American I have to keep my head down at every opportunity, maintain an air of cynical disdain and aloofness from my own country at all times. It works, sometimes. Usually I'm the scapegoat for the world's ills.

"So how do you think the war will go?" I ask her.

"I think it is violence without reason, that it had no reason to begin, that it will certainly not have a reason to end, and that it will outlast our own lifetimes."

This is not something to say to a war journalist. I smile and proffer a pack of Gauloises. They both decline primly.

"They will create monster after monster, bin Laden after bin Laden, Zarqawi after Zarqawi, until they have decimated Iraq, and Iran, and Syria, until they have taken everything."

I'm afraid of losing everything to a war that is thousands of years old. Violence without reason for each generation of man.

I order an Irish carbomb and two Guinnesses on top of that in the next forty-five minutes; Miranda and David follow along. The drunker we get, the lighter the proceedings become. The tension begins to relax; the knotted cords in my back begin to unwind and my face eases into a smile. My shoulders open up and it becomes easier to take everything as it is—oh, it's just war. You're just a war correspondent. After all, you're doing important work, you're here documenting part of history, it's not as if you're on either side of a gun. You're living; your life has meaning. And then another dark thought worms in: How much misery do you have to see before life feels real? But I push that back out of my mind quickly and it's back to merriment.

Dubai nightlife is incredible. It's one of the few places in the Middle East that has any to speak of, the usual Muslim laws being somewhat lax here. Out of the back of a cab I can see the Burj Al Arab building, the luxury hotel that dominates the skyline. It looks like some kind of insectile pod, like a horned worm standing on its hind legs signalling at the sky, looking in vain for some way to climb upwards. The rest of the skyline looks like any Western city, but the street signs, the people, the dry heat of the air even at night mark it as unmistakably Arab. As a Westerner feeling lost I can't do much other than be thankful that I'm not in Baghdad any more; there's no other way to contextualize it.

What can you do, what can you say, when you find love slipping away? goes the song in the club when we arrive. It's an old Northern Soul hit, completely out of place here, though comforting. The bar is sleek and ebony and lit up underneath with blue phosphorecence; it's crowded with tourists of all nationalities wearing suits and evening gowns. David looks for a bathroom and I jockey for a position at the bar. This is always a good one, I think as I struggle to make my presence known to the bartender. I can't seem to wedge myself into the inner circle that crowds the bar. I scrunch myself sideways between two socialites, doing my best to curve a handful of money around their unmoving shoulders.

"Excuse me… excuse me…" I say, drowned out by the music. The bartender fails to register my presence, as do the people on either side of me. If this is any kind of an indicator of my presence as a male who others take seriously, who commands a certain level of respect and is somebody who should be paid attention to and is hence suited as a mate for he has distinguished himself from the breeding pool, then I am failing.

"Excuse me…" The bartender, a woman in a low-cut sheer black dress with gigantic false eyelashes, rushes past me and I try to lean further into the bar, knocking over the Tom Collins glass of the man on my right. His drink streaks across the wood. "Now hang the fuck on…"

Shit. English accent. Essex maybe. I see him as he turns—mid-forties, bulky, head shaved to cover encroaching male pattern baldness, a single diamond stud in his left ear. I can't tell if he's a journalist or some kind of businessman, but he certainly doesn't look particularly pleased with me.

"Shit, I'm really sorry about that, let me buy you another one…"

His face is red. It's gonna be the same old push-and-shove-story-of-the-world-in-microcosm again here. You got in my territory, you looked at my woman, you touched my possessions, you have to die. I root my feet to the ground and wait for a fight. He glares at me like a stuck bull and I meet his gaze, my palms up in the air in the surrender position. He wants to kill me. How's this going to play out? There's no way I stand a chance against him. I can run; I can hope that I don't take too much grievous damage before the bouncers intercede—that's assuming they will, although, then again, this is a classy place and they don't want to scare away their clientele. He's got a red glint in his eyes. "I'm really sorry, let me buy you another…" I consider reaching for my wallet (leave it to an American, I think, to try to solve every problem by throwing cash at it), but decide that the last thing I want him to think is that I'm reaching for something to do him damage with.

We hold in position and then a calm slowly settles over his face as he catches his breath. He seems like a man accustomed to violence. How unfortunate a thing to be accustomed to that is. "No worries, mate," he says. "It was a shit martini anyway." I laugh; in that moment he seems like a massive English Ghandi. If only it were that easy, I think…

When I finally return to the table with our drinks, Miranda is questioning David about his girlfriend back home.

"When was the last time you called her, David?" she asks. He scratches the back of his neck uncomfortably.

"Yesterday morning," he replies. "You know, we have a kind of understanding. I don't have to call her every day, you know, we're comfortable in our bond. I don't want to give her the impression that I'm clingy, you know what I mean?"

"David," she replies. "She's worrying about you constantly. You need to call her every day."

David shrinks a little and then takes the Heineken I pass him.

"I know, I know."

Miranda smiles at me as I hand her the Jack Daniels and Coke she asked me for.

"How long have you been seeing her?" I ask him.

"About a year. We met at Oxford; she's still doing her law degree there. When I was offered this assignment I was thrown into confusion, I'd just met her, I didn't know what to do, I didn't want to put myself in harm's way. But in the end we decided that it was too good of an opportunity for me to pass up. It's only six months, and she can finish her degree anyways. We want to get a flat together in London when I get back."

"What's her name?" I ask.

"Sarah."

"Jewish?"

"Yes, like me… well, I'm half Jewish."

"You are very lucky," I tell him, "that you do not look it. Especially in this part of the world." Miranda sets down her finished whiskey and Coke. "Are you gonna marry her?" I ask.

He blushes suddenly, registers an embarrassed look, and then overcompensates with a cocky grin. "Yeah, maybe. You know, if she's the right girl."

Miranda shoots him a sideways look. "You really should call her, David. It's your turn for the next round, too."

After David gets up Miranda laughs to herself slightly.

"You really look after him," I say.

"Nobody else will. He was a fool to take this assignment and come to the Middle East. So are you for that matter, and so am I. And him, just a child, and Jewish; it is not safe for him in the field at all. He has so much to go back to. I look at him and I think of what they did to Daniel Pearl… it is so easy to make a mistake…"

There is an uncomfortable silence.

"So why did you come here?" I ask her. She hesitates, staring into the bottom of her empty glass, rolling the few remaining drops of liquid around and around.

"Because it's the right thing to do. I can't count on anybody else to stand up and show the injustices that are going on here if I don't. And I wouldn't be able to live without guilt if I didn't use my talents to try and do some good while I'm on this planet. You saw those children… you know what's going on. You know how there's nothing here but chaos. I still believe that there's some kind of decency in this world, and I have to have faith that when things go wrong, people will ultimately fix them if they're shown the problem in enough detail. This is a very wrong part of history. The wrong people are in charge, and everybody knows it. This is a bad time to be alive, but I have to hope that we're all learning our lesson. Part of me thinks that the human race is getting its face ground into its own shit, and if I can help people smell it then I'll have done my duty."

I laugh and finish my Guinness.

"I hope you're right."

"I have to know that I am. Otherwise there's no point. And what about you? Why did you sign up for this?"

"I don't have an answer. Masochism. I was in a nasty divorce, I was offered this, I didn't know what else to do."

"When did you last speak with her?"

"A few months before I left the States. A long time ago. She was a graphic designer when I met her; now she works in a design headhunter firm in New York. She met a guy through work; they got married and he bought them a house in Jersey. Now she's pregnant. That was the last I heard."

"Do you still love her?"

"I did; for a moment there I did."

"I think you certainly must have to try to come here and kill yourself for her. And there's never just 'a moment' with these things, I don't think."

I laugh and look up at the ceiling. Arabesque patterns curl across it, suggesting a sprawling floral landscape. The music pauses briefly while the DJs switch. Suddenly it's less Western fare. A heavy jungle remix of a Kazem al-Saher song starts pounding the walls.

"I think you should call her, John."

I laugh again. David returns with the drinks.

"There's this huge guy who looks like a builder at the bar," he says. "He's so drunk that he's buying rounds for everybody…"

I laugh, my head spinning slightly from drink. The sheer nonsense of the world sometimes…

"I called my girlfriend though. Couldn't get through, she must be at school."

"I hope you left her a nice message," Miranda says.

"Yes, yes I did." He grins. We grin. For a moment I forget everything else. The music is throbbing so loudly now, and the dance floor is so packed, that I have to do the inevitable and suggest a dance. They're both self-conscious; but what else can you do when you've seen that much horror? I goad them into finishing their drinks and then we're pushing our way into the throng.

David dances self-consciously, like a student; he bounces just enough to the rhythm, pressing his thumbs to the tops of his curled-in index fingers and bobbing his hands up and down. The people around us are doing their best to flail with abandon in their expensive evening dress.

I think of the children again, and the chess set. Iraqi POWs with pointy black hoods on their heads. What can I do now? I think. What can I do now except dance? Do my best to forget myself. Enjoy my body while I still have one. What else can I do? I go loose and throw my entire body into the dance, letting it take over completely. What else can I do? I become a blur, harmonized perfectly to the music. I look over and Miranda is doing her own carefully measured dance, carried out with a graceful flowing motion that expresses her essence to me in a way that makes complete intuitive sense; she is communicating herself absolutely. I do my best to side up to her, open up my dance and my motion to make it more inviting, allow her in. She makes no motion to acknowledge me. What else can I do? I dance.

The lights on the dancefloor are blinding. How long has this taken? I think. How long has it taken me to feel comfortable in my own body, with my own existence? What did it take? How much suffering and misery and death did I have to witness to accept the basic sanctity of life?

In the cab home we laugh and tell stories about rabid editors and tales of lost luggage woe. We sing Michael Jackson songs. Everything is happy.

Staring at the ceiling from my hotel bed, alone, I let out a long sigh, close my eyes, and turn over to clutch my pillow as I sleep, like I'm hanging on to a life preserver in the middle of the Atlantic.

My dreams start with a single revelation.

I'm in the fields and I can see a light off in the distance, a glow off the horizon. I run towards it. The night air is sick with crickets, but noiseless otherwise, composed. I'm running through the long grass and trying not to get my feet tangled, uprooting blades here and there as I run.

It's black outside, the moon is hardly there, the stars have shut their doors, but the light on the horizon is just enough to find my way by if I keep focused on it. The lights of the town behind me are fading, a far shore.

I'm alone. I came here to be alone, to be free. In the town I'm a ghost, a gust of air, a boy who no-one knows. Out here, alone, everything I see belongs to me, is me. The sound of barking dogs from the town is carried across the sky.

The exposed skin of my forearms is recoiling from the air, telling me to turn around, go back to the town, but I keep going. The light grows, immensifying; the grass grows longer, filling up with weeds. Trees loom on the horizon, the purple silhouettes of mountains.

They told me never to come here, told everyone never to come here. The fields sprawl outwards; the mirror of my mind in vegetable flesh. My mind as still as the night save for the crickets, the irrepressible background buzz of thought.

The light grows closer, its features become distinct, coarse; it separates into many lights, a hum of them. I reach toward it, picking up speed, and then, in its perimeter, I fall to my knees in the sight of the City of God.

Its pinnacles and spires reach upward, towers of light crawling with the ichor and bile of divinity, the light its blood, its circulation. I fall, the light overcoming me, making of me a shadow by comparison.

And this is the City of God. A blaze of halo, ripping the sky apart. There's one light and there are a million lights, speaking all in unison, every voice contradicting each other, every voice the same. Paths of glowing electric nimbus hovering between all points. A city of angel fury.

Even to kneel in its presence is but to see my own darkness and aloneness in comparison, but to hear the bustle and cacophony of the city, the raging choir of heaven, is to know that there is a way in, gateway upon gateway. There's a way in, a secret sequence of pathways leading to its heart, a road through the byways of the Creator. Many secrets to be learned though no secret could truly be hidden, no shadow could truly remain intact in the luminous face and the monstrous immensity of the City.

I'm surrounded by a Braille of windows lit up along the sides of black skyscrapers, each with a hyperdense symbol just beyond the windowpane, breathing, pulsing, growing with the breath of the universe. An infinity of choices, of masks.

It speaks a single word.

CNN's being nasty again in the morning. I can't escape it. It hovers over me as I have my breakfast eggs and toast and coffee.

Fallujah's been taken. According to the television, the U.S. Marines are now "mopping up pockets of resistance." CNN shows footage, originally from NBC, of a Marine putting a bullet into a wounded and harmless Iraqi insurgent; by the time I'm finishing my coffee and morning cigarette they're claiming that it was in self-defense and that the Iraqi was "playing possum."

Orson's down at the bar too, messing around idly with his Palm Pilot. "Did you read the story in the *Washington Post* about the phosphorous?" he asks me with a sneer.

"No."

"This was a couple of days ago. Nobody's picked up on it. But you Americans are using chemical weapons in Fallujah. White phosphorous rounds." He's saved the article to his Palm Pilot; he pulls it up with the stylus and leans over to show it to me. And sure enough, the Marines are using white phosphorous.

"White phosphorous burns through people completely; it turns them into ash. It can't be put out. It destroys your internal organs if you inhale it. The U.S. has signed treaties saying they will not use it. Once again you Americans have proven yourself to be animals, using dirty weapons just like you accused the Iraqis of."

I clam up. I get hit with a wave of anxiety. I can't stay in this hotel anymore. I can't deal with this existence. I need to get out of the Emirates; I need to be back in the United States. I can't look at these people. I need to crawl as far away from this war as I can get. My breathing starts going haywire, black tidal waves of anxious fear sweep me under. Where am I? How did I get here? How did my life become this? How did the world become this? I'm leaving right now. I'm getting on a plane back to Los Angeles right now and I don't care if it costs me my job, I don't want this job anymore, it's going to kill me. I need to be back in America. I don't care if it's the Evil Empire and everything there is built on a mound of skulls. I don't care. I want to be in LA rush hour traffic listening to talk radio surrounded by three hundred hulking gas-guzzling SUVs, I don't care, I just want to be away from here.

My cell phone rings. It's my editor.

"John. I have an an assignment for you."

Oh no.

"I want you in Fallujah. I want pictures of the aftermath of the battle."

Oh shit.

"But… but you were just telling me it's not safe…"

"Don't turn coward on me now, John," my editor says from his comfortable office in the States. "You were just on the phone begging me for this. Well now you've got it. The fighting's calmed down, you're good to go now."

Oh I don't need this, I really don't need to do this, I should quit right now. Tell him to take you out of this, tell him to have you go take snapshots of festivals in India, anything but…

"OK."

Oh goddamnit why did I say that.

"Great. I have a flight lined up for you in the morning. You should be gone for a week, so bring enough clothing and Iraqi currency. You'll be flying from Basra with the 3rd Battalion 5th Marines."

"Thanks," I reply. Thanks a lot.

Bound for glory am I. I hope I see Miranda again, is all I can think.

I didn't know anything about women in college, I didn't know anything about life, and of course I assumed the opposite, the glory of coming out on the other end of my teenage years leading me to forget that my behavior still wasn't much more than the squirt of a few random hormones. I majored in anthropology and took photos for the school newspaper, and did surprisingly well. By graduation, though, it was only my photography skills that guaranteed me any work, and I quietly congratulated myself on my perseverance.

College was a time of phantom struggles for me. The struggle of balancing work and studying, and meeting the commitments of student life, seemed minor in comparison with the struggle in my head, the struggle for identity. In college you can't help but define yourself, and I defined myself as a victim. I became political. I marched against NAFTA; I marched against global warming. There was an anger in me that I mistook for my identity. I felt I had to hone it, to develop it; I felt it was what would protect me from the big bad world that I had found myself in. The great evils that I found to raise my voice against were only partially drawn from life. Half-quixotically, my fellow radicals and I were able to perform great feats of will and imagination in taking impersonal government or civic policy and projecting our own failings, impotencies and helplessness upon them. It was easy to project every slight, real or imagined, that we had ever experienced upon an abuse of authority. Faceless men in suits would become stand-ins for parents, teachers, bosses, playground bullies, anybody who we had ever been on the opposite side of the boot from. The more we demonized, the better we would feel about ourselves. No wonder protestors are never taken seriously by those in power. It must be a heavy burden to have to play a stern father figure for the world, and become the target of all that sublimated hostility. The manipulative bastards.

Anger. Anger and its drunken brother, hatred, who knows nothing, who sees only his own inadequacy and weakness. Like everything else hatred sees only a mirror. When it rides you, which is almost always, let's be honest, hatred lets you think that you're capable of love. It looks out at the world and anything that it sees that is far enough away, impersonal enough, it can accept. The loving mother stopping to slowly read her child a safety notice on the subway, speaking as if she were sharing the same sense of discovery with her son. The wind through trees in the distance. The way the world seems perfectly ordered and nurturing at times.

And when you let something get close enough, you start to see your own reflection, the resolution gets clearer, you don't have to squint and guess, and then it's over. The ones who gave you birth, the ones who gave you their lives to bring you up. The one who lies next to you in bed at night. The ones who stand by you. Them you tear and shred because you can't let anybody touch you. You hate the sight of them because they love you and you hate yourself and so by extension you have to pulverize their love to bits. Because the dark side always seems so much more real. Failure seems more real. Not having to try seems more real.

With my camera in hand I would exercise my anger. I would document our marches: the preparation, the construction of signs and props, the camaraderie of the group. I would document the mayhem in the streets, the riot cops and the batons, and I would print my photos in the school paper when I got the chance. That was where I met Lili.

Lili was a writer. She was two years older than me. She was majoring in journalism and covering local politics for the paper. Our editor put us on assignment together to cover a labor strike of the local carpenter's union. I was initially bored with the assignment but the more that I listened to her impassioned diatribes on the abuse of undocumented workers by local businesses who were using them to undercut the union, the more I started to care. Rather, I was more and more entranced by her, and her casual professionalism. She was a dancer too. She had short, black curly hair and a body that intimidated the hell out of me; she was the type who liked to aggressively accessorize: giant belt buckles, giant hoop earrings and an always-present backwards black cabbie cap.

She had a certain way of driving me completely nuts; the more she flirted with me the more eager I was to please and of course that got me nowhere. Once I reeled myself back in and stopped trying to win her affections she warmed up to me a little. As we continued working on stories together we became closer; we became a professional team. After a newspaper outing at a bar in town, for which I used my fake I.D., she took me home.

She knew what she wanted and she let me know, guided me. I was still clumsy then. When I asserted myself she became submissive, receptive, guiding me with her submission. We had sex for four hours and then we fell asleep next to each other, our arms on each other, though not embracing. In the morning we showered and she was bashful. We made breakfast together, scrambled eggs and potatoes, and by then we were friends again. We continued like that for another two months. Then she told me she loved me. Immediately I felt that she was trying to control me; assumed that she was saying that only so she could own me, and that she was lying. Her clingy and jealous side began to emerge; I imagined her constricting me like a spider queen, weaving her web around me. She started trying to tell me what assignments to take and which ones to pass up, tried to get me to stop being so politically involved and focus more on school and, the final indignity, how to improve my photography. I was too young to realize that she was doing those things because she did love me, and believed in me, and wanted me to be my best. I assumed she was trying to manipulate me. Our relationship went on like that for another three months, of cold shoulders and misinterpretations. I decided that I needed to get far, far away from her. Everybody needs a scapegoat for their pain. On a rainy Valentine's Day evening in her bedroom I told her that I couldn't be the man she needed, and that it was me (not her), and that my heart wasn't in it anymore. She wouldn't accept it. I told her I was leaving, and then I did. I lost.

"You child," she spat at me through tears. I quietly closed the door to her apartment, on the seventh floor of her complex, and left silently, opening my umbrella. I relished the sorrow of the moment.

You ladykiller, I thought to myself, speaking from the most vicious, and afraid, part of my ego, the bit that it took me a long, long time to realize wasn't necessary to protect myself. As I walked from the apartment into the torrential downpour on the street I turned and looked at the building. She was standing on the balcony, naked, looking at me with a face of utter disgust, and despair, despair that went beyond me, that was unknowable, suffering that I had not alleviated but had only added to.

I had had a lot of passing girlfriends in college, but after I broke up with Lili it was hard to look at myself the same way. A few years later, when I was on assignment in Copsa Mica, Romania, photographing the awe-inspiring pollution caused by the town's carbon black plant, before I met my wife, a hotel cook I befriended asked me if I had a woman waiting for me back home.

"No," I said. "There's nobody waiting for me."

"You don't like women?" he laughed.

"Sure I like women," I came back with. "Just not for very long, you know what I mean?"

When he laughed next, there was a cold, hard edge buried somewhere deep inside. I noticed a wedding band on his finger.

"Oh, so you mean, 'fuck and forget?'"

I laughed, suddenly feeling ashamed and not fully knowing why, not knowing whether his uneasy laughter came from a place of moral disapproval of me or, more worryingly, his own feeling of entrapment, of jealousy for youth and American license.

Some man you are, I said to myself, the same thing I had said to myself the morning after I broke up with Lili, when I woke up and faced myself in the mirror. I thought I could make myself feel better by leaving her, but I didn't. I made myself into a smaller man, and it took me a long time to make it up to myself.

After that my politics faltered. I was still angry, but I spent so much time angry at myself, focusing on my own estrangement from happiness and hardly seeing much else, that I didn't have much energy left over to do much else. Drugs became a priority. My sorrow gained more and more weight, until it stopped becoming a flirtation. Life hurt more and more. It stopped being funny. And then it really stopped being funny. And then it really really stopped being funny. And then I realized that there would never be a punchline. There would never be the moment when the stormclouds cleared and I got my happy ending and I was congratulated for undergoing the spiritual trial of my depression which was only meant to purify me and make me a man. This, I finally realized, was a knock-knock joke. If only I realized then that I was the one telling it.

After I graduated, before I got my first photography job, I spent a summer driving a forklift in a warehouse. It was an important period for me; it gave me time to do my best to stop thinking and, most importantly, to stop measuring myself. One afternoon one of my high school friends, his girlfriend and I went to the city park and swallowed a handful of psilocybin mushrooms each. The trip came on slowly. At first I was paranoid, predictably, that we would be caught. That passed. As I came up I felt the familiar fungal rush, the full-body orgasm. Reality began to run more smoothly. I felt more tapped into the source, loved and forgiven by the world. I looked over at my friends—they had wandered slightly away and were talking, on their own wavelength, doing their own thing.

Normally I would have a panic response; left to my own devices on drugs, my mind can quickly become toxic. This time, however, things went better. I began to concentrate on the sky. It became bigger and bigger, it took on depth, and I began to feel as if I could see gradations of it extending out into space. I remembered when I was a kid, and I would look at the sky and perceive that it was spherical, that I was seeing the curve of the earth. I felt a loving intelligence there, looking down at me; I felt forgiveness and grace raining down upon me from above. My heart began to open up and I could feel the weight of the last few years falling off me, being discarded like sheets of dead flesh. Looking back over my personal failures, I found that I could look at them objectively, and see them for what they were: the education, by trial and error, of the heart of a young man. I could see the pain that I had caused, but instead of seeking to punish myself because of it, I realized that it was better to simply resolve to walk with more compassion in my life. I felt the warm, womb-like caress of the mushroom, backing me up, empowering me to confront the painful parts without flinching or self-hating.

I began to feel something emanating from the ground. I turned and lay face-down in the grass, spreading my palms outward, feeling each individual blade brush against the in-between parts of my fingers. Suddenly I felt I had to hold on for dear life; I could feel the earth spinning and the idea that we could somehow stay put on an orb careening wildly through the emptiness of space became completely terrifying. I grabbed onto the grass and pressed my body to it with all of my strength, hoping against hope that I wouldn't be flung out into the outer darkness.

The force emanating from the ground became stronger, much more tangible. It was a warm, healing, amniotic fluid, pouring through my cells. I clutched the ground tighter, hugging it closer to me. I thought, you're a grown man. What are you doing? What if somebody sees you like this? And then I remembered that nobody knew I was on drugs, that I was just laying down in the park on a lazy Sunday afternoon. I pushed myself further down into the earth. I could feel something emanating from the center and suddenly I couldn't stop thinking like a hippie. I could feel the intelligence of the earth. And it was crying.

Jesus. Jesus fucking Christ, we turned and we raped our own mother, I thought. Jesus fucking Christ. When you're on psilocybin it's not a triviality anymore, it's unavoidable psychic reality. The earth was crying, having to bear the weight of us, having to carry us like Christ carried his cross up Golgotha. Its sorrow was mine.

My own life seemed insignificant in comparison, my inflated dramas and misery; even my rage at the evils of the world seemed trivial. In this light it all looked the same; just more people fighting each other and stomping on the scenery. Dropping into ecological time I saw myself as just one more weed, granted its allotted time to spring up, yearn for the sun, reach its pinnacle and then fall, wilting back into the soil to become compost for future generations.

Suddenly I thought, no wonder they tell you the devil lives in the center of the earth. They want to hide this truth from people so badly.

I curled up into a ball and then sat up, brushing the grass off my arms and face. My friends were still talking to each other a few yards away. At first I wanted to go and talk to them but then I thought, no, stay back; they're talking about something between them that's too personal for you to hear. I stood up and walked over to a park bench, sat down, and began to breathe as deeply as I could, still feeling the warm susurrations emanating from the ground.

I dropped my consciousness to my chest and looked inward. I could feel all the accumulated self-inflicted misery of my life sitting there, hunched on me like an imp, a bruised and swollen abscess deep inside. I put my right hand on it and suddenly I felt that I could heal it; I directed energy from my hand into the chasm in my chest and poured all the healing light and love I could find into it. The abscess began to desiccate; finally, after a few minutes, it burst. Toxins poured forth from it and erupted out of me in a flood; rather than physical bile the infected filth of the wound poured out of me as raw emotion. I began crying, and although I was able to control it at first—it had been almost two years since I had last cried—it quickly turned from small tears into huge, churning sobs. I clutched my hand to my chest, feeling the abscess disinfect and, finally, begin to heal, the broken tissue beginning to knit itself back together.

I looked up and my friends were next to me, looking concerned.

"It's alright," I said. "This is good, this is OK. This is important."

They nodded, held my shoulders. I felt very human. Something bright caught my eye; there were a few tower blocks of apartments across from us, and something luminous and white was fluttering in front of one. It was just a drop-cloth hanging from the edge of a balcony that was being painted, but for a split second I registered it as an angel, and I thought:

You are forgiven.

And the sob that came next emanated from such a deep place that it felt as if it had come from before I had even been born.

When I put my own sorrow next to the misery I have seen in the Middle East, I am shamed. Predictably, I can't think of myself as anything other than a whining, sniveling American brat. But that, in itself, is another trap of the ego. Being alive, in and of itself, is to exist in a condition of suffering. Knowing that you are mortal, and, more pressingly, that the people you love are mortal, is to exist in suffering. Suffering is suffering and, being infinite in nature, there is no measure for it.

All my life I've been floating in the ocean of my senses, struggling to perceive beyond the confines of my own skin. I've looked from north to south and seen only the horizon. I've looked from east to west and seen only the horizon. I've looked at the cloudless abyss above and the black abyss below.

I look and observe, and I preserve with my camera, and what do I see?

I don't see heaven and I don't see hell. I see repeating patterns. I don't see much that's different from day to day. I see people rise up and I see people put down. I see the War that never ends. I see people making love and I see people fucking. I see the money we scramble for. I see people following their dreams, stopping halfway and realizing they've forgotten what they were following. I see those same people forgetting how to have new dreams.

You look at the world's people and take them at face value, and you see the same story. The rich eating the children of the poor. Children born without innocence. A dying and decaying world.

But if you look at them with forgiveness, and if you have forgiven yourself, then you see the very face of God. And that is the true measure of Man.

After that summer I started working as an intern at AP in New York, doing photo developing and waiting for my big chance. I got it when I was assigned to work with Larry Feinman.

It was a very uncertain time in my life. I'd just left school, and begun to realize that artificially inflating my personal emotional shortcomings into major presumed failures wasn't doing much to move me along in life. I was still afraid, still wracked with uncertainty and nebulous feelings of shame and guilt, still flailing in darkness. What I needed, I felt, was a real short, sharp shock, and I got it.

"Ours is a black brotherhood," he told me on the first day I met him. "It's a hell of a way to make a living. Feeding on the misery of others. We're greedy for horror and trauma and the destruction of lives, because without them we go home without a paycheck. And it's the biggest kick I know. Dodging mortal danger to photograph war. Once you get addicted to that, John, you can't go back. You'll get so habituated to the adrenaline that you won't know what to do with yourself when you're not in a war zone. You'll spend three months out in some hellhole snapping photos of eleven-year-olds firing their Kalashnikovs into the air while jacked up on PCP, getting shots of the terrified eyes of soldiers during air raids, photos of starving refugees in remote mountain passes. You'll think you've had all you can stomach and you'll hop on a plane back to the States for three months of recuperation, and you won't be able to take it. You'll be at some party and everybody around you will be talking about how horrible it is the market's down a few points, or how bad such and such movie is, or somebody will spill some red wine on the white shag carpet and it'll cause a huge scene and people will be screeching and you'll be standing there thinking, What the fuck are these people talking about? What the fuck do they know about the world? And you'll have to excuse yourself to the bathroom and you'll be standing there staring at yourself and how many new premature gray hairs you've got, and you'll be thinking, *I can't do this.* You'll stop going out. You'll stay home drinking and smoking dope and running old mental clips of colleagues you've worked with who've been killed, over and over, and you won't be able to face the world, and you'll start to go stir crazy, and then you'll go back. You'll go straight back to combat because after a certain point, you won't understand anything else."

I didn't believe him, of course. I thought he was a bitter man and he was trying to dissuade me from glory, because that's what bitter men do to enthusiastic men.

Larry was from the generation of war photographers who had earned their credentials in the Balkans, and Rwanda. He'd made his living documenting wars that very few people cared about, the ignored atrocities of the Clinton years, that were background annoyances on the nightly news for most Americans. That must have weighed heavily on him.

"What are you afraid of, John?" he asked me while I sat by him as he went through a digital flashcard of photos he had taken on assignment in Kosovo, showing me how to crop and prepare images in Photoshop so that I could do the rest of the card for him.

"I don't know," I replied. "I'm not really afraid of much anymore."

"That's interesting. I don't believe you, of course, but it's interesting that you said 'anymore.' Why is that?"

"I feel like I've confronted fear."

"Those," he snapped back, "are the words of a war journalist, I have to say. That's not a compliment; those are the words that may well get you killed one day. Most of us are like that, though. We tell ourselves that we're going to war in order to document it, because it's a noble calling, but really we're going there to confront fear. Because our lives are run by it. It's the only thing we know."

I'm feeling airsick at the back of the helicopter, hearing Larry's words ringing true in my head yet again. All I can see below is sand; a half dozen other helicopters flank us. The two Marines across from me are looking at me blankly while I clutch my stomach and make occasional gagging motions. They told me not to eat before the flight; of course I went ahead and had a microwave hamburger at the base, thinking it would be small enough not to matter. At present I'm feeling that this was a most unfortunate decision.

"Never rid in a helicopter before?" the Sergeant across from me asks.

"Nope."

"Well if you gotta throw up, don't be shy. Get it out the door and maybe you'll nail a couple of insurgents on the way down."

The chop of the helicopter blades is overpowering my senses and pushing me into trance. The noise begins to scramble my head to the point where I start to hear patterns and words emerge. The blades go "death… death… death…"

The Sergeant across from me is wearing heavy glasses and has a thin John Waters moustache; he's obviously well-built underneath his flak jacket. The jacket's a luxury; it's been too hot to wear armor during the summer. Now that the weather's cooled, U.S. ground force lives are slightly less expendable. During the flight he's been filling me and the Private to his left, who's being shipped to Fallujah for the first time, in on what's been happening on the ground.

"City combat's hellish. When you're in territory that your enemy's been familiar with since they were born, there's a lot of risks you can't afford to take. They'll come at you through alleys, underground passages, secret nooks and crannies that you've got no way of knowing about. One minute you think you're in a cleared area; the next you've got a live grenade in the middle of your battalion. Luckily for us we've just been going ahead and leveling whole city blocks before proceeding into them, demolition crew style."

"Wish we could just neutron bomb the whole place," the Private chirps in with. He's a Chicano kid, nineteen or twenty; he's got "Aztlan" tattooed across his right bicep along with a pair of dice and a clown mask. He's busier spitting tobacco out the window than talking.

"Yeah. I'm sure that would go down just great with the papers. Isn't that right?" he asks in my direction. I nod, my face curled up with nausea. "I'm not gonna say there hasn't been collateral damage in the last week, but it's not like they weren't given a chance. Most of the civilians fled the city before we rolled up, and Prime Minister Allawi's been on the airwaves telling people to surrender nice and easy. If a few insurgents think they're going to do anything other than throw a few nuisances in the way of the greatest war machine in history then they're just suicidal, insane fanatics. Animals deserved what they got."

"Why should they do anything Allawi tells them to? He's been British intelligence's thug since the 1980s; he's a Western puppet and, most of all, he's Shia. Fallujah's mostly Sunni. Why should they think anything other than that he wants them all dead?"

"Fuck it. A towelhead's a towelhead," the Private says. His teeth are stained a dead black with tobacco.

We pass some time in silence.

"Anyways, this's been a triumph of military strategy," the Sergeant interjects after a few moments. "6,000 of us went in there and we brought 2,000 allied Iraqis with us. We put together a task force—we got together Regimental Combat Team 1, built around 1st Marine Regiment, and Regimental Combat Team 7, built around 7th Marine Regiment. Both of those Regiments got two reinforced Marine Rifle Battalions and one Army mechanized infantry battalion. Regimental Combat Team 1 is put together with 3rd Light Armored Reconnaissance Battalion; 3rd Battalion, 5th Marines; 3rd Battalion, 1st Marines and 2nd Battalion, 7th Calvary. Combat Team 7 is almost that well equipped. Then we got Blackjack, an Army Brigade, they were there to keep the enemy away from the Regimental Combat Teams while they went on full frontal assault. That's a lot of firepower, son. That's some of America's finest, fighting men who I have the utmost respect for. Those are men who have earned the right to call themselves Americans, because they know the price we pay to be the greatest country in the world.

"We came in through the north and 3rd Light Armored opened up the attack across the Euphrates; they secured Fallujah Hospital and the two bridges out of the city while Blackjack took out all the escape routes in the south. By the time the sun was up we'd dropped a net around the city and sealed it with complete precision. Then 3rd Battalion, 5th Marines came in through the northwest and took a key section of apartment blocks so we could get an elevated position; we got snipers up on the roof right away taking out the mujahadeen running through the city like cockroaches. That's my battalion; we were running up stairs with machine guns and ammo while in full body armor to get the area secured while the enemy was taking potshots at us with rockets. It was dicey but when you're in action with brave men of that caliber, and you got God above looking out for you, you don't have no fear. You don't think. You stop to think, and you're dead right then and there. You just get the job done.

"Meanwhile we got 2nd Battalion, 7th Calvary and 3rd Battalion, 1st Marines in a double-team doing a slash-and-burn through the city. They're coming down like an angel with a flaming sword, strafing every insurgent they see, leveling pure death through the city at top speed. These fucking insurgents, pardon my language, are getting in their faces, screaming their durka-durka-allah-allah shit, these guys are straight up ready to die, and ready to take as many Marines with them as they can, but our boys just brush them off with complete precision and professionalism. They take the train station in the north end and the engineers blow a hole through the trestle; Bradley tanks pour through and devastate the enemy on the other side. The whole scene's righteous to watch, and don't forget the whole time we've got AC-130 gunships, artillery and aircraft pounding the city. From the positions we've taken we just juggernaut our way into the city core and take the rest of Fallujah. We lost just over a dozen men but we captured or put on ice most of the insurgents in the city; the ones that escaped have to be real cunning sons of bitches."

"Not the kind you'd like to meet in a narrow alley?" I reply. He snickers. I have a hard time with military personnel, especially officers. I find it hard not to automatically see them as stereotypes, and reduce them to the hired-killer caricature I was raised to see them as filling. In the small periods of time I have spent speaking with soldiers, I have largely found them to be, above all else, unaware of the larger context that they fit into. They are, by and large, men who are doing jobs, with little time to ask why they are doing those jobs. Officers, like the Sergeant across from me, tend to have their situation boiled down to a few narrow opinions, but for the most part they're little different from the grunts they give orders to. They're all part of the chain of command, and every part of the chain of command has in common the fact that they have been trained and brutalized to do little more than follow commands. They are very good at their jobs.

"Mind if I take a picture?" I ask. The two men look towards the camera, with little change in their facial expressions. It's almost impossible to keep the camera steady in the helicopter, but I brace it on my knees, toggle a few settings, take a deep breath and manage to come out with a halfway decent digital shot. I get them framed against the endless sand behind them.

Given a moment's respite I start to think about Miranda again, doing the all-too-familiar, and futile, mental dance of trying to figure out what a woman may or may not be thinking. With the short notice of my departure I'd been unable to do much other than pack; I had seen Miranda briefly in the morning, however—she was still awaiting her next assignment. David was nowhere to be seen. When I told her about my flight to Fallujah, her mood immediately darkened.

"I think you are crazy to agree to this, John," she said. "So soon after the fighting? The city's on fire. Why are you agreeing to this?"

The more she expressed concern, the more my own uncertainty began to fade, and the more my own sense of pride and machismo began to assert itself.

"Because it's the right thing to do?"

She gave me a graveyard look.

"I want you to call me in a few days and tell me you're all right," she said. "I have too many dead friends already, John." She handed me her satellite phone number, in an absurdly recontextualized caricature of the age-old mating ritual. I promised to call.

Miranda's been in the game a lot longer than me. War correspondents don't have a very long shelf life. They have breakdowns, they develop debilitating addictions, they get killed. At the very least, they have to witness so much horror and suffer through the senseless deaths of so many friends and associates that after a few years in the field their bravado will be husked out and they'll be frail and shattered. They'll either quit, flip out or crawl back to their home countries to take office positions in their news agencies. There's almost no recognition made in the journalistic profession of the extreme psychological stress that war correspondents are placed in. Professional counseling is not a job perk. We're expected to cope, or look for a less glamorous and "important" job.

"If you're starting to shut down, if you can't feel your emotions, if you feel like you're locked down into a tunnel, if you feel like you're on edge, it may already be too late," Larry Feinman had told me shortly before I took the Baghdad assignment. On edge doesn't exactly work as an accurate descriptor of the last several weeks of my life; doing a flamingo stand on a dentist's drill comes a bit closer.

We're insane, all of us. If we're embedded with troops, we're subjected to the same amount of danger that those troops are. If we're out documenting civilians, we're subjected to the same amount of danger that those civilians are. And we go there by choice, to put ourselves in harm's way like that. I think about Daniel Pearl, who has become a symbol for all of us reporting in the Middle East, kidnapped and beheaded, the videos released by Al Qaeda a year later. We're motivated by pride and more than a touch of voyeurism. We thrive on human misery, all of us, documenting it for the war junkies glued to their televisions and computer screens in the comfort of their own homes. We trawl through the human wreckage, collecting gems of suffering—a child with a shattered brain weeping gore in the aftermath of a mortar attack; a slain combatant being picked apart by wild dogs. We tell ourselves that we are documenting the truth of war so that the politicians and the voters back home can see what they have wrought, see what their racist fear and imperialist greed is responsible for, and our editors never run the worst pictures, tell us never to send them in the first place. They're unmarketable, unpalatable to the taste of the public. And so the truth stays buried. The public sees a few generic images of battle in the streets of Fallujah, sees that we have only lost sixteen American lives in the melee, and says, Oh, well, that's not so bad. That's only to be expected. War is war, after all. And in the meantime, we slaughter and rape and rip and rend to feed a dying machine. And that which the public does not see stays out of the public's conscience, and the machine can continue to run, well-oiled, hands clean. And the existence of the absolute barbarity perpetuated by the American government remains a philosophical problem on the level of global warming or the present-day survival of the Megalodon shark: In the absence of any overwhelming evidence, the problem is easily ignored, and designated the territory of "leftist extremists."

I think of Miranda's children's crusade. If people cannot be forced to acknowledge the reality of war in this age—the age of total media saturation, of digital cameras and weblogs, where an image or story captured one minute can be available for the whole world to see the next—then they will never acknowledge it. They will never bother to look at the fruits of their labors, of their lazy hatred, and the circle will remain uncomplete. Responsibility for these actions will never be taken.

But for the most part those who look for the truth already know it, and those who can't be bothered will never see beyond the lies presented to them by the mass media that has become a monstrosity in our age, a corporate and state-run weapon controlled in total by only a tiny handful of people. And the people who could stop this war—the very ones who authorized it with their ignorance and their trust in men who never had their best interests in mind—remain asleep, curled up in the fetal bliss of their tiny lives, forgetful of their history, of their identities and of the true power that they could wield should they choose. And people like me struggle to show them reality, and we fail, and we only destroy ourselves in the process.

There is, of course, an even more frightening prospect, one that seems even more likely. It is that people do care, and it still doesn't matter.

I put my headphones back on and lean to the right side of the helicopter, being careful not to imbalance it. We're coming up on the outskirts of Fallujah down below. The shuffle gives me The Libertines:

There's a campaign of hate, it's waiting at the school gate. There's a campaign of hate, it's waiting at the school gates…

As we approach Fallujah the sun's almost down; there's a red-gold glow coming off the Euphrates, and off the huge cloud of smoke and debris that is hovering around the city. A trail of it is billowing off it, lit up red by the sun, snaking out across the horizon. The sunset's amazing, one of those holocaust vistas where the sky's painted like sandstone. By the time we're over the city, the sun's down and the major feature we see out the window of the helicopter are the fires lit up sporadically around the periphery and the city core. It would normally be the time for the call to prayer, but we hear nothing, just the sound of machine gun fire and the deep, concussive blasts of mortar explosions intermittently dividing the silence.

The pilot turns to tell us we're beginning our descent; the three of us remain silent as we begin the drop. The wind through the helicopter is incredibly fierce; I clutch my bag and squint against the roar.

We hit the landing pad and settle. There are marines running around getting the helicopter secured; the two guys across from me hop out before everything's hunkered down and then help me out. I wrap a kefir I bought in Basra around my face to keep from getting sandblasted.

They set me up for the night in makeshift housing; they get me a cot and a blanket.

"See if you can get some sleep," the Sargeant tells me. "Got a lot to show you in the morning."

I do my best.

(Continued.)

PAINT ME AS A DEAD SOUL

JHONN BALANCE

Paint me as a dead soul
with a halo of black joy
Medusa in a mirror
etched out in acid
the flesh, the image, the reflection

One who dwells in scarlet darkness
like animals in palaces
drawing blood

The flesh, the image, the reflection
let's complete the illusion

Paint me as you see me
from memory or history
In a fever or a frenzy

Paint your lucid dreams and visions
in a chamber of nightmares
in a temple of locusts
so violent, vile, and vivid

May the colors make you fearful
blind and hypnotizing
in our subterranean heaven

Paint my cunt with dragonflies
my eyes as bright as diamonds
my heart open like an ulcer
or a sacred crimson rose

Bathed in blood
or drowning in my bed
with the fragrance from the flowers
in the gardens of the dead

Paint ghostly foxes, cats and camels
a red dog and a black dog
paint a putrid sunset
in verdigris and violet
ochre, amber, mauve

Four monks
carrying a goat
over the snows
to nowhere

And paint the shades
that come with evening
Peacock angels
dream of leaving

Paint me as you see me
paint me as I see me
Paint me as a Dead Soul

Jhonn can be heard performing this piece
on *The New Backwards* from Threshold House.
(http://www.thresholdhouse.com)

A QUICK TRIP TO ALAMUT: THE CELEBRATED CASTLE OF THE HASH-HEAD ASSASSINS

BRION GYSIN

Can you score at American Express? At Thomas Cook & Sons? At Hertz? Yes, you can in Tehran, Iran… what we used to call Persia.

"Oh, Brion, you *can't* be going to begin your article like that! It would be awful of you. Besides, it might be terribly compromising for poors Shams whom we both liked so much, I thought. I hated his driver, Mammad, of course, but I think Shams is a really nice guy."

So do I. I agree on one hand but on the other it can't do Shams any harm to let the world know he can pull just about anything you like out of a hat in Iran and at the same time I really want to throw a block into his mad plans for getting minibusloads of American Maws up there with blue rinse in their hair and their bifocals on chains around their ropey old necks. Anyhow, I don't think they'd survive it. But I agree he is great. Who else could have gotten the two of us up to Alamut, dressed like we were and with skimpy pimps' pumps on our poor tender feet from the city?

"Oh, it won't be the blue-rinse ladies up in Alamut. It'll be those muscular Germans with varicose veins in their knotty legs and their gray woolen socks in their sandals or hob-nailed boots, all armed with alpenstocks and rucksacks on their backs full of crampons and pitons and long ropes for climbing."

No, it is the British James Bond and Co. Ltd. crew; they have always been the biggest fans of the Old Man of the Mountains in his secret castle of Alamut, ever since the Crusaders sent home intelligence reports about Hassan i Sabbah, Grand Master of the Hash-Head Hashishins, the fanatical Muslim sect who practiced power politics by wielding the knife in the fine art of political murder. Hence our word, Assassin. Marco Polo picked up the word on his way through to China. He reported that the Old Man chose only stout-hearted likely lads for his Fida'i-in, his Adepts whose utter devotion to him and his practices became a fearsome legend from the court of Cathay in the Far East to the court of Charlemagne in the Far West of the then-known world. Kings were killed on their thrones, a prominent Prime Minister was felled as he took a stroll through his own private park. Captured Assassins all told the same story. They confessed under torture that the Old Man of the Mountains had trained them and rewarded them with drugs. Adepts were given a potion which put them to sleep and when they awoke they found themselves in a heavenly garden where fountains were running with honey and wine of which they drank their fill before they fell on passionate maids with flashing eyes and flowing hair who played upon the dulcimer. When the Adept awoke from his dream of Paradise, he was assured by the Old Man himself that come what may he could score for that same stuff forever… after he accomplished his mission. The potion was said to be prepared from the hemp plant, cannabis. All the young heads of the world, all the budding James Bonds of the turn of the First Millennium flocked to his banner.

By the year 1090, the Alamut Academy was the world's finest finishing school for secret agents. The way it worked was elegant, simple. You announce you are starting a commune to beat the Millennium, the next thousand years, in some spot as bare as the hills of Nevada. You make it hard to get in and you announce that once you are in… really IN… you can never get out again. You won't even want to. The young are so needy of something, they beat their way to your retreat but only the pick of them ever even get inside your gate where you make them sit on their hard hungry young asses and wait… wait… wait. When they're really ripe, you take four to ten of them together inside where you feed them and turn them on. You do this in your kennel which you tell them is your chapel, your Chapel of Extreme Experience, lowest grade. Food, music and sex served by chicks and you've got it made. You've got yourself a faithful free worker, a Fida'i, a devoted Dogface. A Dogface must do all the dirty work and you give him plenty of it. If he survives, he may be turned on again, a little higher, and allowed to begin his Basic Training after which he becomes a Rafiq or Private First Class who may move on up to become a Dai. Dais are Sergeants all the way up to the top three officers, Dai-al-Kirbai, who answer only to the Sheik-al-Jabal or Master of Masters, the Grand Old Man himself. Obedience to the Old Man is absolute.

Right from the start, the Assassins exerted an influence out of all proportion to their number. Hassan i Sabbah could point a long bony finger and probe with a knife into the very heart of realpolitik wherever he sent his Fida'i-in. His instructions to them were said to have been *"Nothing is forbidden. Everything is permitted."* Lodges both secret and open branched out through the whole Arab world, all receiving orders from the Old Man in Alamut. A great deal of very special knowledge centered there and not all of it was destroyed in the eventual fall of that capital castle. To this day, however, it remains very difficult to learn much about the initiation of the higher echelons for whom the simple promise of hashish would not be enough to make impatient of this world and oblivious of the personal consequences of their acts. Exactly how they were "sent" is another matter about which one can only surmise that *"You can't let that secret out… it's too dangerous."* Anyone who knew would be in practice for himself. Or is he already?

Hassan i Sabbah died at the ripe age of eighty-four in the year 1124, leaving a tightly-knit network of castles manned by fanatical Adepts whose power spread over another one hundred and thirty-two years, until 1256 when all of them were swept away by the locust-like hordes of the Mongols. Hulagu, grandson of Genghis Khan, unleashed wave after wave and then flying swarms of his hornets up against the imposing pinnacle on which Alamut was built, until at last he could climb into the Eagle's Nest over the mountainous slopes of dead bodies of his own soldiers. The Assassins were slaughtered to the last man and pitched into the valley a full fifteen hundred feet below and the stones of the castle were hurled over after them. What remains of the castles today needs to be searched for. Hulagu's historian, a Persian named Juvayni, wrote: "Of the Old Man of the Mountains and his stock, no trace was left and he and his became but a tale upon men's lips and a legend in the great world." Yes, and the legend lives on all these years later, but what about his stock? Oh, surprise! The Agha Khan of today is the present head of the Sect of Seven, the Ismailis, and he owes his succession to that power and glory thanks to a line which runs right through the long bony fingers of Hassan i Sabbah. But that is a whole other story. Or is it?

Alamut loomed large in my life from the time I first read the *Travels of Marco Polo* in my childhood. I read every version I could find, until I felt I had been there. The legend loomed larger when I grew up and turned on, beginning to have doubts about Inflexible Authority and the nature of the Garden. I read absurdly abstract German theses on Hassan i Sabbah and the mystique of murder. I read French books full of pseudo-romantic rubbish about Hassan's honeyed trap for simple-minded soldiers, making it sound like a pre-World War II Parisian brothel or a branch office of Baudelaire's Artificial Paradise. I read brilliant British travel books by adventure-seeking spinsters, but perhaps the most penetrating book on the real meaning of the mysteries which served the Master in his deadly purpose, is a volume in French signed Betty Bouthoul. The book in itself is a mystery and as such I gave it to my good friend William Burroughs a short time after he had published *Naked Lunch*, before 1960. I explained that I had met the author, a portrait painter in Parisian social circles. She was oddly vague about why she wrote the book or what her sources of research were. Her husband is Maitre Gaston Bouthoul, the lawyer for many of the most famous living painters and he is, at the same time, perhaps the only practicing adept of a very odd discipline indeed… the philosophy of war: polemology. Who else has there ever been in this branch? Clausewitz? Moltke?

Burroughs and I were living in those days in the famously infamous old Beat Hotel on the edge of the Latin Quarter on the Left Bank in Paris. We pored over the book, passing it back and forth. We read and reread it. The crux of the matter, of course, is: How did he do it? And, beyond that: What is the nature of power? Bouthoul teases the reader enough to make you feel that there must be an answer and in the answer lies the key to Control on this planet. Big stuff. Poor Tim Leary had not yet said: "The revolution is over and we have won," but everyone around the Beat Hotel thought that when we put acid in the water supply, that would do it. Burroughs denounced the Garden of Delights as a pernicious weapon of Control, like junk, but we still harkened back to the echo from Alamut, asking ourselves: *How* did he do it?

What was Alamut really like and was there a Garden? Burroughs and I promised each other that one day we would go there to see for ourselves. In the meantime, Burroughs sprinkled his writings with references… even unto the outrageous identification of me with the Master: "See, see the Silent Writing of Brion Gysin, Hassan i Sabbah!" I always felt that Burroughs himself was much more like the Old Man of the Mountains. After all, I have never killed anyone in my life, not even an animal. Burroughs really digs knives and guns: he is forever writing loving details of the specifications of some obsolete repeating revolver… *"and, Splat! A bright red patch of blood splashes across he shirtfront above his belt buckle."* Before I met Burroughs, my beau ideal was a library without comic books but I enjoy and approve his glosses on them, immensely.

When I found myself in Iran this summer, almost by accident, I went to Alamut. Oddly, almost everything I picked up in Tehran had something about the Assassins—the local English-language daily, plus *This Week in Teheran* and the illustrated *Iran Tribune*, as well as the guidebooks put out by *Nagel* and *Fodor*. Most of the information was contradictory and Persian printers' pied type made nonsense out of the rest of it but that seemed to figure. *Fodor* said firmly that the trip should not be attempted by tourists. *Nagel* suggested that if properly outfitted for an expedition, four or five days might be enough provided one took a pack-train of mules, well-equipped and with a thoroughly reliable guide from the city of Qasvin, one hundred and fifty kilometers to the northwest of Tehran. I was planning to set out for Qasvin when my eye caught a sign in the street, saying: *Thomas Cook & Son.* It flashed on me at once that Cook's tours would get me there, unlikely as it sounded to my companion, Lawrence, who was not all that interested anyway because he had his mind set on something else, like meeting some nice friends with a house in the cool mountains and a swimming pool.

I was right: Cooks could do it. I met the VP of the Iranian outfit that runs all three: American Express, Cooks and Hertz. Mr. Mehrzad Shams greeted me with a dazzling smile when I explained my mission: "Alamut? Why, of course. Yes! When do you want to go? Maybe you can go along with the British TV team which is following the track of Marco Polo across Asia. They may have room for you but, if not, I have a young friend who might be willing to take you in his own jeep. He knows the route well. It is the worst road in Iran and maybe the world. One stretch of it took us eleven hours to get through when we went up there last winter but there has been a bulldozer over that bit since then. You'll make it. You might do it in even one day… Make it a real American 'quickie'... Do you want to?"

Noooo! I want to spend at least one night up in Alamut, in the castle itself, I cried. I *must*… I've simply *got* to get to Alamut! I don't know why else I came to Iran. I don't even know why we came to Iran, in the first place. We meant to go to Kabul until the day of the coup and then we found that our charter flight was at least twenty hours long, with the stopover in Moscow and, in any case, at the last minute they switched dates on us so we couldn't go anyway but they wouldn't give us our money back so we changed to Iran at the last minute. It was my idea to fly straight to Isfahan to see all those blue-domed mosques and we hated it. Those bulbous blue domes look like blow-ups of Fabergé Easter eggs left over from the World's Fair of 1625 or something. So we went on to Shiraz and then took a long bus ride across the desert that was supposed to be only twelve non-airconditioned hours long and turned out to be as long as a lifetime. Kerman was OK. We met a family of Persian carpet weavers in their own mud house and the man's old mother was making a pipe of O in the garden, so we swapped tales with her and her cronies. She was an adorably wicked old thing like a lot of old junkies in any clime anywhere. She heated the bowl of her Persian pipe, looking like an oboe with a china egg in it, and then she applied the pellet of almost translucent golden-colored O to it with her fine old fingers, just above the pinhole of the aperture which she reamed out with her iron pin attached to a pair of little iron tongs. She plucked a red coal from the fire in a brasero and held it up to the pinhole in her pipe through which she blew a blast which reddened the charcoal. When it was red enough, she put the O on her pipe to it and sucked in a great blast that went *straight down* into the bottom of her old bellows. She held it as long as she could and let it out in a thin stream of sweet smoke which she blew in the face of her little grand-daughter. She said that at thirty the doctor had told her to smoke for her eyes and she held a government card as an addict. She needed her eyes to make rugs so she smoked thirty pipes a day. "And fly around like a bat all night," I cracked. She cackled like a banshee when that was translated to her. She had darting little blue eyes like pale chips of lapis lazuli set deep in her head. Granny O, we called her.

Shams smiled a truly Persian smile and said: "Maybe you'll find another Granny O up in Alamut."

At this point, I dropped Burroughs' name but Shams shook his head. I mentioned *Naked Lunch*, of which we had found copies for sale in the airport of Isfahan… probably both bootlegged and pirated. I thought someone on the British TV team might have heard of Burroughs or of me, even. One of them was said to be the son of a London illustrator who had done a portrait of Burroughs. I didn't think it worthwhile to add that William had hated it. Anyway, nothing ever came of that project so I went back to the Hotel America where the airconditioner had gone off again or was blowing hot air into the room and Lawrence had gone to a hammam. I hung out in the dingy lobby where the smell of fresh paint gave me asthma, but I picked up Bill. Bill is a candidly insane and utterly mad man-mountain from the pasta pastures of New Jersey, looking like a young professional wrestler with long hair and a truly tremendous torso bulging out of a tank-top above a pair of torn dungaree mini-shorts like Daisy Mae wears around Dogpatch. All this balanced on striped silver and blue platform shoes with high heels which brought his bulky five foot nine up to more than six feet. He had all his fingernails painted in different bright colors of nailpolish and each one had a tiny decal of a flower posed lovingly in the middle of it.

Bill had been stranded for five and a half weeks in the Hotel America, waiting for money. *"John Keats died in Rome, waiting for money from home,"* I quote from my uncollected works. "One thing you can always be sure of: bread never comes through if you need it." From here on I go into a long spiel like the Ancient Mariner coming on strong with his Wedding Guest, about how I once was hung up a whole summer in Rome on the Spanish Steps by the window where Keats died around the corner from American Express and all the time this bread of mine was there, you understand, shoved away in some other file like: Agricultural Loans & Investments, and I'm there every day going crazy and Rome such and oven so even the trade on the steps emigrate out to the beach at Ostia where I can't even follow them because I'm waiting for my bread, see.

I restrain myself from adding anything crude like: You'll do almost any old thing for bread if ya hafta, huh?

Bill goes into *his* song and dance, all about "grabbin' chicks," as he calls it, a-plenty in swinging New Jersey but tough titty in Tehran or so I gather. I get the message but Lawrence cools him out later by telling how he had been raped by a guard in the National Museum that morning: "So I gave in, what else could I do?"

Since he is not a natural Adept, I see no particular profit in enrolling Bill as one of my Fida'i-in. Lawrence I still not sure he wants to go and thinks he would rather buy a Persian rug with his money. Ah, yes, the money. How much is all this going to cost? I don't know. In my insane insistence to Shams that I simply HAD to get up to Alamut, I heard myself saying: "I don't care what it costs." It just goes to show how little I've learned in a lifetime. I tried to retract that unbusinesslike statement but Shams simply smiled like a Persian prince and invited me to a party to meet the boy, he said, who would be driving the jeep. He had one of the oldest family houses up in the hills above Tehran overlooking the city. Why not bring along my all-night bag and sleep in a guest house in the garden? That way we could get an early start before the heat of the day and no need to drive back through the city. Lawrence wanted to come when he heard there was going to be a party. He was still not sure about Alamut but he packed his little shoulder bag and we waited for Shams to pick us up after office hours.

Tehran is built on the steep slope of the foothills of mountains higher than the Colorados. Between the broad streets and the broken sidewalks, wild water rushes down open culverts through the business section, down to the south station and beyond into an inhabited marsh of slum dwellings. It is said in Iran, that only the Shahbanou Farah Diba has ever been down there. Tehran traffic is said not to be the worst in the world but that is a statement for the press, made only by visiting heads of state from the East where, indeed, things may be worse. Westerners crudely declare that it is the most chaotic and dangerous they have ever seen anywhere. One thing about it, it moves. There are no traffic jams unless there had been a thirty-two car collision. Through rivers of carbon-monoxide made from gas cheaper than in Texas, endless streams of cars leap through red lights and green like sex-maddened salmon in mating season, fighting their way up cascades.

Shamas was ramming his jeep through shoals of Iranian-mounted Hillman models made of rusty tin cans, he claimed, and driven by crossing sweepers. There was a touch of class in that last remark and it grew as we climbed into the upper suburbs full of huge houses built by the newly-rich who had all begun their lives in the bottom of the bazaar, he said, shining shoes when they were small and carrying loads on their backs when they were bigger. Some of them have since climbed all the way up into these desirable dwelling areas where one of the first things they do is cut down all the trees so everyone can see their big houses. These shady hills are where old families used to have their country places for the summer, a day's ride out of town when they were built, and only ten to twenty minutes from the office as the highways followed when Tehran mushroomed into a city but, now, there are so many cars on the road that the really rich commute in their helicopters.

"Yes, I'm going to have to get one of those," said Sham's friend, the man in the back seat next to Lawrence. "Right here where we are now on this highway, I used to own twenty-four thousand square meters of real estate. They took eighteen thousand away from me to build this road, leaving me with six thousand meters of real estate. They took eighteen thousand away from me to build this road, leaving me with six thousand meters on which to pay taxes. The trouble is that these six thousand meters are cut off in such a way that I can't even set foot on them without trespassing. They won't let me build an aerial road or dig a tunnel, so I'm thinking of buying a helicopter and building a house here..."

"Of course, you'll have a swimming pool," said Lawrence.

Where we were going, they did... a kidney-shaped swimming pool surrounded by immense weeping willows. The house on the hill was all airy rooms and porticos looking out over a joint I took for Los Angeles. A huge crash-couch under the trees with cushions for twenty-odd turned-on people and a darkboy in a white coat, setting out food and drinks or rolling a joint for you: the place was attractive. Guests gathered like gorgeous moths, as sleek and well-groomed as if they had just clipped out of a chrysalis that afternoon when they woke from their siestas, all Beautiful People. Lawrence sat next to a man who was opening a tin of caviar with care, explaining that this was Golden Caviar and no one in the West no matter how rich he is has ever seen it, let alone tasted any. "Nor in Iran either," quipped somebody out of the dark, "except for breakfast with the royal family. How the hell did you get any of that?"

"I have a little man who brings it to me. He has breakfast every day with the royal family."

"You mean, the Prime Minister? He's dropping in later."

"This is just the milieu I was looking for," purred Lawrence.

I am ashamed to admit that the golden caviar melted in my mouth without going Pop! like I'm used to, so I guess my tastebuds are still back in the delicatessen. I latched onto the bottle of vodka, though, having had a burning thirst ever since I hit Tehran. I found myself raising my glass to the dark eyes of a big blond youth with tanned flesh like a sun-ripened musk melon. There is an old Persian saying: "Women for duty, boys for pleasure but melons for sheer delight." Fucked if he doesn't look like a Fida'i to these old bleary eyes. "Whose trail are you on?" he asks me pointblank. I barely notice that he is actively being attacked by a chick like a golden lizard who is wrapping herself around him. "Whose trail? Why, on yours, Baby," I say with my eyes but my lips say: "Hassan i Sabbah." The gorgeous girl twists around in his arms like a basilisk, eyeing me evenly. Even these narrow blue blinkers of mine have to admit it, she is stunning. He is on one elbow hanging over her, his sheer voile shirt open to the navel. Rolling one evil eye back at me to show me the white of it, this glittering reptile nibbles his nipple. He shifts, groping for cigarettes, bending over to take a light off me while she rolls her python's pink tongue around in his bellybutton. I am completely overcome, as is my condition constantly.

Later, with the vodka bottle empty in front of me, I find myself babbling like the conduit of fresh mountain water which is filling the swimming-pool. Babble like a brook and throw your bread upon the waters, that is my principle. As the Herr Doktor say: "You learn more about people by talking to them than you can by listening to them." Besides I'm in a hurry. I've just picked up on something said a minute ago and I wonder if this trip is really on, after all. From living in Muslim countries for more than twenty years, I long ago came to know that nothing really happens until it has happened. And, even then, you can't always be sure of it. I have just heard someone asking our host and driver-to-be about our trip tomorrow and he said: "What trip?"

Moamer, as I decided to call him, hated us both on sight, for some occult reason. Black-bearded twenty-one year old hairy Aryan, he stood as straight and silent but slight as the Medean spear he seemed to be carrying. A dark Persian Pan, he sulked like James Dean but, as things turned out, he drove better. Antagonism excites me when I am drunk, so I decided to give him my glittering eye routine and lay on him my version of the career of Hassan i Sabbah which runs like this:

My boy Hassan was born in Ray, near present day Tehran, and studied in Nichapour to the east on the old Silk Route to China where he went to a medersa, a boarding-school in which he shared a study with two other boys who are equally famous in history. One of them was known as Nizam al Molk when he became Prime Minister of the then-immense Persian Empire. The other was Omar Khayam, the poet with the jug of wine, who must have been as seductive a character as we find him to be when we read his Rubaiyat. These three got on so well together than they opened their veins and mingled their blood in a schoolboy oath that was supposed to hold good for a lifetime. When Nizam became Prime Minister, he named Omar Khayam state astronomer because he was good at mathematics. Hassan was not but when he came to court on the strength of their romantic bond, Nizam gave him the post of Minister of Finance. While preparing his budget, Hassan sought out the help of Omar with whom he left overnight all the papers pertinent to his financial report which he was to read to the Shah and the assembled court in the morning. When the time came, Hassan picked up his papers and read them aloud, just as he found them. Everyone gasped and then broke out laughing, louder and louder as Hassan struggled on, talking what seemed to be utter nonsense until the Shah stopped him and sent him away in disgrace.

What had happened was that someone, presumably Omar… or was it Nizam?... had not only scrambled the pages but cut them in four and carefully pasted them together again. Now, this is the random process of discontinuity with which Burroughs and I have been working since 1960 when I called them the Cut-Ups. Moamer yawned, naturally, but I plunged on with my story when one of the other guests asked: "Then what happened?"

Hassan i Sabbah went home to Ray in a rage, vowing a terrible vengeance on his old pals for having made a fool of him… he fell ill and did not leave his house for weeks on end. Then, he went walking one night in the dark and empty bazaar where he was not likely to meet anyone he knew but as he passed the one stall still open, a lowly cobbler called out to him, offering him a glass of tea. When he sat down with this poor man, the cobbler said quietly: "Welcome, we have been waiting for you. You are that man." Hassan recognized by certain signs that the cobbler was a member of the secret brotherhood of the Ismailians whose network reached all the way across the Near East to Egypt where the supposed descendants of Fatima, daughter of Mohammed the Prophet, called themselves Caliphs of Cairo with the pretension to rule all of Islam. When Hassan realized the possibilities inherent in such a connection, he said: "Yes, I am that man."

The cobbler gave him the Ismaili code, including the thirty-three handshakes and stuff, so Hassan i Sabbah set off to pick up the threads of this organization along the trade routes which led him through Baghdad and Damascus to Cairo where, as soon as he arrived, he announced that he was not just a member but the Head of the Ismailians. When you join a conspiracy, join at the top. (Unexpected applause at this point from the man with the golden caviar: "Right on!" he cried.) Within a matter of months, Hassan i Sabbah had thrown the city of Cairo into a state of revolution. Was called in by the Fatimid Caliph, he demanded his son and heir as a hostage and, no sooner had he laid hands on this fourteen-year-old boy, than he made off with him in the first boat leaving for Syria. On the way, they were shipwrecked and when they turned up much later in Damascus, the boy he had with him appeared to be only twelve years old, but Hassan i Sabbah stoutly insisted that this boy was the heir to the Fatimid pretensions. Within a few years, they had set up housekeeping together in Alamut and the rest of the story…

"The rest of the story," said the man with the golden caviar, "is that he gave his assassins the sacred mushroom. Hash would not be enough to explain the hold he had over them."

"How about O?"

"Yes, perhaps, O and mushrooms he learned about from the Turkestan steppes where their shamans have always used them. Hassan i Sabbah was a shaman."

"How about the homosexual side of shamanism?"

"I'm sure the Assassins knew about that, all right."

In my excitement, I laid a light hand on Moamer's bare arm, barely brushing it but he sat still and stiff, staring down at the spot as if he expected a cancer to grow there like a mushroom. We were not urged to stay the night, after all, but took a flight home in a taxi down through what I kept insisting was LA. Came the dawn and the reckoning. Despite all the Veganins I took before passing out, I had a horrible hangover and so did Moamer when he showed up late, saying he'd had only two hours' sleep. It did not seem to show in his driving but I clung to the edge of my seat in the open jeep. Shivering Lawrence had come along at the last minute and was stowed away on the top of the things like bedding that Moamer had brought with him. Moamer accepted two Veganins grudgingly and drove like a madman out along the highway to the northwest between desert and bare red mountains. We stopped at Karadj, a market town of one broad unpaved Main Street of one-story stores and gaudy government buildings, lined with trees growing in irrigation ditches flowing with water. Brightly painted and highly decorated with icons and decals and ball-fringe, big fat trucks balled through the dust in which delirious drivers make U-turns and Y-turns and Z-turns while only an occasional X marks the spot of an accident. Wily driving is a matter of pride with the Persians. Moamer dropped into a store run by a Christian Armenian where he brought vodka and beer, ham, boloney, hot dogs and everything which, for good Muslims, is forbidden, not kosher, *haram*.

The air was so hot that you took it into your lungs in short sips, like hot tea. I could hardly breathe. Asthma? I asked myself before bothering Lawrence to get into my bad where I had my Spinhaler and my Moditen. I had taken one Moditen at six, along with two Veganins last night and two more each time I came to again during the night. Also three little old pinkies and then just three more of them later: *Codéthyline Houdé*, free across the counter in France, one tube to a customer since the last scare about *la drogue*. I felt fine, fairly fine: finer than Moamer and that was some consolation. He suddenly whipped the jeep off the road and down into a ditch, or was it a side-road? Moamer croaked like a man coming out of a trance: "Just now, I wake up."

We drove up an avenue of trees which may once have led to a farmhouse but the bulldozers have taken over everywhere in Iran, what with all that good oil money, and new construction in chaos is seen even out here in the bare countryside. Beyond all this mess, the clean mesa land sails up towards magnificent bare mountains all purple and blue and malachite green with copper, no doubt, rising up to a distant peak covered with "eternal" but dingy brown snow. In all this place not one blade of grass grows in the heat of August, only a few ghostly thistles and thorns along the dirt road on which enough dew forms during the night to support them. Yet immense tracts of this totally arid landscape are cultivated during the rainy season. Where there is year-around water on this land, they get three crops a year of all the cereals like wheat, rye, oats, barley and alfalfa which they rotate. All these grains were first domesticated, sown and reaped here in the dawn of our agricultural history.

On the top of the first high ridge marked on my map in Nagel, we stop. "You see that third range of mountains out there? That green spot is just below Alamut." Through my 10 x 40 Japanese binoculars, I can see nothing because the wind buffets my trembling hands but above our heads an eagle is circling as if welcoming us to Alamut which means the Eyrie, the Eagle's Nest. Down the other side of this ridge is *tchaikaneh*, a country tea-house by an oasis in the bend of the road growing around a spring of cold water which comes out of the hillside. Moamer drives up real rugged and leaps from the jeep to put his head under the stream, splashing around for quite a while before we can get a drink. While we are reviving ourselves, the *tchaikaneh*-man comes on shouting and waving his arms about. He is furious because Moamer has run the jeep so far into the red earth moist from the overflow that he has crushed three, no, four blades of grass! Moamer tries to make it a laugh but the man is perfectly serious. The little oasis is precious and fragile, shaded by a ring of pole-straight poplars. The poplar is a Persian tree, first selected and grown along these waterways by the people who gave us the lilac, the apple and pear and the rose and the tulip. The willow and the peach came from China. Hollyhocks are blooming around the door of the little adobe house of the *tchaikaneh*. A willow weeps over the low table on which we eat out of doors.

The *tchaikaneh*-man brought us tea (*tchai* as in China) and truly great bread that looks more like place-mats of heavy brown paper than pancakes. Any Persian who patents this type of unleavened bread and makes it in the States will put pasty white bread out of business. The rest of the meal in this idyllic spot would not be worth remembering if it were not for the melon, THE melon of a lifetime. THE peach, I ate in Georgia, plucking it off the tree where it hung like a golden lantern. THE tomato, I ate in La Ciotat on the French Riviera and THE potato in Tangier. THE melon was not only eaten here, it was cut with THE knife. The moment I saw it, I knew it was THE knife of my life. Perhaps it is just as well I never got to own it, let alone give it to Burroughs who might learn to use it on the upthrust. The knife is an old hand-tempered steel blade which curves and folds into a shank made of the horn of an ibex, justlikethat. Closed, it looks like a fish whose eyes are the ends of the bolt on which the blade hinges. Moamer got it on an earlier trip from the *tchaikaneh*-man in exchange for his opium pipe. I said: "I want one just like it."

"There isn't another one. I'll give you this one if you really want it."

I did and I do but I never got it although I gave Moamer in exchange a knife I had from Burroughs who loves to give them as presents, knowing it is dangerous.

Lawrence was throwing scraps of ham to a foraging hen with one leg in a splint. "If the woman who owns that hen sees her eating ham, then the woman won't eat her… not kosher, *haram*," I said.

"Why, then," said Lawrence, "she'll lay *haram* and eggs."

While we ate, another jeep drove up. "An event to be remembered in the country-side," murmured Moamer, "the meeting on this road of two jeeps."

A dark and plump, slightly dapper city man in a white shirt got out of the jeep with a black case which he gave to his driver who handed him a splendid bunch of grapes and drove off. The man bowed slightly to us as he washed his grapes in the fountain and offered them all to us. We refused politely, insisting he keep some for himself. They were the pick of the vineyard, as good as the *stafidi* in Corinth. Moamer bristled when the man drew up a stool and ordered a tea from the *tchaikaneh*-man. He would eat none of our ham but when I rolled a joint, he accepted it solemnly and pulled on it so long that he had to be asked to hand it to Lawrence who was lying there with his tongue out. Moamer said the man was the visiting male nurse and when I asked what people around there died of mostly, was properly answered: "Death," said Moamer. "There is no hospital and no transportation except his jeep once a month. He's full of shit. He doesn't care for these people."

"Get that Persian princess," Lawrence hissed, "still jiving on that jay."

The poor man looked like he spoke English but he may well not have understood that. We left him there by the fountain, looking wistfully down at his own reflection in the pool with one leg twisted around the other and his arms coiled around him so that one hand under his chin looked like a dove he was fondling. There was something absurdly touching about this post-

Hellenic pose. No need to wonder what he was thinking: the big city and sex, these two wierdos from Paris, the lot.

The road down the far side of the ridge to the Shahrud river was the first on which Moamer had to make two and three Y-turns every time we came to a hairpin bend with a hair-raising, breath-taking drop of what looked like anything from five hundred feet down… down… and down to those silver strands of water at the bottom. And, instead of iron nerves, I had a rusty old hangover deep in my soul. Lawrence was being tossed around in the back like a great Arab lady taking a trip in a howdah but he rallied to pass us a couple of cans of cold beer from the icebox. Out of sheer bravado, we tossed the empty cans into the landscape, thereby polluting the atmosphere. When Moamer got down to the banks of the Shahrud, he nosed the jeep straight out over the banks of a gully so it reared up like a pony and dropped on its four wheels, running smoothly down into the riverbed, just like he knew all the time it would. Only the poor passenger may lose his teeth or collapse with an attack of asthma.

Years back in the old Beat Hotel, I painted a series of pictures I called *"Bathing in the Holy Waters of Alamut."* Thinking these were those, I stripped off to swim. The current is only a couple of feet deep but strong enough to sweep you away for a dangerous joyride down rapids. But the sun was getting low and Moamer said: "You haven't seen the bad road yet." We crossed a military bridge and started zig-zagging an Y-turning up what Lawrence called Mescaline Mountain, because of the weird faces we saw in the rocks. At the top, we penetrated a real spooky tunnel with a winding path through rockfalls from the roof. This boon to weary travelers was put through by Reza Shah who, Moamer said, "took an interest in Alamut." We took a deep breath when we came out the other side for there we were looking twenty miles or more up the Valley of the Assassins. To the left, Lion Mountain, Shir Kuh, rises to something like twelve thousand feet with waterfalls flashing off its bare red flanks, down into the river which runs where it wills through a stony bed almost half a mile wide, twining ribbons of wild water. A huge tawny rock about three stories high stands by the road down below like a sentinel. Far up the valley are two green patches on plateaus at the bottoms of mighty ravines, each denoting a village. If the first one is the Chams Kilaya I find on my map in Nagel, then one of the mightiest Assassins' castles of them all, Maimoun Diz, hangs on a pinnacle some two thousand feet above it. Impossible to identify with certainty even through my 10 x 40 binoculars. With more time one might get a glimpse of it but it takes real mountaineers to get up there, they say.

Our equipment was pitiful. On my feet, I was wearing a pair of pimps' pimps sewn up for me by the Chelsea Cobblers in London. They were so sold and worn that they were comfortable for walking but useless for climbing. They slipped out from under me even on the sidewalks of Tehran. Worse than that, my left foot is totally unreliable since I lose a part of it in a motorbike accident a few years ago. Sure-footed Lawrence was shod with some nifty high heels from Paris on which he tripped about like a goat. Moamer was wearing some Iranian rope-soled numbers with which he ran through rough mountain streams like a gazelle. We had no idea how little food we had with us, for all that had been left to Moamer. When we came to some houses and he had to ask his way, we wondered if we would ever get there by nightfall. We didn't.

When we came to a bridge, we did not take it but ran on up the riverbank for nearly a mile before we turned into the swift-floating water and simply churned upstream through the middle. Water and rocks were flying around us but the jeep did not fail and we made it. Fifty yards upstream, we turned and roared up the bank, coming out int a bucolic countryside of green fields and hedges. The hedges, if studied by a paleobotanist, could give one an idea of the age of the road dating back to the Assassins, surely. The rocky track between hedgerows was made for donkeys and mules and not cars. Water tends to rush down it in streams, carving ruts into torrents. Every so often, an open irrigation ditch cuts calmly across it and the jeep rocks and roars through it, nearly jolting Lawrence out of his palanquin. Moamer runs the ruts like they were roller-coasters until we get stuck and some peasants on their way home with their cattle manage to help us get out again as the sun set swiftly at seven.

Up, up and up and, long after dark, we roared up into the almost perpendicular village of Gazour Khan, immediately after Alamut. There was nothing exciting to do in the village that night until we came, you could see that. Sober-faced children and adults stood around stolidly staring at us. They were all wearing rubber shoes cast in a mould to look like they had laces. All the men wear dreary white shirts and dark trousers. Women wear short pleated skirts over their navy-blue pajama pants and the same shoes as the men. And that is an order! Nearly fifty years ago, now, Reza Shah, father of the present one, issued an order that no one was to wear anything but Western dress and a Pahlavi-peaked cap instead of a turban. As a result, perhaps, everyone acts like a lobotomy case in this country, like they had been amputated of their anima. In any Moroccan village, the same villagers would be smiling and swarming all over you. Some kids do follow us up to the spot where we camp for the night and I notice that the one nearest to me is a dwarf in his twenties. His father is suffering from something in his leg and all I can give him are a few Veganins for the pain. I look in vain for my pinkies, my codeine which cures colds and the belly-ache, mends broken limbs and will cover the first installments of even cancer.

We make camp and Alamut is up there, high overhead in the dark. No question of getting up there and spending the night in the castle as shams and Moamer had done on a previous trip. I am furious. Moamer opens my bottle of vodka and swigs at it, losing the screwcap so that the whole bottle is wasted, later. Then he pulls out his inflatable mattress, pumps it up, sets the better sleeping-bag on it and snuggles down inside without saying Goodnight. There are only two beers left to wash down our sandwiches of ham and boloney rolled in pancakes of bread. To cut the melon, I ask for the knife, OUR knife, and Moamer mumbles he has lost it. There is nothing to do but pack it in so Lawrence gets the remaining sleeping-bag and I roll up in some wet blankets under the stars which we stare at through the binoculars until we are tired of it.

"Just imagine a three-day-long free-fall through the Milky Way?" suggests Lawrence.

I suddenly find I can't breathe, at the mere thought of it. I fumble around in the dark for my Spinhaler and capsules of Intal. Sitting up, I see several lanterns bobbing around in the dark below us in the most alarming fashion. It looks like a meeting. I nudge Lawrence who sits up gasping: "Jeezus, the vigilantes!" Eventually, two pair of legs carrying lanterns pass by in the dark on the far side of the chattering brook beside which we have camped. Perhaps they are afraid of us, they are talking so loudly. Later, a few more of them climb past through the night with hoes on their shoulders. Lawrence is surprised to see they are women. "At this hour!" he exclaims. They are the nightshift of water-workers, redirecting their irrigation ditches down to their fields below. We lie there staring up at the 3D Milky Way some more until I say: "I refuse to believe those are other worlds up there. It is all mere decoration."

Sleep eludes me. The stream two feet away from me is chattering louder since we turned out our lamp. I can hear voices babbling in the brook. Then I hear distinct music and drumming. Are those shepherds and shepherdesses calling out to their flocks in the night or is that the water? I hear martial music and drumming. Are those shepherds and shepherdesses calling out to their flocks in the night or is that the water? I hear martial music like armies with silver trumpets and the wild skirling wail of the Mongol pipes, ancestral voices prophesying war. Suddenly, it is Lawrence beside me, laughing. "Sorry to sound so personal but I've just been seeing our arrival in the eyes of the villagers. There you were wearing nothing, apparently, but your pink Indian shirt, unwinding a long pair of white legs covered with mud which you covered with black velvet pants."

"Tomorrow, I want to look good for my meeting with Hassan i Sabbah. I'm going to wear my gold shirt I was wearing in Cannes when Jodorowsky came in to his press conference wearing the same one."

"You remember that English family that was massacred in the South of France where they were camping?"

"And that German hippie in Turkey the other day."

"And what about *Easy Rider*?"

"Yeah, why don't you roll a last joint with some O in it."

"I'm going to put on my sleep-mask to keep out the stars and start my countdown exercises."

My countdowns are simple enough, something I picked up from the book by Monroe, *Journeys Out of the Body.* Burroughs went into *Mind Dynamics*, or whatever they call themselves now, and says they have slightly different techniques but I've had some real hot-shot successes with my version of this one. My trouble is that I either don't dream or don't remember my dreams on waking. Censor trouble, I suspect. For years, I've claimed that Burroughs diverts my dreams. Be that as it may, I shut my eyes under my sleep mask or leave them wide open as I count down from twenty to zero, making an effort to visualize each number as I go for a spot in space where I say with an attempt at Inflexible Authority: "I fully intend to go out there to meet So-and-So and, when I get back, I'll remember all about it." Sometimes, I have taken quite a hectoring tone. Just as often, or more often than not, nothing happens. This night, of course, I demand to meet Hassan i Sabbah.

The Old Man and I are walking along a high reef of rock looking out over his island, his very last electronically-guarded island, presumably in the Azores. It is late in the day and an ominous lead-colored light floods level across the limited landscape under a low lid of clouds, casting long shadows ahead of us as we climb. Impossible to remember what we were talking about because a trio of his agents, his faithful Fida'i-in, suddenly materializes uncomfortably close behind us, supposedly reporting in to the Old Man. I bristle instinctively but he merely takes a real sloppy salute like he is wiping his mouth with a soiled napkin. I glare at these guys. I know they are supposed to be high-mountain Basque herdsmen, back from Vizcaya on home leave but their eyes look a lot too slanty to me. Something gone wrong in Transmission. I have no time to say this because the landscape erupts behind me. When I whirl around, I can see that our fort on the far side of the island is burning, having fallen under rocket fire. I glare at the Old Man. This is the result of his absent-minded oversight. He forgot to throw in some switch and now all is lost. He looks like a disenchanted Prospero, as played by William S. Burroughs. I glance down at my hands, as instructed by Don Juan, and they are hairy. Am I Caliban? What is the Old Man going to do now? He simply fans out his fine old fingers and raises his shoulders in the old junky shrug. In his deep-set blue eyes, I catch a cold glint of— What is it? The knife-edge of laughter, perhaps? Or is this old Granny O that I have here in front of me?

"That's the life, son," she drawls, "Son cosas de la vida."

In the first light of day, I lie back in my blankets and look up at Alamut through my binoculars. It is higher by far than I thought it would be. "Impossible!" I murmur. The word wakes Lawrence who wants to look, too. "Has someone restored it?" What he refers to are big patches of yellow and red brickwork looking almost brand new, plastered right on the side of the high rocky parapet. The only explanation for these is that the Mongols could not get to them. But how did anyone ever put them there in the first place? Forests of poplar poles must have been tied into scaffolding to cover the cliff-face. Peter Willey, who has written the most recent books about them, says: "The Assassins were at least as capable as the Crusaders—who were responsible for their drugs and murder image—in their brilliant construction of castles, their use of natural land and water resources, their adaptability to political circumstances and their appreciation of the arts. Their system of fortifications was well ahead of its time. Theirs was a very advanced strategic concept of defense in depth which we did not develop again until well into the twentieth century."

Because we dawdled, the sun was well up in the sky by the time we got started. By daylight, we could see that our babbling brook was actually a quick-running cascade, tumbling down through an irrigation ditch bordered by the narrow path up which the night-workers with lanterns had come to regulate their sluices. On the far side of that, yawned a precipitous canyon from which the water had been diverted to serve the village directly below the green platform on which we had spent the night. Looking almost straight up into the light, we could see that Lion Mountain is all striped by such colossal canyons with sharp hogsback ridges between them. Alamut rock thrusts up between a network of these ancient erosions that make it stand out from the rest of the mountainside like a natural fortress on which only eagles would think of building a nest.

Providentially, a man with a mule came along and carried me up the first lap, until we got to the spot where even a sure-footed mule could not go any further. Less sure-footed by far, I slipped off his back to look down the hellish deep pit that still another stream has cut around the back of the castle rock. "Don't fall in!" cried Moamer. I had not thought of it yet but I did then and I went on thinking or dreaming about it for the next couple of days thereafter. Worse than that, I had an all but irresistible urge to throw myself over. Where this urge may be coming from, I'll think about later. For my very entrails were grabbed and my eyeballs seemed to jump in their sockets as I stared out across this almost bottomless red pit at what looked like an emerald saucer hovering in space, hung between the silver rivulet of the stream so far down below and the sun-tipped summit of Shir Kuh towering like an angry cloud above. For a long moment, I could simply not take in what I was seeing, until I looked at it through my binoculars. Then, I could not believe my eyes when I saw it. That far cliff was still in deep shadow and my 10 x 40 glasses are so strong that to see through them clearly demands that one rest them on something solid. My hands trembled and sweat poured down into my eyes. I had the dry heaves, mountain sickness from the thin air at this altitude, and I was gasping with asthma. The bright dancing image I caught, jiggled around like a drop of water on a redhot stove. When my hand was steadied, what I saw was still running like a reflection seen in a windowpane streaming with rain. What is it, what can it be? I kept asking myself. I decide it is Paradise, Paradise garden as seen in a raindrop. So, there really was a garden, I sighed.

Why, there still is a garden, I panted as I climbed on up after Moamer and Lawrence and a small mountain boy who had attached himself to us. I gave him my binoculars to carry, and the copy of *Naked Lunch*, bought in the airport in Ispahan. I needed my hands free for my feet were too big for the goat-bath across the vast curtain of loose rubble which hangs from right under the castle, down and down and on down without a shrub or a blade of grass to cling onto should one make one single mis-step. And there was still worse to come, for, at one point, I heard a cold voice say inside me: "You can't make it." I dared not look down but I twisted around to glance again at the garden and saw that the first rays of the sun had just struck it. All the dew on the poplar trees and green terrace of grass, greener than any seen this side of Heaven, was turned in an instant to vapor. A cloud like one's breath on a mirror burned off this tiny plateau, like a miniature garden on a tea tray hung out over the gulf where Alph the sacred river ran through caverns measureless to man down to a boundless sea. I could not go back, so I scrambled on up to Alamut, gasping like a fish out of water.

At the top of the scree, the solid rock at the peak has been cut through from one side to the other by a tunnel which I would not like to have to stand up in when the wind is blowing. I threw myself on its floor, feeling around for my Spinhaler only to find that I had forgotten it in the pocket of my other shirt. That gave me time to think a few thoughts about my asthma, for it is a fairly new acquisition of mine these last four or five years, instead of the classic asthma which the victims suffer since their childhood. In my childhood, my mother had the asthma, not me. At three or four years of age, I used to like to listen to her chest when she had a crisis of bronchitis, "brown kittens," I called it. Later, she had to get rid of a chow dog she dearly loved because its fur gave her asthma. So, when doing research through some really insane books on modern psychiatry, I cam across this farfetched analysis, I made a note of it:

"An asthma attack is brought about by separation anxiety and means that the patient is trying to inhale his mother, so that he can keep her safely inside his chest in order to feel permanently protected. At times, he has fantasies that she is already within and this brings about a struggle between his ego and the respiratory apparatus 'containing' her."

Wow, does it ever! And who is this inside me, pray, who is trying to push me over? I simply can't look out the front end of this tunnel because the flat roofs of the village are fifteen hundred feet down there beneath my feet and the soles of my shoes are so badly worn that they slip and slide under me even on the paved streets of Tehran, I keep reminding myself. Have I climbed all the way up here to have a wrestling match with the ghost of my mother whose asthma I suffer from only since she died, far away and alone and with misery? Or is this the Old Man, himself, who said to have delighted in throwing strong men over? When the Frankish so-called King of Jerusalem came here to parlay with him, Hassan i Sabbah is said to have simply snapped his long bony fingers at a sentinel posted right up here where I am clinging right now and the boy jumped, snapping to attention in full flight as he flashed past the astonished eyes of the Norman usurper. Burroughs loves this example of Inflexible Authority, and I used it, myself, in *The Process*. I had better be careful.

A severely plain shepherdess of about fourteen, dressed in their national travesty of Western clothes, suddenly appears with three goats behind her and offers me a handful of broken shards of pottery she has culled from the landslide of ruins in this castle destroyed by the Mongols just seven hundred and twenty-three years ago. "Snow came late to the Alborz mountains and the valley of Alamut that winter of 1256," the historian Juvayni records. "Men of a hundred years of age could not remember such a mild winter. It made things easier for the Mongol invader. Hulagu's hordes assaulted the castle with mangonels and the ears of its defenders with wild pipes screaming constantly for three days and nights until the nerves of the besieged cracked and crumbled like the walls of Jericho. At Hulagu's orders, the last Grand Master of the Assassins, Rokneddin the Parricide, was thrown over the same cliff which had provided such sport for his predecessor, Hassan i Sabbah."

Who am I, Rokneddin? Never.

Moamer and Lawrence and the goat-footed mountain boy of about ten, came back at that point to say they had climbed further up and Moamer had even followed the local lad out around the edge of the cliff and down into a sort of cistern cut out of the rock. He claimed that he had been so scared shitless that it had been hard to get back again. There were the remains of paintings on plaster, he said, defaced by centuries of graffiti. I had no desire to see this, ever. I had very little desire to climb further up, either, so I lit up a joint and just sat there transfixed in the niche of some ancient Fida'i sentinel, staring stoned across at the hanging Garden of Delights as it floated over the dark red abyss and into the sunlight like a miniature Paradise planet carved out of jade and flashing with emeralds. "Yakh Chal," the boy said, pointing to it. Moamer laughed. "He says it is called, the Ice Box or the Frigidaire, probably because the sun strikes it so late in the day. Yakh means ice and Cal is a ditch or a hole. Hence, the Icebox..."

The round keep of the castle is the largest heap of stones still standing on Alamut and the goat-path to the upper terraces winds around it. No point in looking down around there, either. The view from the top is like a blow in the brain, overwhelmingly unsettling. Covered with snow and ice as it is in the wintertime, windswept and battered by storms, it must be even more terrifying. Keeping my eyes on my feet to be sure what they were doing, I came with gratitude into what Shams called the court of the castle somewhat grandly. It looks more like a room about ten by sixteen feet which has collapsed and the floor fallen in, filling up a foundation cut into the rock. It holds water or seems to, for a few spiky sedges were sticking up among the fallen hand-hewn blocks of what looked to be limestone. A corner of wall still stands and I had Lawrence take a picture of me in front of it. "For Rolling Stone Enterprises, click!" he cried, clattering away after the mountain boy on his high heels from Paris. When I was sure of what I was holding onto, I craned out with my binoculars and got a really close view of the brickwork. Even the Mongols could not pry it off the cliff-face and it looks as if the bright red and bright yellow bricks had been laid yesterday. When the Mongols were trashing the castle, curtain walls over empty expanses between projecting rocks were easier to kick out completely, but traces of masonry remain on either side of these gaps and one is still crossed by an arch over a hole or horrible chute through which one could slide so easy and glide right down onto the flat roofs of the village except for that deep canyon between us.

Looking around at what remains up there, one is bound to conclude that most of the figures anyone advances about the Assassins are fanciful. First of all, the space is small, no matter what towers and turrets were built on it. For a long time, it was thought that Alamut was the only castle belonging to the sect but several more have been discovered as recently as 1972 and now it is recognized that they had fortified at least three valleys in depth and their strongholds reached out to Syria in one direction and unto the marches of Afghanistan in the other. The capital castle of Alamut may well have been an all but impregnable stronghold, held by but a handful of picked men around the Grand Master who ruled through the power of his mind as well as by his long knife. The long knife, after all, was wielded by one single man at a time. No need of vast hungry armies to pamper.

The final downfall of the Assassins is said to have been brought about by someone named Tousi who had been kidnapped and held in Alamut. By the time Tousi was ransomed, he had learned the weaknesses of the last Grand Master, Rokneddin, who was said to have killed his own father. Tousi gave the plan of the castle to the Mongols on the condition that he would inherit the library of Alamut which has been said by some historians to have comprised the extravagant number of two hundred thousand volumes. Even this number of modern books would need a huge space to be stored and consulted. Ancient handwritten manuscript on parchment would be even bulkier. Nowhere in the ruins as one sees them today would there be place for such a collection. Perhaps what these drivers referred to was the power in these books for the Assassins inspired many other secret societies in Asia and in Europe who adopted their techniques of iron discipline and their philosophy that the end justifies the means. In Europe, their methods of initiation, their method of appointing officers, their emblems and their insignia and other trappings were imitated by such groups as the Knights Templar, the Hospitallers and the Society of Jesus, the Jesuits founded by Ignatius Loyola. Today, Opus Dei in Spain is said to owe much to someone's studies of the Ismailis.

Are there others?

KINGS WITH STRAW MATS

IRA COHEN

I was living in Katmandu, writing poetry and experimenting with astral projection, when I heard that the Kumbh Mela was about to take place in Allahabad. I checked my dervish manual—*The Poems of Rumi*—and it told me to make my way as quickly as possible to this special twelve-year meeting of pilgrims and holy men at the confluence of three rivers—the Ganges, the Jumna and the invisible underground Saraswati.

Over twelve million people were headed by jet, train, oxcart or simply on foot, with the object of bathing at the astrologically perfect moment at the point where the three rivers met. As soon as I read those words of Rumi which proclaimed, "Stop being a water bearer and immerse yourself in the ocean," I got some color film on credit (no easy task in Nepal) and made travel arrangements for Allahabad where I arrived with about $20, dreaming of twelve million third eyes opening simultaneously. After all, the place where the three rivers met was considered to be the external representation of the third eye itself.

The Kumbh Mela takes its name from the Hindu legend which tells how four drops of the gods' holy elixir fell to the earth from a kumbh or pitcher during a struggle with jealous demons. The places where those four drops fell are Allahabad, Hardwar, Ujjain and Nasik, where the famous festivals are held every twelve years. And what was that elixir, if not that most powerful psychedelic, the fabled soma which was known by the ancients to confer instant divinity?

On my arrival, after literally having to smoke my way through hundreds of naked sadhus covered in ashes, I was fortunate enough to meet Ganesh Baba, *High Times'* favorite guru and India's own Mr. Natural, who immediately transmitted to me by psychedelic bullet all I needed to know and gave me a place to sleep besides. It was Ganesh who said, "Someone should write a book called *Kings With Straw Mats*." It would be impossible to estimate how many tons of ganja and charas were smoked during the month-long festival.

The Samadhi Wala, who was about to have himself buried alive for a period of five days without food or water, sings out to me, "Only the Almighty can look after a yogi." Apart from all the drugs used to induce ecstasy and vision, some of the highest yogis and fakirs had their own time-honored ascetic techniques for getting even higher through meditation and the practice of austerities. In search of mystic union with Reality and the acquisition of special powers, they defied all ideas of human endurance, like standing on one leg for twelve years or more, even sleeping while standing with the aid of a hanging swing. Others, known as Ek Bahus or One Arms, hold their arms up for similar periods of time until the arm shrivels into a permanent upright position and the fingernails grow right into the flesh. Other Nagas could lift enormous weights with their cocks, and during one of the processions through the streets of the city, I saw a naked sadhu pulling a carload of saffron swamis by a rope tied to his penis. On that day the townspeople threw over 50,000 rupees worth of marigolds at the feet of the naked holy men as they marched to the river.

Even in your wildest dreams you could never imagine such a circus of high madness, true devotion and showbiz savvy as the Kumbh Mela, which could have absorbed the whole Woodstock nation as if under a single tent. As I stood immersed in the water with tears of inexpressible emotion running out of my eyes and thought, *Here I stand alone among millions,* I began to laugh. We are a multitude moving towards a head...

Taking photographs in such a situation was not always easy. Once, a fat authoritarian figure came down off his elephant to chase me away. Another time, some film was confiscated by the Indian police. Then there was the rain. Even Antonioni with all his government permissions was stopped from filming by a little naked sadhu who had the support of thousands of his fellow yogis, and Antoniom ended by leaving the festival. If you ever want to go to a Kumbh Mela yourself, just take the Kailash 42nd Street Express, don't forget to change at Allahabad, and be sure to bring those two extra arms to hold yourself with.

Om Namo Narayan.

(September 1984.)

Hardwar Journal: The Festival of Kumbh Mela

Now I sit on the banks of Ganga[1], my feet in the river, as I begin this notebook. Everyone has different information about the Mela, but it seems that the main Kumbh begins in Ujjain of March 31, that here in Hardwar the Aard Kumbh, or half Kumbh, will be celebrated on April 13—the main bathing day, with millions expected. The Kumbh Mela occurs every twelve years in four different places—Hardwar, Allahabad, Ujjain and Nasik—but there are annual pilgrimages to each of these sacred sites: a full twelve-year meeting occurring at three year intervals among the four places.

I can hardly lift my arm after cholera shot administered to all people entering Hardwar area (free, or at any rate, covered by a three rupee tax). We meet David on the ghat. He is Scottish, has spent many seasons in Goa and

Manali—now living as a sadhu, or holy man. He holds his hands together, palm against palm, as he salutes the sun before dunking his head three times in the river. As he says, Hardwar is the Gate to Heaven. We have first chilum[2] with him, then go to smoke with two Babas sitting downriver.

Dwarf lady goes by in ricksha with marigolds around her neck. Among the bathers, some few men sifting sand of river bottom with feet and passing mud through straw sieves, looking for treasure left by pilgrims I suppose. They make a strange dancelike movement, gyrating hips as they chum up the mud and stones underfoot. About twenty Indians stop to stare at us and then walk on. Now a leper wearing a Nepalese topi[3] rubs offal off his shoe. He shows me that he has no finger ends. Three wet black children come laughing out of the river and hang over Caroline's shoulder. The Nepali leper is from Jumla. I give him twenty paise. When I was sitting in the bus arriving in Rishikesh near Laxman Jhula, a Tibetan from Kathmandu tried to sell me a black shawl. Everyone is recognizable, familiar and yet a complete stranger. Time to move.

David, the Scottish sadhu, concentrates on douna, the sacred fire: how to make douna, how to feed douna—to keep the fire pure. "Douna is power," he says. "Douna is pure Shakti." If you take care of douna, douna takes care of you. People come and bring charas or leave rupees at douna. Douna is experimental platform for meditation and astral traveling.

Conversation with Indian man from Delhi who has come with his wife and two children plus two sisters-in-laws for bath in Ganga before flying to Iraq, where he works for a Dutch oil company. His eyes light up as he remembers Utrecht. He buys us two glasses of orange juice and we agree that God is One, that all men come from the same place and will return to the same place. In Iraq he will be considered a Kaffir, an unbeliever.

"Life is a game of Karma, crazy life blessed by the Lord. You must play with this power which is pulling you, pushing you. Give away all, receive love—this is divine. We are international divine family," says Mohan Baba, who has just arrived from Germany where he lives with his Canadian wife Jean (Kai Shakti) and two blonde children: Kala Devi and Lord Krishna Johnny. We sit in front of the Ganga, which speeds by us—everything flowing as in the philosophy of Heraclitus. Mohan Baba admires my ring and asks me if I have a ring for him since he has renounced all jewelry as bullshit. I give him my turquoise ring. He is very happy and begins to roll a joint. "When Shiva was holding Ganga, she said, 'Please let me go, O let me flow.'

That is the story as I know it from many generations. All is due to God's mercy." The women bring the baby, Lord Krishna Johnny, back from the Ganga and Mohan rocks him in his arms.

Caroline writes her poem of silence. It is full of gold and yellow shadows. A mixture of magnolia and black musk. They say it will be very hot in Ujjain, dry desert wind and not much water. A special train will take sadhus from Hardwar to Ujjain after April 13. I meet Ananda Puri and Ram Puri (also Americans), old friends from Allahabad and Pashupatinath. She has full jata, hair matted with cow dung hanging in long tresses.

They bring me up to date on Jasper (Ram Giri) and Bom Shankar, a popular irrepressible Nath Baba with many would-be left-hand Tantrics in his coterie. Bom Shankar was taken out of India for the first time to Jbiza and London—stayed drunk most of the time (alcohol is a sacrament in his order) and was arrested by the Spanish police, then finally deported. They also tell me about my old friend, Devananda, with whom they traveled to Tarapit—the great Masan, or Burial Place, on the border of Bihar—which is a veritable storehouse of skulls and bones. There is not enough wood to burn the bodies completely there and the Babas who live in Tarapit decorate their homes with skulls. Shiva was flying through the sky with the body of Sati which he took from the burning pyre when Vishnu, angry because Shiva was ignoring his duties, threw his bolt at Sati's body, cutting it into fifty one pieces. Tarapit is where one eye is supposed to have fallen. Though it would seem macabre, I hear that the sadhus who live there are especially known for their gentleness.

Devananda was devastated when he lost his opium in Tarapit, then found some more and was last seen in Calcutta, where he died. Ananda Puri and Ram Puri invite me to come to Sapta Rishi to see their guru, Santosh Puri. Sapta Rishi named for the Seven Rishis who caught Ganga in their water-pots: they are seven small islands in the river.

A day of full and wondrous things beginning with the walk along the Ganga to Sapta Rishi. The day before I had heard that Ram Nath Agori Baba had left his body. It was as if I already knew it. While walking, I thought often of him, his shaved head and no teeth, giant Nath earrings, black satin gown, his leopard skin and his wild demeanor; his quiet dignity. The first time he saw me I was with Petra and he threw a rupee note into the fire laughing madly and calling out, "MAYA, MAYA." Then he invited us to sit with him and talk the talk. I remember him taken away hobbling from the burning ghat by automobile for advice (he had been Raj Guru to Tribbuvan, former King of Nepal)—then returned in triumph. Or when he held my black book, *Poems From the Cosmic Crypt*, against his forehead and cried "Success, Success" while we stood in front of a burning pyre in Pashupatinath. And hearing Basudeb sing at his side. Heavy Tantra Man Gone Back to Sky. Now hearing at once 10,000 songs to the Mother, Bagala Devi. And the skull was filled with silver.

HARE OM

Sitting in the juice shop I look at beautiful Shiva poster on wall, his exquisite androgynous head with third eye opening in vertical position, flanked by two more heads in profile about to drink the churned-up poison of the sea. Already his throat shadowed with blue. The Face of Glory I carry with me always—Om Namo Shivaya!

(I bow down to you in the name of Shiva.)

The town is full of steamrollers making a heavy din. As one passes, I imagine drummers at the head of a caravan. Sitting on eternal haunches, someone smoking a bidi rolls a big ball of dough and I am reminded of the belly of a middle-aged woman tying up her sari after taking a bath in the Ganga.

New blue and red towers have just been built for police supervision when the Mela really gets underway. A neon Hanuman, the image of the monkey god, springs up out of nowhere, a blinking red light indicating the heart charkra. Caroline points out a beggar with enormous testicles sitting at the roadside. And covering it all, the endless movie music coming out of loudspeakers.

Mind flying, carpet stationary.
Hands flying, eyes stationary.
Spirit flying, Earth stationary.
SILENT CRUSADERS TRANSFER POWER
SPENT LIGHT WEAVES BLIND VISIONS
MIRACLE YOGIS STREAMLINE DESERT COOLER

"If the crowd gets too big, then the mosquitos will come." An old Naga with ashes. Sullen beard washes clothes with soap in river. Eternal moment under water—lotus dream faded with pontoons of light. Hair drying in sun.

Brahma Kumari Mission offers live shows daily. "We have six million branches in your hometown. Please come and take tea." We compare snake rings and do the flying safi trick. Somewhere in the center of the vortex a dark man in a loincloth lights sticks of incense and counts beads. And then the dreamless stone.

If I could only borrow the big Pink Rabbit from the Bidi stand and use it as a prop in the Ananda Akhada of Naga Babas.[4] Program now being simultaneously announced throughout Mela. Great to be smoking Afghani now that the Russians are there. The Afghanis are bringing it by the truckload, trading charas for guns. Try throwing away a fingernail in India. Here everyone knows about it.

Nazar Lagana means applied glance. There are many ways to be invisible. We are in a prolonged dust haze due to wind absence and I see a red shower curtain with earrings walking toward me on brown feet. Put stethoscope in ears and listen to the sound of your own heartbeat. For only one rupee you become your own guru.

Go by foot from Rameshwaram to GoMukh (the Cow's Mouth)—the source of the Ganga—and bring back a pitcher of Ganga water to pour on the lingam of Rameshwaram if you want to be freed from the cycle of death and rebirth. There's nothing like a beggar's squawk when he thinks he's being underpaid. The ghost of Guru Maharaji goes by in a large white suit with mustache. Punjabi woman smokes provocative cigarette.

Dattatreya Giri and Two Ring Baba keep the bagats (the straights) away as they light their chilums and tell us the names of the holiest places. Crystal beads around the necks of Joona Akhada. "Money is like water," Ramuntcho says. "When it is flowing it is good, but when it stays in one place it gets dirty." This is the best, right here is the best there is. Two Ring badmouths a few more bagats and lays his rap on the evening. "Climbing that mountain is harder than German war, they say." And in the not too distant shadows sit the deformed and untouchable beggars like a wall before the river.

"Leave your house and family behind and come to Hardwar right away."

Chello Hardwar

Endnotes

[1] Ganga is the phonetic rendition of the Sanscrit pronunciation of Ganges.

[2] Chilum is a clay pipe used for smoking charas, hashish which is sacred to Shiva.

[3] Topi is a Nepali hat.

[4] Ananda is bliss. Akhada is fraternity. Thus Ananda Akhada is literally Fraternity of Bliss, an order of holy men dedicated to Shiva known as Nagas.

A FEW SCIENCE EXPERIMENTS TO TRY AT HOME

Shoshita Breathwork Rite

A simple technique for dissolving conflicting internal drives or states ("parts" in NLP parlance). Requires a fire (campfire best; a candle will work). Perfect for magicians who work with a "Will" based model of magick.

0. Statement of Intent: "It is my [our] will to become the pure flame of unified will."

1. Light / assemble around fire.

2. Begin connected breathing (simply, breathe deeply and consistently in a circular motion, *without* pausing at all between the in and out breaths; make it one continuous, flowing motion. Look up information on Holotropic Breathwork for further understanding).

3. Imagine self being burned totally by a fire which begins in the right big toe and proceeds to consume the whole body. The connected breath is the bellows which feeds the flame. (This is known as the Kalgni-Rudra in the *Vijnanabharaiva Tantra*.) If desired, the mantra *Om raksharayum tanum dahmami* may be recited internally.

4. Any blockages or conflicting internal voices are imagined as being burned up and reunited with the singular flame of self. Modulate by speeding up or slowing breathing.

5. The "smoke" that is the remnants of the burned blockages is continually exhaled and offered to the goddess Shoshita, who sits in the fire and is in charge of cleaning up leftovers in Tantra.

6. Come down when ready (ecstatic or trance states are to be expected, especially when using a full campfire or fireplace).

–Jason Louv

Magick Memory Past-Life Evocation

1. Identify a trait one is deficient in or a quality which one wishes to develop.

2. Construct a "past incarnation" in which you strongly possessed this quality, or learning a specific lesson important to your current incarnation was the central theme. (Alternately, if one is working with a specific system, create a past life in which "you" were a master of this system.) Treat this as a servitor. Put as much detail and nuance into the story of this other life as you can. Locate it in whatever time period and locale is most appropriate. Assembling pictures of this person or items which "belonged" to them will add effectiveness.

3. Using Crowley's "magick memory" technique, sit in meditation and run your entire life backwards, like a tape on rewind, from the present moment until you find yourself moving past the moment of conception. Don't worry about missing details.

4. You will find yourself in some type of space beyond your present incarnation. A method for moving into other incarnations will be suggested.

5. From this zone enter into the constructed life. Run it forward from conception to death. Pay close attention to the lessons learnt and the parting wisdom of this life.

6. Now run it in reverse. Return to the pre-incarnational zone.

7. Return to your present incarnation and run it forward. Notice how your history changes.

8. Return to the present. Open your eyes. Notice how you feel different.

9. Locate the part of your physiology which feels most affected by this new wisdom. Notice how it feels different. Amplify this feeling. Double it. Double it again. Then, anchor this feeling by touching this part of your body. This will form a mudra for spontaneous recall.

10. See yourself four days, one month, and then eight years into the future. Notice how you have changed.

11. Banish with laughter.

–*Jason Louv*

This ritual is intended to open the gateways between the three phases of consciousness—waking, sleeping and dreaming—and to call into awareness the thread that runs beneath all three, thereby unlocking the secret of the Great Work. This is the first iteration of an illuminatory ritual meant to supercede *Liber Samekh*. It should be fine-tuned with continual use, and may form the symbolic basis of a long-term illuminatory working.

The ritual calls for three participants. At random they should be seated in the north, southwest and southeast. The only materials needed (other than tools for writing) are three masks: a solid black mask, a solid white mask and an "octarine" or suitably psychedelically-colored mask. In lieu of these items, mudras can be used while invoking.

Black/Sleeping: Palms covering face.

White/Waking: Palms covering ears.

Octarine/Dreaming: Palms extended from head like antlers, thumbs touching sides of head and fingers splayed.

0. Banish

1. Magicians link hands. Oath:

"Under three masks
And three forms
Mercury, Salt, Sulphur
Rajas, Tamas, Sattva
Dreaming, Sleeping, Waking
Tripartite God
Hidden God
Creator of the Universe
We invoke thee
Your black mask we invoke
Your white mask we invoke
Your mask of chaos we invoke
All men are but your three masks
We invoke thee."

2. Participants in the southeast and southwest turn towards the participant in the north and visualize a giant, hovering, featureless white mask (the mask of the waking state). The participant in the north invokes the Hidden God in its waking phase as assisted by the other magicians.

"In the north we call you
From darkness cometh
And to darkness goeth
God of light
Open your western gate
Open your eastern gate
You wear our waking days
As your mask of light
All the days of our lives
Are your mask of light
Give us your name
Give us your sign."

Invokers vibrate *"A."*

Ecstasis is attained by the invokee by overbreathing until the "Other" takes over. Writing implements are given for the invokee to record any spontaneously-given sigils or phrases.

3. Participants turn towards the southeast and visualize a giant, hovering, featureless octarine mask (the mask of the dreaming state). The participant in the southeast invokes the Hidden God in its dreaming phase as assisted by the other magicians.

"In the southeast we call you
From darkness cometh
And towards the light goeth
God of chaos
Open your eastern gate
Open your southern gate
You wear our dreams
As your mask of chaos
All our dreams and nightmares
Are your mask of chaos
Give us your name
Give us your sign."
Invokers vibrate "U."

Ecstasis is attained by the invokee by overbreathing until the "Other" takes over. Writing implements are given for the invokee to record any spontaneously-given sigils or phrases.

4. Participants turn towards the southwest and visualize a giant, hovering, featureless black mask (the mask of the sleeping state). The participant in the southwest invokes the Hidden God in its sleeping phase as assisted by the other magicians.

"In the southwest we call you
From the light cometh
And into chaos goeth
God of darkness
Open your southern gate
Open your western gate
You wear our sleeping bliss
As your mask of darkness
All our unknowing nights
Are your mask of darkness
Give us your name
Give us your sign."

Invokers vibrate "M."

Ecstasis is attained by the invokee by overbreathing until the "Other" takes over. Writing implements are given for the invokee to record any spontaneously-given sigils or phrases.

5. At this point all three magicians should be in invocatory trance. All recorded words and signs are pushed towards the middle. The magicians may converse—this may manifest as an argument, a conversation, a chaotic babble or pure glossolalia—until they speak as one voice. Once this is achieved, the magicians vibrate "AUM" in unity until exhaustion. A period of silence—as the manifestation of the Hidden God itself—follows.

6. Magicians link hands. The Attainment:

"Hidden God now manifest
Once dreaming, now sleeping
Once sleeping, now waking
Once waking, now dreaming
Once dreaming, now waking
There is but one beneath all
There is but one mind

Once hidden, now revealed."

7. Banish with laughter!

After grounding, any material talismans recovered should be combined into a single form and then in some way copied, kept and displayed by each participating magician near their places of sleep and work, or other places they will see it regularly during the day.

– *Jason Louv*

Ritual of Ultimate Magickal Smoothness and Überpower

0. Statement of Intent: "It is my will to get a life."

1. Cut your bullshit and your whining.

2. It's really not that important. Seriously.

3. Breathe.

4. Go back to school and/or apply for decent-paying job within your skill set.

5. Spawn.

6. Die.

7. Repeat.

– *Swami Xanax*

The Macroscope: A Magical Tool for World Change

Often we feel like very small cogs in an enormous machine, or sometimes, for a few brief moments, fulcrums on which the entire fate of the planet revolves.

The Macroscope is a meditation technique for identifying the places at which one's magical power can do the most good for the planet and the human race. It serves to align the will with the Divine Will, while keeping the aspirant in the role of a magician, rather than that as a priest.

Let's start by talking about the 2004 Tsunami. A quarter of a million people died, and nearly all of them could have been saved if they had known that they should walk inland quickly thirty minutes before the wave arrived.

Think "psychic communication"—a message of three words, "walk inland now," would have saved an individual life. "Walk inland now. Pass it on" could, in theory, have saved many more. Many of us are used to using divination to get information at least ten times that complex. An average tarot spread with some psychic divination will often render a much more sophisticated understanding of a situation than "Walk inland now. Tell your friends." Many magicians or New Agers have beings that guide them in much more detail than this, or pull similar information directly out of the ether for themselves. Some of us may even have first-hand stories about where information from these levels has changed reality, saved lives an so on. I'm sure there are people reading this who have had those experiences!

The Macroscope meditation is designed to use that latent magical possibility—lifesaving or planet-improving psychic intervention—in a conscious and somewhat organized fashion.

1. Banish

LBRP or equivalent ritual. Hexagram ritual too if you ever use it—the macroscopic aspect of this working makes the hexagram ritual's ability to banish astrological (not just elemental) influences particularly appropriate. You must banish before this meditation for it to have significant effects.

2. Attune

The "Macroscope" is a virtual scientific instrument. An imaginary device which gets more powerful the more people are using it at the same time. Its "seed capital" comes from the lingering energies of events like Harmonic Convergence, or Secret Himalayan Yogis, or Angelic Defence Grids, or any other time when real or imaginary beings have tried to use their consciousnesses on a planetary scale to help influence life on earth for the better. The Buddha could be seen as the patron of the Macroscope.

Visually, the Macroscope is a three-foot sphere which looks like the earth, rendered in translucent blue and holographic green with little points of light for all the conscious entities. A few whales, a lot of people. It defaults to show the material plane but can be tuned for demonic, angelic, devic and other planes of existence, all overlaid on the earth globe. To attune, see the Macroscope either around your body, so you are inside at the center of it, looking out from your heart chakra at the center of the earth, or in front of you, at chest height about two feet away, points of interest rotating into view. Once the image is clear, the Macroscope is enabled.

3. Intervene

Using the Macroscope, find a place where your can "feel" or "know" you can intervene. Set the psychic dials for "show me something I can do to help" and watch for blips. Bigger is better—it shows a place where your energy can make even more of a difference. Focus will on that intervention point. Visualize it like a laser pouring from your heart to that specific situation. If you feel you're in the role of a cop, an aggressor defending against a problem, throw pentagrams or other juju symbols down the beam. If you're a guide, or a protector, try other sigils.

When you feel done, or when you've got definite effects and are ready for the next target, move on.

4. Coordinate

Individual intervention is a warmup excercise when using the Macroscope. Because of resonance effects, compound interest and other aspects of synergy, the Macroscope works better when many beings are coordinated on a single task. This requires a leap of faith. You have to be willing to believe that the Macroscope is an interface to an objective reality: that billions of beings are trying to help. The more you can believe that as an objective truth, the more effective the Macroscope ritual can be.

If you can bite off mere prayer as psychic action, then everybody praying to God is visible as a helper. Billions of Christians, Muslims, Hindus and others light up. If you think that a meditator counts, Buddhists beyond count appear. These are the big pools of energy in the Macroscope system. But a lot of it is very undirected and uncoordinated. That's where you come in. Visualize being allocated an energy pool: a slab of potential energy from these undirected good will pools. Who allocates you this energy? A long question. You can believe in Buddhas or Angels and it all works the same.

As a focus for these undirected prayers for a better world, re-attune. See the places with all of this extra energy you can focus it to intervene.

Repeat as necessary until done. The process can take on a life of its own once you really let go into it—round after round of coordinate, attune, intervene. You can burn out—if you tap into deeper levels of the Macroscope ritual, you can find yourself feeling like an extension of the Buddhas or an

Angel among Angels or various other Archetypal Divine Forms. It can be highly addictive, so limit your exposure to what your life can sustain.

5. Dismiss

When you're done with your "shift," dismiss the Macroscope. Feel the sphere dissolve into your aura, expanding into the thirty to fifty-foot radius sphere around your body. By dissolving the Macroscope into your aura over time, you'll become attuned to Macroscopic Reality, i.e. the reality of these energy currents, intervention opportunities, etc. You can begin to feel like a member of an enormous team, all helping and cooperating to try and make the world a better place. It's a little like joining a secret society or something... those on the Staff... the conscious crew-members of Spaceship Earth.

6. Banish

You can't go leaving the Macroscope in your aura unbanished, or you'll find weird things accumulating. Once your aura has absorbed it, Banish. Hard. Let the entire model go completely and return to your regular life.

As a magician, the Macroscope as a ritual symbol has a lot more going on than appears at first sight. Firstly, the banishings before and after use make this a lot more than a New Age ceremony—they prepare a space in which the magician has indicated they are serious about this as magical work. That intention, and the purification of the space, can actually allow the consciousness of the magician to purify to the point where their Will can become aligned with the Praxis Mundi—the Will of the World. The Macroscope can be seen as an interface to the Divine Intelligence of the Earth (why yes, there is a Hebrew name for that... and they use it a lot in the Golden Dawn rituals!). After all, all of those displays and maps showing where things are... that stuff isn't really "inside" the magician. If there's any good info there, it's likely coming from "outside." Whatever that means!

– *Shivanath*

2012: The Return of Quetzalcoatl
Daniel Pinchbeck
Tarcher, 2006

Daniel Pinchbeck's *2012: The Return of Quetzalcoatl* is a continuation of the adventures he described in *Breaking Open the Head*. As a fan of that previous account of his "psychedelic journey into the heart of contemporary shamanism," I have been very curious to find out what Pinchbeck has been up to since his initation into the worlds of ayahusca, DMT, iboga and psilocybin.

The first half sets a good pace and is built up on ideas and experiences that are more or less canonical and well-documented, and it is thrilling to see them all lined up in order. Pinchbeck has done his homework and explores areas that many self-conscious psychonauts tend to avoid; for example, while lingering on the subject of crop-circles, he avoids trying to prove or disprove the phenomena and instead interprets our mass-rejection or mystification of them as a tender spot in our culture that exposes how tenaciously humans are clinging to an understanding of the universe that is unraveling out from under us. His vision of these last few years leading up to the end of the Mayan calendar—and life as we currently know it—is potent and infectious, and I began to make a list in my head of friends that I ought to lend this book to when I finished it.

However, as the book marches on it becomes evident that there are undeniable problems with not only his theories, but his motivations as well. The dissolution of his family life (due in no small part to the adventures he endures) coincides neatly with an impairment in his focus. While anyone with a magical bent to their thinking is able to catch the synchronicities and cosmic giggles that propel one forward through life, few people magnify those coincidences to global significance and apply them to the fates of everyone around them. Pinchbeck is honest about calling himself out when he senses his insecurity or baser instincts polluting his quest, and then his keen self-analysis eventually leads him back on track again. For every one of those moments, however, the reader will pick out two more in which Pinchbeck leaps from conclusion to conclusion with frighteningly subjective abandon, feats which no adept would ever perform without a firm grasp on oneself and one's limitations. That the ordeals resulting from his sloppiness ultimately lead to Pinchbeck's receiving a profound annunciation (from the great Quetzalcoatl itself) is cold comfort indeed: by the time this transmission occurs, the reader's head is likely to be so sore from repeated smackings that it can't possibly accept Pinchbeck's revelation as more authoritative than anything one might cook up on one's own, given enough bark-scrapings and jungle voyages. And by the time Pinchbeck begins handing over the bullhorn to prophets whom even he considers to be of dubious value, such as Dreamspell Calendar inventor José Arguilles, mental-health breaks between chapters become necessary.

With so many people in the world clamoring for Apocalypse, it can be hard to avoid playing that game. This book pulls you into it, at first calmly inviting you to play, then later begging and demanding that you finish what you started. There were many points where I had to put the book down for a couple of days so I could fairly weigh his ideas; his background matches my own in so many ways that it was easy to get swept up in agreement with his lyrical voice and his incredible citations from countless scientists, thinkers and miscellaneous holy folks—but his book does not hold up to the level of scrutiny that he holds his role models to. In laying the book aside and trying to follow his arguments to their logical conclusions, I found that they seemed to dissolve without his voice there to energetically perpetuate them. I began to see this book, however bold and inspiring, as the product of a very neurotic and conflicted person. By the end, when Pinchbeck finds himself struggling to shake himself free from the influence of Santo Daime practitioners and New Age healers, his theorizing seems almost frantic. However, I will say that my own worldview feels very sharpened by reading it—having to constantly dis- and re-assemble my own philosophy before Pinchbeck's dark mirror was strenuous exercise that left me refreshed and exhausted by turns.

I actually feel pretty concerned for the guy, because I believe the transmission he's been given by Quetzalcoatl is legitimate, and that his work is significant and enlightening, even ennobling—to him. Unfortunately, being a writer, he is oriented toward broadcasting everything he thinks and experiences and projecting it onto the world at large, which leads to not only some grievous errors in literary judgment, but also inters him in a self-made prison of "prophecy." Without his ability and drive to write and deliver his prophecy to the masses he sees as teetering on the brink of Apocalypse, he'd probably be enjoying an incredible period of enlightenment. However, without the impulse to include and save us all somehow, I doubt he would have ever set out on this journey to begin with. Because of it, he experiences the most intimately documented magical breakdown I've ever come across. By the end of the book, at the point where he's hoping the reader will finally be prepared to absorb the significance of Quetzalcoatl's message, his words practically spasm on the page.

To offer contrast, not long afterward I re-read the end of Alan Moore's comic *Promethea*. The last fifth of the series depicts the Apocalypse as a massive, inevitable unifying shift in consciousness, using artwork and fictional characters to illustrate almost exactly the same ideas that Pinchbeck delivers. I was struck by the differences. Despite drawing from many of the same paradigms and sources, the work of Moore's team is just plainly superior—more succinct, gentler, less subjective and more challenging than frightening. It is also more persuasive and more believable, despite being embedded within a comic book. Moore makes the Apocalypse game seem like an unavoidable fact of existence in our modern world, but one that the individual is free to conceive of however they will; in addition, Moore lays out sketches of the Eastern and Western magical traditions, giving would-be voyagers a leg up in discovering original prophecies of their own. Pinchbeck starts out with the same idea, and the first two hundred pages of *2012* is authentic as only an autobiography can be, but as he presses on and his inexperience and insecurity begin to catch up with him, ultimately the only way he can reconcile them is to imagine that we are all in the same boat as he is—and it happens to be one where his help is needed to steer. With all due respect, I'd rather go over Niagara Falls in a barrel.

I'd still recommend Pinchbeck's first book to almost anyone, especially to those taking tentative steps toward exploring worlds just outside our own, but the second book seems only recommendable as a warning of what an individual will go through if one takes the path of initiation without having done the necessary work on oneself over a natural amount of time. I'm grateful to have read this, but I'll have reservations about picking up his next one—that is, if it turns out that they are still printing books in the years leading up to the great Arrival.

A mystic may swim through the same water that a madman drowns in, but if his connection to this world or to his will is not strong, then he will also be crushed by the same gravity that everyday human slobs effortlessly walk their tiny dogs through. In racing through a lifetime's worth of initiations in just eight years, this seems to me what Pinchbeck is running up against; in the closing of the book he leaves an uncertain image of what his life is now or what he plans to do with his hard-earned prophecy. He is as human an Apocalyptic prophet as one could dream up, a neurotic New Yorker struggling to stamp out willful ignorance and self-obsession on both a personal and global level.

– *Tom Blunt*

An Age for Lucifer: Predatory Spirituality and the Quest for Godhood
Robert C. Tucker
Holmes Publishing Group, 1999

Excellent book on predatory dynamics worth a hundred cheap occult books on "the left-hand path," recommended to me by Richard Metzger. The (late) author spent the 1980s researching claims of Satanic abuse and came to the conclusion that there's no such thing. His supplementary thesis, however, is that of a Satanic abuser "archetype," or, as he puts it, a new phase of human evolution, a predatory human being whose singular drive is to devour.

Tucker describes a "religion of devouring," a de facto new religion of our age, whose adherents, who he calls Luciferans, continually attempt to possess and consume the spiritual and life energy of others in order to become more than human, the final impulse being that of devouring and supplanting God. This is an excellent description of the true "sinister path," those who make their way in the world by struggling to gain control over others. He cites corporate CEOs, New Age tyros, politicians and pyramid climbers of all types as being exemplars of the Luciferan, though he is clear that it is an archetype that can be found in all walks of life. I thought specifically of the mass craze over Robert Greene's *The 48 Laws of Power* and *The Art of Seduction*, those most modern of books on black magick.

The Luciferan model of spirituality is the Darwinian and the impulse is to Eat. As Tucker says, "a new human predator has appeared, and is learning how to thrive by exploiting other humans in various ways—physically, emotionally, cognitively and spiritually. Although human in form and origin, the new human is evolving. As with all other beings, its core impulse must be to survive by accumulating personal energy and power through predation. Unlike most other predators, however, the new human must expand the predatory field to include not just plants and animals, but the life energies of unevolved lower-order human beings as well."

If one accepts Tucker's conclusions, it becomes hard indeed not to see the entire world as a predatory hierarchy. Hierarchy, of course, is the calling card of Hell—notice all those ranks of spirits in the Medieval grimoires (although one suspects that if the *Goetia* were re-written today, Hell would more closely resemble an endless, ineffective corporate bureaucracy than a feudal demense). Much of the religious, occult and New Age worlds, for instance, are unveiled as massive soul-energy snatch-and-grab operations, although that should have been apparent anyway.

The problem, however, is that once accepting the lizard-brain reality of the Luciferans, it's hard to escape. Much of Tucker's book reads not so much as an objective critique as it does wishful thinking, creative willing of a scenario into reality and, in many places, as an open invitation to the predatory and Luciferan world.

As a "reality tunnel" in the Wilsonian sense, then, Luciferianism has little to offer but the loss of one's humanity. To worship at the Church of Devouring is to live in a world defined solely by devouring. "Don't play cards with Satan," the singer Daniel Johnston once said, "he'll deal you an awful hand." How many Faustian bargains have *you* seen work? After all, to live as a predator, you have to accept one minor detail: that you, too, will one day be eaten.

–Jason Louv

Voice of the Fire
Alan Moore
Top Shelf Productions, 2004

In his postscript to *The Name of the Rose*, Umberto Eco notes that so many diverse cultures have invested the rose with significance for so many centuries, that as a symbol, it has become practically void of meaning—but what is the metaphoric weight of a single flower to that of one of the four elements? In the course of *Voice of the Fire*, the element's true nature proves to be ever-evasive yet constantly radiant, at times even brilliant.

Originally published in 1996 in the UK, comics writer Alan Moore's first novel has recently been given its American debut by Top Shelf. Forsaking a continual narrative and spanning some 6,000 years, the novel consists of twelve chapters, all of which are set in or around the English city of Northampton during the month of November. As Northampton has been Moore's hometown for the duration of his life, and November is the month of his birth, *Voice of the Fire* can be taken as a piece of "site-specific" writing in which Moore seeks to get a firmer grasp on the history of the city and his own life. He goes about this psychogeographical experiment by delving into the strata of local legend and history from 4000 BCE to 1995, picking up uncanny details and strange connections along the way.

The origins of this unusual novel most certainly lie in Moore's 1994 decision to become a magician (think Aleister Crowley or Austin Osman Spare), and *Voice of the Fire* is one of his first works to directly reflect the impact of that choice. Although it is impossible to summarize Moore's complex beliefs in a single statement, it is useful to note that for Moore, magic is a way to explore questions about the nature of creativity: What is happening to the artist when he is creating art? What kind of sources are being tapped into during the act of creation?

However, since the history of magic and witchcraft is also the history of secrecy and persecution, the novel presents an array of characters trying to understand both their experiences with the supernatural as well as the reactions of the people around them. The encounters range from the comparably mundane to the utterly fantastic—from a fisherman who discovers that the whole population of his village has disappeared without a trace, to witches who conjure up imps to do their bidding.

In his best comics, Moore combines fascinating stories with complex structural arrangements, always careful that his formal innovation remains a crucial aspect of the entire work—readability and coherence are never sacrificed for the sake of a clever gimmick. *Watchmen*, for instance, uses shifting time frames and parallel narratives, gathering momentum by simultaneously developing numerous related stories across space and time. *From Hell* revisits the Jack the Ripper murders by drawing from a stockpile of relatively ordinary historical characters and occurrences and fusing them into patterns of great narrative force.

The skill for marrying emotional resonance with formal fireworks survives the change of medium intact. Although he joggles time frames and bases many of his stories upon elaborate premises, Moore's main fascination in *Voice of the Fire*, rests upon our human conception of the world—how it has become increasingly more familiar to us, while at the same time retaining an innate sense of mystery.

The first two stories, which are also the longest ones in the book, introduce the overall intent of the work. In "Hob's Hog," a young boy learns for the first time that shamans like the Hob-man truly exist, their aura of power derived from a place outside the normal boundaries of the world:

> *She is now say of stick-head men, and of they saying-path. [...] Say she, for make this saying-path they stick-head men is want of a strongness and a queer glean that is not hind-whiles in of they. A strongness that come from other world, in neath of dirt, where is they spirit walk.*

The second story, called "The Cremation Fields," features a young trickster who manages to get herself close to a dying "cunning-man." While patiently waiting for the old man to reveal the location of his treasure, she listens to his troubles in persuading his child to accept the duties of the shaman. The opinions of the cunning-man's son go on to show that magic has been old-fashioned for a terribly long time—even in 2500 BCE:

Garn will not take up the task, and sets a face against his duty. Says he's not a cunning-man and makes work as metal-monger, which he thinks a craft more fitted to our time. He says he does not care to know the old and secret ways. We cannot talk save that we quarrel, so we do not talk at all.

By suggesting that life's mysteries far outweigh the accumulated knowledge of any human being, Hob and layman alike, the conclusion of the story sets the tone for the tales to come. In this light, *Voice of the Fire* becomes a series of initiations, twelve licks of the flame occurring at the same time.

Despite the obvious changes in character and incident, such a structure still contains the potential for monotony; but Moore is attuned to this danger, and consequentially varies the tempo and texture of his narrative. His prose is both rich and precise, largely rid of the purple excess found in his early comics such as *Swamp Thing*. Still, Moore is a passionate wordsmith who enjoys the richness of language – whether drawing together an extended mesh of metaphors or describing the minute details of his setting, his forceful style can approach sensory bombardment; a quality that owes something to the prose of Iain Sinclair. But even if Moore may be a spendthrift of words, he's far closer to a lavisher than a wastrel. For example, here is how the narrator of "The Head of Diocletian," a Roman official who has been sent to Britain to investigate cases of coin forgery, gives his first impressions of London and its denizens:

When I came to Londinium a half-year since, I thought it hunched and squalid, breeding ugly humours, pestilences in amongst the jetties and the narrow yards, pooled urine yellowing there where the cobbles dip. The locals, hulking Trinovante fishermen or shifty Cantiaci traders, had a pleasing insularity, despite their sullenness. They kept amongst their own kind and made little fuss, yet fresh from home I thought the city Hades; they its fiends and chimaera.

In another chapter, a pair of witches are being burned alive in the year 1705; one of them relates their shared history, and reaches an epiphany of sorts:

Beneath the base of every flame there is a still, clear absence; a mysterious gap between the death of substance and the birth of light, with time itself suspended in this void of transformation, this pause between two elements. I understand it now, that there has only ever been one fire, that blazed before the world began and shall not be put out until the world is done. I see my fellows in the flame, the unborn and the dead.

Though the general atmosphere of the novel verges between dread and transcendence, humor plays a major role in the proceedings, sometimes even taking the center stage. This is certainly the case with "Confessions of a Mask," in which a head on a spike receives a new neighbor. "Did you know, Sir, there is something in your eye?" he, a freshly decapitated head, asks his more careworn companion, whose laconic reply is: "Yes, I did. Unless I am mistaken, it's a lump of coal."

Voice of the Fire aligns itself with Moore's other magical "works" of the period, particularly his performances with the grandiosely named *The Moon and Serpent Grand Egyptian Theater of Marvels*. As he makes evident through these works, the essential assumption behind magic is that an overlay of meaningful symbolism can be assigned to the world. These symbols in turn can be used to build up a conceptual structure which somehow yields results that couldn't be reached as easily (or at all) by other means. Like religion, philosophy, and other systems of thought, magic tries to strike a balance between so-called reality and its kaleidoscopic distortions. But the thing that seems to separate magic (or at least certain types of magical thinking) from most other models of thought is its willingness to revise its foundations and practices. Magic revels in the complexities of human experience, and doesn't consider all that ragtag data in the back of our heads as a nuisance. Rather, magic welcomes the distortions and paradoxes that form such a considerable part of the human consciousness, and tries to turn these notions into something truly worthwhile.

In numerous interviews over the past several years, Moore has stressed the close relationship he perceives as existing between magic and art. In fact, Moore sees the two as completely intermingled, and this is precisely what is interesting about his writing, the public manifestations of his magical thinking. In Moore's recent work, one individual's flexible set of tools for dealing with the relation between reality and consciousness produces a series of elegant signs and symbols, an artistic clockwork connecting the individual to the universe. A working becomes a work of art, and the unsuspecting reader is none the wiser.

By telling twelve tales centered around the element of fire, Moore has embraced the myriad potential meanings it evokes in the reader's imagination. After all, it's just the matter of a jump-cut from the fire beneath a cauldron to the burning pyre of a witch hunt, or from the purifying white light of Pentecost to the tormenting flames of hell. Indeed, this contrary pairing of the extreme states of purification and torment seems to be something that Moore is aiming at in *Voice of the Fire*: to relay in prose the white heat of life.

– *Ismo Santala*

It's no surprise, given the current episteme of authenticity through "extremes"—and I use this word with all the bungee-cord, *Fear Factor* baggage entailed—that we find ourselves in the midst of a full-on tryptamine chic. In addition to the promise of dropping out of local space-time continua, of communing with a network of pre-anthropoid, auto-corrective jungle intelligences, ayahuasca and its ilk fold you into the club with a built-in hazing process—to wit, you get to dry-heave and lose control of your bowels for an hour or so before, perhaps during, and maybe even after your communion with Aztec death gods in some inter-dimensional air-pocket.

On top of all this glamour, the tryptamine family holds the allure of being an elite commodity within the traditional dealer-user circuit of weed, coke, uppers, downers and so forth. You really have to know the right people. My own DMT-clan experience, until last July, had been of mail-order scores of obscurely sfumato legalities, ground-up perennials smoked in bongs, and utter disappointment. It was with very low expectations, then, that I guzzled down a syringe filled with a dose of the wholly synthetic 5-MeO-AMT suspended in Captain Morgan's rum—"a very reliable solvent," the Guy insisted. In addition to having that re-assuring, Erowid-nerd demeanor these grey-zone "research chemical" people always seem to have, this part-time dealer moonlighted, or daylighted, as a subway operator for the NYC MTA, setting the whole trip up in a suggestive Casey Jones framework that was not lost on me.

It's hard to say whether the rum did forfend a chemical breakdown—of the AMT varietal, not myself—as the stuff had been sitting in my crisper drawer since the New Year (it had been purchased from Casey along with some other alphabet-soup research chemical and a few tabs of crystal meth shellacked with some vaguely empathetic compound; in the prevailing lingo, "ecstasy"). Given that I was flying to California for good in a month, the clock was ticking on this very liquid, maybe even controlled, substance, and hell, what else was I going to do six days into the sweltering daze of the embarrassing Queens summer blackout, the final *coup de theatre* that concluded my sojourn in the City? And so it was under the guidance of book-lamp that I dosed myself two fingers of the tragically un-hooky 5-Me0-AMT and Captain's and hunkered down amidst the cat hair and city dust for what I hoped to be a cheap Friday date with whatever entities this shit would cozen down.

So was my losing streak with the tryp-trip finally set right? Well, surely did I puke and shit, the latter in densities and coral shades that only psychedelics and malt liquor can secure. Check. No real conversations with angels or devils *stricto sensu*, although there was a quite otherworldly conference call with hostesses of a Metairie sub/dom houseboy party. In between maintenance trips to the toilet, tethered to my 99 cent store emergency land-line, I listened as, several states away, an unscreened slave-boy—a hasty last-minute replacement who turned out to be a halfway house schizoid junkie—cast aside all protocols of proper servitude and tried to mix with his betters. Had I been sober, would I have so agilely processed this arcane, darkly sybaritic rite transmitted in disembodied form, as bustiered matrons very literally kicked their errant slave down two flights of front steps for all to see, buck naked, into the small hours of Big Easy night? While I was never properly evicted from my body—sadly, not so my friend down South, apropos of her landlord—I felt what I would call a greater fluency in bilocation, the miracle of which modern telecommunications both allow and make us take for granted. Time was dilated, though not to the extent you get with your stronger LSD, but enough that I set out for my Saturday afternoon appointment at eight a.m., at which point I discovered that I was unable to ride a bicycle, which for me is really saying something. Several hours later, the AMT-spirits guided my wobbly legs through the mostly powerless blocks of Queens to another stereoscopic vista of places and times: a rave had been staged in the middle of the day, in the courtyard of an art museum, starring one of the pioneers of 1980s acid house. Surely this all must mean *something*, I thought as my sleep-depped frame lean-danced to a DJ set I'd had a ticket to see in Detroit, fifteen years earlier, only to have it cancelled and future-transmitted to a perhaps even more desolate setting, now reveled to with the glowing interest of delay-relay. Surely.

So, no, the wisdom of the Amazon did not feed me with the Gnostic riches of its root work—and matters of synthetic proxy aside, it's well that it did not. Synthetics have their own sympathetic storehouses, cities their own psycho-historical networks. What business do I have running off to suck vines in South America when it's in the concrete jungle that I live, where the competitively dank, telluric tendrils of the MTA route to me an elixir to convene with this dislocated, shorted-out landscape on its own terms? In this sense, my experience was as appropriately authentic, organic, and I would even say *macrobiotic*, as I could have asked for.

And I might never touch tryptamine or New York soil again.

Two thumbs up.

– Shaun Frenté

"MY DARK PLACES" (AFTERWORD TO THE 2014 EDITION)

JASON LOUV

This book scares the shit out of me.

There. I said it.

Ultraculture Journal One is the product of an extreme mindset, and an even more extreme time. I assembled it in 2007, after hauling myself out of the worst two years of my life. I was twenty-six years old, living in Prospect Heights, Brooklyn, putting it all together in the very, very early dark ages of print-on-demand technology; I'd just moved back from Vancouver, British Colombia after being very unceremoniously thrown out of the country by the Canadian authorities.

Previous to this unfortunate border run-in, I'd been living in the suburban outskirts of Vancouver, more than halfway insane and convinced that my entire reality was being used as a weapon against me for my self-perceived crimes-against-existence.

Prior to *that*, I'd been working as a full-time editor at the then-infamous Disinformation Company, a publisher that specialized in putting out the kind of counterculture material that I had taken *just a bit too seriously*. I'd released a book called *Generation Hex*, a compilation of writing by young anarchist occultists, the type of person I fancied myself to be.

Generation Hex was a magick spell to "find the others," that old hackneyed saying of Timothy Leary's, and it sure worked. I suddenly found myself transformed from being a shy, numbingly awkward, intelligent, moody post-adolescent and into the Dark Shaman of the Apocalypse, a punk politician for mass consciousness change. Unfortunately, the mask wasn't me. It was a construction, a live-action role-playing game that suddenly got very, very real. I found myself totally surrounded by occult people—not the most balanced, grounded or healthy lot in the world—playing "that guy," the Upstart Magician—not the most balanced, grounded or healthy persona in the world.

Throw a lot of psychedelics and rougher drugs into the mix, the harsh poverty and grind of being a young writer in New York and, finally, an ill-conceived move away from New York and my support network (however severe the living conditions) for a girl I was convinced was "the one," and you have the recipe for a very, very hard early-twenties learning experience. With one added difference: Magick isn't a game. At least it had *stopped* being a game, and become all too real.

I found myself surrounded by all sorts of—yes, colorful—but very deeply maladjusted people. Voudon houngans; Hindu demagogues; multiple hierarchical and controlling occult orders; people one slip away from becoming professional occult assassins for the mob (yes, this exists). I had moved in to my own personal hell-realm hallucination, a mish-mash of comic books, role-playing games and enough *real* occult hoodoo bullshit, surrounded by enough people who *truly* took it all *very* seriously for the whole scene to quickly become utterly terrifying—at a soul level.

In the end, what bailed me out was basic common sense, remembering that there were a lot of people who loved me for me despite the nonsense I had gotten myself wrapped up in and, most of all, the ability to finally tell the truth to myself instead of spending my time convincing myself how hardcore occult I was. As Philip K. Dick said, "reality is that which, when you stop believing in it, doesn't go away." And in a way, the most important "magick" of all was finding out what the thing that doesn't go away is.

Not the arcane Qabalistic charts, not the mind games, the NLP, the spooky clothing, the spooky way of talking-like-you-know-secret-things, the drama, the freaky-deaky sex magick… no, what's left is *you*, and the rest falls off like the scab it can now be seen as, the scab from your own unresolved wounding.

This present book is the record of what happened next (and my article "A Grammary" here seems completely disordered to me now, a giant infodump of information that I had not yet properly processed and contextualized; my views of magic now are, thank God, so calm, simple and elegant in comparison). The book is also, by-and-large, about the Tantric and non-dual "enlightenment" traditions of India, because that was the reality I decided to move into after letting go of the maze-like nowheres-ville of left-handed chaos magick, Hermeticism, Neuro-Linguistic Programming and Voudon—a.k.a. *siddhi chasing*, nearly all of it, though these days I have a newfound appreciation of Western magick from a more balanced, grounded perspective.

Most specifically, the book focuses on the deeply convoluted and factitious Nath Sampradaya, an ancient renunciate tradition of dope-smoking Sadhus, who rejected the caste system of India to wander as naked, itinerant beggars, enmeshed totally in meditation in wild and lonely places, completely dependent on the hospitality of the people around them for sustenance. True anarchists and magicians, who had rejected the life script and personality that had been given to them in order to become totally free from bondage, who covered themselves in ashes in order to symbolize that they had already died, at least to the world of *samsara* or social illusion.

This was an idea that deeply appealed to me—and a lineage that I formally entered, after a year's sojourn as a Sufi dervish to jump-start my heart—because I felt like I'd burnt myself to a crisp with magick, that there was no way out, no hope, and the only option was to essentially start life over. Bear in mind that this was also halfway through the second Bush administration, and it was easy to feel that way about the world, too. (Still is, sometimes.) So start life over I did, with none of the old crap left except for that raw non-dual awareness of Self. No hoodoo, no tricks, no bluffing, no nonsense.

Shortly thereafter I found myself with nothing left to my name except a trash bag full of clothes and a Nepali *trishul*, a magical weapon sacred to the god Shiva—Lord of Yoga, Lord of the Naths—as well as a printout of the true secret cipher key to the *Book of the Law*. There are people in the world who might have murdered for that printout. I left it on the G train to Queens, as a symbolic gesture that I no longer needed that old occult nonsense, took the trishul and moved on to start my new life.

I got a job in advertising, on Madison Avenue. I reinvented myself, did yoga, meditated, spent some time with Hindu gurus, focused on chasing girls instead of chasing the dragon of magick. Instead of my previous enamorment with the occult, I became enraged by it, and spent a lot of time trying to talk people younger than me out of involvement with it, playing the all-knowing guru at the all-knowing age of twenty-six.

Then, just when I had begun to put myself back together, Lady Jaye Breyer P-Orridge—a Santeria high priestess and half of the Breyer P-Orridge pandrogyne who, with Genesis Breyer P-Orridge, I considered (and still consider) my root guru—died tragically. Here was real death. Real ashes.

The ideas in this book were the ones that were occupying my mind, the ones that carried me through that time—enlightenment, renunciation, samsara, karma, dharma, seeing-through-it-all. Though you never really see through it all, of course. You just find yourself in a new illusion, a new game, wearing a new mask and new clothes.

But I liked being an anonymous nobody, covered in ashes. The pressure was off. It was, all in all, not a bad way to wait out the end of the Bush years.

I recently read a book called *Shadows on the Path* by Abdi Assadi, an acupuncturist and therapist who spent decades going through his own painful spiritual journey only to find that while the fancy, overhyped techniques of "spirituality" gave him an inflated sense of at-one-ment with the universe, they didn't heal his personality, or his shadow. That work, of course, has to be done on its own—you can't count on the light at the end of the tunnel to fix you.

The book probably would have been a good one for me to read at the time—these were the struggles I was facing, first attempting to heal my own shadow by plunging head-first into it and dredging the depths of demonology and drug use, and afterwards simply attempting to *shut it off* with Vedantic mysticism and a series of messy, boundary-free, unhealthy (because I was not healthy) romantic relationships with New Age healers and Lightworkers that I expected to mother me. Neither approach fully worked. It was only later, as I entered my thirties, sobered up, began to settle down into the functional routine of adult work life and entered therapy (the Reichian version) that I began to truly do the work of healing the personality.

But back to the present volume: When I originally published *Ultraculture Journal*, I announced, perhaps hastily, that I planned to make it the first in a series of six, one a year up till 2012 (that might have been a bit of an anticlimax, in retrospect), as a kind of update of Aleister Crowley's *Equinox*.

However, it was the process of actually becoming an integrated and healthy human being and functional member of society, instead of simply shouting, loudly, about spiritual techniques—actually stress-testing the material until a workable fusion emerged, capable of actually producing a healthy adult—that consumed my time, instead of simply promoting systems I had not fully mastered, with an authority I had not fully earned.

I spent years cleaning up after what I perceived to be my mistakes, mistakes that were probably just inevitable learning experiences and universal hard knocks, looking for karmic absolution at the feet of Hindu gurus and, later, back in the Himalayan mountains at 13,000 feet drinking *bhang* tea in ancient shrines dedicated to Shiva, Ganesh and Ram, seeking to purge the lingering darkness of my years in the occult. I gave it all up. I moved to Los Angeles, worked day jobs, cultivated relationships and took care of the business of daily life, slowly letting go of the burden of cosmic madness.

And thank God.

It took me six years to be able to write about any of this publicly, and with any kind of clarity. Until 2012, I was *terrified* to write about magick in public again. I didn't want to dredge up old conflicts, re-open old wounds or do any further damage to my career. But I am inextricably linked with the Work, for better or worse. And Ultraculture—an idea I had when I was sixteen—will not leave me be. Through a series of hedging moves in my life, I found myself forced to take that Work up again, and in 2012 re-started Ultraculture as a website—more to confront my own fears than anything else, and show the universe that I wasn't scared or superstitious anymore, no longer scared of being myself, as bizarre as I had become. Because no matter how much others tried to taint magick for me, or knock me down for it, or disillusion me from it, *I love magick.*

The real magick. Not all the evil convoluted satanic pedo horseshit. My magick, my connection to the universe, as it started: an exploration into the mystery of existence, an exercise in living fully and being free. Free from control, free from the mind and the ego, free from limitations. *Real magick.*

So here I present to you, once more, my problem child. And may you, hopefully, learn more from my mistakes than anything else, and attain to Peace, Freedom and Happiness in this lifetime, my wish for all beings, sentient and insentient.

–Jason Louv, Los Angeles, 2014

SOME TECHNICAL POINTS ON THE 2014 REISSUE OF THIS BOOK

The original edition of *Ultraculture Journal One* (published at Lulu) contained two essays that have been excised from this edition.

The first is the essay "David Bowie and the Occult" by the Swiss O.T.O. researcher Peter-R. Koenig. Though he initially gave approval for its publication, he afterwards requested it be removed in order to save it for a later book. You can read the original at his Ordo Templi Orientis Phenomenon Web site at www.parareligion.ch/bowie.htm

The second is the essay "The Man With the Tattered Smile" by "Mordant Carnival," a Northern Tradition practitioner who requested her essay (about working with the Norse god Loki) be withdrawn. That request has been honored on republication of the book.

Perhaps fittingly, I believe that the excisions of these two essays makes for a more focused, purer form of the book. It is, in its present form, much more thematically cohesive than the original edition, keeping a tighter focus on Eastern Tantra and the highly aligned current of Thee Temple ov Psychick Individuals (of which I include the essays by Brion Gysin and Jhonn Balance). It is my hope that this edition stands not only as a record of the occult underground but as an important document in the study of the development of Eastern religious traditions in the West—which it is.

CONTRIBUTOR INFORMATION

Jhonn Balance, 1962-2004, born in Mansfield, England, co-founder of "sidereal soul" industrial group Coil with Peter Christopherson, collaborator with Psychic TV, Current 93, Nurse With Wound, Death in June, Nine Inch Nails and others. Will be remembered as a natural visionary and shaman in the same way that Austin Osman Spare is now considered.

Joel Biroco is an enigma. He is the classic model of a person who will be famous when they are dead. He has written every day of his life since the age of twenty-three. He is now forty-eight and lives in London. He has published under more names than he can remember. He has just finished his third novel, writing as opposed to reading. The first two got burnt. Apparently, he is an occultist of international repute. He doesn't fuck about. He has a website at www.biroco.com.

Prince Charming. I am the soon to be notorious acrobat/nude dancer/poet/playwright who will scandalize sex-obsessed Hollywood during the the summer of 2007. I will haunt Hollywood's hotel lobbies, nightclubs and casinos, radiantly naked except for an elegant sable wrap, a pet spider monkey hanging from my neck and a silver cod-piece packed with cocaine. Multi-talented, I see no boundaries between my personal life and my taboo-shattering performances. As such, I will be the sexiest warlord in the universe. www.prince-charming.net

Ira Cohen (born February 3, 1935) is an American poet, publisher, photographer and filmmaker born in New York City to deaf parents. During the 1960s, he traveled to Tangier, where he published the magazine *GNAOUA*, featuring William S. Burroughs, Brion Gysin, Jack Smith, and Irving Rosenthal. He also published *The Hashish Cookbook* under the name of Panama Rose. He continued to travel until 1980, when he returned to New York City, where he now resides.

Elijah. You are all ABOMINATION! ABOMINATION!! ABOMINATION!!!

Ganesh Baba, formally known as Shri Mahant Swami Ganeshananda Saraswati (or Giri) and informally as the Psychedelic Swami, carried two usually distinct lineages, the Lahiri line of Kriya yoga, as taught by Shri Lahiri Mahasaya, Shri Sanyal Mahasaya, Shri Tripura Charan Devsharma, and Shri Swami Sivananda; and the charas-smoking Naga line, through the Dasnami order of the Alaknath Akhara in Bareilly. Born in about 1890 in Orissa and educated in Calcutta at the height of the British Raj, he spoke perfect Victorian English and took pride in weaving contemporary thought with the ancient teachings to which he was heir. Ganesh Baba lived in India and Nepal most of his life, but spent several years in the United States and in France. He died in 1987.

Brion Gysin, 1916-1986, born in Canada, expelled from Surrealist Group in Paris by Breton, lived extensively in Morocco, rediscovered Cut-Up method and helped create Dreamachine along with Ian Sommerville. Painter, writer, Adept of ferocious import.
enig

Lamda is a writer, musician, short filmmaker and magickal practitioner. His current projects include public art performances and scoring film soundtracks. His new short film *Flowers & Smoke* (an attempt at ultrahuman contact through the use of flowers and smoke) is soon to be available to the public. (www.aceofdiscs.com)

Lalitanath. I born I lived I soon to die.

Jason Louv lives in New York and is well-traveled on all planes. He edited *Generation Hex* (Disinformation, 2005) and the forthcoming *Thee Psychick Bible* with Genesis P-Orridge. He eats dark forces for breakfast, and is emotionally unavailable, but totally worth it.

Dave Lowe was born in New York City and grew up near San Francisco. He has lived and worked in Australia, Thailand, Vietnam and the Maldives. Along the way, Dave has collected a varied array of encounters and experiences, from Africa, India and Asia, which form *The Lowe Road*, his first travel book. When he's not writing, he's working in marketing, and is currently based in South East Asia. He met the editor of this book on a train in India.

Hans Plomp, born in Amsterdam in 1944, one of the nozems associated with Provo, noted poet, author of more than twenty books, founder of Ruigoord Cultural Free Zone, and founding member of the Amsterdam Balloon Company. He lives in Amsterdam.

Genesis Breyer P-Orridge. STOP IT! Stop being possessed by characters written by others. Rebuild your SELF from the FOUND UP! Change the way to perceive and change all memory. http://www.genesisp-orridge.com

Johnny Templar is buried in the tomb of Christian Rosenkreutz along with a portable DVD player.

Shivanath is a representative of the ancient Nath Sampradaya, possibly a bad example of a human being but a fairly decent little saint, for those of debauched tastes and low standards. His day job is rewriting reality in the environmental, humanitarian and military domain for clients as diverse as you if something causes you to get evacuated from your house, the purple circle, the hexagon and the little tree in the corner.

ARTICLE HISTORIES

"A Interview With Monica Dechen Gyalmo" by Prince Charming was written especially for this volume.

"The Amoral Way of the Wizard" by Lalitanath is published in print for the first time in this volume.

"Are You a Skin?" by Johnny Templar was written especially for this volume.

"Black Mass" by Jason Louv was written especially for this volume.

"Causal Cosmogeny and Cosmology" by Ganesh Baba is published in print for the first time in this volume.

"The Day I Went to Fetch the Acids" by Joel Biroco is published in print for the first time in this volume.

"Eternalicious" by Shivanath originally appeared in a self-published print edition.

"General Order Master" by Genesis Breyer P-Orridge first appeared, in part, in *The Wild Palms Reader*, St. Martin's Press, 1993. It appears here in its unexpurgated form for the first time.

"A Grammary" by Jason Louv was written especially for this volume.

"Kings With Straw Mats" by Ira Cohen was originally published in *Ellipsis*, Vol. 5, No. 5, 1996, and will also be published in *Ira Cohen: A Dissolute Life Spent in the Service of Allah*, forthcoming from Autonomedia.

"I Married My-Self" by Lamda is published in print for the first time in this volume.

"Notes of an Alchemist" by Ira Cohen will be republished in *Ira Cohen: A Dissolute Life Spent in the Service of Allah*, forthcoming from Autonomedia.

"Paint Me as a Dead Soul" by Jhonn Balance is reproduced by permission of the Jhonn Balance Estate and is published in print for the first time in this volume. Jhonn can be heard performing this piece on the forthcoming album *The New Backwards* from Threshold House (http://www.thresholdhouse.com).

"The Parable of Lamion" by Elijah appears in print for the first time in this volume.

"A Quick Trip to Alamut" by Brion Gysin is reprinted with permission from the private archive of Genesis Breyer P-Orridge.

"The Sayings of Ganesh Baba" as gathered by Ira Cohen were originally published in *Ins and Outs*, vol. 1, July 1978.

"S/He is Her/E" by Genesis Breyer P-Orridge was originally published in a limited edition (500) chapbook, New Way On Press, 2000. See www.genesisp-orridge.com for more details.

"Tantric Picnic" by Hans Plomp appears in print for the first time in this volume.

"Trishuls, Tibetans and Tsunamis" by Dave Lowe is published in print for the first time in this volume and is excerpted from a longer work in progress.

APPENDIX. A BRIEF OUTLINE OF THE PARABLE OF LAMION BY FRATER ALIYA (ELIJAH)

Started Febuary 3, 2006

Reference
The Book Buggalou (Attack of the Munchee-Chee)
Frater Aliya
The Book Blue
Frater Elijah
The Book Gamma-go
Frater Fantastico
The Book of Conjuration
Frater Fantastico
The Book of Chaste Lightning Frater
The Book of Batz Moru
Frater Aliya
To include
Atheist Inclusion
Taoism Default
The Alpha and Omega
Christ & The morning star
Luciferous-Christos
Unity & Love in Shadow-light
Stigmata Shubu Stigmata | Stigmata
| Shubu-Stigmata
| con Shubu
The HolyGhost
The HolySpirit
The Great Houses of Lamion
House OM
All Supernal Cap issues
Moment Misericordia: The Thumb-Concentration (AOS + Buddha)
The All-Now
Barbelith & Thee Invisibles The All not-Now and the induction principle of inclusion. Metrics of the All-Now
The All
The Now
\ The Palace of Serenity \
The Great Wall
The Delegation
The Pearl of Inverted Synthesis
Shadow Spooge
5-Golden Rings
The First Lawful Expression of the Tetra-Cubular Grammatrix — Pentagrammaton
— Messiah
The Consortium
House of the Eternal (Eternal Halls of Lamion)
House of Beth-Qol
The Children of Beth-Qol
Tiyet
Luciferous Christos Unity and Love in Shadowlight
Moglthox
Mogltox
Mogle
Set as Isolate Intoxication
The Triple Goddess
Harakhan
Astu-Yevix (Ay-Ya)
Ye-Amon
Green Jesus
Hanna
modifications and inclusions
House of Akasha
The Akashic Record (individual levels, pan-out lounges, zeitgeist, all).
Akashic Record of Initial Nephi Interactives
Zod-Kasian Akashic Record
Animal Akashic Record
Sekhmet, Baast/ Bast, Raven, Coyote, Gaia, Pele, Scarlet Eldarath
Hall of Images
Yetziratic Interactives, Akashic Record(s)
Factions
Faction Paradox
The Tao Ordinance(s)
Squoon-Jheel and the Fractal Mosaic
Dizzy chicken, dorje-wheel-arrat CCM, and Bhagavadgita at the Green Oasis with the proper administration & liberation of all great beings con shubu stigmata
Ordinances and Dictates
Consumate Dictate
The Law of Three
— One for all and All for one
The Pirate's Law — Arghhh!
Our Reservation
Ginger Snaps Principle
All Laws of Chaos [LOC]
Moments, Days and Pages
The Day of Dream 0
The Day of Dream 1
The Day of Dream 2+
The dream of the Roc
The Skiing Dream
The Updates of the Dream Gate and the Dream Master (see the Lord of Yoga & lawful PMB states with Nephi EA-components and comfort issues).
Moment Mephisto and the undoing of the Triadic-Wyrms
The Day of the 7-Palms
The Revere of the 7-Seas
Metatron
Unicursal Day
The Day Rememberance
The Day of V.V.V.V.V. and the SQ/SG going buggalou
Moment of Solace
Dolphin Day and the Aeon of Animals and inclusion of Abramelic Will
Pages of Summary and the p.s. pages
Page 365, 366, 367
The Day of Hera Elios
The night of Wimbledorf
The Liberace Underground
Aiye Wedo Moment
The Ghede Moment of the original Suns of the earth
The Octrig-Shoggothalis
The Ghede-dense-zombie-alleviation moment of Melchizedek & Buddha
The Expungings
The Ionic universe.
Algolian-Dense-Shadow-false void variations of the demi-planes of Lamion.
All modular life undone.
All Spider Goddesses & Spider Queens undone.
\ via appropriate expression of the tetra-cubular grammatrix
\ see Buddha and the Alpha and Omega.
All Pit of 66 and Bes-Qol undone, expunged and appropriated.
All Saturnian Ophidian Machines Undone and Universal connectives via the Sephira of Yesod (Shaddai-El-Chai Adonai Joey) dimensionality of the Terran system set.
Lamionic game of thrones, game of thrones.
Tenth Degree Roles

Model Supremacy
Supernal Caps (see Batz Moru) and Initiation
Consensual Reality; Model Supremacy (Skandhas); Reality Fields
The Great Wall
The Transfinite Array
The Transfinite (layerz)
The "Separation" (Yetziratically—Of the mind of man) and the Purification.
Skandhas and relations to perceptions
Higher Dimensionality
Intelligences
Reality Interactives
The Lawful and Unlawful Paths (of the Tree, and Dayside, Nightside & Astriellic & Krlamic pathways) all put to 7'th aeon functionality.
The Vengeful Dead and the Bardo (Bardic Shaper Bardo).
The B.S. issue 333 zero-point issue with reality governance directionals and the Horizon-Bon Pa and the Tulpatudes (LGOH/Isaac issues)
The Great Wall
Skandhas (conceptualization vs. "Ophidian technologies" vs. MS)
The Witches' Sabbat
Between
BetweenZ
The path of initiation
The great wheel
The undoing of Typhon
The Shem
The Shem Ha Mephorash
The Intelligences, Horizon, The Goetia
Aeonics
Time as a quasi-aeon, Skandha, Emit-Ecaps, Layers, Dream-Gate. Relations to the hours/set sexual theme, the lamionic/astriel branch offs, the tranny-tetragram relations, tetracubular expressions, the sphere (outside/between)—Stereographic projection. Transyuggothian (mara-maya-magic mirror), 789

The three Aeons

Formula of Osiris, "whose word is so that men worshipped Man, thinking him subject to Death, and his victory dependent upon Resurrection. Even so conceived they of the Sun as slain and reborn with every day, and every year." (Heart of the Master) of Osiris in Equinox of the Gods: "the second [Aeon] is of suffering and death: the spiritual strives to ignore the material. Christianity and all cognate religions worship death, glorify suffering, deify corpses." "Crowned and conquering child, who dieth not, nor is reborn, but goeth radiant ever upon His Way. Even so goeth the Sun: for as it is now known that night is but the shadow of the Earth, so Death is but the shadow of the Body, that veileth his Light from its bearer." (Heart of the Master) "The Aeon of Horus is here: and its first flower may well be this: that, freed of the obsession of the doom of the Ego in Death, and of the limitation of the Mind by Reason, the best men again set out with eager eyes upon the Path of the Wise, the mountain track of the goat, and then the untrodden Ridge, that leads to the ice-gleaming pinnacles of Mastery!" (Little Essays Towards Truth, "Mastery")

Other aeons

The future Aeon, which is seen to eventually replace the present one, is the Aeon of Ma'at. According to some-such as the Aeon of Ma'at has already arrived. For others, (among them Nema, and the Horus-Maat lodge) it is present as a backwards-flowing current grounded in the future.

Temporal aspects

There is a debate as to the temporal span of an Aeon. On the one hand it is argued that an Aeon lasts 2000 years in accordance with the astrological ages generated by the procession cycles of the earth's axis (ie; the 26000 year "platonic year"), while on the other, Crowley himself suggested that the Horus Age may last as little as 100 years, and that the Aeons might not be uniformly defined in terms of duration. Still another point of view suggests that an Aeon is better interpreted in light of the Gnostic model in which Aeons (or Aions) are considered as stages or spheres of influence in terms of the development of an energy. As such, in this view an Aeon is not Chronological at all, and it is possible for several Aeons to co-exist on the Earth at one time. Contemporary earthly existence of "prehistoric" cultures, patriarchal structures, and Horus-influenced bastions of individualism, are cited as support for this hypothesis of heterogeneous Aeonics.

Glossary

MAA KHERU | (Egyptian, "See the Fallen One!") When uttered aloud, allows the soul to proceed to the underworld and there win the power of the gods. Wade Baskin defines it (sp. Ma'kheru) as an Egyptian sorcerer and literally means "Magic Word" or "Voice of Truth" (Ma'at). In the sense of a vow only the actual hieroglyphs can tell us the correct translation:

MA'AT | The divine feather and balance, as well as the Goddess of Truth and Justice. In the judgment of the dead, Ma'at weighs the feather in the balance against the soul. The Aeon of Ma'at is to follow the present Aeon of Horus, and was inaugurated in 1948. In vulture symbolism compare Hebrew Meth, "death."

All that, however, merely scratches the surface of the Egyptian understanding of Ma'at. It is the basic principle of Kamite tradition and the link to the Gods. Here is where China and Egypt share in making ritual so important, which is how the Egyptians knew Ma'at. In "Her Bak" we learn that Ma'at is the key to the reason for man's life and the key to the mystery of Egypt itself. It is the mediation between man and the gods and serves, moreover, as a bridge between all disparities. When we ignore tradition, we soon drift into error. One of man's more noticeable failings is a lack of perseverance, but whenever we emphasize anything, we call up the opposite of emphasis, i.e. spontaneity and change: Priest vs. Shaman. Evil, then, is ignorance caused by the absence of Ma'at. Gnosis—the knowing of the divine names—brings us back. Ma'at is the necessary balancing of the paradoxes of wisdom and that is why it is characterized by a feather, so the necessary balance can be extremely subtle.

The Aeon of i (I-dot) and the inclusion of all syzygies
Transyuggothian and "assimilated conceptions" with the Mara-Maya-Magic Mirror progression via BARBELITH.
1-1 function definition, Onto & dijectivity
Trans Aeonic Bridges & Dirac Delta Trains
The Great Wall Time as a Quasi-Temporal Aeon
The Holy-Octahedron and the Configuration of Space
The Mutagenic School Caps
All Unlawful Ophidian (abomination technologies) undone returned
All Computer Components returned to proper placements; the release of the original P.O.L. space-ship model entity which was trapped between [Elohim-Elijah-#26]
See the PMB-Hypnogogic model correction with comfort issues in mind and also see the HOLY-GHOST, Buddha along with the Alpha and Omega.
Shadow-Time Aeonics and Incarnate issues AMI
Tesselation of the Sphere ("5d-Sphere transmogrification point model of Seper Yetzirah") \ 0 - 5 dimensions
PMB States "Patanjali Modulates Babalon" (Hypnogogic Models and the infinite world model and difficulties resolved)
Loop-d-loop repeat model (deja-vu) resolutions via 767
The Aeon of Animals
Definitions of Will
767 Issues (757, 747, 737, 727, 717, 777, 787)
No non-initiates involved
Pacts of Innocence & the Aeon of Shaitan.
Non-involvement of the Church of Satan, Temple of Set, IOT, or any other Magickal (or mundane) organization.
Must be admitted face-to-face.
Cannot leave Las Vegas
Must abide by Consumate Dictate and "What Buddha Say" (see House OM).
Supernal Caps issues ATB (see Batz Moru ~ House OM)
Akashic Record (in parking lot & stigmata inclusions day) and F-False Void Point-to-point inclusive of Model Supremacy [MS]
Comfort Manifestation Issues (including Animals ~ Dolphin Day)
Correction of Nephi issues and un-lawful crossing over (zod-kasian or otherwise)
Emit-Ecaps models and relations to Skandhas Point-to-point Aeonic Maps (SQ/SG/F-F void conceptions see MS)
Aeonic Words & the XO role(s)
Thelema, Agape, Aughm
Ipsos
Manifestation, Festat, Allala, Abrahadabra, Horizon
The word of the Aeon of Shaitan Satan—Undoing of the "Oberion" and the inclusion of the outer supernova shell of quliiphoth with the first lawful expression of the tetracubular grammatrix,
The Silent Aeon (see severence issues), Aeon of Isis, Osiris (Amun-Re & remembering of Osiris), the Book of Life, the Aeon of Ma'at / Mu-ion
Fissle, and festat levels
The "Nu-Flusion"
The Holy Yechudim and the Partzufim
The Neverending Story & akashic record.
The Endless (Gaiman)
The Horizon of ETERNITY & The Computer [perfected] \ All-Now
YHVH-AUPQ-NO-ZIROH-AUPQ-YH-VH-YHVH-AHIH-YHVH-AUPQ-HORIZON-AUPQ-YHVH
YHVH-AUPQ-SAOH-AUPQ-YH-VH
YHVH-AUPQ-AOH-AUPQ-YHVH
YHVH-AHIH
The P.O.G. | Lamionic Pylonic Outer Gateways and Underdark/ "Underearth"
The Demi-planes of Lamion
Shadow-Planes, A.'.A.'.A.'. & A.'.A.'. variations and purifications, expungences and aeonic defuncts
The Mechanical Worm/Wyrm
The Ancient of Days (The Ancient of Days of the Parable of Lamion)
Ampt and the Ma'atian Gnosis \ The Feather and the dot \ The Feather
The Aeon (Creation, Bornless, Harpoorkraat, Ra-Hoor-Khuit, Set, Grendel)
The Tattwas
Akasha and the dot. Inclusion of the tattwic schemes in the

conceptualization of
the transfinite array.
Consummate Dictate
Tetragrammaton
Include the Transgen-
der schema\
The Horus-Set-
Maat-333-"astriellic"
conceptions
the Nephi
The Unlawful expres-
sion of a "tetra-cubu-
lar" grammatrix.
The Lawful Expres-
sion of a tetracubular
grammatrix and 777
see delegation and
consortium
the 4-Trees and the
crossing over into the
Lamion Continuum
{absolute liberation
for all Zumanity
[see skandhas/
Humanity, also see
Transfinite]
} see the "pages of
summary" and the
"p.s. pages"
BLBK (BLIQ index-
ing)
The Quantum Regis-
try index
The Quantum Matrix
The Day of 365, 366,
367 and the emptying
of Horizon BetweenZ.
People
BRAHMA
Brahman
Wakantanka
St. Germain
Germain-Sophie
The Great Spirit
The God Beings \rez
classes\
Nema, Nemo, Pro-
methea
Daimonic Intelligence
Angels
Devils
Demons
Jinn
Mind
Skandhas
The Witchy-Poos
Edward Kelly & John
Dee
The
Venerable Bead
Franz Bardon
Aleister Crowley
Austin Osman Spare
Aos
Zos vel Thanatos
The Alpha and
Omega
Prophet (E)
Alan Moore
Trimegistus
Trimegistus
the Person
Hermes, Mercury &
Tahuti
Hermes, Mercury
Tahuti
Promethea
the role & role model
Too-Tay-Too-Ta
Tnchen-Too-Ta
trimegistri of the
Lamion Continuum
Atu
Atu "phi-indepen-
dence"
The AB TARO, The
Arcana of Inversions,
The Book of Wild'ng
and Atavism, Book
231 relations
The Great White
Brotherhood (aka)
Guru-Chela
The Lamion Contin-
uum
The Scarlet Brother-
hood
A.'.A.'.
A.'.A.'.A.'.
Babalon
The Fallen
The Scarlet Gash
The Celestial Bureau-
cracy
Buddha
BLBK—Bird Lady
Buddha-Kind
Buddhakind—(see
consumate dictate
and Batz Moru) all
Buddhakind, Bodhi,
Bodhisattvas and
universal servants
or similartudes
protected by outer
robe of illumination
and parametrizer
issuences. All Buddhas
can experience any
form of consciousness
without being affected
in any way always.
Amoghasiddhi
Shakyamuni
Akshobhya
Jambhalas
Amitabha
Ratnasambhava
Ratnas—Jewel
Aksoybhum
Avalokitesvara
1,000 Armed Chenz-
rig
Taras
Green Tara
White Tara
Yellow Tara
Orange Tara
Blue Tara
Black Tara
Crimson Tara
Purple Tara
Brown Tara
Raiden
Chang-ti
Amaratsu
Kuan Yin
Kuan Yuan
Kuan Yin & Kuan
Yang
Pantanjali
The Lord of Yoga
The Triple Goddess
Paladine Magere
Takhisis
Shetakisis
High-Priestess-Shakti
(Horizon Atu)
No-One was involved
H. P. Blavatsky
Solar Logos
Logoidal Functions
True Logoidal Func-
tions
False Logoidal
Function
Initated Logoidal
Functions
The Fallen Shekina
The Severence Aeonic
Issues
Pentacost-Inclusion
and
"The Rite of
Ascension"
"False" Void concep-
tions
"False-False"
Wilson / Leary
8-circuit model and
extensions
Thee Essentials of the
Sublime—The Lord
of Yoga
The later stages of
Adept study.
Initiated study as an
evolutionary trend
Belief established
from novitiate
\Fundamental tools
\ {One way into the
higher schematics of
that particular branch
~ to all branches.}
Will, Desire, Belief
\See Book of Wild'ng
by Julian
\{Axis Aleph, Mem,
Shin}
Ritual Basics, Set-up,
Structure
\The orchestration of
the alphabet
| Rhythm, Style, Flow
|The intent and car-
rying out of the intent
~ Fueled by Desire
| Expression of Will ~
Honing thereof
| The Praxis of Ritual
(Meta-graphically as
in a logical progres-
sion)
| Becoming. The
Study of Skandhas
Triage
\Buddhism

ALSO AVAILABLE FROM ULTRACULTURE

MONSANTO VS. THE WORLD: The Monsanto Protection Act, GMOs and Our Genetically Modified Future • Jason Louv

$4.49 Paperback • $2.99 Kindle • Available Now on Amazon.com

Monsanto—one of the largest agriculture and biotech companies in the world—creates genetically engineered seeds and food, or GMOs. They've also brought the world toxic chemicals like DDT, PCBs and even Agent Orange.

But who is Monsanto really—and why do many see them as one of the most evil companies in the world? Are GMOs and genetically engineered food the solution to world hunger, or a shockingly dangerous threat to our health? And does Monsanto really, as some suggest, secretly control much of the United States' agriculture and food departments? What are they hiding from the public?

All of these questions rocketed to the forefront of the American dialogue when Barack Obama signed into law the Farmer Assurance Provision, or "Monsanto Protection Act"—which critics claimed would give Monsanto immunity from the federal government. "Monsanto vs. the World" puts to rest the myths and shows the shocking reality, delving into the science of GMOs, the political machinations of Monsanto in Washington and around the world, and showing what you can do to keep GMOs off your plate.

In Monsanto vs. the World, which cites nearly one hundred scholarly journals, books, studies, articles and even Monsanto's own documents, you'll discover the details of:

• Monsanto's long history of creating—and covering up the effects of—toxic chemicals and weapons

• Monsanto's powerful lobby that has tendrils in the FDA, the USDA, the EPA—and even the White House

• What GMOs and genetically engineered organisms are—and how they may be hazardous to your health

• How Monsanto is using GMOs to suppress small farmers and invade the world

• How to keep GMOs off your plate and make sure you're eating fresh and healthy food

For less than the price of a lunch, get the crucially important information that will change how you see your food forever—and that will keep you and your family eating healthy instead of GMO.

24245015R00219

Made in the USA
San Bernardino, CA
18 September 2015